Sound Work:

Composition as Critical Technical Practice

SOUND WORK

COMPOSITION AS CRITICAL TECHNICAL PRACTICE

Edited by Jonathan Impett

Leuven University Press

Table of Contents

7   INTRODUCTION: MUSIC-MAKING AND STORYTELLING
Jonathan Impett

15   TOO COOL TO BOOGIE: CRAFT, CULTURE, AND CRITIQUE
IN COMPUTING
Alan F. Blackwell

35   ILLUSIONS OF FORM
David Rosenboom

79   WHAT TO WARE? A GUIDE TO TODAY'S TECHNOLOGICAL WARDROBE
Nicolas Collins

89   TOWARD A CRITICAL MUSICAL PRACTICE
Ann Warde

105   THE COMPOSER'S DOMAIN: METHOD AND MATERIAL
Nicholas Brown

117   DISSOCIATION AND INTERFERENCE IN COMPOSERS' STORIES
ABOUT MUSIC: THE RENEWAL OF MUSICAL DISCOURSE
Jonathan Impett

137   PLATES

153   THE IMPOSSIBILITY OF MATERIAL FOUNDATIONS
Scott McLaughlin

171   THINKING *LIVENESS* IN PERFORMANCE WITH LIVE ELECTRONICS:
THE NEED FOR AN ECO-SYSTEMIC NOTION OF AGENCY
Agostino Di Scipio

195   EXPERIMENT AND EXPERIENCE: COMPOSITIONAL PRACTICE AS
CRITIQUE
Lula Romero

219   DESIGNING THE THRENOSCOPE OR, HOW I WROTE ONE OF
MY PIECES
Thor Magnusson

231   A FEW REFLECTIONS ABOUT COMPOSITIONAL PRACTICE THROUGH
A PERSONAL NARRATIVE
Daniela Fantechi

247   TEMPORAL POETICS AS A CRITICAL TECHNICAL PRACTICE
Karim Haddad

277   COLLABORATIVE CREATION IN ELECTROACOUSTIC MUSIC:
PRACTICES AND SELF-AWARENESS IN THE WORK OF MUSICAL
ASSISTANTS MARINO ZUCCHERI, ALVISE VIDOLIN, AND CARL FAIA
Laura Zattra

295   *PARLOUR SOUNDS*: A CRITICAL COMPOSITIONAL PROCESS
TOWARDS A CYBERFEMINIST THEORY OF MUSIC TECHNOLOGY
Patricia Alessandrini and Julie Zhu

319   CHANGING THE VOCABULARY OF CREATIVE RESEARCH:
THE ROLE OF NETWORKS, RISK, AND ACCOUNTABILITY IN
TRANSCENDING TECHNICAL RATIONALITY
Ambrose Field

335   DESIGNING AUDIENCE–WORK RELATIONSHIPS
Marko Ciciliani

355   ONLINE MATERIALS

357   NOTES ON CONTRIBUTORS

365   INDEX

Introduction

Music-Making and Storytelling

Jonathan Impett

This volume is concerned with storytelling: the stories composers tell about composition, to themselves and to others. In the past, the self-reporting of composition has tended to consider the areas in which it aspires to be innovative, or the theories—musical, aesthetic, social, scientific, technological—that have informed the work, rather than the activity of composition itself. The knowledge presented in such cases often lies *outside* composition. There is no lack of accounts by composers demonstrating how their work embodies this theory or that principle, or introduces a new technical concept. There is no shortage of investigation of the ontology and epistemology of the "work" as a persisting historical cultural phenomenon, but the technologies and context of composition have undergone a paradigm shift. The present, to repurpose a phrase, is another country.

In contemporary science, the role of storytelling is increasingly recognised not only in science communication but also in its self-image and hence in scientific practice (Davies et al. 2019). In the discussion of music creation, several factors contribute to the urgent need for new discourse, new voices, and new kinds of story. The cultural landscape is transformed, and with it the perceived role of "art" music and the nature of public critical discourse. In a prevailing atmosphere of individualism, the commonality of creative experience is all the more important—both among artists themselves and with their audience. And composition is largely supported as an activity of knowledge-production, as research, rather than as creative development per se. We need, therefore, to tell more material, honest, and useful stories—to seed discourse, to find resonances, to encourage critical engagement.

To paraphrase Brian Ferneyhough ([1982] 1995), composition walks a tightrope between formalism and the arbitrary, a process informed by theory and intuition, constraint and contingency, expectation and experience. It is a continuous, situated, iterative process of inscription and reflection in which its models, metaphors, aspirations, obligations, tools, and technologies all play a part; it has a narrative, or rather multiple narratives (Impett 2016). This process and its products embody assumptions, choices, and intentions that have significant implications for the position, role, and impact of artist and artwork alike—critical implications, whether the artist chooses to regard them as such or not. The artefacts of composition—however notated, improvised, virtual, embodied, or technologically implemented—are hybrid technical objects and require a technicity of engagement on the part of artist and listener.

The hypothesis of this volume is that we might rather consider composition as a design process, and that we might usefully study its dynamics and decisions in the spirit of what Philip Agre described as *critical technical practice*. Agre developed his ideas in the context of his work in artificial intelligence (AI), at a moment of deep transformation in that field, of moving from "mentalist" to "interactionist" models. His fundamental insight is that individual practice—what he described as "the practical logic of computer work" (Agre 2002)—is indivisible from the social context and implications of its products; they constitute a single critical activity:

> The word "critical" here does not call for pessimism and destruction but rather for an expanded understanding of the conditions and goals of technical work.... Instead of seeking foundations it would embrace the impossibility of foundations, guiding itself by a continually unfolding awareness of its own workings as a historically specific practice.... It would accept that this reflexive inquiry places all of its concepts and methods at risk. And it would regard this risk positively, not as a threat to rationality but as the promise of a better way of doing things. (Agre 1997a, 22–23)

Agre criticises conventional accounts that present work and theory as a mutually justifying pair—one as the natural embodiment of the other—as insufficient. Such accounts hide narrative, decisions, and parameters, avoid critical context. Instead, he outlines a practice that is reflective in two directions: in terms of what it actually involves—intentions, conditions, means, theory, actions, constraints, events—and in terms of its context—cultural, social, technological, and, in our case, artistic and even personal. He describes a single disciplinary field: "one foot planted in the craft work of design and the other foot planted in the reflexive work of critique" (Agre 1997b, 155). This is not the place to hazard a reductive summary of Agre's concept, but we must point to a recent resurgence of interest in areas such as software studies (Kitchin and Dodge 2014), intelligent design (Somerson and Hermano 2013), architecture (Parisi 2013), and artificial intelligence itself, which has been massively re-energised with recent advances in machine learning. Like the artefacts of these fields, music inhabits a liminal material state, is heavily dependent on the means of its realisation, retains its identity across manifold instantiations, is adaptive to the context of its embodiment, and is the product of deep concept, abstract imagination, and painstaking technique and experiment.

In critical technical practice, reflection and its articulation are integral and essential to the process; there is no single model any more than there is a single model of composition. This volume explores the potential of critical technical practice (CTP) as an ethos and discourse for the articulation and sharing of knowledge production through composition across styles, practices, and contexts. The technological context, materials, and practices of composition have always been closely coupled. The wider cultural role and understanding of composition as an activity has been transformed with each technological paradigm shift. This volume considers the new cultural, professional, epistemic, and institutional situation of composition in the particular contexts of the wide range of current technologically enabled practices: music information retrieval, live coding, live notation, intelligent instrument-building and hacking, interactive, autonomous, and algorithmic approaches, distributed creativity, sound art, and computer-assisted composition. As an inherently reflexive approach, CTP brings implications for the development of these same contemporary practices.

The opening chapters consider the relevance and potential of critical technical practice in music from wide perspectives. Alan Blackwell's "Too Cool to Boogie" sets the scene by locating Agre's thought in the field of artificial intelligence, its issues and subsequent developments. Critical technical practice presents a critical response to the impasse of AI in the 1980s; technical and philosophical views are inseparable if the field is to realise its potential for good, and this relationship is reflected in the stories practitioners tell about their own work. The author explores Agre's thought by situating it in a specific instance of his own practice: studying funk bass. The interaction of technical methods with the embodied, situated, complexly motivated narrative of human practice emerges as the object of critical reflection.

David Rosenboom's magisterial "Illusions of Form" presents a body of creative thought that has evolved in parallel and kept pace with the developments that have produced the concept of CTP, the current 4E view of cognition (embodied, embedded, enacted, extended), and recent advances in biotechnology. Rosenboom invokes Agre's ideas to construct a critical reflection on the development and implications of his own radical concept of *propositional music*. Received boundaries of genre or discipline are abandoned, not to indifference but to a new mode of artistic-technical-scientific endeavour—an *artscience*, its methodology informed by the current concept of emergent engineering. Composition becomes an activity of world-model building, an imaginative process that engages with the cognitive processes of performers and listeners alike, using means and models derived from and developed with advances in science and technology. Through examples of neuromusical propositions, musical configuration spaces and emergent collaborative projects, Rosenboom lays the ground for a new artscience discourse. In his vision, critical technicity is in operation throughout the acts of composition, performance, and listening.

The software-hardware binary central to current technology-based practice is examined in Nicolas Collins's "What to Ware?" He suggests a taxonomy, a series of axes along which their different affordances and constraints might be understood. This illuminates the artist's selection of tools as a series of conscious choices, all informed by a fundamental critical question in art, that of truth to materials—in this case, whether music made with electronics should sound like electronic music.

Collins's fine-grained analysis of craft is complemented by Ann Warde's broad recontextualising of the very activity of composition. She pursues a process of substitution to explore the prospect of a "critical musical practice," such that composition becomes a way of imagining and modelling "a world we'd *like* to perceive and experience—an environment: a social, physical, tactile environment." Warde performs a further inversion: by seeing music *as a* technology, she presents it as having a wider function in its own present. These substitutions shed new light both on the wide relevance of Agre's ideas beyond their apparent subject area, and on the potential role of music as a critical instrument.

The intimate dance of the technical and the critical is explored in Nicholas Brown's "The Composer's Domain." The essentially transdisciplinary nature of the work of composing with computers emerges from two case studies. Such work becomes a way of interrogating both assumptions about music-making and the world-views embodied in technology; it proposes alternative ontologies for music and poses new questions concerning our relationship with the natural, cultural, and engineered world we inhabit. At the heart of this music is the fulcrum between the digital and the mechanical, developing the thesis of the chapter by Nicolas Collins. The abstraction, conditionality, and absolute nature of the digital are balanced by the situated and responsive materiality of the ways in which the work is shared.

The editor's "Dissociation and Interference" considers the relevance, implications, and enactment of critical technical practice in the current environment of art as knowledge production. Crucial differences emerge between CTP and actor–network theory: a CTP approach addresses the significant gap in current music discourse between material and social perspectives. Agre insists on the identification of moments of dissociation and interference as a key component, and this is discussed in the context of the practical business of composition.

McLaughlin, Di Scipio, and Romero examine particular aspects of contemporary composition, as they emerge from the writers' own practices—aspects with broad common resonance. Scott McLaughlin pursues the question of material indeterminacy in "The Impossibility of Material Foundations." The composer sets the conditions for the development of a relationship between performer and an unpredictable and unstable performance environment—a combination of technique and instrument. This essentialises and microexamines the situation that effectively obtains in any "conventional" performance. A touchstone comes from Agre, in his description of such a process as "embrac[ing] the impossibility of foundations, guiding itself by a continually unfolding awareness of its own workings as a historically specific practice" (1997a, 23). Composition is thus acknowledged as a situated experimental process, the recursive exploration of the infinite possible networks conceived as a "phase space."

Agostino Di Scipio puts forward a view of live electronic music as an inherently critical practice in "Thinking *Liveness* in Performance with Live Electronics." His chapter begins with a comprehensive historical survey of practice and concepts. Di Scipio's concept of liveness involves not simply human presence or "real-time" operation—itself a very plastic idea—but the real lived time and space of performance. He proposes the *performance ecosystem* as an operative unit, such that system and site are coupled in performance. Critical technicity runs through practice and performance into their social context: "By way of turning the hybrid constitution of techno-ecosystems into phenomenologically shared auditory events, these mediators audibly expose the human, all-too-human reality of our pervasive technological condition."

In "Experiment and Experience," Lula Romero resists the notion of mastery—of craft or materials. In the pursuit of openness of relationship between composer and work, she finds Cage's apparent rejection of the subject insufficient as a response. Instead she sees a continuous intra-action between composer and materials; the resulting music is a product of their interference. Such openness becomes a process of continuous critique, evading commodification and offering alternative world models. This critique is confronted with each technical decision: the spatial distribution of multiple possible outcomes, the design of and negotiation with systems. Romero proposes a reformulation of the composer as a feminist subject.

The accounts of Magnusson, Fantechi, Haddad, and Zattra set out from very practical aspects of contemporary composition practice. Metacompositional thought in the design of a performance system is a theme developed in Thor Magnusson's account of his development of the Threnoscope, a live coding environment. As a mode of compositional inscription, code has its own dynamics in terms of imagining and structuring work—or rather potential work—and in its dissemination and reuse. Here it becomes a context for experimentation as well as a creative tool; conventional categories of modes of practice and expertise dissolve as questions of music theory, cognition, technology, interface, and instrument design provoke and inform one another. Projects such as the Threnoscope invite us to dynamically re-evaluate notions of design, composition, performance, improvisation, and collaboration.

The activity of com-posing—the putting together of music—is predicated at some level on a conceptual model of the resources and materials to be used. The management of resources—their representation, their perceived or ascribed relationships, their disposition—is so fundamental an activity, so practical, that it may seem pre-technical and is certainly lost in most accounts of practice. Instead, the decisions it embodies reflect a critical stance that informs all its artefacts. Daniela Fantechi explores this topic in "A Few Reflections about Compositional Practice," a refreshingly candid account of personal practice as revealed in a series of case studies. Awareness of choice—of taste, of the changing objects of attention and of provisional, variable parameters of categorisation—evolves from an autoethnographic discipline to a guiding critical stance. This generates a narrative of form emerging from levels of compositional memory and the inherent temporality of the material.

Karim Haddad's "Temporal Poetics" presents a way of conceiving musical time and of manipulating the temporality of musical entities mentioned by Fantechi. This is contiguous with the roots of Western mensural notation in the ars nova, but also with Hölderlin's assertion of rhythm as the essential property of art, of nature, and of knowledge. Computer-assisted composition restores the flow of time to the working environment; the temporalities of imagination, experimentation, composition, and performance modulate each other. Haddad's approach recognises the particular temporality of materials while being situated in both the historical flow of musical culture and a critical exchange with contemporary technology.

Music research has recently focussed on collaborative work in contemporary music creation; we might more accurately observe that music research has recently come to take note of the extent to which collaborative or distributed processes are vital to music creation in general. As the technological possibilities available to musicians have proliferated, distributed technical expertise has become crucial at the stage of composition. A very particular mode of collaboration obtains in institutional studios where composers are invited to work with the assistance of technical experts. Laura Zattra examines the dynamics of such situations in "Collaborative Creation in Electroacoustic Music," by exploring three cases in detail. Useful terms derive from design practices; workflow, communication, and the co-evolution of musical imagination with technical experimentation emerge as significant factors. The complicity, empathy, creativity, and openness of the assistant are crucial, and yet their professional status is not always resolved.

Finally, Alessandrini and Zhu, Field, and Ciciliani present visions for new ontologies of music, each taking a unique critical stance and exploring its ramifications for their technical practice. Patricia Alessandrini's feminist multimedia monodrama *Parlour Sounds* is the case study at the heart of her chapter with Julie Zhu. In the spirit of Haraway-inspired cyberfeminism, the project challenges predominant practices of technology, confronting those of music with those of the domestic environment. Such displacement brings the work into new critical relationships with many aspects of its production and context: the collaborative processes of composition, of interface design and construction, the physical location of work with music technology, the relationship of art with daily life, and the power structures at play in the soliciting and production of music. Cyberfeminist principles inform the proposal of an alternative to dominant paradigms of electronic music, and a theoretical framework in which roles and distinctions between composition, design, improvisation, and performance are blurred.

Ambrose Field seeks to change the vocabulary of creative practice from another perspective. Much compositional activity now happens in an academic context, where it is supported and expected to explain itself as research. This transition has been extensively discussed: from the epistemological implications to the ways in which it reflects a new mode of supporting cultural and creative development. From the composer's perspective, however, such discussion has largely been concerned with defending creative freedom or claiming epistemological relevance. Instead, Field addresses the question of the practice itself directly. When creative practice also becomes experimental practice, what are the ramifications for both the self-image and the practical behaviour of the practitioner? Field considers the formulation of questions and especially the development of new approaches to workflow, which he describes as "the creative envelope."

If the practices of music creation are to enter a more dynamic phase of critical awareness, the relationship with the listener, audience, or co-participant becomes crucial. For whom is this work intended? How is it to be received, in what circumstances and with what expectations of attention or investment?

Marko Ciciliani's "Designing Audience–Work Relationships" explores this in detail through three of his audiovisual projects—performance/installation hybrids. They work with time, space, and multiplicity of phenomenon to experiment with modes of social and individual interaction. Hall's "proxemics" provides a metric of intimacy. Patterns of temporality and attention emerge from the engagement of performers and listeners, not as an epiphenomenon but within the scope of compositional imagination, design, and critical reflection.

Through such processes of critical technical reflection, of detailed discussion of the practical narrative of composition, common themes emerge from this multiplicity of creative practices. Technology is present not for technology's sake, but because our evolving relationship with technology is one of the defining paths of our current state. A systems view of practice and its artefacts appears often, just as the mid-century visions of cybernetics are informing recent work in the new AI—currently searching for ways to confront its own hidden assumptions, tastes, and prejudices. Above all we see references to building models of possible worlds; David Rosenboom's *propositional music* stands as paradigm in this regard.

Composition is not the sudden, unitary embodiment of an idea but a situated, distributed, time-extensive activity. And the products of this activity, of these decisions, reflect world views and values; they propose new models. If we are to talk about music in material ways and music is to do its important work in the world, then composers must begin to have new kinds of conversation with each other and with the wider community. It is hoped that this volume will contribute to such a development.

References

Agre, Philip E. 1997a. *Computation and Human Experience.* Cambridge: Cambridge University Press.

———. 1997b. "Toward a Critical Technical Practice: Lessons Learned in Trying to Reform AI." In *Social Science, Technical Systems, and Cooperative Work: Beyond the Great Divide*, edited by Geoffrey C. Bowker, Susan Leigh Star, William Turner, and Les Gasser, 131–57. Mahwah, NJ: Erlbaum.

———. 2002. "The Practical Logic of Computer Work." In *Computationalism: New Directions*, edited by Matthias Scheutz, 129–42. Cambridge, MA: MIT Press.

Davies, Sarah Rachel, Megan Halpern, Maja Horst, David Kirby, and Bruce Lewenstein. 2019. "Science Stories as Culture: Experience, Identity, Narrative and Emotion in Public Communication of Science." *JCOM: Journal of Science Communication* 18 (5): A01. https://doi.org/10.22323/2.18050201.

Ferneyhough, Brian. (1982) 1995. "Form—Figure—Style: An Intermediate Assessment." In *Brian Ferneyhough: Collected Writings*, edited by James Boros and Richard Toop, 21–28. London: Routledge. Essay written 1982; first published 1984 in French translation (*Labrys* 10).

Impett, Jonathan. 2016. "Making a Mark: The Psychology of Composition." In *The Oxford Handbook of Music Psychology*, edited by Susan Hallam, Ian Cross, and Michael Thaut, 2nd ed., 651–66. Oxford: Oxford University Press.

Kitchin, Rob, and Martin Dodge. 2014. *Code/Space: Software and Everyday Life.* Cambridge, MA: MIT Press.

Parisi, Luciana. 2013. *Contagious Architecture: Computation, Aesthetics, and Space.* Cambridge, MA: MIT Press.

Jonathan Impett

Somerson, Rosanne, and Mara L. Hermano, eds. 2013. *The Art of Critical Making: Rhode Island School of Design on Creative Practice.* Hoboken, NJ: Wiley.

Too Cool to Boogie

Craft, Culture, and Critique in Computing

Alan F. Blackwell

University of Cambridge

This chapter is based on a lecture originally structured as an extended riff on the disco classic "Boogie Oogie Oogie"—recorded in 1978 by A Taste of Honey and featuring a famous bass solo by the songwriter Janice Johnson. The original lecture, delivered by a professor of computer science and would-be disco bass player, was prefaced by an image of the author posing in front of his academic bookshelves, wearing the traditional ceremonial gown of Cambridge University while sheepishly holding his Fender bass.

The talk itself was structured to follow the lyrics of that song, with each section developing a theme inspired by one line. Copyright constraints make it impossible to quote those lyrics verbatim in this published version (unfortunately there are no established conventions for music sample licensing in academic writing). However for disco enthusiasts who would like to listen along, I provide time codes (with Spotify links to the original seven inch single edit) at the start of each section.

The inspiration for this approach (notwithstanding the fact that I had been working on the "Boogie Oogie Oogie" bass part when I should have been preparing an otherwise disco-less talk) had been the song's origins. That well-known story, as reported by Ed Hogan (2021), is:

> While playing before a staring, apathetic audience during a gig at an airbase in San Bernardino, CA, Johnson improvised these lyrics: "If you're thinking that you're too cool to boogie / we've got news for you / everyone here tonight must boogie / and you are no exception to the rule."

So the theme of this chapter is the contrast between, on one side, Janice Johnson's airbase audience, who I will use to represent the formalised bureaucratic systems (and corresponding academic theories) of the military-industrial complex, and, on the other side, the funky boogie band insisting that these guys have to get up on the floor—stepping into the world of practice.

My perspective on critical technical practice comes from analysing this intersection, and in particular investigating the ways in which Philip Agre's own research in artificial intelligence had encountered and engaged with a central contrast between systematised theory and embodied practice.

15

Cool (00:45)[1]

Computer science and artificial intelligence were born during the period of World Wars, when national dominance, from the 1920s through the Cold War, was largely determined by which bloc had access to the most powerful technologies. Cybernetic missile controls, code-making and -breaking, and radar surveillance all played critical roles in developing the material infrastructure, skilled practices, and managerial systems of developments in information technology.

Many founders of these disciplines had either served in the military (often as radar engineers, codebreakers, or communication specialists), or were subsequently funded during the Cold War era by military research programmes. Despite the inevitable mavericks and visionaries that might be found among original thinkers of any era, the prevailing institutional culture reflected the post-war male conventions of the time—photographs show chess-playing boffins, bespectacled engineers in front of oscilloscope screens, and tweedy seminar audiences. Alison Adam, in her feminist history of AI (1998), accurately observes this milieu in which the paradigmatic technical challenge for intelligence was taken to be a machine able to play chess rather than (at the height of the normative post-war gender roles critiqued by Betty Friedan as *feminine mystique*), going home to help their wives cook meals, change diapers, or iron shirts.

More recently, it has been argued that the whole enterprise of artificial intelligence, in which some fundamental essence of intelligence will be abstracted from the human body in order to be mapped onto a machine, could only be imagined from a position of privilege—among white men for whom the body presents no constraint to a person's imagination or opportunities (Devlin and Belton 2020). Gender critique of AI is not the central theme of this chapter, but must be remembered as an ever-present underlying concern, especially given the gendered imagination of AI itself, in which "sexy robots" from Fritz Lang's Maria in *Metropolis* to Alex Garland's Ava in *Ex Machina* reflect a constant stream of misogynistic fantasy and retribution. While killer robots such as the Terminator may be gendered male, the ideals of the AI servant, whether Joseph Weizenbaum's pioneering chatbot Eliza or Apple's Siri, are unfailingly gendered as female (Adams 2019). As often noted, the Turing test ideal of performance was itself originally posed as a test of gender, a tragic juxtaposition with Alan Turing's own persecution and death within the homophobic and misogynist norms of the Cold War era.

This, then, is the context in which AI is "too cool to boogie"—the infrastructure of command and control, the post-war culture of masculine repression, and a tradition of academic enquiry that is abstract, symbolic, and mathematical rather than messily embodied.

---

1   spotify:track:2PCPgUVvFDBMDZJBVKMZQI#0:45.

NEWS FOR YOU (00:54)[2]

As discussed throughout this volume, the key concern in Agre's agenda of critical technical practice is expressed aphoristically as follows: "Technology at present is covert philosophy; the point is to make it openly philosophical" (Agre 1997, 240).

In Agre's own case, this agenda arose from two perspectives, clearly reflected in the two halves of his book *Computation and Human Experience* (1997). One of these perspectives probes the ways that the AI methods of the 1980s start to fail, when faced with physically embodied tasks—and Agre's book includes the source code of his AI system as evidence of his technical progress towards that problem. The other pays critical attention, drawing on insights from science and technology studies, to the ways that such technical failures point towards philosophical problems in the enterprise of symbolic AI.

Agre's own AI research, and the core of his critique, is based in the technical methods used before the more recent explosion in neural network and machine learning methods. Now known as "good old-fashioned AI" (GOFAI), at the time Taste of Honey recorded "Boogie Oogie Oogie," this type of research was "symbolic AI," dedicated to showing the ways that reasoning-in-general (i.e., abstracted from bodies) could be equated with symbol-processing. This was both a theory of mind (that the brain contains symbols, and that humans reason by manipulating those symbols) and an engineering method (in which computer programs use symbolic names to label pieces of computer memory). As a thoughtful technologist, Agre became increasingly concerned about the ways in which these two aspects of AI—theory of mind and engineering methods—did not match up with each other as smoothly as many researchers assumed.

A key problem was the fact that a computer program can be written using any words at all as the internal labels (e.g., the names of variables and functions), but will behave in exactly the same way, regardless of what those labels are. It makes no difference if the programmer writes x = y + 2; fred = mary + 2; or aubergine = happiness + 2. Once the program is running, each of those pieces of code would be functionally identical. Programmers should always be alert to the meaninglessness of the labels that appear in their code, but Agre observed that AI researchers, when discussing the philosophical implications of their work, would often elide this important distinction. If a piece of source code in an AI system reads truth = belief + intention, programmers can easily start to talk about that code as if it related to actual human beliefs and intentions, forgetting to test whether their argument remains valid if the word "belief" is (perfectly validly) replaced with "aubergine."

This important point is closely related to the "symbol grounding problem" (famous from John Searle's Chinese Room argument), a philosophical question in symbol-processing AI that asks how the computer is able to relate its

---

2 spotify:track:2PCPgUVvFDBMDZJBVKMZQI#0:54.

internal representation to the world outside. Agre's own technical research for his PhD at the MIT AI Lab addressed the problem of how a program can reason about a situation in the world, rather than just the relationship between internal symbols. As with many researchers at the time, he tested his approach using a simplified "toy world"—in his case, a computer game in which a penguin (Pengi, the name of his program) simulates embodied action by navigating virtual blocks to escape a virtual maze.

The problem with many toy-world methods of the 1970s and 80s (including my own AI research at that time [Blackwell 1989]) was that the methods effective in virtual worlds seldom turned out to be equally effective in the real world. Virtual toy worlds, inside the computer itself, are completely predictable—every aspect is known, because the programmer has constructed this world. In contrast, attempts to apply AI in the real world encoded knowledge about more complex problems in the form of "expert systems," where the programmer collects expert knowledge about some specialist domain such as medical diagnostics or military tactics, and uses the resulting set of symbolic relations to answer questions or suggest plans in terms of those symbols (Forsythe 1993).

The biggest problem with such systems seemed to be that they failed to capture common sense—for example, a medical system might prescribe drugs for a patient who is already dead. If none of the experts had thought to mention the common-sense fact that dead patients would not be given drugs, then it is easily possible that no programmer would think to include this fact in the code. Towards the end of the symbolic AI era, large investments were made in attempts to capture and encode all common-sense knowledge in the world, so that this database could be used as a basis for less fragile reasoning. The most ambitious of those projects, CYC (Lenat 1995), employed hundreds of computer science PhDs over a period of decades, working on rigorous ways to encode what turns out to be millions of pieces of common-sense knowledge—including many statements that would be obvious to any child.

This key problem in symbolic AI—that the theoretical relations within the system, however sophisticated, may not relate to the common-sense knowledge of embodied human experience—can be directly attributed to the central issue addressed in this chapter. They are examples of a disembodied technology that is too cool to boogie.

Although a fundamental problem of GOFAI, this problem has not gone away in the current era of machine-learning-based AI. Apparently dramatic successes of more recent "deep learning" AI systems continue to be demonstrated in toy worlds. The first major success of Google's DeepMind research division was, once again, learning to play a computer game (Mnih et al. 2015). Their demonstration of learning to play the game *Breakout*, while its internal programming is vastly more complex than Philip Agre's Pengi, seems on the surface to be remarkably similar in the toy-world problem it is trying to solve. Even the most dramatic success from DeepMind, the AlphaGo system whose tournament success against the world Go champion provoked worldwide consternation over humanity's latest defeat by machines, took place in the toy world of the Go board—another virtual refuge for those who are too cool to boogie—a place where common sense does not apply, embodiment is irrelevant, and the closed world is fully defined by the rules of the game.

Agre was by no means the only thinker from the disco era who had noticed the fundamental problems of building systems that were based on disembodied symbolic theories. As a young researcher, Agre corresponded with peers in other disciplines and was influenced by senior figures who had been drawing attention to these problems. A few well-known examples across these decades include management theorist Horst Rittel (Kunz and Rittel 1972; Rittel and Weber 1973), who drew attention to "wicked problems" that could not be solved through AI-like processes, sociologist Lucy Suchman (1987) who documented the failure of AI systems to do "situated planning," and computer scientist Paul Dourish (2004), who pointed out the ways in which the word *context* can be used to sweep the hardest problems of embodiment under the rug, in the hope that nobody will notice.

Everybody here (01:01)[3]

If the origins of critical technical practice lie in the problems of AI during the disco era, how might the problems originally addressed by AI researchers be relevant to the theory and practice of music? Music AI research is of course a substantial field of investigation, extending to classification and recommendation systems, synthetic instruments, generative works, and compositional tools. Core questions in critical technical practice apply to many of these, and other chapters in this book touch on relevant issues. But at this point in my own argument, it is important to note that the core issues of embodiment and symbol-processing in computer code are equally relevant to digital music systems.

To illustrate, I present three vignettes from my own observations of symbol processing methods in the work of research collaborators, which despite shared research concerns are located in the quite distinct situations of an art gallery, a dance studio, and a techno rave.

In March 2006, music AI researcher Nick Collins, with harpsichordist Dan Tidhar, baroque recorder player Inga Maria Klaucke, and composer Julio d'Escrivan, presented a programme entitled *Baroqtronica: The Art of Machine Listening* at the Kettle's Yard gallery in Cambridge.

This inaugural public presentation of Collins's Ornamaton system was described as follows:

> A new artificial musical lifeform will be unleashed to accompany the instrumentalists as they play an original sonata. The computer's role will be to provide additional ornamentation to the performer's parts. To this end, it is equipped with machine listening technology, simulations of the human ability to track the beat and key, and the capability to find and extract salient note events and reuse them algorithmically. The score (for the human players) is written as a large da capo aria where on the repeat, the humans will gradually play less notes and thus the Ornamaton will be challenged to gradually provide more. The Ornamaton is

---

3 spotify:track:2PCPgUVvFDBMDZJBVKMZQI#1:01.

autonomous and generative, so once set in motion it requires no human input, and
its actions, whilst of course constrained by its programming, will be unique to the
particular performance. (Collins 2006)

The Kettle's Yard gallery is a distinctive space. Originally the home of curator
and collector Jim Ede, the furnishings, including many works by the post-
war generation of British artists, have been preserved as a public museum in
exactly the arrangement Ede left them. A concert series takes place in the largest room of the house, knocked through between two of the four old cottages
Ede acquired. Early arrivals to a concert can lounge on furnishings apparently
preserved since the 1950s, while the rest of the audience sits on folding chairs
arranged around the piano and stairs, among Ede's household objects, paint-
ings, and sculpture. This domestic, consciously anachronistic, setting seems
ideal for *Baroqtronica*. However, the musical culture of this city tends more
towards the Baroque than the contemporary, and there are probably more a
capella choirs in Cambridge than there are electronic composers. The genteel
staging is thus presented as if it were a classical recital, with a small speaker
stand discreetly placed between Dan's harpsichord and Inga's music stand. The
evening is an intriguing novelty, with polite applause from series-goers who
had been invited to imagine how Bach might have ornamented performances
of his time, if he hadn't been constrained by how fast he could play the notes.

The location of my second vignette is the rehearsal studio of Wayne
McGregor's Random Dance, one of the world's leading contemporary companies. McGregor, who is also principal choreographer for the Royal Ballet, has for
years collaborated with scientists in many disciplines, challenging his dancers
to work above all with their minds, and with research processes integrated into
their work. One extended project explored the potential of a Choreographic
Language Agent—a piece of AI software that might help bridge the creative
processes between the language of dance and its practice. Early work on the
CLA drew on research into sketching and software design, inviting dancers to
explore and label three-dimensional moving forms developed within a branching space of design alternatives. But despite earnest experimentation, computers appeared to be unwelcome additions to the dance studio. The working life
of a dancer is above all focused on the body, and the process of creation is one
of co-present bodily interaction. The CLA software was unsympathetic to these
basic requirements, with language but no body, while operating its keyboards
and 3D controllers constrained the dancers who could otherwise have been
moving freely.

The location for my third vignette is a basement nightclub in the centre of
Birmingham, the venue for an Algorave hosted by the Network Music Festival.
After speaking at the conference during the day, we carried equipment over
beer-sticky disco carpets, past black-painted walls and ceilings, to set up our
live coding rigs in the DJ booth. Performing as the Humming Wires, the author
projected live-coded visuals to accompany Sam Aaron's electronic dance
music. Our improvisations drew on imagery from our laboratory, including a
piece named *Titan* in which a collage of images from the derelict control panel

of the pioneering Titan mainframe included controls to "BOOTSTRAP START" and "DISABLE LEFT PARITY." A small audience of electronic music enthusiasts occasionally danced to the pumping bass, but mostly held pints of beer while standing to watch the gradually elaborated codes.

Each of these vignettes represents a setting where technical systems and abstractions are inserted into an embodied performance context. Although the software systems are all innovative, description of the software innovations alone would be completely inadequate to capture either the essential characteristics of the situation, or the most critical questions for their respective research agendas. They are already technical, and also sites of practice, but with tensions between abstract theory and embodied experience that demand a critical technical practice in music and dance software to at least the extent that Agre advised for AI research software.

No exception to the rule (01:08)[4]

Do the latest generation of machine learning (ML) systems represent a different kind of AI, and an "exception to the rule" with regard to the critique I have presented so far? In some ways, these systems are certainly very different to the GOFAI symbolic AI systems that were the focus of Agre's concerns. For a start, the program code doesn't contain arbitrary symbols of the kind described above. Mostly the program code of ML systems relates to statistical training and mathematical optimisation of a model reflecting the data the system has been given. That "model" is encoded as a set of numerical parameters describing relationships between data—and the implications of this kind of model for music research are discussed further in the next section. To the extent that these mathematical relationships might be interpreted as representational "symbols," there is no longer any mystery of the kind expressed as the symbol grounding problem. On the contrary, we know precisely what grounding there has been—the model is grounded in the training data it was given.

The relationship between training data and machine-learning AI systems, or indeed any kind of statistical "big data" algorithm, is no longer a question of obscure philosophical critique. As I write, during the 2020 coronavirus pandemic, national protests have caused reversals of government policy over the use of an algorithm to statistically normalise the predicted grades from cancelled school exams. The word *algorithm* is no longer the potential inspiration for an underground nightclub trend—for example, "Hacking meets clubbing with the 'algorave'" (Cheshire 2013)—but rather a metonym of dystopian and inhuman control: "Why 'Ditch the algorithm' is the future of political protest: Students challenging the A-levels debacle have exposed the anti-democratic politics of predictive models" (Amoore 2020).

---

4   spotify:track:2PCPgUVvFDBMDZJBVKMZQI#1:08.

The ethical and political problems inherent in machine-learning AI are increasingly a focus of concern for commentators and policymakers, as it becomes clear that these methods simply acquire and replicate the biases of the data they have been trained with. Use of public data sets has resulted in systems that replicate public racism, sexism, and other forms of prejudice, leading to frequent occasions where universities, technology companies, or public agencies withdraw both published research data sets and the systems created from them. In some fields of AI, such as facial recognition technologies, the racial biases are so entrenched and the consequent reinforcement of systemic racism so severe that there have been calls for the whole field of research to be halted.

Public awareness of algorithmic bias is now well developed, and many commentators are aware of the way that training data is the primary source of such bias. There is also growing awareness of the economic inequities in the way such training data is acquired and monetised, both in the practices of "surveillance capitalism" (Zuboff 2019) and in the unregulated labour markets through which people are recruited to create training data in low-income countries or at rates far below the minimum wage (Moreschi, Pereira, and Cozman 2020).

Contemporary society is facing many challenges arising from these legal and commercial developments, and many of the issues just mentioned have an impact on music and the creative industries. But in the context of this book, a critical, but less-often noted, question relates to the way that machine-learning-based AI can be used in apparently creative contexts.

Generative machine learning systems (at the time of writing, most widely associated with the Generative Adversarial [neural] Network or GAN), use their training data not only to construct a statistical model corresponding to the training data provided, but also to generate completely new instances of data that will be compatible with the same model. At the time of writing, the GPT-3 system has been used to demonstrate entertaining, sometimes impressive, pastiche. While often nonsensical at a logical level, the output of this system quite recognisably imitates the style of the training examples it has been given (Bender et al. 2021).

In terms of musical composition and performance, use of such systems clearly demands further application of critical technical practice, and is indeed no exception to Agre's rule that we must be overtly philosophical in understanding the relationship between the (formal) mathematical models, and the (embodied) data sets and their application.

Just to be clear, at the time I write this, I am not aware of any generative machine learning system that has produced particularly impressive results in music composition. My critical concerns are drawn from the well-known successes (and subsequent concerns regarding training bias) of GAN methods in image synthesis, and dramatic recent advances in text synthesis as demonstrated in the GPT-3 system. Nevertheless, there is no technical reason to doubt that similar or related methods will be effective in music synthesis, and that the same critical problems will apply in all these creative domains.

The key dynamic, I claim, in all these situations is that we humans have always found it fascinating when a mechanical system—an *objective* entity belonging to the purely material world of objects—exhibits behaviour that appears to be *subjective*, belonging to the world of intersubjective reciprocity that is the foundation of social relations. The classical narratives of statues or machines coming to life, and the frightening consequences as humans employ them or fall in love with them, are repeated from Pygmalion, to the Golem, to Karel Čapek's Robots, E. T. A. Hoffmann's Sandman, and innumerable repetitions in our contemporary popular culture.

According to this interpretive dynamic, machine-learning AI *appears* to exhibit subjective behaviour precisely because it *does* exhibit subjective behaviour—the millions of observations of human subjectivity that have been collated and stored in its training data. In one early and disturbing demonstration of GANs, a system trained on pornographic images produced new images that were stylistically pornographic, reproducing the subjective experience of glimpsing pornographic images, while not actually containing any recognisable parts of human bodies or pornographic acts. A more recent demonstration of bias in GANs showed that missing details of President Obama's face would be reconstructed as the face of a white person because of the racist subjectivity through which the training data had been collected. These systems might be regarded as "subjectivity factories," dedicated to collecting (through their training data) human subjectivity, and packaging it to be replayed.

I have argued, along with others, that the illusion of mechanical agency, derived from real but invisible humans, is no more than sophisticated puppetry—a reality that was advertised long ago in the naming of Amazon Mechanical Turk, which is one of the leading labour exchanges for the unregulated collection of subjective judgements, but named after the famous hoax in which a mechanical chess player had a human hidden inside it (Blackwell 2021).

In the creative arts, there is a well-established discourse in relation to such hidden labour or passing off others' work as one's own. A machine learning AI system such as GPT-3, if claimed to demonstrate original subjective creativity rather than acknowledging that it is reprocessing the subjective creations of others, might be described as an enterprise of institutionalised plagiarism. Indeed, many commercial products and research prototypes are quite capable of directly replicating phrases and sentences that were literally stored in their training data. If we consider everyday applications such as machine translation systems, how surprised would we be to find that the output phrase is an exact quotation from a poem, from Wikipedia, or indeed from an anonymous worker inside the Mechanical Turk? Whether or not the plagiarism involves exact quotation, recent demonstrations have crossed the line between pastiche and passing-off to an extent that could certainly be legally contested for works still under copyright, avoided only through the expiry of copyright in a widely reproduced demonstration that a GAN trained on the works of Rembrandt could then output a perfectly convincing "new" Rembrandt. Such technical achievements, while impressive when understood to be the work of a machine, would be deeply problematic if (as some AI pundits claim) the machine is to be treated legally as if it were a person.

The legal, ethical, and commercial implications of using these technologies within the creative arts are almost wholly untested at present. Copyright law was framed in relation to certain methods of mechanical reproduction, often privileging the business needs of publishers over and above the many previously established conventions of quotation, attribution, or collective authorship that might have been applied in specific and distinct cultural settings. Nevertheless, attribution of authorship is one of the rights recognised in the Universal Declaration of Human Rights—and there are few musical traditions in which it is considered appropriate to obscure or deny the original creator of a tune or technique, even where it has been shared freely. Unfortunately, it appears that misattribution and denial is fundamental to the enterprise of puppetry that is the basis of machine-learning AI. Further advances in GAN applications seem likely to make this worse, for example through the methods of "authorship obfuscation," a field apparently created in the hope of protecting whistle-blowers or human rights activists (e.g., Brennan, Afroz, and Greenstadt 2012), but in practice a set of techniques that could render plagiarism almost undetectable.

These, then, are the ways in which the latest advances and continued research into machine-learning-based AI are no exception to the rule of critical technical practice. Philosophical critique remains essential, as this section has demonstrated, especially in relation to the (explicit or implicit) claims made by technology developers for their AI systems. However, the configurations of the body in relation to theory, and the sociotechnical contexts in which practice is conducted, continue to change fluidly. Critical technical practice is not a set of knowledge, but a set of processes. In the remaining sections of this chapter, I provide some concrete illustrations of what these look like, in relation to my own experience of technical advances.

ON THE FLOOR (01:16)[5]

As an example of a music research context in which the statistical modelling approaches of machine learning AI might be applied, this section gets up on the floor (of the laboratory) with an overview of the Virtual Violins project, established as an interdisciplinary collaboration between professor of mechanical vibration Jim Woodhouse, professor of auditory neuroscience Brian Moore, and professor of music and science Ian Cross, with the author joining that team as an advisor to research being conducted by Claudia Fritz. The goal of this project was to gain improved understanding of the acoustics of the violin, through precise measurement of the vibration characteristics of a range of violins, followed by synthesis of new "virtual" violins in which the vibration was modified in controlled ways. Although the mathematical methods used in this project are not technically the same as those used in machine learning research at the time of writing, the overall approach is broadly similar to the logic of generative machine learning systems described in the previous section—first,

---

5 spotify:track:2PCPgUVvFDBMDZJBVKMZQI#1:16.

collect data that is representative of some phenomenon of interest; second, use the data to construct a statistical model that characterises that phenomenon; then third, generate new data using this model.

Statistical modelling of complex data often uses a geometric analogy, in which data samples can be considered as points in a multidimensional space. If a group of points in the training data are considered to be similar, the modelling task is to describe the region within the space that contains all such similar points. As a simple example, imagine teaching a machine learning system to recognise the concept "New Zealand." We can do this with a two-dimensional space, where the dimensions in this case would be latitude and longitude. The system might be trained by repeatedly telling it the map coordinates of various towns in New Zealand. After receiving numerous examples, the system would eventually learn that the concept "New Zealand" can be applied to the region in this two-dimensional space where the latitude dimension of all the training examples is always more than 35 but less than 46, while the longitude dimension of the training examples is always more than 176.5 but less than 178. The more locations are provided, the more precise these bounds can be made (including, potentially, the more accurate non-rectangular shape of the country). If the geometric model is sufficiently accurate, then it can also be used to "generate" a new location that might be a new town, or the site of a future town.

Practical machine learning systems are more complex than this simple example, but only in the number of dimensions, which is so large (often hundreds, thousands, or millions of dimensions) that it is difficult to imagine the geometry in any intuitive way. In particular, just as with visual perspective projections of 3D scenes into 2D, points that are actually very far apart in multidimensional space might appear close together when seen from a certain angle.

In the Virtual Violins project, the many dimensions of interest for statistical modelling include the different ways in which the body of a violin can vibrate (up and down, side to side, end to end, and across the f-holes), and the many ways in which we describe and perceive the sound of violins. The mechanical design of the violin has evolved so that the action of the bow on the string produces a rich and mathematically complex sound with an extremely wide range of frequency components beyond simple harmonics. The body of the violin has evolved to enable the multiple different vibration modes, each adding a further layer of resonance and damping. In addition to the many dimensions of these mechanical features, there are also many dimensions of interpretation that can be applied to the sound. The expert violinist hears the sound in terms of other instruments they have heard, of the characteristic tone of particular performers, of the expressive goals of different composers, and of the vocabulary of character and connoisseurship developed by critics, sound engineers, makers, adjusters, dealers, and collectors of violins.

The goal of our research, when considered at the most abstract level, was to construct a set of statistical models that would allow us to relate these many dimensions to one another, defining the metaphorical region of "violinness" within this complex space of perceptual acoustics, but also learning which regions in the space might be more desirable than others, and what mechanical properties cause one violin to be better than another. If represented statistically, of course, this would allow us to "generate" new violins with a sound that is both desirable and characteristically that of a violin, but potentially even better than could be achieved with physical materials.

The research itself proceeded empirically, getting "up on the floor" with violins, violinists, makers, and others to interview, measure, and observe. There is of course an existing body of theory, already based on observation and measurement of violins using scientific instruments. But the theoretical descriptions had never been fully adequate to explain all the characteristics that make one violin sound better than another, or why different people might prefer different instruments. Our multidimensional statistical modelling approach allowed us to create a "map" (in many dimensions) of the different timbres that can be created through varying the mechanical characteristics, and understand the ways in which some descriptions of timbre are more or less similar, in their perceptual implications, to others (Fritz et al. 2012).

This project offers an illustration of how statistical learning methods might produce models that give some insight to inform musical practice. Such models can be used in directly generative ways, for example (in one strategy) to generate new timbres that lie interestingly and ambiguously *between* recognised ways of making or playing the instrument, or (in another strategy) to extrapolate the sound *beyond* that of any known violin for enhanced or dramatic effect.

As mentioned, the statistical models of the Virtual Violins project, while multidimensional, are still far simpler than those created in state-of-the-art machine learning AI systems. But this simplicity does allow a degree of intuition, in understanding how the mechanical object (the violin) is related to embodied modes of perception (by both player and listener), and how these relationships might be predicted or mediated by a statistical model. The ways that embodied practice, skill, and connoisseurship are all implicated in the interpretation of violin sound, and hence these models, is also clear. As the use of machine learning AI systems in music acquires many more statistical dimensions, and ranges further from intuitive understanding, these fundamental characteristics of embodiment are likely to become harder to recognise and appreciate.

Boogie oogie oogie (01:20)[6]

This second technical case study is a reflection on my own experience of playing the song "Boogie Oogie Oogie," and the context of that experience within an embodied technosystem. As an amateur double bass player for over three decades, I had played in many good quality orchestras, occasionally under famous conductors, and often alongside professionals. I can play much of the standard concert repertoire passably, and can contribute to performances in many other genres, so long as I have a score to read. Yet I seldom listen to orchestral music by choice, and would go out of my way to hear bass-heavy dub reggae,

---

6   spotify:track:2PCPgUVvFDBMDZJBVKMZQI#1:20.

funk, techno, or drone metal rather than a string quartet or a piano sonata. So I jumped at the chance, when the excuse presented itself, to buy a fretless Fender bass for my teenage guitarist daughter, justifying the expense because I could also do with a more convenient instrument for those gigs where I would have been amplified anyway.

As it turned out, my daughter rapidly became a far more expert player than I did, successfully auditioning on bass guitar to gain a conservatoire place. But at the time I was preparing the talk on which this chapter is based, I was still taking lessons in the hope of becoming sufficiently proficient to play the music I enjoyed. Unfortunately, despite years of performing experience, and many years teaching and publishing on the peripheries of music research, I had seriously underestimated the degree to which the practical mastery of these two very similar instruments might vary. Almost all these differences can be characterised as embodied, practice-based, and arising from a technosystem of material culture, media technologies, and embodied cognition.

Some of these differences will be very well known to anyone who has strayed across the boundary between Western pop music and Western academic or art music. Although the two bodies of practice can in principle be described in terms of the same fundamental theoretical formalisms—temporal rhythm, harmonic modes, melodic shape, and the relations between them—in practice, there is surprisingly little commonality for the instrumentalist. Despite my two instruments being almost identical in their theoretical musical function, even small differences became obstacles when they are opposed by thirty-year habits. The double bass (which I will refer to as "contrabass" from here, since both instruments are simply called "bass" in normal rehearsal and performance) is held vertically, with strings from left to right. The guitar is held horizontally, with strings from top to bottom. The "top" (uppermost) string on the guitar is the low E, while the "top" (pitched) string on the contrabass is the high G. The neck of the guitar is shorter, meaning that the hand does not need to stretch so far, but the shorter distances allow notes to be played with all four fingers, while contrabassists (in the low register) use only three, meaning that even the simplest scale is played quite differently. The fret positions are numbered as for a guitar, while the contrabass hand positions are counted idiosyncratically with half steps. The left-hand technique is thus completely different (and would have been even more different, if not for the fact that I had bought a fretless guitar). The distance between the guitar strings is half that of the contrabass, making it impossible to produce sustained tone with a finger placed between them, making the right-hand technique also completely different, even by comparison with pizzicato contrabass, and so on.

Yet adjusting the accumulated habits of thirty years' muscle memory was only the starting point for my struggles. A contrabass player is always given a score, never expected to play from memory. A funk band does not welcome music stands onstage. Even where bass guitar parts are shared online, or written out for a student, they are notated as tablature (tabs), rather than pitch and rhythm staff notation. The rhythm does not even appear on the tab, other than counting beats, meaning that the student must listen to a recording to know how the part should sound. A contrabass player would be considered incompetent if they needed to hear a recording in order to interpret a score. A competent band guitarist should have no need to consider individual notes at all—they are given chords, or simple key progressions, and expected to improvise and fill the actual notes within the conventions of a particular genre. All these differences required sustained attention and determination on my part, and I never came close to achieving the last of them.

So these are the practically embodied experiences of music-making that were uppermost in my own reflections at the time I prepared this talk. The contrast between, on one hand, the formal theory (almost identical musical structure and logical layout of the instrument) and, on the other, the quite distinct embodied practice that would be required for me ever to perform "Boogie Oogie Oogie" with a disco band appeared rather extreme.

Once this investigation had started, there were further opportunities for critical technical practice extending beyond the observations I have made so far. All these practical considerations—the use of recordings or not, teaching from tabs versus scores, learning chords rather than bow techniques, and so on—are trivially familiar to any music teacher, professional musician, or even any teenager who has played in both the school orchestra and a rock band. So the experience of being too cool to boogie had already been a feature of my own teenage years, sadly preserved ever since.

A more distinctive set of observations relates to the technical infrastructure and evolution of funk and disco bass, which I naturally interrogated in relation to my previous involvement in the Virtual Violins project. In the course of that project I had, of course, taken my contrabass to the engineering laboratory in order to compare its vibration characteristics with the other members of the violin family we were studying. Like any experienced string player, I was familiar with the evolution of the instrument; with the advances that had been made in the composition of the strings, their tuning and range; the player's stance; the size and weight of the instrument; and the practical techniques and limitations arising from these. Like all members of the research team, I was alert to the subtle interplay between the ways that composers use tone colour of particular techniques in orchestration, the traditions and personalities of the different orchestral sections, the distinct teaching traditions for each instrument, and the influences of collectors and connoisseurs in relation to the work of luthiers and adjusters. All these factors, evolved over centuries of the Western classical music tradition, are integrated into a cultural technosystem such that no single factor can be isolated from the others in causal or interpretive analysis.

It is rare for quite such close attention to be paid to disco as a musical genre. Furthermore, it is hard to gain the necessary critical distance for understanding technical innovations that have all taken place within the past few decades rather than across centuries. The fundamental theoretical insights of the Western music tradition have been achieved over a timescale that must be counted in generations, rather than in research grants. However, it seemed to me at the time I was making this analysis that there was at least as much opportunity for critical technical practice in the disco as on the concert stage. The technosystem of the funk bass guitar is still evolving, but has already achieved a critical vocabulary, a pedagogy, a tradition, and numerous innovators and virtuosi.

I insist on calling the funk bass a technosystem, rather than (as might be done with the violin) a skilled tradition of instrument-making and technique, because of the extent to which electronic devices and circuits are fundamental components of the practice. Advances in pickup and amplifier technology had changed the role of the bass in popular music throughout the twentieth century, from 1920s recordings in which only a tuba could match the volume of drums in a rhythm section, to the more sophisticated recording methods that allowed contrabass players like Milt Hinton and Jimmy Blanton in the 1930s to extend the range of techniques beyond the basic need for volume. The invention of electric bass guitars provided instruments that were both robust and sensitive, to the extent that the slap of strings on a fingerboard (unavoidable when plucking a contrabass fast and loud, and generally deprecated among orchestral players) became an optional gesture rather than an unavoidable necessity.

A key technical development, now so ubiquitous that it could be considered almost an external part of the instrument for a working disco bassist, just as the bow is part of the instrument for an orchestral contrabass, is the audio compressor circuit—either as an effects pedal or built-in to many dedicated bass amplifiers. The compressor reduces the amplitude range of the guitar's output, so that subtle gestures and melodic passages can be easily heard, while the loud percussive slap of the strings against the instrument complements rather than obliterates the rest of the sound. This electronic addition has changed the practice of instrumental technique, which in turn offers new opportunities for stylistic arrangement as the bass becomes able to play a greater role as a percussion instrument. In many funk numbers the bass has become the lead instrument, with the compressed slap and pop being the auditory signature of the genre. Janice Johnson, as bass player and songwriter for "Boogie Oogie Oogie," is an appropriate figurehead for this understanding of the instrument as technosystem, within a critical technical practice.

No more (01:23)[7]

Previous sections in this chapter have discussed the problems of embodiment in artificial intelligence, both classical symbolic GOFAI and machine learning approaches using statistical big data, followed by considerations of how critical issues of embodiment and statistical acoustic analysis can be observed in music research and (reflective) instrumental practice.

In this final section, I return to the intersection of practices in AI and in music, in order to understand the future potential of bringing together Agre's critical frame, developed from the discourse of AI and computing research, alongside the discourse of music research.

---

7   spotify:track:2PCPgUVvFDBMDZJBVKMZQI#1:23.

A key reference is the work of sociologist of science Andrew Pickering, who has explored the "mangle of practice" in which scientific theory is entangled with, then challenged and disrupted by, the material world of the laboratory with its tools and instruments (1995). At first sight, Pickering's work, as with many others engaged in laboratory studies, might appear to be heading in the opposite direction from Agre. Where laboratory studies tries to recognise the practice underlying the theory, Agre's main goal was to recognise the (philosophical) theory underlying the technical practice of the AI programmer. But this apparent opposition is largely a consequence of the peculiar epistemology of AI as a discipline. AI itself, albeit through technical devices, makes direct claims about knowledge, considers itself to be building knowledge systems, and to the extent it is a science (as opposed to a work of imagination—the branch of computer science that tries to make computers work the way they do in films), appears to be creating knowledge about knowledge.

So Agre's complaint that AI researchers are doing covert philosophy is solidly justified. If we inspect their philosophical claims more carefully, this draws attention to problems such as those of social context and embodied cognition that have largely been the concerns of this chapter. There are, of course, branches of Western philosophy that are concerned with knowledge in relation to society and embodiment. Where AI research might prefer to place itself within the positivist legacy of enlightenment natural philosophy, where observation and empirical evidence could be uncontested replacements for skilled argument as the ground of academic enquiry, many of its technical applications are more appropriately understood from the perspective of phenomenology, proposed by Husserl specifically because he saw the need for a science of culture that might address the apparent failings of natural science methods when turned towards human experience.

Phenomenological methods and accounts have indeed been widely applied in the critical analysis of computing technologies, drawing on Agre's pioneering work among others. Recent classics in this genre include, for example, Paul Dourish's *Where the Action Is: The Foundations of Embodied Interaction* (2001), from another AI researcher-turned theorist of user experience and human–computer interaction (HCI). There is a substantial community of computer science academics on the boundary of science and technology studies and HCI, including the present author. This group, as advocated by Agre, does draw directly on critical traditions in philosophy, for example in the recent MIT handbook on *Critical Theory and Interaction Design* (Bardzell, Bardzell, and Blythe 2018) that juxtaposes classic texts in critical theory with reflection and commentary by HCI academics. Many of these authors directly acknowledge the legacy of Agre, and refer to their own work as critical technical practice (e.g., Dourish et al. 2004).

Even though Agre's thinking is so well established within one branch of computer science, the AI researchers to whom he addressed his original critique are still mostly unaware of this work. To the extent that AI researchers are concerned about social issues relevant to their creations, they generally pursue these either through "AI for Good"—attempts to create AI systems that would alleviate poverty, prevent climate change, and so on—or by joining other AI researchers for meetings on "fairness accountability, and trust," where the main focus is on adding these FAT attributes as additional features of AI systems, rather than questioning the philosophical foundations of the whole enterprise.

An alternative would be to turn closer attention towards the practice of AI itself—and here, scholarship regarding practices in music may be more directly relevant (and developments in AI reciprocally relevant to music in turn). One question that has been a major direction of enquiry for the author is the understanding of software production as a craft, in which the programming language is considered to be a tool, and the data to be a material (or, as also happens in more abstract AI research, and potentially in future ML, reversing code and data). There is broad interest in the activity of programming as a craft, for example in a 2018 conference jointly hosted by the Psychology of Programming Interest Group and the Art Workers Guild of London. All AI research is grounded in programming (the original "hacker" culture was closely associated with the MIT AI Lab), and there was a long tradition in the GOFAI era of exploratory programming in which insights were achieved through creating, running, and modifying experimental code in interactive environments such as the LISP REPL (read evaluate print loop). Similar practices continue in machine learning and data science research, where the Python language is interactively created, run, and modified in computational "notebooks."

In recent years, these same craft practices, originally developed for AI research, have been adapted for musical performance, with the REPL a core foundation of many live coding languages. Just as GOFAI coders created improvised extensions and dialects of their programming languages, in order to explore new conceptual structures, many in the first generation of live coders also made their own languages with which to improvise code onstage. The resulting interplay between performance and craft is resulting in phenomenological reflections on this new form of computational musical practice, and on the materiality and craft of coding (Boverman and Griffiths 2014; Blackwell and Aaron 2015). Presenting technical practice as performance, and in front of an audience ("show us your screens," as the TOPLAP live coding manifesto exhorts), makes public this verso of critical technical practice. Contemporary technologies should certainly be open to critique, as Agre observed. But they must also be understood as practice—resulting from human activity, a craft as well as a science, both visible to and accountable to a public. The musical performance practice of live coding is precisely such an opening-up, offering a direct and explicit alternative to the technical configuration of music as industrialised consumer product.

Forms of consumption in which music, and indeed AI technology, can be understood as anything other than a human enterprise might appear to be a peculiarly Western conceit. In many other cultural knowledge systems, including those of the Pacific where I have recently been investigating alternative conceptions of AI, technology is understood to be embedded in relations of materiality and practice through principles such as *whakapapa*—the Māori systems of genealogy that recognise the origins and descent of both the things we make and the ways we make them (Chitman, Māhina-Tuai, and Skinner 2019). Music and AI are both endeavours in which the material arts and the performing arts are brought together in integrated and embodied systems of knowledge. The two can continue to draw on and learn from each other, and reflective practitioners should engage in both craft and critique, both embodied and curious, 'til they just can't boogie no more.

REFERENCES

Adam, Alison. 1998. *Artificial Knowing: Gender and the Thinking Machine*. London: Routledge.

Adams, Rachel. 2019. "*Helen A'Loy* and Other Tales of Female Automata: A Gendered Reading of the Narratives of Hopes and Fears of Intelligent Machines and Artificial Intelligence." *AI and Society* 35: 569–79.

Agre, Philip E. 1997. *Computation and Human Experience*. Cambridge: Cambridge University Press.

Amoore, Louise. 2020. "Why 'Ditch the Algorithm' Is the Future of Political Protest." *Guardian*, 19 August 2020. Accessed 12 March 2021. https://www.theguardian.com/commentisfree/2020/aug/19/ditch-the-algorithm-generation-students-a-levels-politics.

Bardzell, Jeffrey, Shaowen Bardzell, and Mark Blythe, eds. 2018. *Critical Theory and Interaction Design*. Cambridge, MA: MIT Press.

Bender, Emily M., Timnit Gebru, Angelina McMillan-Major, and Shmargaret Shmitchell. 2021. "On the Dangers of Stochastic Parrots: Can Language Models Be Too Big? 🦜." In *Proceedings of the 2021 ACM Conference on Fairness, Accountability, and Transparency*, 610–23. Accessed 18 March 2021. http://faculty.washington.edu/ebender/papers/Stochastic_Parrots.pdf.

Blackwell, Alan F. 1989. "Spatial Reasoning with a Qualitative Representation." *Knowledge-Based Systems* 2 (1): 37–45.

———. 2021. "Ethnographic Artificial Intelligence." In "Artificial Intelligence and Its Discontents," special issue, *Interdisciplinary Science Reviews* 46 (1–2): 198–211.

Blackwell, Alan F., and Sam Aaron. 2015. "Craft Practices of Live Coding Language Design." In *Proceedings of the First International Conference on Live Coding*. Zenodo. http://doi.org/10.5281/zenodo.19318.

Bovermann, Till, and Dave Griffiths. 2014. "Computation as Material in Live Coding." *Computer Music Journal* 38 (1): 40–53.

Brennan, Michael, Sadia Afroz, and Rachel Greenstadt. 2012. "Adversarial Stylometry: Circumventing Authorship Recognition to Preserve Privacy and Anonymity." *ACM Transactions on Information and System Security (TISSEC)* 15 (3): article 12. https://doi.org/10.1145/2382448.2382450.

Cheshire, Tom. 2013. "Hacking Meets Clubbing with the 'Algorave.'" *Wired Magazine*, 29 August 2013. Accessed 12 March 2021. https://www.wired.co.uk/article/algorave.

Chitman, Karl, Kolokesa Uafā Māhina-Tuai, and Damian Skinner, eds. 2019. *Crafting Aotearoa: A Cultural History of Making in New Zealand and the Wider Moana Oceania*. Wellington: Te Papa Press.

Collins, Nick. 2006. "Ornamaton." Programme note for *Baroqtronica: The Art of Machine Listening*, Kettle's Yard, Cambridge, 19 March 2006. Accessed 12 March 2021. https://composerprogrammer.com/music/mar19.pdf.

Devlin, Kate, and Olivia Belton. 2020. "The Measure of a Woman: Fembots, Fact and Fiction." In *AI Narratives: A History of Imaginative Thinking about Intelligent Machines*, edited by Stephen Cave, Kanta Dihal, and Sarah Dillon, 357–81. Oxford: Oxford University Press.

Dourish, Paul. 2001. *Where the Action Is: The Foundations of Embodied Interaction*. Cambridge, MA: MIT Press.

———. 2004. "What We Talk About When We Talk About Context." *Personal and Ubiquitous Computing* 8 (1): 19–30.

Dourish, Paul, Janet Finlay, Phoebe Sengers, and Peter Wright. 2004. "Reflective HCI: Towards a Critical Technical Practice." In *CHI'04 Extended Abstracts on Human Factors in Computing Systems*, 1727–28.

Forsythe, Diana E. 1993. "Engineering Knowledge: The Construction of Knowledge in Artificial Intelligence." *Social Studies of Science* 23 (3): 445–77.

Fritz, Claudia, Alan F. Blackwell, Ian Cross, Jim Woodhouse, and Brian C. J. Moore. 2012. "Exploring Violin Sound Quality: Investigating English Timbre Descriptors and Correlating Resynthesized Acoustical Modifications with Perceptual Properties." *Journal of the Acoustical Society of America* 131 (1): 783–94.

Hogan, Ed. 2021. "Janice Johnson: Artist Biography." AllMusic. Accessed 11 March 2021. https://www.allmusic.com/artist/janice-marie-johnson-mn0001664199.

Kunz, Werner, and Horst W. J. Rittel. 1972. "Information Science: On the Structure of Its Problems." *Information Storage and Retrieval* 8 (2): 95–98.

Lenat, Douglas B. 1995. "CYC: A Large-Scale Investment in Knowledge Infrastructure." *Communications of the ACM* 38 (11): 33–38.

Mnih, Volodymyr, Koray Kavukcuoglu, David Silver, Andrei A. Rusu, Joel Veness, Marc G. Bellemare, Alex Graves, et al. 2015. "Human-Level Control through Deep Reinforcement Learning." *Nature* 518: 529–33.

Moreschi, Bruno, Gabriel Pereira, and Fabio G. Cozman. 2020. "The Brazilian Workers in Amazon Mechanical Turk: Dreams and Realities of Ghost Workers." *Contracampo—Brazilian Journal of Communication* 39 (1). http://dx.doi.org/10.22409/contracampo.v39i1.38252.

Pickering, Andrew. 1995. *The Mangle of Practice: Time, Agency, and Science*. Chicago: University of Chicago Press.

Rittel, Horst W. J., and Melvin M. Webber. 1973. "Dilemmas in a General Theory of Planning." *Policy Sciences* 4 (2): 155–69.

Suchman, Lucy. A. 1987. *Plans and Situated Actions: The Problem of Human-Machine Communication*. Cambridge: Cambridge University Press.

Zuboff, Shoshana. 2019. *The Age of Surveillance Capitalism: The Fight for a Human Future at the New Frontier of Power*. London: Profile Books.

Illusions of Form

David Rosenboom

Composer, Valencia, CA

FRAMEWORKS

Extraction

Perceiving forms enacts *extraction*. Forms are extracted by perceivers that are themselves extractions marked by closed boundaries within environments (brains, algorithms, or other natural or artificial machinations). Perceiving forms involves extracting differentiable entities from continuously emerging and evolving phenomena that can be stored and referred to as parts of the fine structures of particular *nows*, each with its synthesised past and projected future (Rosenboom 2018b). In cognition, the boundaries of forms are extracted from interactions among exogenous inputs and endogenous syntheses of representations suitable for storage. Histories and perceived time are extracted from resyntheses. Perceiving forms also engenders perceiving *perceiving forms* and perceiving *perceiving perceiving forms*, up to Nth-order, recursive, self-referential frameworks, which also include extracting the forms of perceived perceivers (von Foerster 1984, 2014). Perceiving and cognising forms are active, imaginative, creative processes (Rosenboom 2014a).

In 1967, at the University of Illinois in Urbana-Champaign (UIUC), I was fortunate to be a student in a graduate seminar offered by the great composer and systems theorist Kenneth Gaburo called Studies of 20th Century Theoretic Systems. The fifth lecture in that class was titled "An Incipient Theory of Structure" (K. Gaburo 1976). It was a reading, indeed a performance, in which many repetitions of the word "extraction" were juxtaposed against a large variety of terms, statements, gestures, and vocalisations. At several points in the presentation, a specific juxtaposed statement was delivered, "At this point (or at some previous point or points) some of the previous statements may have collected relationally to form a group or groups. If so, each element in each collection would have been extracted, recursively, from its ordered place. In addition, each collection would have been an extraction, recursively, from all statements given" (ibid., [3]).

At the end of the performance, a series of six inferences were presented, each investigating specific contextual conditions for relations among elements in the long list of juxtapositions to form groups. The final inference presented a proposition: "The five statements, i.e., inferences ONE through SIX, satisfy the minimal conditions for an incipient theory of structure, and are, in themselves, an extracted group from the Universal set of statements which could be made regarding the structure of this composition, as well as those which should be made regarding the subject: STRUCTURE" (K. Gaburo 1976, [9]). The key here is that, like in Gaburo's *extraction* composition, the relationships forming groups are extracted through perception and cognition, and the processes for achieving this are recursive and emergent. The great second-order cyberneticist Heinz von Foerster remarked, "I am always seeing form as a structure of relations that can also have different structures of relations than their elements" (2014, 166). Inevitably then, perceivers of forms *are* essential, dynamical parts of the forms being perceived, along with all their differentiations, boundary conditions, and environments. The *eye of the beholder* beckons investigation into the nature of illusion.

Propositional music—models

I sometimes joke that, in the evolution of culture, the primary purpose of labels should be to make themselves obsolete as soon as possible. So be it with *experimental music*, which to my mind, simply underscores the artist's license to establish a unique practice with agency and effectiveness outside the definitions of established practice. So be it also with *propositional music* (Rosenboom 2000c), though after writing about it for some decades now, it still maintains its utility as a conceptual screwdriver for exploring *critical practice* among artists and artist-philosophers, who make work "spanning literary and theoretical discourses" and operate "across art in all its forms and across culture in all its locations" (G. Smith 2018, front matter description). With some degree of consistency, Gregory Bateson's methods for elucidating "metapatterns" connecting mind to nature (1980), and thus to thinking, leaning, and creativity among seemingly diverse domains of human thought and creation, have motivated me to take frequent retrospective looks over my highly heterogeneous work trajectories, now spanning more than five decades in music and its allied arts and sciences, to extract "ideas that connect." This has always revealed self-luminous, sometimes surprising, connecting threads tying together ideas about evolution and emergence within the unfolding nature of musical forms, including those on the scales of individual compositional formulations as well as the superimposed histories of multiple genres and methodologies. This periodic retrospective analysis has become a productive critical practice. Pointedly put, these emergent notions in creative music-making commonly begin with *musical propositions*.

Propositional music is a point of view about composing, in which composers might build proposed models of worlds, universes, evolution, brains, consciousness, or whole domains of thought and life, and then proceed to make dynamical musical embodiments of these models, inviting us to experience them in spontaneously emerging sonic forms. Propositional musical thinking is also contextualised now in the genreless climate from which new generations of musical practitioners are drawing surprising and extraordinary inspirations.

Such a practice fuels creative music methodologies by explicating this idea of *propositional music* as an approach to composition, improvisation, analysis, and adjacent areas of interdisciplinary—or perhaps *anti-disciplinary*—thought. According to this view, composing involves proposing models for whole musical realities, emphasising the dynamic emergence of forms through evolution and transformation. Their correspondence to proposed realities navigates a profound and complex meeting place for creative license and scientific verification. This is an area where music, science, and philosophy can meet in deep theoretical territory, one in which distinctions may collapse into a new kind of *artscience*.

Ideas about morphogenesis, music as a vehicle for exploring human knowledge, the emergence of global properties, the nature of forms, comprehending initially undefined or imponderable forms, and more meet naturally in this terrain. Furthermore, when we combine this with currently emerging *neuromusical propositions* (Rosenboom 1997; Nijholt 2019), we can be catapulted down our hierarchies of presumption towards necessary first principles again and again, questioning our understanding of evolution and categorisation. Following Frederik Stjernfelt's analysis of Charles Sanders Peirce's categories of *dicisigns* as basic elements in semiotic cognition that even reach down the evolutionary ladder to primitive metabolism (Stjernfelt 2014), we might soon discover a *biomusical semiotics* emerging from neuromusical propositions. Out of this can come inspired rethinking about musical creativity and the profoundly integrative powers of auditory perception—enhanced by musical experience—to *hear* relationships among diverse phenomena and find clues to hidden orders of complexity and unsuspected patterns. With *active imaginative listening* we can learn to distinguish the features of complexity and parse subtle relationships among newly differentiable entities (Rosenboom 2014a).

Propositional music often requires collapsing distinctions among a priori formal percepts in order to investigate the nature of self-organising and emergent musical forms. Along with this comes a concept I call *dynamic dimensionality*, which has implications in both the arts and physical sciences. Dynamic dimensionality invokes the idea that the dimensions of description for processes and forms may continuously materialise and dematerialise. This is analogous to actions of parameterising articulators of forms and processes and their comparative complexities and viewing them as dynamic, not fixed.

Other important composing tools in this work have included: musical configuration spaces with contingent and adjacent possibilities, extended musical interface with the human nervous system, and active imaginative listening as performance and as composition.

In earlier writings on *propositional music*, I tried to challenge the cognitive superglue that seems to bind *form* and *cause* in Western minds—that forms always result from the actions of hierarchies of ordering agents. This worldview obscures the role of minds as order-seekers that extract distinctions among things like sculpture and unformed lumps of raw material. "What we refer to as formed, . . . is usually imbued with the intelligence of the forming agent, which we somehow distinguish from the natural order of the unformed lumps" (Rosenboom 2000c, 213).

Propositional music similarly addresses the activity of model building as one of process. It uses the idea of a *model* as a multi-dimensional framework inviting active engagement in exploration and discovery inside a propositional world. This is not about proposing imperialistic prescriptions for viewing models as hypothetically precise representations of worlds presumed to be unquestionably *real*—real as replicable in the sense of scientific positivism. It is more about a process of discovering palpable substance than about verifying representations of the represented.

We situate the word *propositional* here in a way allowing it to address semantic and aesthetic propositions separately from the idea of provability. The artist here *proposes* in the process of making, and through critical feedback, refines and enriches the field of possibilities for interactive extraction that the making process can produce for the *interactee*.[1]

Of course, the word *proposition* has morphed through myriad presumptive definitions and posited interpretations since the ambiguity of Aristotle's *protasis* (Baratin et al. 2014). We take a mediating position between, on the one hand, idealistic, scientific unification and mandated realist testing, and on the other hand, free *what-if, as-if* experimentation in arts and aesthetics with no realist mandate. Still, musical propositions result in sensible things. We imbed research in process with emerging knowledge rather than in product and coded knowledge. This is critical to the reflexive nature of propositional music practice.

Such practice embraces continuous questioning and avoids conclusiveness. Semantic mappings and assessments of meaning are, thus, always evolving. In the natural human quest for stability, this is hard to cognise. It reminds us of the shock to logical positivism delivered by Kurt Gödel's discovery of incompleteness, described here by Rebecca Goldstein: "The idea that the criteria for semantic truth could be separated from the criteria for provability was so unthinkable from a positivist point of view that the substance of the theorem [incompleteness of arithmetic] simply could not penetrate" (2005, 160).

Later in this chapter, I provide some descriptions of music and media examples from my own *oeuvre*, which are offered to describe examples of specific methodologies for composition, performance, improvisation, and interdisciplinary thinking in this domain. The intention is to outline some premises with which to approach making propositional music and some fundamental steps to consider in constructing systems for composition and improvisation with these ideas. Perhaps they will also stimulate ideas about ways to work with naturally emerging networked interactivity, how substantive phenomena can spread through complex dissipative and resonant processes, implications of the *infosphere*[2] for propositional art-making, the relationship of propositional music to society, and potential sources of new mythology for our culture.

---

1   The term interactee was introduced to me by the brilliant installation artist Sara Roberts.
2   The word infosphere refers to the environment of information enfolding human society, analogous to the atmosphere, biosphere, etc., and usually used in reference to electronically reproducible and transmittable information.

Qualities of change—form as cognitive synthesis

Time is manufactured in music. Music is not *of time*, it creates experienced time through a distribution of *nows* in meta-time-space. (See Rosenboom 2018b for further elaboration.) We may view individual cognitive temporalities as labels for the dimensions on which we *move* in multidimensional, parameterised spaces in order to articulate and extract information about the other dimensions. We note that multiple times (nows) are not imbedded in a meta-time-space. Therefore, perceiving multiple times isn't possible, at least within the dimensional structure that perception materialises inside cognition. Perceived time may also be thought of as a means of generating shared experiences among observers sufficiently *close* to each other about information articulated on the remaining dimensional axes.

We regard this as an anisotropic process, because we experience things individually as one *thing* coming *after* another. *Afterness* is contingent upon storage and memory processes that also engender comparisons and judging *beforeness*. Much of this is relatively unconscious, except when disciplines of internal analysis bring it into awareness, and new consciousness arises. Describing apprehensions engenders dimensionality, axes with scales of measure enabling comparisons, and similarity and dissimilarity judgements among phenomena. Dimensionality (number of discrete dimensions) is then variable and emergent, creating virtual spaces in which strongly entangled things are viewed as *close* to each other, and weakly entangled things are considered *far* apart. Tactual and kinaesthetic senses are necessary for judging close and far. Emergent dimensionality, though, may stimulate imagining an isotropic view of the axes of motion, enabling cross- and auto-correlations forward and backward. It may be fanciful, or maybe not so fanciful, then, to envision a *time-eye-in-the-back-of-the-head* (Rosenboom 1984).

A first illusion about forms is that forms are fixed. Rather, forms are emergent. A second illusion is that stability can be achieved by pre-stating the dynamics among components of forms. The multiplicity of adjacent possibilities among component parts prevents that. Theoretical biologist and complex systems researcher Stuart Kauffman has shown again and again that as reasonably complex systems evolve, the branching possibilities for future system states, produced by the recombinant adjacencies of component parts, explode. For biological systems, this expansion is such that only a tiny portion of possible pathways can be explored during the anticipated longevity of the universe (Kauffman 2016). Furthermore, how boundaries are drawn, delineating what the component parts of a system are and separating them from each other, also involves uncertainties. Consequently, the ability to pre-state the branching pathways a system might follow is extremely limited. This is not adequately described by applying commonly understood notions of randomness. It is, rather, more about what is, indeed, *knowable*.

Attempting to pre-state outcomes into imagined futures, the states of which cannot themselves be pre-stated, can lead to self-contradictions and other illusions when applied to the perception of forms. Each present moment, a *now*—multiple *nows* may be possible—contains a synthesised past and imagined future (Rosenboom 2018b). Energy, matter, time, and space can interact in ways that collapse useful distinctions among them, questioning their designation as primary. In quantum field theory, a particle can be said to carry its own proper time with it inherent in the waveform of its mass. *Wave* and *particle* are only words representing concepts. In critiquing quantum field theory, Sunny Y. Auyang writes, "Recollection is a kind of imagination occurring in the present" (1995, 179). The role of the past in making predictions and identifying forms is a subtle, non-trivial, creative exercise.

The idea of *precedent*—that the way something was observed or judged to be determined in a particular way in the past should determine how it should be judged or determined in the future—suddenly comes under a light of scrutiny. Two musical analogies come to mind: my own *A Summary History of Humans in the World* (2017) and John Cage's *Lecture on the Weather* (1976). In my *A Summary History . . .*, a video plays showing a hand writing a series of nineteen lines of text with a fountain pen on watercolour paper, capsulising (my view of) how human culture got from forming habits to experiencing non-correspondence among models for tools—deterministic engineering—with ever-expanding observation abilities, beginning with this first line,

habits develop in primitive states engendering sustainable forms
— to —>,

and ending with these lines,

a non-correspondence of idealized tools with the behavior of the universe at
observable extremes slowly becomes evident
— to —>
illusions of "law" and "precedent"—even of "form"—may be at play here
— to —>
now what do we do? (Rosenboom 2018c)

Along with this fixed video, a solo performance emerges, in which interactive software captures samples from the history of musical material developed through improvisation, and makes the samples available for the performer to build new musical forms with collaged histories and in-the-moment extensions. (See MF2.1 in the online repository for this book to view the complete work.[3])

Cage's *Lecture . . .* also questions the idea of precedent in this excerpt from its opening, spoken preface: "Of all professions the law is the least concerned with aspiration. It is concerned with precedent, not with discovery, with what was witnessed at one time in one place, and not with vision and intuition. When the

---

3 Access the online repository at https://orpheusinstituut.be/en/sound-work-media-repository. Further details of the repository can be found in the appendix to this book on p. 355.

law is corrupt, it is corrupt because it concentrates its energy on protecting the rich from the poor. Justice is out of the question. That is why not only aspiration but intelligence (as in the work of Buckminster Fuller) and conscience (as in the thought of Thoreau) are missing in our leadership" (Cage [1976] 1979, 4). Following the full preface, twelve speaker-vocalists deliver texts extracted by means of I Ching chance operations from the writings of Henry David Thoreau, along with film by Luis Frangella and extraordinary field recordings of thunder and other sounds by Maryanne Amacher. I was fortunate to both assist in the production and perform in the world premiere of *Lecture on the Weather* on 15 June 1976 with Cage at York University, Toronto, in collaboration with the Canadian Broadcasting Corporation. The CBC commissioned the work in observance of the Bicentennial of the USA. The experience was transformative and occurred during a particular atmosphere of discussion in international contemporary music communities about composers and political action. French philosopher Michel Foucault's commentary seems relevant here, "We could . . . say that the law works in the imaginary, since the law imagines and can only formulate all the things that could and must not be done by imagining them. It imagines the negative" (2007, 47).

Perceived forms may be more appropriately thought of like verbs, items of action, rather than like nouns, items of distinction that only seem to be fixed. *A chord is a verb, not a noun.* Forms evolve through actions of perception and cognition, internal endogenous data reduction, and the synthesis of *idiologs* (mental images entangled in memory).[4] Form emerges via *holarchical*[5] processes resulting from simultaneous, up-down, evolution on macro- and micro-scales of time, space, energy, matter, dimensions, complexity, and cognitive extension. The marked description of a particular form results from both bottom-up and top-down evolution mediated by feedback. Its concretisation is illusory.

Forms are also extracted from environments. Environments receive the effects and retain the tracings of emerging forms within them. Environments bear witness to entangled forms dynamically evolving. Individual observers obtain information about dynamical systems and evolving forms from fragments of their environments. If particular effects (tracings) of those systems and forms impinge with considerable *redundancy* upon multiple fragments of their environments, then multiple observers will obtain information about these systems and forms that seems coherent and consistent. They will then agree and judge them as stable and relatively fixed.

This brings up an idea about environments as broadcast mediums. Intelligent entities leave imprints on environments, and detection (extraction) of information (regularities/irregularities) from environments by other receiving

---

4   A more detailed definition of idiolog would be: the form of processes involved in representing the idea of a quality. Usually used in reference to the encoded form of human percepts or sensory-motor or expressive qualities residing in the electro-chemical activity of the brain's neural networks and memory. (See also a discussion of qualia later in this chapter.)

5   In previous publications, I have used the term holarchy when referring to structural entities that result from simultaneous evolution on both macro- and micro-scales and have both bottom-up and top-down dynamical building processes (Rosenboom 1997, 2000c).

entities completes a communication channel. An analogy in quantum physics emphasises the environment as a communication channel through which observers learn about physical systems. In this case, multiple observers obtain information from fragments of the environment. Observers do not extract their data about a system by directly measuring it, rather "a vast majority (if not all) of our information is obtained *indirectly* by probing a small fraction of the environment" (Ollivier, Poulin, and Zurek 2004, 1).

The extraction of presumptions about palpable forms depends on boundary determinations segmenting component parts, amplification of selected parts (combined effects of attentional focus and lateral inhibition of neighbouring phenomena), and redundancy (reinforcing multiple observations judged to be coherent). "An operational notion of objectivity emerges from redundant information as it enables many independent observers to find out the state of the system without disturbing it" (Ollivier, Poulin, and Zurek 2004, 4). "The whole idea of redundancy is that it allows one to be sloppy in decoding the message and still 'get it right'" (4). "Objectivity comes at the price of singling out a preferred observable of S [a system] whose eigenstates are redundantly recorded in E [an environment]" (3). "Hence, observers probing fractions of the environment can act *as if* the system had a state of its own—an *objective* state" (3). This brings up the idea of "Quantum Darwinism—the idea that the perceived *classical reality* is a consequence of the selective proliferation of information about the system" (3).

Boundary setting is particularly important in decoding musical forms. It is also critical in assessing the fine graining (as in granular synthesis) necessary for measuring degrees of order or entropy in a collection. It enables groupings to be extracted with internal contingencies in space-time among sublevel parts from which local sequences and local times emerge. Perception of form involves perceiving and extracting presumed contingencies. This enables detection of hierarchies, a kind of data reduction enabling the formation of memories, and thus, personal time. Cognition makes form from entanglements among endogenous and exogenous inputs. The result: form emerges in cognition, and forms are *propositions*. Finally, realities are propositions, and emergent mind is built from a tangled network of mini-reality propositions with interacting resonances. We might call this *searching for form*, or *form-finding* among a field of adjacent possible forms.

In his foundational *Laws of Form*, G. Spencer-Brown writes: "a universe comes into being when a space is severed or taken apart. . . . By tracing the way we represent such a severance, . . . [we] can begin to see how the familiar laws of our own experience follow inexorably from the original act of severance. . . . At this stage, the universe cannot be distinguished from how we act upon it, and the world may seem like shifting sand beneath our feet" (Spencer-Brown 1972, v).

Forms are built in cognition from intertwined endogenous and exogenous processes that can even be trans-sensory. They are fundamentally emergent and *holarchical*, arising from observed regularities and complexities extracted among lower-level units that are modulated by downward feedback from high-level integrative functions. Emergent, holarchical forms also evolve through the feedback processes of *critical contemplation*. These can be second-order reflections on reflection as well as primary feedback from initially reflecting.

Critical analysis of the *role* of observations when misperceived as causal energies making forms appear static is also pertinent here. Wimsatt (2013) proposes the idea of *generative entrenchment*, in which extracting presumed regularities leads to *tendencies* for forms to grow in robustness or persistence and increase in complexity as a result of *factors* guiding those tendencies. This is quite distinct from characterising forms as resulting exclusively from law-like, physically deterministic, causal fabrications. Thus, critical analysis of interdependencies among observation, perception, thought, form, and cause is crucial in propositional music practice.

Buddhist logic views reality and the forms we extract from it as moving and thoughts as static constructions. The legendary Buddhist philosopher Nāgārjuna writes (stanza 48), "If a mind apprehends a form with inherent existence then the mind will apprehend its own nature. Such a mind has arisen from causes and conditions, so it is a dependent arising which lacks inherent existence. In the same way, form does not exist truly, so how can that mind apprehend a form with true existence?" (Komito 1987, 90–91).

In thinking about how we describe systems producing forms, we might invoke these two delineations:

> *Formal*—systems and forms described by simple axiomatic or combinatorial formulations; but, due to incompleteness, in formal descriptions, some questions always remain that are undecidable within the system. *Continuous*—systems and forms are much more difficult to describe, because they have dynamic indeterminacies; introducing discrete factors to try to simplify the descriptions nearly always reduces *continuous* models to *formal* models.

Another approach invoked in propositional music could be:

> *Ponderable*—systems and forms that are thinkable, not necessarily in language or signs, rather in musical intellect; this may require viewing ponderability within entirely new cognitive paradigms.

Returning to Nāgārjuna (stanza 45), "Neither does inherently existent form, having the nature of elements, arise from elements nor from itself and not even from others. Therefore, it does not exist, does it?" (Komito 1987, 90).

The mouse and the sequoia—scales and stability

The time and space perspectives of form perceivers mediate what is retained in memory as palpable substance. Forms with greater temporal and spatial extent than a perceiver's—perhaps something like typical lifespan or breadth of time and space scale awareness and cognitive extension—may appear stable: architectural forms, protons, apparent laws of nature, a sequoia tree, musical traditions. Forms with far less temporal and spatial extent than a perceiver's may appear unstable, fleeting, or ephemeral: quantum resonances, individual nows, neural impulses, unpremeditated thoughts, a mouse, radical musical appearances.

Human-made musical forms exist largely in relatively mid-range or short-range material extensions. One individual sonata is short-range. *Sonata form* is mid-range. Perhaps all individual sonatas can be heard as particular short-range manifestations of the same mid-range composition: *Sonata Form*. That form is historically emergent, shaped and continuously evolved by many contributors. In contrast, *raga* forms in Indian classical music are culturally emergent, not owned by individuals, yet continuously evolved by the multiple generations of an entire culture, who inject their short-range, spontaneous, creative impulses, which influence evolution. So is the case with the *blues* in Afrological music, a continuously realisable form with infinite possibilities for variations in expression. Composer-performer Wadada Leo Smith has described an integration of evolutionary progression and underlying continuity in jazz, from bebop through simpler forms of hard bop and on to emerging complexities in extension bop: ". . . but the basic music form did not essentially change because the use of the song form and the blues continued to hold this new music within" ([W.] L. Smith 1973, [18]).

We could say then that stability is a relative matter. René Thom suggests that "forms that are subjectively identifiable and are represented in our language by a substantive are necessarily structurally stable forms" (1975, 14). We note here the use of *subjectively identifiable* as key. All forms are subject to perturbations within their environments, and here we are making subjective similarity judgements among multiple iterations of an entity or phenomenon to decide whether it can be called *stable*. This, though, is also a matter of the scale of observation. The most stable musical drone we can produce is likely to reveal wild and scattered instabilities when viewed with a temporal microscope. This, in fact, is a primary proposition underlying my composition *Two Lines* (Rosenboom 1989). The most stable, very long drone I could play on a viola was analysed for microscopic pitch variations, inevitably resulting from physiological dynamics in playing. The variations were then greatly amplified and quantised into the pitches of a score, which composer-performer-philosopher Anthony Braxton and I realised many times in duet form (Rosenboom and Braxton 1995).[6] The result seemed to exhibit very complex behaviour, yet somehow sensible as not being random. Later multi-dimensional complexity analysis revealed that, indeed, attractors around certain pitch tendencies could be found in the notes. Stability and irregularity, in this case, proved to be two factors dancing in intricate balance.

If compositional acts involve situating conditions in environments that engender emergent processes in which forms may be extracted, and if these relationships emerge through selective, recursive, networked processes that are continuously evolving, then composition is a kind of *critical creative practice*. Music-making of this kind involves unconstrained, continuously evolving

---

6   A recording of *Two Lines* can be streamed at https://www.dramonline.org/albums/david-rosenboom-two-lines.

technical practice, and situates spontaneous music-making as a critical synthesis of composition, research, and performance in *propositional music*.

Intelligence?—Recursive reflexivity and critical practice

We speak about musical intelligence, or intelligence in general, as if we know what it is. Instead, we experience that knowing primarily in the negative; that is, we believe we know, or at least can sense, when intelligence is *not* present. Elsewhere, in writing about paradigmatic parallels and complementarities among experiences in experimental musical composition and some of the primary problems in interstellar communication, I have proffered an idea about regarding *intelligence as a field*. This idea emerges from considering the variety of forms in which intelligence could possibly manifest itself, and particularly, the vast range of physical and temporal scales on which it could manifest. In the search for extra-terrestrial intelligence, or closer to home, non-human intelligence, we must confront the possibility that, because the nature of the intelligence we search for *cannot be known in advance*, and if we engage in such a search only with the perspective of our familiar presumptive models, we might miss apprehending what we search for. This is similar to the problem of approaching a new and unfamiliar form of music without the openness of perception and cognition required to find and recognise the intelligence within it. We simply miss it! To make matters worse, the propensity to regard intelligence as *knowable* leads to causal forming—extraction—of what is regarded as *artificial*, technical forms of something that is *unknowable*.

There are many strong correspondences in what is described above with Phillip Agre's critiques of artificial intelligence (1997a, 1997b). To his critiques, I add the observation that it is interesting to wonder about how we can make artificial versions of something that is defined with only vague presumptions. Agre's inoculation for this disease is *critical technical practice*. "A primary goal of critical technical work, then, is to cultivate awareness of the assumptions that lie implicit in inherited technical practices" (Agre 1997a, 105).

A critical technical practice is one that rethinks its own premises as routine work. We know that classical engineering design principles eventually fail when they are relied upon to create forms objectified to be fault-free, entirely predictable, and fully controllable. Alternatively, *emergent engineering* principles, developed through investigating complexity dynamics, value adaptability over perfect stability.[7] Process is more sustainable than product.

Agre continues, "To this end, it is best to start by applying the most fundamental and familiar technical methods to substantively new ends" (Agre 1997a, 105). An example of this in contemporary music is the prepared piano. Centuries of design engineering have gone into developing the piano to a high level of engineering perfection in an attempt to best serve its presumed purposes. In the twentieth century, though, composer-performers found a new purpose for the instrument by inserting objects inside its mechanisms to open

---

7 See Krakauer (2019) for a detailed description of the objectives of emergent engineering.

new worlds of sounds. Today, ironically and productively, prepared piano techniques have also been codified and perfected to a very high technical level.

With the development of electronic music, the idea of standardisation in musical instruments was challenged. Previously, an instrument was considered a thing to be mastered, worthy of performers spending lifetimes practising with tools to be relied on by composers for predictable results. Electronics, though, is best thought of as a malleable medium, like clay. Literally, composition, performance, and instrument design began to merge and distinctions among them collapsed. A prime example of this is the legendary SalMar Construction of Salvatore Martirano, which was developed through years of critical refinement in composing, performing, and engineering practice until an individual's personal, integrated, musical system became embodied in circuitry (Rosenboom 2020a).

Artificial intelligence purports to be able to enact artificial reasoning, partially to demystify itself. But is this intelligence? Intelligence is recursively self-reflective and can implement reasoning about reasoning. Artificial reasoning has not been shown, in my judgement, to be able to enact *musical intelligence*. For example, the quest to build improvising programs with presumptive models about what music or a musical style is generally fails. However, other approaches, in which the instrument essentially does a kind of research on the actions of an improvising performer, and then makes the results available to the performer to activate at will, are much more useful. In my work, *Predictions, Confirmations and Disconfirmations* (Rosenboom 1992d, 2012b), a software tool that I wrote, called Hierarchical Form Generator (HFG), uses a simple, partial model of perception to parse improvised input into low-level units (like musical phrases), potentially combine them into higher-level groupings using an expectancy measure derived from extracted patterns, and make the results available to the performer to call up and transform within a continuing improvisation. This tool evolved through critical practice and refinement, beginning with an interactive brain-computer music interface (BCMI) project in the 1970s (Rosenboom 1997). It is not, however, a tool that presumes any extant model of musical form, style, or genre. It permits improvisation to begin from a point of spontaneous intention arising. Its richness grows with the improvisor's proprioceptive skills (practical) for interacting with a self-generated musical environment tuned and sharpened (limiting) through practice and feedback. (See MF2.2 for an introductory talk I gave in 1991 after writing HFG, followed by my first performance with it.)

This practice imbeds research inside creation along with documentation and new frameworks for discovery. It includes establishing ever-evolving principles of interactivity and extending notions of tools. A continuous collapsing of distinctions among terminologies also fuels this critical practice. "By the end of the story, though, deeper technical issues about representation and learning will have arisen through reflection on difficulties encountered along the way" (Agre 1997a, 106).

Concurrent complexities—adaptation and dynamics

Recent developments in understanding complex adaptive processes play a significant role in this new musical landscape. Again, music provides an environment for experimentation. Complexity can be *heard*. It is a phenomenon of apprehension. It is tempting to regard apparent complexity as special and likely to have resulted from intelligent initiation. In perception and recognition, *simplicity* and *complexity* are relativistic and complimentary terms. Cultural artefacts may appear to have simple forms in relation to the perceived complexity of nature. A simple, large-scale form, like a building, may result from a complex arrangement of small parts. The apparent simplicity in the outer form of a sand pile may result from an immensely complex fitting together of grains. The temporal structure of music offers many analogies. A musical drone may appear simple. However, when one listens to it actively for a very long time, the subtle variations in its microstructure may reveal limitless complexity. Similar exposure to apparently random noise (like a waterfall) can activate resonant, recognising circuits, such that many recognisable things are heard inside the noise. The stochastic arrangement of a cloud of sounds may have simple direction in its overall movement. It may be a fundamental trait of adaptive organisms to develop correlations between the derived complexity-simplicity of a perception and the projected complexity-simplicity of a source or cause of that which is perceived. Such correspondences may not always be borne out, and this might be critical to keep in mind when interacting with unknown intelligences. The digit sequence of π appears complex, but can be produced by applying simple rules. Similarly, we dream of discovering simple rules, which when applied, could produce a whole universe. Music composition today includes corresponding ideas.

Note that these notions about complexity differ from some common, impressionistic meanings in music, which tend to equate complexity with something that is difficult to hear or described as unpleasant and "hard" to listen to. We know we can hear, or learn to hear, and make fine discriminations between sound aggregates produced with different probability distributions, or different applications of set orderings. We may not be able to discern the generative methods behind them, but we can differentiate among various results. To each result, we ascribe a sound *quality*. As always, effortful practice opens doors. Without that, the fantastic plasticity of our nervous system will dutifully allocate the brain's resources to becoming ever more efficient at tuning in what is common and tuning out what is uncommon. It isn't unreasonable to question whether this kind of adaptation in intelligence has survival value for the species. Becoming more skilled at tuning in what is common may enhance agency in slowly evolving environments, but it may also narrow focus and increase rigidity in apprehending forms.

It is undeniable from disciplined, active imaginative listening experience that we can hear, or learn to hear, emerging global phenomena from the underlying critical masses of interacting parts. They relate to what we can hear in nature. A way musicians might assist in studies involving the sonification of complex data sets is to contribute what we know about ear training and audiolising sonic objects. It is often ignored in both the visualisation and the sonification fields that, though we can come up with an endless list of clever ways to audiolise or visualise data, perceptual mechanisms are pliant and respond very well to training. Musicians interested in complexity know that the musical ear can be trained to follow high-speed transformations in complex, sonic relationships. Such training, however, may require very large amounts of practice. The results, however, are clearly evident (Rosenboom 1992a).

My recent work with BCMI (Rosenboom and Mullen 2019) and with a variety of interactive instrumentation concepts has led to the idea of what I call *concurrent complexity*. This begins with placing boundaries around two (or more) systems with internally networked parts that exhibit *interaction states* with each other. For example, in interactive music, one system might encompass a brain with proprioceptive agencies, and another might be an instrument with self-organising affordances (Tanaka 2010). Many other examples can be imagined, more simple and more complex. Preliminary, promising work in analysing dimensional complexities found in music and the EEGs (brainwaves) of active imaginative listeners indicate that correspondences may be observed, and indeed, heard. Particular correspondences may then be delimitated as inter-action states. For musical performers and instruments, these interaction states can be treated like compositional elements, just like *notes*. Of course, there are many ways to investigate, define, and measure what we call complexity that may have utility in creating interactive composition and performance systems: complexodynamics, multi-scale entropy, mutual information, sophistication, holographic complexity, and more (Aaronson 2011; Antunes and Fortnow 2007; Birbaumer et al. 1996; Carpentier et al. 2019; Costa, Goldberger, and Peng 2005; Cottrell and Montero 2017; Mainzer 2007).

Studying concurrent complexity models for music and interactive systems opens new cognitive spaces for potential artistic practices. Hearing complexity is a part of perceiving, parsing, and apprehending sonic scenes. This involves detecting emerging regularities from complexities among lower-level units, aspects of symmetry, energy, and endurance, and reflexively evaluating the role of observations as possible causal energies in extracting and making forms.

Complexities observed among resonant networks, acoustic, neural, and others, suggest some principles for emergent forms in art and music.

- A multiplicity of interacting parts is needed.
- Recognition of differentiation among parts is required along with the simultaneous understanding of higher-order unity.
- Phase transitions towards complex structures in a system's dynamics occur at critical points in the process.

Predictions and memory become part of the description of any present moment.

- What is perceived as complex is relative to the observer's perceptual reference scale.
- Extension and prolongation lead to nested, local cycles and larger, global hypercycles in an emerging structure.

- *Power law scaling* among components on small local and large-scale global extensions enables the system to exhibit metastability, common functioning over a wide range, while considerable variation and adaptability takes place among behaviours on each individual scale.

Expressive forms can have elastic distinctions among component parts that can also transcend the idea of information always being carried in sequential symbol strings. René Thom asserts that when we speak of *information*, we should really be talking about *form*. He then expounds on the idea of *topological complexity* for forms and also reminds us: "It is sometimes said that all information is a message, that is to say, a finite sequence of letters taken from an alphabet, but this is only one of the possible aspects of information: any geometric form whatsoever can be the carrier of information, and in the set of geometric forms carrying information of the same type the topological complexity of the form is the quantitative scalar measure of the information" (Thom 1975, 144–45).

Representation and notation—mappings and semantics

Interactive systems permeate our culture: interactive devices, interactive software, interactive installations and artistic realisations, new methods for communicating and new ways of engaging in signifying meaning and new semantic forms. Naturally, interface design—not only via technology—has become a vigorous discipline that is widely discussed, talked about, and taught. As the very conception of what music can be has also evolved, especially in the twentieth and twenty-first centuries, concepts about the functions, meaning, and efficacy of various kinds of music notation have also evolved. Notation has moved from its role in Western classical music as a tool to concretise iconic musical objects into a vast open arena of new functions in the processes of creative invention, realisation, transcription, and co-creation. Performance is process. Notation functions best when viewed as an *interface* in performative interactivity.

Pianist-writer Virginia Gaburo (1977) provides a possible starting point for opening things up: "Meaning takes place in the mind. The sensibly perceivable symbol acts as a stimulus to mental activity" (25) and "musical notation need not be merely inscribed musical sound—a translation with attendant losses and gains of possible indicators of meaning: nor need it be inscribed directions for the production of sound   a contract" (33). Make a mark. A representational system then begins—notation. When a formal representational system (absolute mapping) is constructed with structurally stable states enabling emergence of markers for a descriptive language, minds may then create semantic realisations of propositional worlds by attaching meaning to markers in the representation system, and through co-communication and co-evolution, the system then becomes dynamic and continuous again with its attendant natural uncertainties and adjacent contingencies.

Agre's criticism of AI discourse as conflating representations of things with the things that they represent also bears on misunderstandings about the interface nature of music notation. Notation is an invitation for interaction, not a perfectly precise representation. It is more like a window through which the creators of the notation (composers) and those interacting with the notation (interpreters, performers, interactees) view and co-create with one another.

An illusion of form arises from the persistent confusion of the exogenous with the endogenous, in parallel with Agre's pointing out how confusions in AI result from conflating representations with the represented (Agre 1997b). This persistence seems inherent in human nature, which means discipline is required to transcend it. Galileo describes a 1632 discussion about deception of the senses in which his character, Simplico, complains,

> . . . according to Copernicus one must deny one's own sensations. For, this principle by which we go around with the earth is either intrinsically ours or external to us (namely, a case of being forcibly carried by the earth); if it is the latter, (since we do not feel being forcibly carried) we will have to say that our sense of touch does not feel the very object being touched and does not receive its impression in the sensorium; but if the principle is intrinsic, then we will not be feeling a motion deriving from within us, and we will not be perceiving a propensity perpetually inherent in us. (Galileo 1997, 217)

There is a parallel in Agre's critique of artificial intelligence with the critique here of objectified forms. Agre points to a "strategic vagueness" in AI vocabulary (Agre 1997b, 142). Establishing degrees of vagueness versus precise delineations in structural parameters can be a very useful tool in the intentional forming of interactive strategies for musical engagement. As mentioned earlier, intelligence itself, despite an endless and useful search, has no fully satisfying definition. Intuitively, one can joke that nobody knows what intelligence is, but everybody knows when it isn't there! Despite many attempts to pin it down, in which some practitioners invest astonishing levels of belief, a degree of essential vagueness remains. So, AI could be said to engender artificial vagueness. Then, what is *real* vagueness, and what is *artificial* vagueness? And finally, can artificial vagueness actually be created with discrete state machines (computers)? There is a similar problem with viewing notation as definitive description. Strategic vagueness can also function as a very useful and intentional tool in composition.

Elsewhere, I suggested that the ideal mental state with which a musician may approach a new kind of musical notation might be similar to that of the SETI astronomer looking for extra-terrestrial messages (Rosenboom 1992c). An essential condition of this state would be maintaining the openness of perception and cognition required to find and recognise a form of intelligence, the nature of which cannot be known in advance. This is critical. This newly recognised intelligence would, no doubt, have arisen from a process of evolution that may also not be knowable (Rosenboom 2003). The nearly limitless variety of ways in which intelligence may emerge is not predictable. The ways in which musical intelligence may be imbedded in new notation is limitless. The musician interactee must extract that intelligence to materialise meaningful results.

Notation may also stretch beyond the visual, diagrammatical, pictorial, and verbal. I have used sounds as scores, in which musicians listen to sounds provided as the signifiers of the score. Here we investigate sounds as signs, sounds as semiotic elements, and sounds as propositions.[8] My work *On Being Invisible* (1976–77), which could be described as an attention-dependent sonic environment in which the environment evolves in response to feedback from detecting auditory event-related potentials (AERPs) in a performer's brain, evokes a kind of semiotic sonification framework that is mutually dependent upon the design of an instrument and the behaviour of the listening performer.[9] Insook Choi (2018) has provided a thorough analysis of these kinds of sonification frameworks, particularly with respect to biological information, listening, and emergent behaviour.

Choi's analysis offers a strong foundation for further development in this domain. She draws on Peirce and reminds me of his illustration using sound and air to dissect elements of consciousness. In *Illustrations of the Logic of Science*, Peirce writes ([1878] 1934, section 395), "In a piece of music there are the separate notes, and there is the air." He describes how a single sound may exist in air for a long time and "might be present to a sense from which everything in the past was as completely absent as the future." He contrasts this with the air, "the performance of which occupies a certain time, during the portions of which only portions of it are played. It consists in an orderliness in the succession of sounds which strike the ear at different times; and to perceive it there must be some continuity of consciousness which makes the events of a lapse of time present to us." Thus, we hear the air via the individual notes, but do not directly here it. By this, he distinguishes things that are present at every instant and those that have beginnings, middles, and ends and present themselves in succession. The two objects thereby distinguished are sensations, of which we are continuously conscious, and thoughts, which are apprehended in successions of sensations. "Thought is a thread of melody running through the succession of our sensations," states Peirce. There is music in this formulation.

Deviant resonances—interfaces and instruments

Instruments, too, can be intentionally designed with a degree of strategic vagueness. They also contain unintentional vagueness, noises, deviant resonances, that can be sources of discovery. Cybernetic uncertainties, emerging from self-organising evolving dynamics, underlie fundamental unpredictability, in that there is no certain succession of states within a known repertoire of states. The differentiables in the system are also subject to fundamental uncertainties, in measurement and interaction dynamics, resonant emergence and interaction, facilitative coincidence and inhibitory coincidence, reinforcement, reduction, cancellation, relaxators, attractors, repellers, feedback interaction, and more.

---

8 Stjernfelt's extensive exploration of "decisigns beyond language" is very pertinent here (2014).

9 Numerous performances and recordings of *On Being Invisible* have been produced and released over the years. For a good technical description of the work, consult Rosenboom (1997). (See MF2.3 to hear examples.)

In the late 1970s, I drafted "a speculative program for the development of optimal input structures for performance-oriented electronic musical instrumentation" (Rosenboom 1987, 569).[10] It was ambitious. "We can now conceive of the design of instruments which can contain a stored repertoire of complete models of musical reality, are heuristic and adaptive, are capable of doing instantaneous research on an input stream being received to extract salient features with which to differentiate among potential outputs, and of disseminating information around a network of shared resources serving the high-level, real-time needs of an evolved ensemble of human performers" (569). It also completely redefined musicianship technique to extend "far beyond the development of physical and proprioceptive skills in the performance of specific musical vocabularies to include the imbedding and activation of formal structures and entire musical models in an often spontaneous, musical context" (569). Of course, AI was making its way into musical instrument design. "Our idea of performance can then include such forms of interaction as querying associations of attributes, context contingencies, implications, associations, and conceptual dependencies" (580).

What can it mean to *play* such instruments? Maintaining the idea of *play* in instruments imbued with the ability to enter the domain of interactive composing co-creatively with a performer brings up many fascinating questions (Rosenboom 1992b). Where are the various definitions of play imbedded in the interaction states of two complex adaptive networks—naturally intelligent organism (performer-composer) and artificially intelligent system (musical instrument). What are the potential stimulus-response mappings in such instruments that can both extend and support human capabilities?

Kristin Erickson has developed an intriguing merger of algorithmic music and human theatrical performance (Erickson 2018). In her constructions, human beings with opinions, feelings, and urges act within a framework of algorithms, with humans playing roles of logic gates to self-determine their own performance outcomes. To implement this, she developed hardware-software components, in particular, "a browser-based platform for generating, organizing, and distributing performance instructions called Telebrain" (ibid., 337). This creative blending of AI and non-AI with humans and machines is very intriguing.

Imagine the following mappings as a thought exercise, like Gaburo's *extraction* composition. Think of the label *key press* as a *sign*, a *representation*, for the *detection of any discrete event*, a *stimulus* sensible in the structure of an *instrument*: detecting a P300 peak in an event-related potential (ERP) within a brain's EEG, the rising of a seismic wave in the Sun, activation of a strong resonance in a physical object, anything determined to be a *musical event*. A correlative compositional exercise is to answer the question: *What is a musical event?* Any answer is a proposition. Observe that the propositional responses increase in cognitive scope and globality as this list of juxtapositions proceeds.

---

10   This document was originally drafted during a period of significant collaborations with electronic systems designer Donald Buchla in anticipation of forming a non-profit research organisation. It was later published in *Perspectives of New Music*.

Event		Propositional response
key press	→	pure wave with fixed pitch
key press	→	synthesis patch producing fixed pitch
key press	→	fixed pitch with velocity shaping (piano as example)
key press	→	playback stored audio sample
key press	→	fixed sequence of "notes"
key press	→	fixed deterministic generative algorithm
key press	→	fixed remapping of stimulus-response correspondences for given key
key press	→	fixed remapping of stimulus-response correspondences for entire keyboard (set of sensible stimuli)
key press	→	non-linear deterministic generative algorithm
key press	→	genetic algorithm
key press	→	pseudorandom deterministic generative algorithm
key press	→	probabilistic generative algorithm
key press	→	random (subject to quantum uncertainties) generative algorithm (noise)
key press	→	self-organising system
key press	→	cognitive model of composition/improvisation/ performance
key press	→	cognitive model of music
key press	→	domain of musical thought
key press	→	musical thought itself
key press	→	system of thought
key press	→	idea of thought
key press	→	thought
key press	→	idea of consciousness
key press	→	consciousness
key press	→	idea of sentience
key press	→	sentience
key press	→	self-organising universe

Fanciful or not, we get the point.

Next, we can ask this question: How do we know when and where the key was pressed? A few more questions and observations emerge.

- Detection of any presumably discrete event involves uncertainties at its edges. Deep consideration of this phenomenon may generate very interesting and artistically valuable concepts.
- A piano key is a complex, non-linear mechanical system. A switch is simpler; but then, how do we know precisely when it was closed, and what is interesting about what we can't know?
- Perhaps musical control over the dynamics of boundary detection is essential for *interesting* instruments. The more perfect the stimulus-response mapping is, the *less* interesting the instrument may be.

- Internuncial computation between stimuli and responses offers rich opportunities; but, the more it strives for perfectly reliable predictability, the more it departs from being a valid representation of natural phenomena, in which an inherent unpredictability is always present.
- An enormously potent area for study and creativity now involves this question: *What are the best stimuli to choose for a brain-computer music interface (BCMI) work, and how do we classify them?*

Concepts surrounding the nature of *resonances* are important in this arena of exploration (Rosenboom 2020b). We can imagine the nature of *predictive resonances*, those emerging within the predictabilities of classically engineered systems, and *deviant resonances*, those ballooning out from in between the boundary distinctions of any system or model, interacting in ensemble with each other and creating rich territory to explore for interactive systems that are adaptively engineered (Rosenboom 2019b).

We asked what it means to *play* an algorithm. We might also ask how we got from Simplico's time in 1632 to now, when we play them all the time. Multiple time and space contexts for composition, performance, sound histories, and interactive constructions are all malleable and can be directly modulated and intentionally imbedded inside instruments as part of propositional music thinking—instruments for *music of many nows.*

Thinking composition into being—as situating—as invitation

How do we distinguish sound, perception, hearing, listening, and music? Perhaps, it may be useful to place them in a possible landscape of experience. Here's an attempt. *Sound* is simply *things as they are. Auditory perception* is a *bridge between sound and hearing*, a link between the nature of things and experience. *Hearing* is *observing our sensory input* in its totality and *knowing our mechanisms for synthesising memory engrams, our inner representations for sound experiences. Listening* is *active practice with the interaction of our own nature and sound as it is.* If we are *making music*, we are *being ourselves with the decisions and actions we make in order to invent inner and outer worlds involving sound.* Practising music-making involves attempting to know and understand these decisions and actions.

How does this work in cognition? Heinz von Foerster presents a sequence of propositional mappings (1984).

COGNITION → computing a reality

He then anticipates an objection: that he is replacing an unknown term, *cognition*, with other unknown terms, *computation* and *reality*, that are "even more opaque than the definiendum" (von Foerster 1984, 294). He then inserts the word *descriptions* as a possible solution.

COGNITION → computing descriptions of a reality

However, to be consistent with the sequential, hierarchical nature of sensory information processing, he adds loopback recursion for descriptions and computations, which makes it *holarchical*.

COGNITION → computing descriptions of descriptions of descriptions . . .

Finally, he proposes "to interpret cognitive processes as never ending recursive processes of computation" (ibid., 296).

COGNITION → computations of computations of computations . . .[11]

To serve the musical context of this writing, I extract the following propositions:

MUSICAL COGNITION → computing musical propositions
and
COMPOSITION-PERFORMANCE → activating musical propositions.

If musical cognitive processes involve thinking, then we are *thinking composition into being*. Propositional music involves thinkable musical processes that also include *rethinking* thinking and *rethinking* rethinking thinking. Things are *things* when we think them into being. Propositional music includes imagining critical frameworks for rethinking musical practice in all its dimensions as regular routine work. There is no end point, no arrival.

To ward off any misinterpretation, it is not my intention to situate music solely within the realm of thinking in its most abstract understanding. The point of inception for any music arriving might lie anywhere, including what appears to be enactment flowing from some ineffable instantiation. Pierre Schaeffer points out that what he terms abstract music may begin with mental conception followed by notated expression (representation) and concrete performance (2012). In counterpoint, he describes alternatively that composition may also begin with experiencing concrete materials and then flow through stages of experimental drafts on to substantive making.

Some reflection on thinking and spontaneous creation may be germane here. For example, in my view, the term *free improvisation* is a misnomer. No matter how spontaneous improvised actions might feel, they are always enacted by an entity that has grown and evolved its self-structure to enable best functioning. In this case, I regard the *performing entity* (human being) as the *composition*, and that as an improviser—and everyone needs to improvise in some aspects of life—one can choose to *compose one's self* by *composing one's practice*. Improvisations will ensue from self-nature and self-conditioning. We can question whether true improvisation is non-algorithmic, emergent from unknowable, unprestatable adjacent possibilities among musical, non-language-based, thoughts.

---

11 I've slightly rewritten the last two of von Foerster's diagrams. He drew loops in his text that are rendered here as iterations of words: descriptions of . . . , and computations of . . . .

Theoretical physicist David Bohm proposes we think of *thought as movement*, and that the essence of movement may be in the *intention* to move (1994). It may be a vehicle propelling us to grasp and label what we presume to be knowledge; but I add, *thought is not an entity that can know*. As musicians, we sometimes experience what we regard as interruptions in executing complex demanding performances that we blame on thinking. Our musical proprioceptive systems honed by practice should be sufficient, and perhaps necessary, to reach the illusion of perfection. Perhaps, though, it is *thinking with self-consciousness about thinking* that is the source of the interruptions, and thought, perhaps musical thought, still functions in the underlying mechanisms. Back to Bohm, then, "So could we also say, 'can the movement of thought be aware of itself?'" (1994, 123).

To this we add something about ineffable components we recognise and experience in musical inspiration: intuition, feelings, sensations, urges, passions and spontaneous thoughts, intentions and memories. These are self-evident parts of the *nows* of human experiences. Neuroscientist and multidisciplinary aficionado Edgar E. Coons asks, "How can we increase our attentions to the NOWNESS 'propositions' of experience?" (Coons 2019). The focus of Coons's propositions in this case is on the idea of *qualia* as key to understanding the information imbedded in each experienced NOW.

Qualia arise from the endogenous sensibilities extracted from perceived, delineated phenomena. In this chapter, we have referred to entanglements among exogenous inputs and endogenous syntheses as part of the process of extracting forms. Initially, as Coons describes, these remain private, internally felt entities. Coons asserts further that the human impulse to make them somewhat public, to unlock them in expressive representations has yielded "huge benefits" and "makes us so UNIQUE" (2019). Organising and synthesising memories—creative data reduction within hierarchies of contingent, regenerative relations among parsed components—leads to drawing boundaries around and labelling qualia. Materialising palpable exogenous things from perceived endogenous activity in organising experiences brings internalised qualia into a public space and evokes representations: visual, vocal, tactile, sonic, and so on.

The word *quale* refers to something that cannot be treated quantitatively or in a relational manner. This distinguishes it from measurable *sensation*. Qualia can also refer to phenomena "that are not strictly sensorial, such as the impression of knowing or . . . states of the propositional type (such as believing that P or desiring that Q)" (Proust 2014, 877). The domain of experience we label music may enable non-denotatable qualia. Music can function as an internally self-sufficient, non-representational practice. In this sense, it can provide a powerful outlet for externalising and sharing non-labelable, non-languageable qualia.[12]

12　This does not exclude making sounds that are imitative or representational, like bees buzzing, a horse's hooves on cobble stones, fog horns, etc.

We should note that a vigorous dualist debate has raged around the idea of qualia for a long time, the detailing of which is beyond the scope of this chapter. Suffice it to say that for our purposes, we treat qualia as not being reducible to physicalism. It is hard to expunge felt experiences from the debate with purely functionalist approaches. Here again is a deep theoretical territory wherein science and art might meet in fruitful dialogue.

We conclude this section by again asking the question, what is composition? We consider an answer proposition by imagining the possible pathways from endogenous (private) experience to making exogenous (public) experiences. We can posit:

- Imagining *as* composition
- Imagining *as* performance
- Listening *as* composition
- Listening *as* performance
- Composition *as* situating
- Composition *as* inviting
- Composition *as* co-creation
- Form *as* cognitive synthesis
- Composition-performance as situating cognitive synthesis
- . . . . *as* . . . .

Perhaps, as composer-writer-theorist François Bonnet asserts, all that we have created so far is just an invitation for music to reveal itself, and that "What we call music is not music, rather invocations for music to appear. . . . Music is always yet to come" (Bonnet 2020).

*　　*　　*

Choose your universe—a few propositional music narratives from recent compositions

We preface this section with suggestions for a few principles in systematic, propositional music practice. Bear in mind that all involve collapsing distinctions among composition, performance, listening, and imagining.

- Consider all interaction to be a process of co-evolution of autonomous agents with each other and their environment, the procedures of which lead to emergent order. These are potentially best implemented with adaptive network structures.

Begin with procedures that return to first principles of composition:

- *Choose your universe*—choose the universal set or domain of compositional attention and the kinds of distinctions that will be made as a result of compositional thought and choice.
- List the potential generative relationships among distinctions in the universal set, that is, how it will be ordered.

- Determine the dimensions of description and scales of measure for parametric values to be used.
- Describe the dynamics and margins of uncertainty associated with making distinctions among entities placed along the parametric scales.
- Design the compositional pragmatics needed to make arrangements among the distinctions in the universal set.
- Consider interaction states as communication and compositional objects, that is, each condition and/or mode of interaction becomes an element for compositional design.
- Consider all interactive processes to have many *nows*, many versions of a present.
- Consider the effects of uncertainties in observables and uncertainties in representations as parts of compositional designs.
- Regard the resulting models as propositional.
- Consider necessary cultural evolution to be as important as technological evolution for this to work with our species.

Could the above actually be considered a *piece*, a *practice*, a way of *working*, a way of *thinking*, a practice with continuous looping back? Yes, this is a continuous, analytically critical practice, fully integrated with spontaneous creativity at its core.

Here are some notes on a few examples from my recent work.

THINKABLE PONDERABLE BEGINNINGS—APPARENT ORIGINS AND TRANSFORMATIONS

Quartet for the Beginning of a Time *(2019)*

The existence of a beginning is not provable, only thinkable, ponderable. This compositional story may at first appear paradoxically to rely on the idea of a fixed score. To be sure, when the work is viewed inaccurately as being fully represented by marks on paper coming from a lexicon of traditional Western symbols, many things look relatively fixed. Then again, some are not so fixed. A structure lies under the surface, in which a key operator guiding the formation of musical materials is the degree of *diffuseness* versus *clarity* applied to particular musical parameters.

First, here are some of the key sources of inspiration. One is imbedded in the range of meanings and concepts associated with the word *gravity*: force of attraction, warped space, black hole creation, big crunch, seriousness, momentousness, urgency, consequence, precariousness, perilousness, and so on. Of course, this quartet acknowledges Olivier Messiaen's grand masterpiece *Quartet for the End of Time* and the tragic circumstances under which it was composed during World War II. My *Quartet for the Beginning of a Time* also underlines the persistence of hope and the infinite cycles of renewal and beginning in the universe. But it also emerges during a time of extraordinary angst about divisions in our world, uncertainties about the sustainability of human occupancy on the Earth, and great inequities in distribution of means for agency in human lives.

Though I am not providing arguments credible to professional cosmologists, I possess an informed, hard-to-describe morsel of doubt about the reality of the widely accepted theory of *inflation*, which is thought to follow the Big Bang at the presumed beginning of the universe we believe we are aware of inhabiting. This standard theory requires an infinitely dense, gravitational singularity at the point of the Big Bang, where the known regularities of physics (laws) break down, and even the idea of *knowing* might be undefinable.

In the late 1970s, particularly around the emergence of my series of pieces labelled with an umbrella title, *In the Beginning*—(with various subtitles) (Rosenboom 1978–81, 2012a) (see MF2.4 for recordings), and in the 1984–85 multi-movement work for percussion soloist with instruments interfaced to a live computer-electronics system, *Zones of Influence* (Rosenboom 2014b) (see MF2.5a and MF2.5b, respectively, for audio and video recordings showing a performance of the complete work), and the violin-piano-percussion trio *Champ Vital (Life Field)* (Rosenboom 2012b) (see MF2.6 for a video showing a performance by the California E.A.R. Unit), I explored compositional paradigms with a kind of black-hole/white-hole diametrical model. Various musical structure parameters were thought of as producing differentiable musical shapes or contours that were mapped into a multidimensional space. The axes of the spaces were scaled in two ways: *linear correlations* of shapes with each other and *mutual information* measured among pairs of shapes. Both were explored as being potentially analogous to perceivable and quantifiable similarities and differences among shapes and were used in transformation processes, for example, in gradually transforming one shape into another. The black-hole/white-hole idea appeared when both stochastic and deterministic tools were used to introduce mutations into the shapes and observe *trajectories* in the multidimensional scaling spaces, as newly transformed shapes appeared and were heard. By tuning the tendencies in these processes, shapes might tend to decrease their distance (perceivable difference) from each other until a maximum packing, with maximum order around a fixed tendency, would occur, and differences would disappear into a maximally ordered black hole. Injection of disorder might then cause an exploding emergence from a conceptual white hole into new listening territory. One section of a composition might tend in one direction and another in an opposite direction—into a musical black hole and out of a white hole, for instance. It was possible to create very exciting and dynamical musical territory with these tools in both fixed scores and more open interactive constructions.

Other ideas for this cosmological conundrum have been proposed. Some invoke the notion of prior universes or multi-dimensional stars collapsing onto an event horizon, from which a new universe emerges, something like the one we believe we inhabit (Afshordi, Mann, and Pourhasan 2014). Of course, the word *prior* already presumes particular knowledge of time, which is also being examined and re-examined these days with newly emerging propositional models. There is also a holographic principle bearing on this, relating physical laws acting on a volume with different laws acting on a boundary surface. This invokes a potential illusion about gravity stemming from what is known as the Maldacena Conjecture (Maldacena 2005).[13]

I chose to use the geometric form of the *catenary* as a tool for organising musical parameters in my *Quartet for the Beginning of a Time*. A catenary is a curve formed by gravity when flexible cords hang freely from pairs of fixed points near a strongly gravitating body. Thus, a symbolic relationship to gravity is maintained. To make the score, sets of catenaries were laid on their sides, rotated horizontally, and placed along a progression of emerging time.

The amounts of space between sides of various catenaries are related to degrees of diffuseness or clarity applied to particular musical parameters: clarity of tonal reference dissolving into atonal fields and re-emerging later, clarity of perceivable pitch evolving into and out of relatively non-pitched sounds, independence versus synchronicity among players, relational simultaneities, temporal densities and speeds, and shifting *complexodynamics* among simple versus compound time forms and melodic shapes. This measured diffuseness both challenges the perception of palpable forms and invites creative endogenous synthesis of forms by active imaginative listeners.

When an initial set of closing catenary curves reaches a dense horizon, ahead of a point where they meet at a common centre of gravitational focus, sounds and motion stop suddenly. A short, loud sound marks the singular point, ø, where the set of closing catenaries and a set of reopening catenaries touch. Sounds and motion remain imperceptible briefly until they re-emerge after the opening catenary curves cross over another density horizon. These expanding curves guide musical forms that articulate a new time. An endlessly rising harmonic progression leads into and out of this process, linking back to the complex dynamics of human interactions within an evolving universe. (See plate 2.1.) (See MF2.7 for a video showing excerpts from a preview performance of this work.)

Notation styles vary throughout the course of the work, from relatively fixed, through insertion of unsynchronised parts, to symbols for raw sounds laid out in a *musical configuration space* (Rosenboom 2019c).

---

13   Also known as AdS/CFT (anti-de Sitter/conformal field theory) correspondence, this is an idea in the arena of theories about quantum gravity and the holographic principle, in which a description of a volume of space can be encoded on a lower-dimensional boundary to the space. For more critique and discussion, see Penrose (2004).

Quartet for the Beginning of a Time, Score, p. 3

Figure 2.1a

Figure 2.1a–c. Three example pages from the *Quartet for the Beginning of a Time* score, moving from the relatively fixed form of upwardly modulating harmonic spirals being smeared with glissandi, to non-tonal and rhythmic complexities with unsynchronised bracketed parts beginning to appear, and to a configuration space of symbols for raw sound types.

Quartet for the Beginning of a Time, Score, p. 8

Figure 2.1b

Quartet for the Beginning of a Time, Score, p. 11

CS4
156

configuration space of possibilities

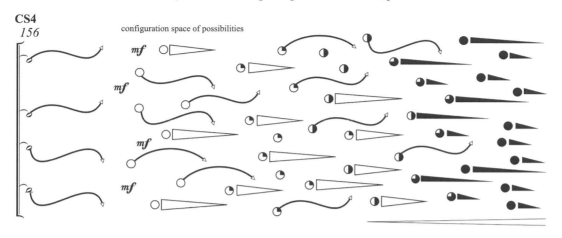

CS5
160

increasing speed and temporal density

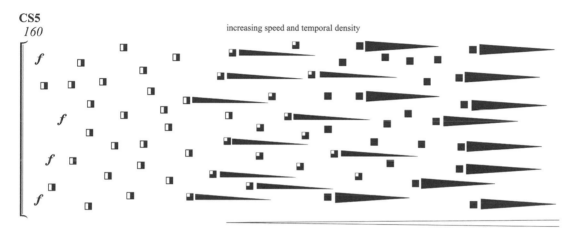

CS6
164

loosing perceivable pitch

noise pulse

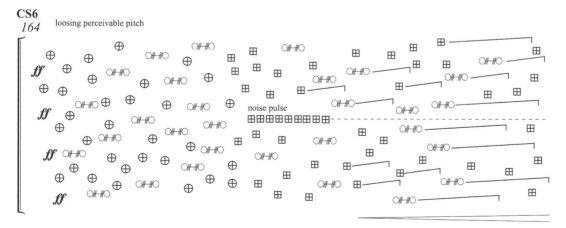

Figure 2.1c

TRANSIENT ADJACENCIES—MULTIPLE NOWS

Earth Encomium *with* Nothingness Is Unstable *(2017)*

Non-existence is charged with the potential for existence, a powerful field of potential energy, like a battery, out of which existence can always explode. Non-existence is compressed like a spring, an imbalance waiting for movement to release a version of space defined by this movement. Matter-space is just movement, dramatically transformed by our emotional intellect into a conceptualisation of power and the forms with which we perceive it.

Another way to think about it is that nothingness usually collapses into somethingness—the phenomenal particularities of experience. Kauffman considers how our boundaryless universe could come into existence: "... from the *possible, thus from nothing actual*, a new way to ask: 'Why something rather than nothing?' ... 'Because the universe *could* become, and perhaps because it could become complex'" (Kauffman 2016, 214). Musical particularities, *musics of many nows*, containing fine structures with created pasts and futures, also spring from initially undefined singularities of experience into multiple dimensions of mutual interactivity.

Two compositions are combined here in an integrated form. They are linked together with a system of *harmonic orbits*. These orbits can be heard in ever-descending spirals within spirals that create multi-dimensional harmonic loops. Perhaps mixed feelings of homage, pathos, and inevitability somehow reside inside these descending loops. In *Earth Encomium*, the loops are interpreted in a solo for piano and electronics. The piano's raw acoustic sound is parsed into specific spectral elements, which in turn ring a bank of software-based, complex digital resonators that are also tuned to the same harmonic orbits. In *Nothingness Is Unstable*, delicate natural sounds collected in field recordings in Indonesia and the United States activate the same banks of complex digital resonator circuits. Live acoustic inputs also activate the resonator banks in counterpoint with the field recordings (see plate 2.2). Eventually, more intertwining harmonic orbits can be blended in with instruments that can be computer activated. In my performances this has typically been a Yamaha Disklavier piano playing chords exceeding what can be performed with two human hands.

This music was originally commissioned by Harvestworks Digital Media Arts Center in New York to be presented with the unique Geluso 3D sound distribution object at the 2017 New York Electronic Arts Festival at ISSUE Project Room in Brooklyn. I developed algorithms for sound diffusion with Geluso's object, which consists of a six-speaker array that must be suspended in the centre of an audience space. The speakers work in pairs, pointing in opposite directions along X, Y, and Z axes. Individual sounds can be positioned in the 3D space by precisely controlling the phase relationships of the sounds sent to individual speakers in the array. Audience members can navigate this space with their ears, and the sound perspectives will vary for individuals located in separate parts of the space.

This led me to also create a modified version of the diffusion software that I could use in performances with a 6.2 surround system when the Geluso object was not available. This version produced a quasi-3D experience, which was not the same as with the Geluso object, but did create a unique surround-sound experience that I had not heard before. I have used this approach in many performances since that time. A stereo mix-down version can be heard on my double CD *Deviant Resonances* (Rosenboom 2019b). (See MF2.8 to hear this version.) I dedicated this immersive musical wrapping to our stressed planet.

When possible, a series of close-up images of textures found in the natural world are projected with superimposed text. The penultimate image shows a quotation from Sun Tzu's *The Art of War* (Sun-tzu 2003, 37). (See MF2.9 for a concert video including a performance of *Earth Encomium*.)

Choose Your Universe *with* Natural Scores *(2018)*

This is a newly developing work in which a process of continuous, endless beginnings belies the very idea of style. A genre-less musical world unfolds. This work reflexively recycles itself. It is intended to draw both listeners and performers into a set of complimentary and contrasting sound worlds that challenge the meanings of *natural* and *artificial*.

The instrumentation is based on analogue electronics that are not *played* by hands, only by the acoustic inputs from separately played instruments. So far, I have used a five-string electric violin. The electronics are *played* only by sounds from the violin. My analogue instrumentation does not use oscillators. Rather, libraries of carefully composed waveforms, either originating in field recordings or extracted from prior performances are employed. In the later case, the idea is for the work to be continuously cumulative and evolve by means of playing with its histories. The work can also be realised in multiples, as long as other performers engage in the subtle articulation of the work's intentions. So far, a duet version has been performed successfully with composer-trumpeter-technologist Sarah Belle Reid, using instrumentation compatible with the concept. (See MF2.10 for a video showing excerpts from a performance of this duet version.)

Regarding the conceptual scores for this work, the idea is that they also continuously evolve with their histories. New score components are generated in response to new performance experiences. There is no fixed score, rather a collection of articulated concepts represented in various ways to be used as interactive guides. Here are two examples. The first is a set of word juxtapositions.

Potential framing, something emerging . . .

Intrinsic Spin	< - >	Existential
Harmonic Loops	< - >	Gravity
Multidimensional Oscillator	< - >	Dimensionality of Time
Glide Paths	< - >	Field-less Change
Fields	< - >	Curvature
Resonance Network	< - >	Spontaneous Singularities
Potential Dimensions	< - >	Discontinuities
Dilation	< - >	Continuities
Coherence	< - >	Reductionist
Highlighted Identity	< - >	Infinite Uncertainties
Apparent Discreteness	< - >	Contacts
Quasi-coherence Structures	< - >	Bounded Tension Field
Emergent Dimensionality	< - >	Differentiations
Essential Tension	< - >	Spontaneous Resonance
Marking	< - >	Integration
Holistic	< - >	Salience
Abstractive	< - >	Contiguous
Causal	< - >	Contingencies
Binary	< - >	Exciter Function
Dissipating Resonances	< - >	Decoherence
Polarized Fields	< - >	Particle Horizon
Adjacencies	< - >	Qualitative
Convergent Dimensionality	< - >	Apparent Continuum

Not propositional opposites, sense of compositional pairings . . .
DR 3/29/2020

Figure 2.2.

The second example shown in plates 2.4a–c includes three images selected from a book of drawings I call *Natural Scores*.

Synthesising transformed histories

Battle Hymn of Insurgent Arts *(2018)*

From time to time, an artist's eternal aesthetic investigations into the evolution of humanity in the universe can encounter detours when it is necessary to search for light in times of great divisions. Far from obfuscating the ongoing aesthetic agenda, however, such detours can serve as key informants. The irresistible impulse is to not look away, and to reach for the values of equality, tolerance, and access, while simultaneously trying to avoid causing harm in reaching for the non-absolute of perfection in practice. From time to time, I have engaged in making "musical interventions"—exploring ways to confront forces of division with music. Over time, a collection of pieces with socio-political content resulted. They emerged from contemplating the perplexing,

Figure 2.2. A component in continuously evolving score elements for *Choose Your Universe*.

pluri-perspective character of what could be a principled aesthetic regime of political order. How could such a regime arise and be nurtured from within the natural flesh of society and "the ungraspable identity of the people that makes democracy an enigma"? (Plot 2014, 25).

Battle Hymn of Insurgent Arts is written for brass quintet with electric rhythm section and electrified singer delivering a new setting of Mark Twain's little-known rewrite (ca. 1900) of lyrics for the *Battle Hymn of the Republic (Brought Down to Date)* (Twain 1972, 15; Rosenboom 2018a). Twain's pen was, in part, energised by his reaction to politics surrounding the Philippine-American War, "Mine eyes have seen the orgy of the launching of the Sword...." The score for this work uses relatively standard notation, suitable for the pointed message of the work. It encourages the singer to use electronic voice processing of their own design, though, and includes a somewhat transformed *Battle Hymn* chorus and a brief nod to Ray Charles's 1972 album *A Message from the People.* (See MF2.11 for a concert video including a performance of *Battle Hymn of Insurgent Arts.*)

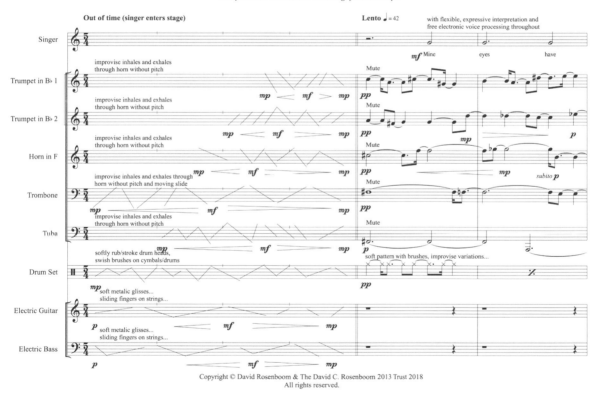

Figure 2.3.

Figure 2.3. First page of the score for *Battle Hymn of Insurgent Arts*.

David Rosenboom

LISTENING AS PERFORMANCE AND COMPOSITION

The Experiment *from* Hopscotch *(2015)*

In 2015, an extraordinary collaborative opera project, called *Hopscotch—A Mobile Opera for 24 Cars*, was produced in Los Angeles by The Industry opera company. Conceived and directed by Yuval Sharon, several composers and writers created a narrative and music in which the city of Los Angeles became a character, and audiences experienced performances inside limousines driving them from place to place, where site-specific scenes were also performed (Sharon 2015).

Among the compositions that I wrote for this opera is a scene called *The Experiment*, with a libretto written by Erin Young (Rosenboom 2015, 2019b). It engages audience members as participants in a paradigm that involves *listening as performance and composition*.

In this scene, a principal *Hopscotch* character, Jameson, reaches a personal crisis. In his desperate search to understand the meanings of heaven and hell and the liminality of imagination and reality, Jameson pursues the path of a mad scientist probing for illusive clues in the brain and mind, which he believes will answer his dilemmas. Audience members don headbands that transmit their brainwaves to software that extracts features common to particular states of mind mediating their reactions, especially those that might indicate agitation, alert shifts of attention, and a meditative focus. When Jameson sings questions to the audience, features detected in their group brainwaves—averaged together in a kind of hyper-scanning—call up a mix of pre-recorded responses sung or chanted by a soprano in three distinct styles, again representing the presence of agitation, alert shifts of attention, and meditative focus. In this way the states of the group mind hearing the questions—they begin relatively simply and slowly become more challenging—determine the mix of vocal replies heard in a collage of song. The brain responses direct which song styles will become momentarily dominant in an ever-shifting musical landscape. Finally, when audience members' brainwaves exhibit significant and sudden changes all at the same time, a special chord sounds to signal the group mind shifting in synchrony. From this, Jameson derives his answers. Ironically, his blind determination dooms him to declare the conclusions most consistent with the substance of his own imagined reality. (See MF2.12 to hear a recording of *The Experiment*.)

The propositional model of this work calls to mind how exogenous and endogenous creative actions intermingle in creating meaning. As von Foerster writes, "the listener and not the speaker determines the meaning of a sentence" (2014, 81). In retrospect, the specific case of *The Experiment* also brings to mind how Julian Jaynes's prescient investigations of *bicameral theocracies* from decades ago may bear significant relevance to this scenario (Jaynes 1976). The full libretto for *The Experiment* unfolds a narrative in a non-linear fashion that also integrates stories about migrants that are especially relevant to south-western US history.

Two other recent works that enact listening as performance and listening as composition, also employing BCMI (brain-computer music interface), are *Portable Gold and Philosophers' Stones (Deviant Resonances)* and *Ringing Minds* (Rosenboom 2019b; Rosenboom and Mullen 2019). (See MF2.13 for a recording of *Portable Gold and Philosophers' Stones (Deviant Resonances)*; see MF2.14 for a concert video that includes an explanation of how *Ringing Minds* works and a performance.) Works preceding these that involved measuring auditory event-related potentials (AERPs) in performers' brain signals, which could be described as self-organising attention-dependent environments in performance, include *On Being Invisible* (see MF2.3, referenced earlier), and *On Being Invisible II (Hypatia Speaks to Jefferson in a Dream)* (Rosenboom 1997, 2000a, 2000b, 2019a). (For a video showing recorded imagery with electronic sound and voices, as they might appear in a live performance, see MF2.15.) All these works involve Nth-order cybernetic feedback configurations, sometimes also enfolding creative transformations of histories and socio-cultural engagement.

The Experiment

Part 2: Jameson's Questions

Music: David Rosenboom
Text: Erin Young

These are declarative questions. Each one is articulated by a specific chord, sometimes containing only a few notes, like bugle calls, sometimes lyrically chromatic. After posing each question to the audience, Jameson stops and listens to a vocal collage of answers sung in response. The collective brain states of the audience members control a mix of three distinct types of vocal responses, corresponding to states of agitation, shifting attention and/or alertness, and a singular focus exhibiting minimal shift in brain state. After listening for a time appropriate to allow each response collage to be experienced musically, Jameson interrupts with the next question. The questions progress in darkness and aggressiveness. Though it is possible to vary the order of the questions in response to how the audience reacts, this general progression should be maintained. Question 11 should always be the last one.

Place breaths as needed. Work with natural rhythms of speech. Black and white notes indicate only relatively shorter and relately longer durations. The music is not metric, rather flowing with the rhythms of the thoughts. Interpret freely and expressively. Graphic spacing suggests speeding, slowing, notes close or separated. Syllables may be sustained between notes.

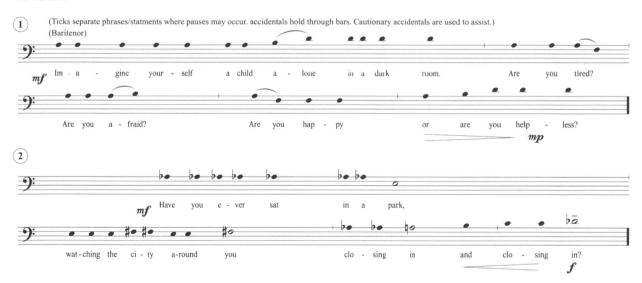

Figure 2.4a–d.

Figure 2.4a–d. Examples of *Jameson's Questions* and the three kinds of vocal responses mixed by audience group-brainwave spectra in *The Experiment*.

The Experiment

Part 2: Answers (A) Agitation

Music: David Rosenboom
Text: Erin Young

Pitched chanting/speaking, always with a sense of urgency, agitation, alarm, rhythmically incessant, with a quick, exigent sense of time and rapid tempo.

(Soprano/Mezzo-soprano)

This section mightalso accompanied by an instrumental ripping sound, like claws ripping fabric. (Violin overpressure could be used.) This is optional.

Figure 2.4b.

The Experiment

Part 2: Answers (B) Shift in Attention/Alertness

Music: David Rosenboom
Text: Erin Young

Speak each part like a newscaster delivering a suddenly breaking story. Use pitched speech on the notes of the chords indicated to create three versions of each numbered answer text. The first version should be on the lowest note of the chord. Slightly delay each subsequent version—second on the middle and third on the top note—by listening to each preceding voice and following that as quickly as the mind will alow to create a short human delay.

(Soprano)

Don't close your eyes. The darkness in your mind is thicker than the darkness of the room.

The edge of the park, the beginning of the city, the roads, the streetlights, the concrete building, the door, the windows, the small apartments, the roof, the smog, the blue sky and the nothingness beyond it.

I forgot everything, every moment of sitting on my couch, hours of driving endless miles, every day I crouched over my computer. It became a colorless spot inside everything else that mattered, every fight, every kiss, every moment you smiled and I smiled, and we could see it.

It told me to learn patience. I wanted to know more. It told me to wait, but I couldn't. It told me goodbye, and I left. It watched me leave. I never looked back.

A shift, drifting in the rising current, falling in the crashing stream, the fading morning, the failing dusk, the coming morning, the birth, and the death, a cycle of creation and destruction.

Figure 2.4c.

The Experiment

Part 2: Answers (C) No Reaction/Focus

Music: David Rosenboom
Text: Erin Young

Place breaths as needed. Work with natural rhythms of speech. Black and white notes indicate only relatively shorter and relately longer durations. The music is not metric, rather flowing with the rhythms of the thoughts. Interpret freely though thoughtfully. Graphic spacing suggests speeding, slowing, notes close or separated. Syllables may be sustained between notes. Dynamics are improvised and may be shaped in rehearsal or recording sessions.

(Ticks separate phrases/statments where pauses may occur. Accidentals hold through bars. Cautionary accidentals are used to assist.)

(Soprano with wide range)

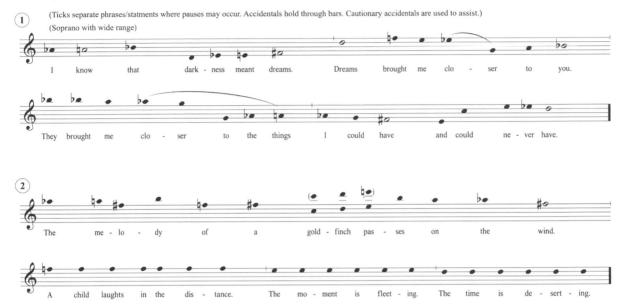

Figure 2.4d.

(See plate 2.5 for an image of the software control surface developed for *The Experiment*.)

CONFIGURATION SPACES—EMERGENT TIME

Unverifiable Intuitions (2016)

Some of my scores are constructed as *musical configuration spaces* with contingent and/or adjacent possibilities. The term is loosely related to how it is used in physics as a tool for mapping the possible states of a system. Various ways to navigate these spaces are developed for each configuration.

Unverifiable Intuitions is a solo for creative pianist (Rosenboom 2016). There is no metre. Only relatively longer and shorter notes are shown. Time is emergent. It depends upon the pianist maintaining a still and inquisitive mind. The score is constructed in four continuous sections, each beginning with a musical "Question" followed by a musical "Investigation." The "Questions" are all related to one another. The pianist determines their own progress through the piece, guided by listening actively and imaginatively to the interacting symmetries and asymmetries emerging from the resonant sound fields within each "Investigation." Music appearing between bold bar lines makes up what are called *musical units*. Each one is characterised by a particular musical cohesiveness and is interpreted as a distinct entity within the structure. *Unverifiable Intuitions* was written for renowned contemporary music pianist Satoko Inoue.

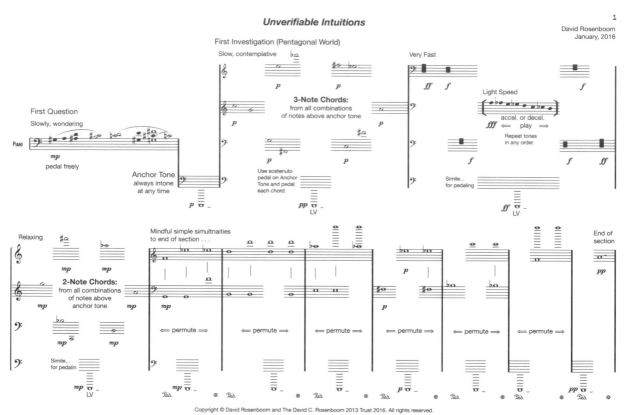

Figure 2.5.

COLLECTIVE INTERACTIVE EMERGENCE—INTELLIGENCE AS A FIELD

Swarming Intelligence Carnival (2013)

Interactively collaborative and emergent projects have been a focus of periodic investigations throughout my work. This example was a spectacle with dance, video, and music, realised with my major collaborators, legendary dancer-choreographer-painter-film-maker Sardono W. Kusumo, and composer-performers Otto Sidharta and Dwiki Dharmawan. It was the opening event of the 2013 World Culture Forum held in the Lotus Pond of Garuda Wisnu Kancana (GWK) Cultural Park in Depasar, Bali, Indonesia. The venue is a trans-

Figure 2.5. "First Question" and "First Investigation" from the score to *Unverifiable Intuitions*.

formed, limestone quarry, which we transformed again into an instrument for making art. Hundreds of artists were involved in this collective creation.

Elsewhere, I have written about a concept in which the phenomena of intelligence can be thought of as existing in a field (Rosenboom 2003). This project examined the dynamics of swarming behaviour as a form of global intelligence, as a field that can emerge from the unified actions of many members of a large group. In particular, the intention of this convergence of artists was to demonstrate a culture that can emerge when open minds mutually reinforce each other in forward-looking action.

Part of our task was to organise an emerging art form with nearly six hundred participating musicians, dancers, and other artists. A primary conceptual tool we used was to mimic simulations of swarming behaviours (flocks of birds, schools of fish, swarms of insects, and other animal groups) with sets of very simple rules for movement, enabling this very large group to organise its mass movements in, out, and around a very large outdoor venue.

Well in advance, we took measurements of the acoustic properties of the Lotus Pond, by capturing its audio impulse responses, to see how it transforms sound, to capture the rhythms of its echoes and find its resonate frequencies. With this data, I was able to transform soundscapes from field recordings of swarms in nature and sounds from urban human swarms. For the performance we were able to make use of an immense 5.1 surround-sound system installed along the ridges of the venue's high limestone walls. I was then able to play these transformed sounds back into the Lotus Pond, producing doubly transformed soundscape compositions, and mix them to create an immersive live-electronic musical surrounding for the event.

Other collaborating artists used video projection mapping to fit related images onto the rock wall surfaces of the venue. These were also meant to depict dynamic behaviours of swarms in geometric patterns and forms from nature. Finally, hundreds of dancers and musicians moved in swarming choreography, circling continuously, in and out of the Lotus Pond. This was meant to celebrate the beautiful complexity of humanity for all the international cultural emissaries attending this unique World Culture Forum. Artists have ideal minds for intuitively comprehending the nature of complexity. (See plates 2.6a–f.) (See MF2.16 for a video showing selected views from this event.)

*   *   *

Concluding commentary

Hopefully this tour of ideas reveals some of the places where languages of sciences and arts can meet fruitfully in deep theoretical territory. Our habits of description lie at the centre of this terrain. By being open to collapsing distinctions among formal percepts in a reflexively critical practice, though, we may find the means to cognise and describe a kind of useful *artscience discourse*.

Music now is experiencing a kind of post-instrumental practice—at least in the classical sense—where notation is a thin transparent surface at the interstices of co-creative representations. We can explore stripping temporal contexts from sounds and examine both the possibilities and the limitations of trying to imbed knowledge in waves. We can usefully perform with histories, both on micro-time scales, with recording, sampling, and delay technologies, and on macro-scales, by unpacking artefacts of musical archaeology in collages of *nows*.

Nothing in this invalidates in any way musical actions that have been created in our synthesised pasts or will be created in our projected futures. In the acts of drawing boundaries, we also create endless beginnings and endless endings. Could they be called *pieces*?

The arts are well primed to work with constant critical awareness that when we construct modes for describing phenomena for the essential purposes of co-communication and collaboration, we also narrow the possible pathways to substantively experiencing those phenomena. By delineating what algorithms in discrete state machines can do, we also confront the possibly non-algorithmic aspects of brains, thinking, intention, and self-identification in thought. *How do we know that knowing is happening?*

Spontaneous music-making in our age of malleable technologies and emergent forms challenges us in particular ways. Agre investigates improvisation in relation to complexity, planning, and environments: "I propose that activity in worlds of realistic complexity is inherently a matter of *improvisation*. By 'inherently' I mean that this is a necessary result, a property of the universe and not simply of a particular species of organism or a particular type of device. In particular, it is a *computational* result, one inherent in the physical realization of complex things" (Agre 1997a, 156). He focuses improvisation on "the continual dependence of action upon its circumstances" (156), in contrast to AI's focus on actions being dependent upon *planning*, which is itself an extremely challenging idea to break down. Attempts to integrate computation with musical improvisation are rife with conundrums. Agre continues, "The Cartesian roots of contemporary computational ideas obstruct the project of reconceiving 'computation' in interactionist terms" (159). Furthermore, in the list of complexity, planning, and environments, it is also necessary to situate *improvisation in social structures*.

So, what are we representing with our mappings of natural phenomena (brains, hands, bodies, ecosystems, asteroseismologies, energy-matter-time-space dynamics . . .) onto the parameters articulating our propositional music systems? What is the size and complexity of the algorithm required for me to always know that my thoughts of raspberry gelato will eternally map to E♭ major, and why do I care?

Here is a potential description for a kind of experimental music activity:

- Integrated mind-body energy enacts supposed empirical measurements of proposed differentiable categorisations to which it attaches meaning for creating shareable propositional models of temporary causation, from which emerge proposed mappings of observables onto propositional worlds of differentiables inside a chosen world of entities and their comparative relationships in scales of measure—a propositional world we choose to call musical—*choose your universe*.

References

Aaronson, Scott. 2011. "The First Law of Complexodynamics." *Shtetl-Optimized* (blog). Accessed 21 April 2021. https://www.scottaaronson.com/blog/?p=762.

Afshordi, Niayesh, Robert B. Mann, and Razieh Pourhasan. 2014. "Black Hole at the Beginning of Time." *Scientific American*, August, 37–43.

Agre, Philip E. 1997a. *Computation and Human Experience*. Cambridge: Cambridge University Press.

———. 1997b. "Toward a Critical Technical Practice: Lessons Learned in Trying to Reform AI." In *Social Science, Technical Systems, and Cooperative Work: Beyond the Great Divide*, edited by Geoffrey C. Bowker, Susan Leigh Star, William Turner, and Les Gasser, 131–57. Mahwah, NJ: Erlbaum.

Antunes, Luís, and Lance Fortnow. 2007. "Sophistication Revisted." University of Chicago. Accessed 21 April 2021. https://people.cs.uchicago.edu/~fortnow/papers/soph.pdf.

Auyang, Sunny Y. 1995. *How Is Quantum Field Theory Possible?* New York: Oxford University Press.

Baratin, Marc, Barbara Cassin, Sandra Laugier, Alain de Libera, and Irène Rosier Catach. 2014. "Proposition / Sentence / Statement / Utterance." In *Dictionary of Untranslatables: A Philosophical Lexicon*, edited by Barbara Cassin, translation edited by Emily Apter, Jacques Lezra, and Michael Wood, 859–74. Princeton, NJ: Princeton University Press. First published 2004 as *Vocabulaire européen des philosophies: Dictionnaire des intraduisibles* (Paris: Seuil; Robert).

Bateson, Gregory. 1980. *Mind and Nature: A Necessary Unity*. Toronto: Bantam Books.

Birbaumer, N., W. Lutzenberger, H. Rau, G. Mayer-Kress, and C. Braun. 1996. "Perception of Music and Dimensional Complexity of Brain Activity." *International Journal of Bifurcation and Chaos* 6 (2): 267–78.

Bohm, David. 1994. *Thought as a System*. London: Routledge.

Bonnet, François J. 2020. *The Music to Come*. Rennes, France: Shelter Press.

Cage, John. (1976) 1979. "Preface to 'Lecture on the Weather.'" In *Empty Words*, 3–5. Middletown, CT: Wesleyan University Press. First published 1976 in *Lecture on the Weather* (New York: Henmar Press).

Carpentier, Sarah M., Andrea R. McCulloch, Tanya M. Brown, Sarah E. M. Faber, Petra Ritter, Zheng Wang, Valorie Salimpoor, Kelly Shen, and Anthony R. McIntosh. 2019. "Complexity Matching: Brain Signals Mirror Environment Information Patterns during Music Listening and Reward." *Journal of Cognitive Neuroscience* 32 (4): 734–45.

Choi, Insook. 2018. "Interactive Sonification Exploring Emergent Behavior Applying Models for Biological Information and Listening." *Frontiers in Neuroscience* 12: 197. https://doi.org/10.3389/fnins.2018.00197.

Coons, Edgar E. 2019. "From RATionalize to ARTionalize." From a talk given at the Institute for Doctoral Studies in the Visual Arts and personal communications.

Costa, Madalena, Ary L. Goldberger, and C.-K. Peng. 2005. "Multiscale Entropy Analysis of Biological Signals." *Physical Review E* 71 (2): 021906.

Cottrell, William, and Miguel Montero. 2018. "Complexity is Simple!" *Journal of High Energy Physics*, article 39. https://doi.org/10.1007/JHEP02(2018)039. Preprint version available at https://arxiv.org/pdf/1710.01175.pdf.

Erickson, Kristin Grace. 2018. "Performing Algorithms." In *The Oxford Handbook of Algorithmic Music*, edited by Roger T. Dean and Alex McLean, 335–42. New York: Oxford University Press.

Foucault, Michel. 2007. *Security, Territory, Population: Lectures at the Collège de France 1977–1978*. Edited by Michel Senellart. Translated by Graham Burchell. New York: Picador.

Gaburo, Kenneth. 1976. *Paper Play: Extraction*. San Diego, CA: Lingua Press.

Gaburo, Virginia. 1977. *Notation (A Lecture to be Performed by Solo Speaker to Attentive Audience)*. La Jolla, CA: Lingua Press.

Galileo Galilei. 1997. *Galileo on the World Systems: A New Abridged Translation and Guide*. Translated and edited by Maurice A. Finocchiaro. Berkeley: University of California Press. First published 1632 as *Dialogo . . . sopra i due massimi sistemi,*

Tolemaico, e Copernicano (*Dialogue on the Two Chief World Systems, Ptolemaic and Copernican*) (Florence: Landini).

Goldstein, Rebecca. 2005. *Incompleteness: The Proof and Paradox of Kurt Gödel*. New York: W. W. Norton.

Jaynes, Julian. 1976. *The Origin of Consciousness in the Breakdown of the Bicameral Mind*. Boston: Houghton Mifflin.

Kauffman, Stuart A. 2016. *Humanity in a Creative Universe*. New York: Oxford University Press.

Komito, David Ross. 1987. *Nāgārjuna's "Seventy Stanzas": A Buddhist Psychology of Empiness*. Text translated by Tenzin Dorjee and David Ross Komito. Ithaca, NY: Snow Lion Publications. Includes a translation of the Śūnyatāsaptati of Nāgārjuna (c.150–c.250 CE).

Krakauer, David C. 2019. "Emergent Engineering: Reframing the Grand Challenge for the 21st Century." In *Worlds Hidden in Plain Sight: The Evolving Idea of Complexity at the Santa Fe Institute 1984–2019*, edited by David C. Krakauer, 349–55. Santa Fe, NM: Santa Fe Institute Press.

Mainzer, Klaus. 2007. *Thinking in Complexity: The Computational Dynamics of Matter, Mind, and Mankind*. 5th ed. Berlin: Springer.

Maldacena, Juan. 2005. "The Illusion of Gravity." *Scientific American*, November, 57–63. Accessed 22 April 2021. https://inpp.ohio.edu/~inpp/nuclear_lunch/archive/2009/maldacena_illusion_of_gravity_qpdf.pdf.

Nijholt, Anton, ed. 2019. *Brain Art: Brain-Computer Interfaces for Artistic Expression*. Cham, Switzerland: Springer.

Ollivier, Harold, David Poulin, and Wojciech H. Zurek. 2004. "Objective Properties from Subjective Quantum States: Environment as a Witness." *Physical Review Letters* 93 (22): 220401. https://doi.org/10.1103/PhysRevLett.93.220401.

Peirce, Charles S. (1878) 1934. "How to Make Our Ideas Clear." In *Collected Papers of Charles Sanders Peirce. Volume V: Pragmatism and Pragmaticism*, edited by Charles Hartshorne and Paul Weiss, section 388–410. Cambridge, MA: The Belknap Press of Harvard University Press. First published 1878 as the second of Peirce's "Illustrations of the Logic of Science"

(*Popular Science Monthly* 12: 286–302).

Penrose, Roger. 2004. *The Road to Reality: A Complete Guide to the Laws of the Universe*. London: Jonathan Cape.

Plot, Martín. 2014. *The Aesthetico-Political: The Question of Democracy in Merleau-Ponty, Arendt, and Rancière*. New York: Bloomsbury Academic.

Proust, Joëlle. 2014. "Quale, Qualia." In *Dictionary of Untranslatables: A Philosophical Lexicon*, edited by Barbara Cassin, translation edited by Emily Apter, Jacques Lezra, and Michael Wood, 877–78. Princeton, NJ: Princeton University Press. First published 2004 as *Vocabulaire européen des philosophies: Dictionnaire des intraduisibles* (Paris: Seuil; Robert).

Rosenboom, David. 1978–81. *In the Beginning*—(scores for a series of nine works). Valencia, CA: David Rosenboom Publishing. Available to download from https://davidrosenboom.com/compositions-2.

———. 1984. "On Being Invisible, I. The Qualities of Change, II. On Being Invisible, III. Steps towards Transitional Topologies of Musical Form." *Musicworks* 28: 10–13.

———. 1987. "A Program for the Development of Performance-Oriented Electronic Instrumentation in the Coming Decades: 'What You Conceive Is What You Get.'" *Perspectives of New Music* 25 (1–2): 569–83.

———. 1989. *Two Lines*. Valencia, CA: David Rosenboom Publishing; Hanover, NH: Frog Peak Music. Available to download from https://davidrosenboom.com/compositions-19811990.

———. 1992a. "Complex Adaptive Systems in Music." Unpublished talk given at the 124th Meeting of the Acoustical Society of America. Abstract published in *Journal of the Acoustical Society of America* 92 (4): 2403.

———. 1992b. "Interactive Music with Intelligent Instruments—A New, Propositional Music?" In *New Music across America*, edited by Iris Brooks, 66–70. Valencia, CA: California Institute of the Arts; High Performance Books.

———. 1992c. "Music Notation and the Search for Extra-Terrestrial Intelligence." In *Frog Peak Anthology*, edited by Carter Scholz, 103–6. Hanover, NH: Frog Peak

Music. Republished in *Leonardo* 26, no. 4 (1993): 273–74.

———. 1992d. "Parsing Real-Time Musical Inputs and Spontaneously Generating Musical Forms: Hierarchical Form Generator (HFG)." In *Proceedings of the 1992 International Computer Music Conference*, 186–89. San Francisco: International Computer Music Association (ICMA).

———. 1997. *Extended Musical Interface with the Human Nervous System: Assessment and Prospectus*. Rev ed. Leonardo Monograph 1. San Francisco, CA: ISAST. First ed. published 1990. Available to download from https://davidrosenboom.com/writings.

———. 2000a. *Invisible Gold: Classics of Live Electronic Music Involving Extended Musical Interface with the Human Nervous System*. Pogus Productions, P21022, compact disc.

———. 2000b. "Music from—On Being Invisible II (Hypatia Speaks to Jefferson in a Dream)." On *Transmigration Music*. CDCM Computer Music Series 30. Centaur Records, CRC 2490, compact disc.

———. 2000c. "Propositional Music: On Emergent Properties in Morphogenesis and the Evolution of Music; Essays, Propositions, Commentaries, Imponderable Forms and Compositional Methods." In *Arcana: Musicians on Music*, edited by John Zorn, 203–32. New York: Granary Books / Hips Road.

———. 2003. *Collapsing Distinctions: Interacting within Fields of Intelligence on Interstellar Scales and Parallel Musical Models*. Valencia, CA: David Rosenboom Publishing. Available to download from https://davidrosenboom.com/writings.

———. 2012a. *In the Beginning (1978–1981)*. New World Records, 80735-2, 2 compact discs.

———. 2012b. *Life Field*. Tzadik, TZ8091, compact disc.

———. 2014a. "Active Imaginative Listening—A Neuromusical Critique." *Frontiers in Neuroscience* 8. https://doi.org/10.3389/fnins.2014.00251.

———. 2014b. *Zones of Influence*. Pogus Productions, P21074-2, 2 compact discs.

———. 2015. *The Experiment*. Valencia, CA: David Rosenboom Publishing. Available to download from https://davidrosenboom.com/compositions.

———. 2016. *Unverifiable Intuitions*. Valencia, CA: David Rosenboom Publishing. Available to download from https://davidrosenboom.com/compositions.

———. 2018a. *Battle Hymn of Insurgent Arts*. Valencia, CA: David Rosenboom Publishing. Available to download from https://davidrosenboom.com/compositions.

———. 2018b. "Propositional Music of Many Nows." In *Tradition and Synthesis: Multiple Modernities for Composer-Performers*, edited by Dusan Bogdanovic and Xavier Bouvier, 121–42. Lévis, Québec: Doberman-Yppan.

———. 2018c. *A Summary History of Humans in the World*. Vimeo video, 17:08, posted by "David Rosenboom," 24 April 2021. Accessed 28 April 2021. https://vimeo.com/541144268. YouTube video, 17:08, posted by "David Rosenboom," 25 April 2021. Accessed 28 April 2021. https://youtu.be/dDSH9meVf0E.

———. 2019a. *Brainwave Music*. Black Truffle Records, BT048, 2 LPs.

———. 2019b. *Deviant Resonances: Live Electronic Music with Instruments, Voices and Brains*. Ravello Records, RR8009, 2 compact discs.

———. 2019c. *Quartet for the Beginning of a Time*. Valencia, CA: David Rosenboom Publishing. Available to download from https://davidrosenboom.com/compositions.

———. 2020a. "Exploring Compositional Choice in the SalMar Construction and Related Early Works by Salvatore Martirano." In *Between the Tracks: Musicians on Selected Electronic Music*, edited by Miller Puckette and Kerry L. Hagan, 113–51. Cambridge, MA: MIT Press.

———. 2020b. "Resonance Morphogenesis." In *Spectres II: Resonances*, edited by François J. Bonnet and Bartolomé Sanson, 65–72. Rennes, France: Shelter Press.

Rosenboom, David, and Anthony Braxton. 1995. *David Rosenboom / Anthony Braxton: Two Lines*. Lovely Music, LCD 3071, compact disc.

Rosenboom, David, and Tim Mullen. 2019. "More Than One—Artistic Explorations with Muilti-agent BCIs." In Nijholt 2019, 117–44.

Schaeffer, Pierre. 2012. *In Search of a Concrete*

Music. Translated by Christine North and John Dack. Berkeley: University of California Press. First published 1952 as *A la recherche d'une musique concrète* (Paris: Seuil).

Sharon, Yuval (concept and direction). 2015. *Hopscotch—A Mobile Opera for 24 Cars*. Performed by The Industry. Accessed 23 April 2021. http://hopscotchopera.com.

Smith, George. 2018. *The Artist-Philosopher and New Philosophy*. New York: Routledge.

Smith, [Wadada] Leo. 1973. *notes (8 pieces) source a new world music: creative music*. N.p.: self-published.

Spencer-Brown, G. 1972. *Laws of Form*. New York: Julian Press.

Stjernfelt, Frederik. 2014. *Natural Propositions: The Actuality of Peirce's Doctrine of Dicisigns*. Boston, MA: Docent Press.

Sun-tzu. 2003. *The Art of War*. Edited and translated by John Minford. New York: Penguin Books. Text written c. fifth century BCE.

Tanaka, Atau. 2010. "Mapping Out Instruments, Affordances, and Mobiles." In *Proceedings of the 2010 Conference on New Interfaces for Musical Expression (NIME 2010)*, 88–93. Sydney, Australia: NIME.

Thom, René. 1975. *Structural Stability and Morphogenesis: An Outline of a General Theory of Models*. Translated by David Fowler. Reading, MA: W. A. Benjamin. First published 1972 as *Stabilité structurelle et morphogénèse: Essai d'une théorie générale des modèles* (Reading, MA: W. A. Benjamin).

Twain, Mark. 1972. *A Pen Warmed-Up in Hell: Mark Twain in Protest*. Edited by Frederick Anderson. New York: Harper & Row.

von Foerster, Heinz. 1984. *Observing Systems*. 2nd ed. Seaside, CA: Intersystems Publications.

———. 2014. *The Beginning of Heaven and Earth Has No Name: Seven Days with Second-Order Cybernetics*. Edited by Albert Müller and Karl H. Müller. Translated by Elinor Rooks and Michael Kasenbacher. New York: Fordham University Press. First published 1997 as *Der Anfang von Himmel und Erde hat keinen Namen: Eine Selbsterschaffung in 7 Tagen* (Vienna: Döcker).

Wimsatt, W. C. 2013. "The Role of Generative Entrenchment and Robustness in the Evolution of Complexity." In *Complexity and the Arrow of Time*, edited by Charles H. Lineweaver, Paul C. W. Davies, and Michael Ruse, 308–31. Cambridge: Cambridge University Press.

What to Ware?

A Guide to Today's Technological Wardrobe*

The School of the Art Institute of Chicago

At some point in the late 1980s the composer Ron Kuivila told me, "we have to make computer music that sounds like electronic music." This might appear a mere semantic distinction. At that time the average listener would dismiss any music produced with electronic technology—be it a Moog or a Macintosh—as "boops and beeps." But Kuivila presciently drew attention to a looming fork in the musical road: boops and beeps were splitting into boops and bits. Over the coming decades, as the computer evolved into an unimaginably powerful and versatile musical tool, this distinction would exert a subtle but significant influence on music.

Kuivila and I had met in 1973 at Wesleyan University, where we both were undergraduates studying with Alvin Lucier. Under the guidance of mentors such as David Tudor and David Behrman, we began building circuits in the early 1970s, and finished out the decade programming pre-Apple microcomputers like the KIM-1. The music that emerged from our shambolic arrays of unreliable homemade circuits fit well into the experimental aesthetic that pervaded the times (the fact that we were bad engineers probably made our music better by the standards of our community). Nonetheless we saw great potential in those crude early personal computers, and many of us welcomed the chance to hang up the soldering iron and start programming.[1]

The Ataris, Amigas, and Apples that we adopted in the course of the 1980s were vastly easier to program than our first machines, but they still lacked the speed and processor power needed to generate complex sound directly. Most "computer music" composers of the day hitched their machines to MIDI synthesisers, but even the vaunted Yamaha DX7 was no match for the irrational

---

*   This essay began as a lecture for the "Technology and Aesthetics" symposium at NOTAM (Norwegian Center for Technology in Music and the Arts), Oslo, 26–27 May 2011, revised for publication in *Musical Listening in the Age of Technological Reproduction* (Collins 2015). It has been further revised for this publication.

1   Although this potential was clear to our small band of binary pioneers, the notion was so inconceivable to the early developers of personal computers that Apple trademarked its name with the specific limitation that its machines would never be used for musical applications, lest it infringe on the Beatles' semi-dormant company of the same name—a decision that would lead to extended litigation after the introduction of the iPod and iTunes. This despite the fact that the very first non-diagnostic software written and demonstrated at the Homebrew Computer Club in Menlo Park, California, in 1975 was a music program by Steve Dompier, an event attended by a young Steve Jobs.

weirdness of a table strewn with Tudor's idiosyncratic circuits arrayed in unstable feedback matrices. One bottleneck lay in MIDI's crudely quantised data format, which had been optimised for triggering equal-tempered notes, and was ill-suited for complex, continuous changes in sound textures. On a more profound level, MIDI "exploded" the musical instrument, separating sound (synthesiser) from gesture (keyboard, drum pads, or other controller)—we gained a Lego-like flexibility to build novel instruments, but we severed the tight feedback between body and sound that existed in most traditional, pre-MIDI instruments and we lost a certain degree of touch and nuance.[2]

By 2015 MIDI no longer stands between code and sound: any laptop has the power to generate directly a reasonable simulation of almost any electronic sound—or at least to play back a sample of it. Computer music *should* sound like electronic music. But I'm not sure that Kuivila's goal has yet been met. I still find myself moving back and forth between different technologies for different musical projects. And I can still hear a difference between hardware and software. Why?

Most music today that employs any kind of electronic technology depends on a combination of hardware and software resources. Although crafted and/or recorded in code, digital music reaches our ears through a chain of transistors, mechanical devices, speakers, and earphones. "Circuit benders" who open and modify electronic toys in pursuit of new sounds often espouse a distinctly anti-computer aesthetic; but the vast majority of the toys they hack in fact consist of embedded microcontrollers playing back audio samples—one gizmo is distinguished from another not by its visible hardware but by the program hidden in ROM. Still, whereas a strict hardware/software dialectic can't hold water for very long, arrays of semiconductors and lines of code are imbued with various distinctive traits that combine to determine the essential "hardwareness" or "softwareness" of any particular chunk of modern technology.

Some of these traits are reflected directly in sound—with sufficient attention or guidance one can often hear the difference between sounds produced by a hardware-dominated system versus those crafted largely in software. Others influence working habits—how we compose with a certain technology, or how we interact with it in performance; sometimes this influence is obvious, but at other times it can be so subtle as to verge on unconscious suggestion. Many of these domain-specific characteristics can be ignored or repressed to some degree, just like a short person can devote himself to basketball; but they nonetheless affect the likelihood of one choosing a particular device for a specific application, and they inevitably exert an influence on the resulting music.

---

2 For more on the implications of MIDI's separation of sound from gesture see Collins (1998). One magnificent exception to the gesture/sound disconnect that MIDI inflicted on most computer music composers was Tim Perkis's Mouseguitar project of 1987, which displayed much of the tactile nuance of Tudoresque circuitry. In Perkis's words: "When I switched to the FM synth (Yamaha TX81Z), there weren't any keydowns involved; it was all one 'note.' . . . The beauty of that synth—and why I still use it!—is that its failure modes are quite beautiful, and that live patch editing [can] go on while a voice is sounding without predictable and annoying glitches. The barrage of sysex data—including simulated front panel button-presses, for some sound modifications that were only accessible that way—went on without cease throughout the performance. The minute I started playing the display said 'midi buffer full' and it stayed that way until I stopped" (email, Tim Perkis to Nicolas Collins, 18 July 2006).

I want to draw attention to some distinctive differences between hardware and software tools as applied to music composition and performance. I am not particularly interested in any absolute qualities inherent in the technology, but in the ways certain technological characteristics influence how we think and work, and the ways in which the historic persistence of those influences can predispose an artist to favour specific tools for specific tasks or even specific styles of music. My observations are based on several decades of personal experience: in my own activity as a composer and performer, and in my familiarity with the music of my mentors and peers, as observed and discussed with them since my student days. I acknowledge that my perspective comes from a fringe of musical culture and I contribute these remarks in the interest of fostering discussion, rather than to prove a specific thesis.

I should qualify some of the terms I will be using. When I speak of *hardware* I mean not only electronic circuitry, but also mechanical and electromechanical devices from traditional acoustic instruments to electric guitars. By *software* I'm designating computer code as we know it today, whether running on a personal computer or embedded in a dedicated microcontroller or DSP. I use the words *infinite* and *random* not in their scientific sense, but rather as one might in casual conversation, to mean "a hell of a lot" (the former) and "really unpredictable" (the latter).

The traits

Here are what I see as the most significant features distinguishing software from hardware in terms of their apparent (or at least perceived) suitability for specific musical tasks, and their often-unremarked influence on musical processes:

- Traditional acoustic instruments are three-dimensional objects, radiating sound in every direction, filling the volume of architectural space like syrup spreading over a waffle. Electronic circuits are much flatter, essentially two-dimensional. Software is inherently linear, every program a one-dimensional string of code. In an outtake from his 1976 interview with Robert Ashley for Ashley's *Music with Roots in the Aether*, Alvin Lucier justified his lack of interest in the hardware of electronic music with the statement, "sound is three-dimensional, but circuits are flat."[3] At the time Lucier was deeply engaged with sound's behaviour in acoustic space, and he regarded the "flatness" of circuitry as a fundamental weakness in the work of composers in thrall to homemade circuitry, as was quite prevalent at the time. As a playing field for sounds, a circuit may never be able to embody the topographic richness of standing waves in a room; but at least a two-dimensional array of electronic components on a fibreglass board permits the simultaneous, parallel activity of multiple strands of electron flow, and the resulting sounds often approach the

---

3 Quotation drawn from memory. I can find no transcript of this outtake in the available documentation of the recording session.

polyphonic density of traditional music in three-dimensional space. In software most action is sequential, and all sounds queue up through a linear pipeline for digital to analogue conversion. With sufficient processor speed and the right programming environment, one can create the impression of simultaneity; but this is usually an illusion—much like a Bach flute sonata weaving a monophonic line of melody into contrapuntal chords. Given the ludicrous speed of modern computers this distinction might seem academic—modern software does an excellent job of simulating simultaneity. Moreover, "processor farms" and certain digital signal processor (DSP) systems do allow true simultaneous execution of multiple software routines. But these latter technologies are far from commonplace in music circles and, like writing prose, the act of writing code (even for parallel processors) invariably nudges the programmer in the direction of sequential thinking. This linear methodology can affect the essential character of work produced in software.

· Hardware occupies the physical world and is appropriately constrained in its behaviour by various natural and universal mechanical and electrical laws and limits. Software is ethereal—its constraints are artificial, different for every programming language, the result of intentional design rather than pre-existing physical laws. When selecting a potentiometer for inclusion in a circuit, a designer has a finite number of options in terms of maximum resistance, curve of resistive change (i.e., linear or logarithmic), number of degrees of rotation, length of its slider, and so on; and these characteristics are fixed at the point of manufacture. When implementing a potentiometer in software all these parameters are infinitely variable, and can be replaced with the click of a mouse. Hardware has real edges; software presents an ever-receding horizon.

· As a result of its physicality, hardware—especially mechanical devices— often displays non-linear adjacencies similar to state-changes in the natural world (think of the transition of water to ice or vapour).[4] Pick a note on a guitar and then slowly raise your fretting finger until the smooth decay is abruptly choked off by a burst of enharmonic buzzing as the string clatters against the fret. In the physical domain of the guitar these two sounds—the familiar plucked string and its noisy dying skronk—are immediately adjacent to one another, separated by the slightest movement of a finger. Either sound can be simulated in software, but each requires a wholly different block of code: no single variable in the venerable Karplus–Strong "plucked string algorithm" can be nudged by a single bit to produce a similar death rattle (Karplus and Strong 1983); this kind of adjacency must be programmed at a higher level, and does not typically exist in the natural order of a programming language. Generally speaking, adjacency in software remains very linear, while the world of hardware abounds with abrupt transitions. A break point in a

---

4   Composer John Bowers borrows the term *anisotropy* from material sciences to describe this behaviour (private conversation, Newcastle upon Tyne, UK, October 2019).

hardware instrument—fret buzz on a guitar, the unpredictable squeal of the STEIM Cracklebox[5]—can be painstakingly avoided or joyously exploited, but is always lurking in the background, a risk, an essential property of the instrument.

· Most software is inherently binary: it either works correctly or fails catastrophically; and when corrupted code crashes, the result is usually silence. Hardware performs along on a continuum that stretches from the "correct" behaviour intended by its designers to irreversible, smoky failure; circuitry—especially analogue circuitry—usually produces sound even as it veers towards breakdown. Overdriving an amplifier to distort a guitar (or even setting the guitar on fire), feeding back between a microphone and a speaker to play a room's resonant frequencies, "starving" the power supply voltage in an electronic toy to produce erratic behaviour—these "misuses" of circuitry generate sonic artefacts that can be analysed and modelled in software, but the risky processes themselves (saturation, burning, feedback, under-voltage) are very difficult to transfer intact from the domain of hardware to that of software while preserving functionality in the code. Writing software favours Boolean thinking—self-destructive code remains the purview of hackers who craft worms and Trojan Horses for the specific purpose of crashing or corrupting computers.

· Software is deterministic, while all hardware is indeterminate to some degree. Once debugged, code runs the same almost all the time. Hardware is notoriously unrepeatable: consider recreating a patch on an analogue synthesiser, restoring mix down settings on a pre-automation mixer, or even tuning a guitar. The British computer scientist and composer John Bowers once told me that he had never managed to write a "random" computer program that would run, but was delighted when he discovered that he could make "random" component substitutions and connections in a circuit with a high certainty of a sonic outcome (a classic technique of circuit bending).[6]

· Hardware is unique; software is a multiple. Hardware is constrained in its "thingness" by number: whether handcrafted or mass-produced, each iteration of a hardware device requires a measurable investment of time and materials. Software's lack of physical constraint gives it tremendous powers of duplication and dissemination. Lines of code can be cloned with a simple cmd-C/cmd-V: building seventy-six oscillators into a software instrument takes barely more time than one, and no more resources beyond the computer platform and development software needed for the first (unlike trombones, say). In software there is no distinction between an original and a copy: MP3 audio files, PDFs of scores, and runtime versions of music programs can be downloaded and shared thousands of times without any deterioration or loss of the matrix—any

---

5 See http://steim.org/product/cracklebox/.
6 Private conversation, Norwich, UK, January 2004.

copy is as good as the master. If a piano is a typical example of traditional musical hardware, the pre-digital equivalent of the software multiple would lie somewhere between a printed score (easily and accurately reproduced and distributed, but at a quantifiable—if modest—unit cost) and the folk song (freely shared by oral tradition, but more likely to be transformed in its transmission). Way too many words have already been written on the significance of this trait of software—of its impact on the character and profitability of publishing as it was understood before the advent of the World Wide Web; I will simply point out that if all information wants to be free, that freedom has been attained by software, but is still beyond the reach of hardware. (I should add that software's multiplicity is accompanied by virtual weightlessness, while hardware is still heavy, as every touring musician knows too well.)

· Software accepts infinite undos, is eminently tweakable. But once the solder cools, hardware resists change. I have long maintained that the young circuit-building composers of the 1970s switched to programming by the end of that decade because, for all the headaches induced by writing lines of machine language on calculator-sized keypads, it was still easier to debug code than to de-solder chips. Software invites endless updates, where hardware begs you to close the box and never open it again. Software is good for composing and editing, for keeping things in a state of flux. Hardware is good for making stable, playable instruments that you can return to with a sense of familiarity (even if they have to be tuned)—think of bongos or Minimoogs. The natural outcome of software's malleability has been the extension of the programming process from the private and invisible pre-concert preparation of a composition, to an active element of the actual performance—as witnessed in the rise of "live coding" culture practised by devotees of SuperCollider[7] and Chuck[8] programming languages, for example. Live circuit building has been a fringe activity at best: David Tudor finishing circuits in the pit while Merce Cunningham danced overhead; the group Loud Objects soldering PICs (programmable integrated circuits) on top of an overhead projector;[9] live coding versus live circuit building in ongoing competition between the younger Nick Collins (UK) and myself for the *Nic(k) Collins Cup*.[10]

· On the other hand, once a program is burned into ROM and its source code is no longer accessible, software flips into an inviolable state. At this point re-soldering, for all it unpleasantness, remains the only option for effecting change. Circuit benders hack digital toys not by rewriting the code (typically sealed under a malevolent beauty mark of black epoxy) but by messing about with traces and components on the circuit board. A hardware hack is always lurking as a last resort, like a shim bar when you lock your keys in the car.

---

7 See http://supercollider.sourceforge.net/.
8 See http://chuck.cs.princeton.edu/.
9 See http://www.loudobjects.com/.
10 See http://www.nicolascollins.com/collinscup.htm.

- Thanks to computer memory, software can work with time. The transition from analogue circuitry to programmable microcomputers gave composers a new tool that combined characteristics of instrument, score, and performer: memory allows software to play back pre-recorded sounds (an instrument), script a sequence of events in time (a score), and make decisions built on past experience (a performer). Before computers, electronic circuitry was used primarily in an instrumental capacity—to produce sounds immediately.[11] It took software-driven microcomputers to fuse this trio of traits into a powerful new resource for music creation.

- Given the sheer speed of modern personal computers and software's quasi-infinite power of duplication (as mentioned earlier), software has a distinct edge over hardware in the density of musical texture it can produce: a circuit is to code as a solo violin is to the full orchestra. But at extremes of its behaviour hardware can exhibit a degree of complexity that remains one tiny but audible step beyond the power of software to simulate effectively: the initial tug of rosined bow hair on the string of the violin; the unstable squeal of wet fingers on a radio's circuit board; the supply voltage collapsing in a cheap electronic keyboard. Hardware still does a better job of giving voice to the irrational, the chaotic, the unstable (and this may be the single most significant factor in the "Kuivila Dilemma" that prompted this whole rant).

- Software is imbued with an ineffable sense of now—it is the technology of the present, and we are forever downloading and updating to keep it current. Hardware is yesterday, the tools that were supplanted by software. Vinyl records, patchcord synthesisers, and tape recorders have been "replaced" by MP3 files, software samplers, and ProTools. In the ears, minds, and hands of most users this is an improvement—software often does the job "better" than its hardware antecedents (think of editing tape, especially videotape, before the advent of digital alternatives). Before any given tool is replaced by a superior device, qualities that don't serve its main purpose can be seen as weaknesses, defects, or failures: the ticks and pops of vinyl records, oscillators drifting out of tune, tape hiss and distortion. But when a technology is no longer relied upon for its original purpose, these same qualities can become interesting in and of themselves. The return to "outmoded" hardware is not always a question of nostalgia, but often an indication that the scales have dropped from our ears.

---

11 Beginning in the late 1960s a handful of artist-engineers designed and built pre-computer circuits that embodied some degree of performer-like decision-making: Gordon Mumma's "cybersonic consoles" (1960s–70s), which as far as I can figure out were some kind of analogue computers; my own multi-player instruments built from CMOS logic chips in emulation of Christian Wolff's "co-ordination" notation (1978). The final stages of development of David Behrman's "homemade synthesizer" included a primitive sequencer that varied pre-scored chord sequences in response to pitches played by a cellist (*Cello with Melody-Driven Electronics*, 1975) presaging Behrman's subsequent interactive work with computers. And digital delays begat a whole school of post-Terry Riley canonical performance based on looping and sustaining sounds from a performance's immediate past into its ongoing present.

Hybrids

Lest you think me a slave to the dialectic, I admit that there are at least three areas of software/hardware crossover that deserve mention here: interfaces for connecting computers (and, more pointedly, their resident software) to external hardware devices; software applications designed to emulate hardware devices; and the emergence of affordable rapid prototyping technology.

The most ubiquitous of the hardware interfaces today is the Arduino, the small, inexpensive microcontroller designed by Massimo Banzi and David Cuartielles in 2005. The Arduino and its brethren and ancestors facilitate the connection of a computer to input and output devices, such as tactile sensors and motors. Such an interface indeed imbues a computer program with some of the characteristics we associate with hardware, but there always remains a MIDI-tinged sense of mediation (a result of the conversion between the analogue to digital domains) that makes performing with these hybrid instruments slightly hazier than manipulating an object directly—think of controlling a robotic arm with a joystick, or hugging an infant in an incubator while wearing rubber gloves. That said, I believe that improvements in haptic feedback technology will bring us much closer to the nuance of real touch.

The past decade has also seen a proliferation of software emulations of hardware devices, from smart phone apps that simulate vintage analogue synthesisers, to iMovie filters that make your HD video recording look like scratchy Super 8 film. The market forces behind this development (nostalgia, digital fatigue, etc.) lie outside the scope of this discussion, but it is important to note here that these emulations succeed by focusing on those aspects of a hardware device most easily modelled in the software domain: the virtual Moog synthesiser models the sound of analogue oscillators and filters, but doesn't try to approximate the glitch of a dirty pot or the pop of inserting a patchcord; the video effect alters the colour balance and superimposes algorithmically generated scratches, but does not let you misapply the splicing tape or spill acid on the emulsion.

Although affordable 3D printers and rapid prototyping devices still remain the purview of the serious DIY practitioner, there is no question that these technologies will enter the larger marketplace in the near future. When they do, the barrier between freely distributable software and tactile hardware objects will become quite permeable. A look through the Etsy website reveals how independent entrepreneurs have already employed this technology to extend the publishing notion of "print on demand" to something close to "wish on demand," with Kickstarter as the economic engine behind the transformation of wishes into businesses. (That said, I've detected the start of a backlash against the proliferation of web-accessed "things" [see Arieff 2014]).

Some closing observations

I came of age as a musician during the era of the "composer-performer": the Sonic Arts Union, David Tudor, Terry Riley, La Monte Young, Pauline Oliveros, Steve Reich, Philip Glass. Sometimes this dual role was a matter of simple expediency (established orchestras and ensembles wouldn't touch the music of these young mavericks at that time), but more often it was a desire to retain direct, personal control that led to a flowering of composer-led ensembles that resembled rock bands more than orchestras. Fifty years on, the computer—with its above-mentioned power to fuse three principle components of music production—has emerged as the natural tool for this style of working.

But another factor driving composers to become performers was the spirit of improvisation. The generation of artists listed above may have been trained in a rigorous classical tradition, but by the late 1960s it was no longer possible to ignore the musical world outside the gates of academe or beyond the doors of the European concert hall. What was then known as "world music" was reaching American and European ears through a trickle of records and concerts. Progressive jazz was in full flower. Pop was inescapable. And composers of my age—the following generation—had no need to reject any older tradition to strike out in a new direction: Indian music, Miles Davis, the Beatles, John Cage, Charles Ives, and Monteverdi were all laid out in front of us like a buffet, and we could heap our plates with whatever pleased us, regardless of how odd the juxtapositions might seem. Improvisation was an essential ingredient, and we sought technology that expanded the horizons of improvisation and performance, just as we experimented with new techniques and tools for composition.

It is in the area of performance that I feel that hardware—with its tactile, sometimes unruly properties—still holds the upper hand. This testifies not to any failure of software to make good on its perceived promise of making everything better in our lives, but to a pragmatic affirmation of the sometimes messy but inarguably fascinating irrationality of human beings: sometimes we need the imperfection of things.

References

Arieff, Allison. 2014. "Yes We Can. But Should We?" *Re:form*, 15 September 2014. Accessed 19 March 2021. https://medium.com/re-form/just-because-you-can-doesnt-mean-you-should-252fdbcf76c8.

Collins, Nicolas. 1998. "Ubiquitous Electronics—Technology and Live Performance 1966–1996." *Leonardo Music Journal* 8: 27–32.

———. 2015. "Semiconducting: Making Music after the Transistor." In *Musical Listening in the Age of Technological Reproduction*, edited by Gianmario Borio, 291–300. Abingdon, UK: Ashgate.

Karplus, Kevin, and Alex Strong. 1983. "Digital Synthesis of Plucked-String and Drum Timbres." *Computer Music Journal* 7 (2): 43–55.

Toward a
Critical Musical Practice

Ann Warde

Independent scholar

Philip Agre's article "Toward a Critical Technical Practice" (1997b) emphasises the practical usefulness of applying life experience to the development of artificial intelligence. In his case, artificial intelligence is realised using computer programs to model human ways of occupying our world. The title of this chapter substitutes **musical** practice for *technical* practice, questioning, from the perspective Agre describes, whether music might be usefully understood also as a way of modelling our experiences of the world. Perhaps music might model a world focused, in particular, on those experiences we perceive as individuals. And, from this viewpoint, music composition might be conceived as providing an opportunity for those who construct music to model a world we'd *like* to perceive and experience—an environment: a social, physical, tactile environment—one that, as individuals, we might enjoy living within.

A critical approach to music composition helps us, as we attempt to build these kinds of models, to correctly construct an environment we desire, so that we get it right. A critical approach requires asking questions, from as many perspectives as we can, about the details of our work, but also about why we make the specific musics we do, why we might want to live in the world we are composing, and what other alternative worlds we might also consider constructing, in order to find ourselves focusing authentically on experiences peculiar to each of us as composers.

Michael Dieter, in his essay "The Virtues of Critical Technical Practice," refers to several works by Jacques Rancière, for whom "art is always defined as something more than itself, since aesthetics functions as at once removed from the political and simultaneously located within its sphere of influence by forever holding out the possibility of another world" (Dieter 2014, 221).[1] Dieter himself links this definition of art to the process of critical technical practice: "Indeed, CTP's double act of craft and critique invites reflection on transformations in sense and perception that occur through a suspension of 'means' and 'ends' across sociotechnical experience" (ibid., 218). Perhaps it is this suspension of "means" and "ends" that leads a practitioner into art? "Means" suggest a focus on how a practitioner proceeds—the method that is used—while "ends" suggest a focus on results, on considering just what it is that is intended to be

---

1   Dieter's references are to Rancière's *The Politics of Aesthetics* (2004) and *Dissensus: On Politics and Aesthetics* (2010).

produced, and for what purpose. Suspending a focus on the "how" may lead a practitioner along an unanticipated path of "otherness"—straying from a usual (and perhaps habitual) way of proceeding. Coupling this different pathway to a holding-off on just what it is that one envisions as an end product, and refraining from articulating exactly why one might want to produce whatever actually results, suggests heading away from a familiar location, and perhaps towards something less definite, but nonetheless encompassing what might be hoped for. However, with no definite end in sight, and no clear path on which to travel, one is left only with one's becoming, with a recognition of the process in which one is embedded—suspended in between the lack of a well-travelled, familiar route and the absence of a clearly anticipated, expected destination.

Sensory perception

Dieter's suggestion of a set of "transformations in sense and perception" that happen within this kind of experience links his statement to Agre's probing of his (Agre's) own lived, sensory, experience as a source for the development and construction of intelligent systems. Agre's ideas—unusual and groundbreaking inside the world of artificial intelligence tool development in which he was enmeshed during the 1990s and early 2000s—represent a node within a network of conceptualisations not only proposed by the thinkers he himself draws upon in his writings, but also those engendered by earlier thinkers, and by Agre's contemporaries working in other fields.

Grounded in an observation of the priority of direct experience, these ideas overlap and intersect Agre's focus on sensory experience as a key mechanism through which we come to know our world and to understand our interactions within that world, including those with other people and with our surrounding environment. This perspective includes the notion of basing the development of work (for ourselves as individuals) on unpredictable, essentially unforeseeable, "input," derived from our physical encounters and experiences of interacting with, and simply living in, the worlds we occupy—that is, doing what we do as humans.

Throughout this chapter I've made observations of ideas and perspectives that emerge when I substitute—in extracts from Philip Agre's article—the word **music**, or the word **composition**, for the words *technology* and *AI* (with some latitude, and alongside a few related word substitutions that are unmarked). In addition, because I am interested to explore notions related to the concept of *newness*, I have also in almost all cases replaced Agre's word *new* with related but alternate words. Substituted words are indicated within Agre's texts by **boldface** type.

In the section of Agre's paper called "Waking Up" he explains his engagement in a process of observation and analysis: the observation of his own, personal activities, as he lived his life from day to day.

> . . . writing out the full details of an actual episode . . . would raise an endless series of additional questions, often unrelated to what I was looking for. It is hard to convey the powerful effect that this experience had on me; . . . I was motivated . . . by a passion to explain to my fellow **composers** how our **musical conceptualisations** had cut us off from an authentic experience of our own lives. (Agre 1997b, 146, edited)

I find the idea of "authentic experience" suggestive. For a composer, perhaps this might be some kind of authentic experience of listening—a kind of listening that places the details of our perception of sound *before* our interpretation, and before our identification of it. This theme seems to be an important one. It points to an idea of *lived experience*, or some might say *direct experience*. We may turn to the American pragmatist philosopher Charles S. Peirce (1839–1914) for a comment on this particular categorisation of experience:

> . . . continuity, regularity, and significance are essentially the same idea with merely subsidiary differences. That this element is found in experience is shown by the fact that all experience involves time. Now the flow of time is conceived as continuous. No matter whether this continuity is a datum of sense, or a quasi-hypothesis imported by the mind into experience, or even an illusion; in any case it remains a direct experience. For experience is not what analysis discovers but the raw material upon which analysis works. This element then is an element of *direct experience*. (Peirce 1958, section 535, italics added)

Victoria Welby, a British philosopher and thinker active at the turn of the twentieth century and well known to the European and American scientific and intellectual communities of her time, maintained a wide-ranging correspondence with multiple thinkers and inquirers, including Charles Peirce. Near the start of her 1903 book *What Is Meaning?*, in conjunction with her interest in establishing an educational foundation—in early childhood—that might foster the development of thoughtful and actionable adults, Welby tells us:

> When we understand that "Sense" is the central thing as means of (1) all experience; (2) all interpretation; (3) all knowledge; (4) all conduct; (5) all prediction; and that the forms of language are merely means of conveying this in its highest, as well as its simplest forms, we shall use all possible means for concentrating the child's interest upon it. . . . The child must therefore everywhere and always be imbued with the sense that the one thing first needful is Sense, and the idea that, having this, all things may be added . . . (Welby 1903, xxix)

Using personal perceptions rooted in concrete experiences as a basis for constructing approaches and procedures to produce work—including artwork— is an idea that also resonates independently within multiple fields, through the practice of employing analogy and metaphor as a means of developing knowledge.

ANALOGY AND METAPHOR

This method of peering—through the use of generative metaphor—into potentially unfamiliar ways of comprehending and interpreting textual information is also a central focus of Philip Agre's. His 1997 book, *Computation and Human Experience* (Agre 1997a), probes deeply into the multiple, distinctive roles that analogy and metaphor may play in the development and construction of the computer technology underlying artificial intelligence. Through an exploration of their function within other, related, projects, I will investigate a few specific uses of analogy and metaphor within the languages we employ to describe and explore musical experience. Integral to this approach is a focus on an inclusive notion of musical composition, one that encompasses all methods for constructing plans, realising conceptualisations, and developing skills, in preparation for the making and performance of music.

The approach introduced at the start of this chapter—an attempt to uncover multiple meanings of a text through substituting specific terms for others—was also practised by Victoria Welby. Her 1903 *What Is Meaning?* specifically focuses on developing this technique, which she calls *translation*, within her "Significs" approach to investigating how language is used to convey sense and meaning. This technique mirrors my word substitution procedure.

> . . . there is a method both of discovering, testing, and using analogy . . . and this may be called in an extended sense Translation. (Welby 1903, 126)

> The mere attempt to state one subject in the terms of another, to express one set of ideas in those words which seem to belong properly to another, changing only the leading terms, could not fail, if done systematically and critically, both to enlighten us on points of connection or correspondence which have not been suspected, and also, perhaps, to reveal ignorance in some cases where we have taken knowledge for granted. (Ibid., 128)

The process of transporting one's perceptual observations from the region of sensory, felt experience into the region of, perhaps, a cognitive model, in the form of an experience of art—one intended to engage perception—connects to Welby's notion of just this kind of process of a translation of sensory experience into "intellectual" understanding. The process itself relies on observing, within sets of contrasting ideas, intersections among characteristic similarities, and, simultaneously, distinctions that may articulate meaningful differences.

> The . . . idea of Translation in all its applications implies, of course, the careful recognition of Distinction, and starts from the conception of Equation. Its use is seen wherever there is a presumable unity implied in differences which can be distinguished. . . . An answer to those who would doubt the validity of a translation of the physical into the mental is supplied by the word sense itself. (Welby 1903, xxii)

Let us now apply Welby's practice of *translation*, as a means of employing analogy and metaphor towards the development of knowledge, to additional extracts from Philip Agre's writings. By stepping out of one contextual environment and into another, still surrounding ourselves for the most part nonetheless with an identical verbal description, let us see to what extent we might encounter a sense of altered boundaries, and whether the potential might emerge for developing a larger conception of a fluid, continuously evolving sense of musical boundedness and constraint.

Boundaries and limits are entangled with our attempts to distinguish compositions from instruments, and composers from performers—attempts that often present us with collections of intriguing ambiguities. How might we further engage with this kind of useful uncertainty?

> Every **music** fits, in its own unique way, into a far-flung network of different sites of social practice. Some **musics** are employed in a specific site, and in those cases we often feel that we can warrant clear cause-and-effect stories about the transformations that have accompanied them, either in that site or others. Other **musics**, not unlike electric lighting and the telephone, are so ubiquitous—found contributing to the evolution of the activities and relations of so many distinct sites of practice—that it requires considerable effort to understand their effects on society . . . (Agre 1997b, 131, edited)

Here (from this "translated" version of the beginning of Philip Agre's essay "Toward a Critical Technical Practice") an idea seems to emerge that music might somehow be capable of tangibly bringing about changes—transformations—within society, and perhaps that is one of its purposes, one of its uses. The precise nature of this change is likely specific to the circumstances within which music happens: the more restricted and restrained the circumstances, the more pointed and clear the effects. On the other hand, far-flung, disconnected, distinct circumstances seem to cloud our understanding of music's effects, complicating them—making these effects difficult to discern.

The range of musics people listen to and have listened to, sounds they call and have called music, is extraordinarily diverse. Perhaps what is most striking, however, is the process of listening . . . the same music can be heard as astonishingly different both to different people and to the same person at different times.

Listening combines our perception of sonic structures, unfolding in time, with our own personal listening histories. In this way, listening embodies musical intelligence, or sometimes, simultaneously, multiple musical intelligences. Through coming to understand a specific listening process—one that each of us, as a conceptualiser of music, personally experiences—we can, through composing music, construct musical intelligence. I think this is what Michael Dieter refers to when he contrasts "the recovery of actual lived experiences" with "transcendental categories for all possible experience" (2014, 225).

But how does a composer make her way towards the construction of a distinctive, alternative, out-of-the-ordinary listening experience—that model of a visionary world we'd like to inhabit? As we know, it is not easy—nor would we want it to be: it is, of course, through encountering and overcoming obstacles within the compositional process that we find ourselves happening upon an unfamiliar perceptual environment, a different musical experience.

In the section of "Toward a Critical Technical Practice" called "The Fallacy of Alternatives," Agre articulates some of the difficulties we may encounter. His descriptions help clarify the details and implications of obstacles, and thus they may assist us in uncovering solutions.

> It is useful . . . to distinguish four reasons why it is difficult to create alternatives to the standard methods of **music composition**. First, it is difficult to become aware of the full range of assumptions underneath existing practices, from **compositional** methods to genre conventions to metaphors. Second, having formulated an alternative intuition, it is difficult to reduce that intuition to a novel **musical** method—an **unfamiliar** type of artifact, or an **unconventional** way of building artifacts. Third, having invented a **different compositional** method, it is difficult to prevent that method from being construed as "nothing new" within the elastic boundaries of existing **musical** schemata. Fourth, having coupled an unusual **musical** method with an **uncharacteristic** way of talking about the phenomena, it is difficult to apply the method to any real cases without inventing a lot of additional methods as well, because any worthwhile system will require the application of several interlocking methods, and use of the existing methods may distort the novel method back toward the traditional mechanisms and the traditional ways of talking about them. (Agre 1997b, 152–53, edited)

> When **composers** look at an innovation and pronounce it nothing radically **innovative**, they will be wrong in some ways and right in others, and it will require tremendous effort to determine which is which. Critical practice is essential to make sense of such things, but the goal of this practice should be complex engagement, not a clean break. (Ibid., 151, edited)

Music as technology

Might considering music as a technology be another way to encourage a redrawing (dynamically, evolutionarily) of its boundaries? If we consider music composition as the building of an alternative world, and music itself as a technology, that would suggest there are perhaps two instances of a critical musical practice we might be able point to: a keen awareness of the multi-dimensional layers of intersecting factors that inform and shape how the world that is modelled by the composition is perceived and interpreted, and an insightful recognition of the wide range of potential circumstances within which the composition might be encountered. A critical engagement with all factors, circumstances, attitudes, habits, and sensibilities that contribute to the composition as a perceived experience is an auspicious way to assist the composition itself in becoming a living, authentic, effective entity.

Technology is a capability, a thing that can do or perform something. What might music do? What are its capabilities? And, if the activity of making music is a technology, does it have a purpose? A use? How might we use it, how might we make it useful?

"Music is literally inconceivable without technologies." This observation by Jonathan Impett (2016) articulates a central theme underlying the multiple, wide-ranging viewpoints voiced and illustrated by contributors to the Orpheus Sound Work 2016 research seminar. His statement nudges us to think more broadly about how we might understand what technology is. One path we might take is to explore how technology might be distinguished, on the one hand, by its connection to science (as in Agre's discussions) and, on the other, by its connection to the arts (in our discussion here).

> I imagine a building in which the arts are met by technology and the sciences on their common ground. They all investigate, stipulate, create, and exploit systems. They are all faced with the puzzles and the functions of structure. And their aims and results complement one another because of their difference. While the sciences observe or stipulate systems that are *to be analogous* to an existent truth or reality, and while technology stipulates and creates systems that are *to function* in an existent truth or reality, the arts stipulate and create systems that are analogous to an existence *desired to become* true or real. (Brün [1970] 2004, 172)

The composer, thinker, and computer music pioneer Herbert Brün's framing of these definitions of science, technology, and the arts, via conceptualisations that are formulated through the use of parallel syntax, can help us investigate details of distinctions between these three activities. And, at the same time, through acknowledging their basic commonalities, his use of language also points to other, potentially ambiguous (and thus, I would suggest, useful), interconnections.

All three activities (science, technology, the arts) stipulate systems. The indication of a process of *stipulation* suggests a connection to Dieter's "suspension of 'means' and 'ends' across sociotechnical experience." That is, not defining explicit means or ends may be understood to invite a creative imagining of those means and ends, while firmly established means and ends may instead simply invite response and reaction. Through his articulation of this approach, perhaps Brün is pointing to the notion of models; that by "system" he implies an interconnected set of interdependent parts, which is used to conceptualise an aspect of our present accumulated experience, or of our potential future experience.[2]

All three of these activities focus on the construction of some kind of model—not actuality, not reality, but a *representation* of experience. And, because a model (even in the case of technology—but there is more to say about this) is not actual experience, but an interpretation of experience, it is important that a freedom from assumed limitations is clearly articulated. We may be required to react to our perception of some aspect of our everyday physical world (perhaps a cat crosses our path and we must step around it to avoid stepping on it). However, a model of that world, articulated as a "system," is a conceptualisation that can be considered from multiple perspectives without any undue repercussions. Again, some technologies may appear to be exceptions; however, computer technology is *not*. In fact, this is one of its potential pitfalls, discussed incisively in Agre's chapter "Abstraction and Implementation" (1997a, 66–88). A message here is, do not place a constraint where none is required.

---

2   These insights into Herbert Brün's use of the word *stipulate* are informed by a discussion with Michael Brün (his son).

Building on the idea that these three activities focus on the construction of models of experience, Brün specifies that science and the arts represent *analogies* of a present or future "existent truth or reality." Technology, however, is intended *to function* in an "existent truth or reality." We may ask, does a technology actually function as intended? *Must* it actually function as intended? Perhaps in some cases may it be most useful if it is repurposed?

Technology's model is a physical model, and because it is intended to function in the current world, it embodies aspects of that world. Musics also embody aspects of the current worlds in which they are made and in which they happen. Brün's distinctions among science, technology, and the arts have to do primarily with the relationship between the purposes of our model-making and aspects of time. They imply either an accumulated past that informs an existent present or a desired future.

An "existent truth or reality" is the *present moment*, and from the viewpoint of a performer (who is also a listener), music itself (the lived experience of music) *is* a technology, intended to *function* (to "work") in the present. And, interestingly, as a result of the inevitable embeddedness within the particular contextual details that define the time in which both music and technology happen— as they move ahead into the future—music, and other technologies, carry with them the trappings of the time and place in which they are experienced. That is, we often associate past times, specific places, and particular occasions with our contemporaneous experience of a specific musical event, brought to mind by sounds that may refer to that event, and that may suggest that we reach back to remember, in a sense to re-live, our experience of its specific characteristics. This remembrance may also happen in connection with our use of a specific piece of technology, be it a specific model of a toaster, of a car, or of a distinct version of a piece of computer software.

Brün's definition of technology also specifies that it "functions"—it works; it is intended to accomplish something. He specifies that technology is intended to function in relation to the world within which it is applied and used, that is, "an existent truth or reality." From the point of view of a performer who in some way makes use of a musical plan, some kind of musical roadmap—a set of actual or potential patterns of sounds that the performer intends to realise— this conception of technology might also describe an aspect of music. It may suggest, in addition to being an art (a system that is "analogous to an existence *desired to become* true or real"), that music itself is at the same time a system intended to "function in an existent truth or reality." That is, music itself must "work." Whatever its intention, that intention must be able to be realised.

This is the case even if the music involves written notation that is technically impossible to perform (for instance in some works by Christian Wolff). This impossibility presents a challenge to the performer, and, as part of the performance of the composition (the application of the music as technology), the performer confronts and grapples with this challenge.

Reiterating our initial statement: music also requires technologies—systems that facilitate the production of sounds in the present moment. And, these sound configurations, however they are produced—and *because* they are produced—are also systems that can, from yet another listening perspective, be heard (perceived) as "analogous" to an "existent reality," one that enfolds these musical sounds in a present, *perceptual* time frame. The interpretation of musical experience, then, as a *perceptual* activity that can be observed, measured, and situated (perhaps musicologically, or psychophysically) in a contextual environment, also allows it to be understood as a system *analogous* to an "existent reality"—music can be understood also to be a science.

So it appears, to some extent, that science, technology, and the arts all tend to take part in one another's distinctions. On the one hand, all are bound up in one or another way with the observations assigned to science: the arts are, for instance, intended to be observed, and, as they undergo the process of being constructed, they must observe themselves. And, each constructs, in at least one or another of its aspects, systems that are intended "to be *analogous* to an existent truth or reality" (which I'm understanding as the present time and environment). On the other hand, nonetheless, at the same time, science, technology, and the arts must all in some respects be *functional* within the present time and environment.

However, perhaps, when we consider the characteristics of "an existence *desired to become* true or real"—a future orientation—might we suggest that this distinction belongs uniquely to the arts? Science must be of the moment, although its models can predict a future time. And, the realisation of the prediction itself, based on information gathered from an "existent truth or reality," does itself necessarily belong to that reality. Also, in a strict sense, science is not in a position to venture beyond the data it has collected, since, without data, science cannot engage in its processes of measurement.

While the arts function in the present, and they stipulate "systems that are analogous to an existence *desired to become* true or real," their associated technology must at the same time function in the present. However, if technology is intended to bring about a system that is "analogous to an existence *desired to become* true or real," that technology itself must be envisioned as one of the arts: it must be a *technology desired to become* true or real.

My point here is that Brün's descriptions illustrate multiple, entangled, interconnections between these three activities, and—perhaps because of these entanglements—to some extent each can be described by the definition attributed to the others. Might these interconnections extend to the technology of artificial intelligence, and might links between technology and the arts extend to include an interrelationship between artificial intelligence and music?

MUSICAL COMPOSITIONS AS ARTIFICIAL INTELLIGENCE

Music is an art. As we have seen, according to Herbert Brün's definition, it is thus one of multiple arts that "stipulate and create systems that are analogous to an existence *desired to become* true or real." This thought merges with the notion of engaging in a critical practice in order to correctly build an environment we'd like to inhabit. This is a potential purpose of music, one with which we initially began our discussion.

My question now is about musical compositions. How might they function within this process, specifically, as methods for the construction of musical activity and experience? Perhaps we might first consider what kind of endeavours we understand a composer to engage in, with the intent to construct a musical composition. In his chapter in the present book (p. 117), Jonathan Impett suggests: "We . . . use the term *composer* here to refer to all such artists who take responsibility for conceiving and producing a musical phenomenon that has some degree of boundedness and identity, regardless of how reproducible it might be or at what remove composers stand from a listener's experience. On some level, at some point, they com-pose—they put together."

So, then, what specifically might a musical composition entail, as a "putting together"? Perhaps a merging of conception and production involving at some level a methodology, a blueprint for an activity, for which the composer takes responsibility. Perhaps we might say it is the "how"—the "how" of making music, the "how" of Christopher Small's *musicking* (1998). That is, suppose we say a musical composition is an answer to the question, How do we make (practice, perform, perceive) this music? Then we might suggest that the composition is the "methodology" that answers this question.

We have seen that music can be understood to function as a technology, and that it requires technology in order to happen (most obviously it makes use of instruments, as technologies—from the human vocal apparatus to trombones, kanjira, and sheng, to electronics and computers for music-making, sound-art construction, and sound production and presentation).

Might we also consider the process and activity of composing and constructing music to be a technology? Perhaps we might even venture to say that musical compositions are technologies for constructing musical/aesthetic experiences—particularly if we understand the word *aesthetic* to mean a methodology or a practice: a way of doing something.

A musical composition can be a "how" of making music (a way, a method, a practice) at all levels of complexity. It may encompass notation (but not necessarily), conceptualisation, knowledge of specific performance practices, an ability to realise those performance practices, and knowledge of context(s) within which specific musical activity is embedded.

Authentically listening to our lived experience might facilitate the building of musical compositions that embody an unfamiliar (because we are just now observing it) yet perhaps strangely comfortable feeling (because this experience is our own)—a feeling of oneself experiencing a world within which one fits and finds one's place. This description of the process of composition embodies a kind of imaginary, visionary intelligence, suggesting that musical compositions may be correctly called *artificial* intelligence because they are models or representations (or imitations?) of a personal human intelligence.

Let's step back to consider how we might understand what *intelligence* is, and how we might understand what *artificial* is. If artificial intelligence is understood, in fact, to be some kind of manufactured intelligence, perhaps, then, might it also be understood to be a "how" in a way similar to musical composition?

Investigating the etymology of the word *intelligence* brings us to its sixteenth-century Latin roots: *inter* (between) and *legere* (choose). So, perhaps *intelligence* implies an ability to *distinguish*, to choose between, to perceive degrees of difference, a process that we might understand as underlying, and possibly facilitating, its current definition: "the ability to acquire and apply knowledge and skills" (Lexico 2021b). *Knowledge* we may understand as "awareness or familiarity gained by experience of a fact or situation" (Lexico 2021c). Might we extend this definition to include an awareness or familiarity gained through *personal* experience, that is, our own perceptual experience?

Perhaps the "putting-together" of a musical composition defines, describes, and presents a set of perceptual distinctions. Perhaps it defines, within itself, *what makes a difference*. To the extent that a piece of music "stipulates" (proposes) and creates a system "analogous to an existence *desired to become* true or real," this system, the composition's system, may comprise a *system of distinctions*—a system that within itself defines *what makes a difference* in relation to "an existence desired to become true or real," and a system that possesses the ability to draw upon and to apply knowledge ("awareness or familiarity gained by experience of a fact or situation").

A look at the etymology of the word *artificial* connects it to the word *artifice*, from the late Middle English *ars* (art) and *facere* (make)—with the current definition: "made or produced by human beings rather than occurring naturally, especially as a copy of something natural" (Lexico 2021a). That is, might we consider an artificial intelligence to mimic our human intelligence (which itself is marked by its ability to identify distinctions)? If we suggest that musical compositions are plans and conceptualisations for the production of systems defining and articulating specific, bounded collections of distinctions, then perhaps we might consider music compositions themselves as artificial intelligences. And, if we already understand music compositions as technologies for constructing musical/aesthetic experiences, then they may be also considered to be artificial intelligences if they are understood as acting in ways that overlap the function(s) of computational artificial intelligence (AI) as it exists in our contemporary world.

What, then, about artificial intelligence itself? Agre's concern for *technical* practice indicates that AI is meant to be a technology (which, according to Brün, "stipulates and creates systems that are *to function* in an existent truth or reality"). However, it is a specific kind of technology, and its development and application is generally considered to be within the realm of science (again, Brün's definitions tell us that "the sciences observe or stipulate systems that are *to be analogous* to an existent truth or reality").

Stepping back, perhaps, might we consider the idea that artificial intelligence, and, indeed, any musical composition, is at once a science, a technology, and an art? Its construction involves stipulation (we do not know its means or ends), observation (we must observe ourselves as bearers of intelligence and sources of information for creating models of intelligence), and construction of a concrete system (creation). A computer program operating as an artificial intelligence (like a musical composition) is intended "*to function* in an existent truth or reality," while at the same time it is intended to form an analogue or model—both from a practical standpoint, and from the standpoint of its reliance on data and information existing within the "truth or reality" inside which it is conceived and constructed. However, its apprehension, its result, its "output," by a perceiver, experiencer, and/or listener, is intended to be "analogous to an existence *desired to become* true or real."

AI, MUSIC, AND NON-HUMAN RESEARCH

While grounded in my study of music (as a student of Alvin Lucier, and—vicariously—of John Cage [through my own investigations, and in-depth conversations with composers who worked with him]), my own direct engagement with these questions of listening, perception, and identification of sound comes most recently from my work for a period of ten or twelve years with the science of animal vocalisations—sounds animals make that appear to represent some kind of communication. Much of my activity has been focused on whale sounds. The blue whale, the largest whale, when it sings (*singing* is a bioacoustics term for animal sounds that are sequentially ordered), makes two distinct sounds, called notes: one is an amplitude-modulated tone ("A"), the other is a frequency-modulated tone ("B"). Each sound is about thirty seconds long and has a fundamental frequency of about 17 Hz. The animals make a variety of patterns using these notes, for instance, A A B A A B, or A B A B . . . (McDonald, Mesnick, and Hildebrand 2006; Oestreich et al. 2020).

What fascinates me about these sounds is the extraordinarily different perceptual scale they represent. Because the fundamental frequency is so low, as humans we most likely will be able to perceive these sounds only through the use of a hydrophone positioned so close to the animal that it captures the energy of the sound's upper harmonics. If we are lucky enough to be able to experience this, when we listen to the amplitude-modulated tone, we will hear a set of slow pulses, just a little faster than one per second. However, if we speed up playback of the sound, so that the time is compressed and the pitch is raised, we, as humans, hear a quick series of pulses, ending in a slightly longer pulse, all of which, rather than a series of pulses, we perceive as one coherent sound (this can be heard in MF4.1 in the online repository for this book).[3] This experience provides us with clear evidence that the myriad organisms occupying our planet Earth perceive this Earth in vastly different ways. And it is an instance of one category of direct listening experience that informs my sense of compositional and musical boundaries.

When we compose music, is our intention really directed to the goals of constructing specific "use cases" for specific purposes, versus musics for "general use"? And when a specific use for a music is met, what happens when it finds itself in a different environment, one whose requirements are different? Then at that point it both is something that may become reinterpreted—so its initial

---

3   https://orpheusinstituut.be/en/sound-work-media-repository. Further details of the repository can be found in the appendix to this book on p. 355.

reasons for being constructed are perhaps lost or overlooked—and at the same time may introduce ideas and methods that prompt exploration, borrowing, and the development of unfamiliar musics within the environment it now occupies.

I think Agre, in his re-evaluations of how the development of artificial intelligence tools might proceed, is pointing to a lack of interaction with actual real-world problems that could be potentially addressed by AI, and also, perhaps more so, he is pointing to abstract approaches to the development of AI that are not based on an examination of human behaviour (in all its complexity). Rather he seems to suggest that a firmer foundation for AI development may lie with experimentation and refinement of algorithms invented for specific applications, those that appear to have acquired lives of their own.

Interestingly, Agre's insights continue to represent an important area of investigation for the machine learning community interested in developing solutions to pressing real-world problems, as revealed in "Machine Learning That Matters," by computer scientist Kiri Wagstaff (2012), and Hannah Kerner's "Too Many AI Researchers Think Real-World Problems Are Not Relevant" (2020).

The final paragraphs of Agre's essay shed light on the actualities of attempting to create a model—an *artificial intelligence*/**musical composition**—of this kind of environment: one in which we find ourselves to fit, and in which we enjoy the experience of being ourselves.

> **Musical** research can only develop from within the **composer's** own practical work, and it will only progress when the **composer's** experience is neither channeled by self-reinforcing conceptual schemata from inside the field nor delegitimated by incommensurable philosophies from outside of it. . . .
>
> A critical **musical** practice will . . . require a split identity—one foot planted in the craft work of design and the other foot planted in the reflexive work of critique. Successfully spanning these borderlands, bridging the disparate sites of practice that **compositional** work brings uncomfortably together, . . . will require . . . the exploration of alternative work practices that will inevitably seem strange to insiders and outsiders alike. This strangeness will not always be comfortable, but it will be productive nonetheless, both in the esoteric terms of the **musical** field itself and in the exoteric terms by which we ultimately evaluate a **musical** field's contribution to society. (Agre 1997b, 155, edited)

Returning to the non-human animal sounds I've been working with, I wonder, might we consider these sounds also to be a kind of technology? This could make sense if we think of their communicative function as a technological function . . . that is, in terms of Merriam-Webster's dictionary definition of technology: "a capability given by the practical application of knowledge" (2021).

It is difficult to ascribe knowledge to non-human animals, since we cannot access the mechanisms underlying their thought processes. However, perhaps our lack of understanding can be a basis for constructing, in this case, an abstraction of the notion of knowledge. So, we could say these sounds might constitute a technology that is a capability given by the practical application of *a model of intelligence*. Or, the practical application of an artificial intelligence.

In this way a musical composition, as an artificial intelligence itself, could be used to probe this other model, the model of a non-human intelligence (itself also an "artificial intelligence"). Which might mean the art of musical composition, along with its essential usefulness as a contributor to our perceptual understanding of possible worlds, also just might be a useful means for exploring the ways in which non-human animals might use sound to communicate.

REFERENCES

Agre, Philip E. 1997a. *Computation and Human Experience*. Cambridge: Cambridge University Press.

———. 1997b. "Toward a Critical Technical Practice: Lessons Learned in Trying to Reform AI." In *Social Science, Technical Systems, and Cooperative Work: Beyond the Great Divide*, edited by Geoffrey C. Bowker, Susan Leigh Star, William Turner, and Les Gasser, 131–57. Mahwah, NJ: Erlbaum.

Brün, Herbert. (1970) 2004. "Technology and the Composer." In *When Music Resists Meaning: The Major Writings of Herbert Brün*, edited by Arun Chandra, 163–76. Middletown, CT: Wesleyan University Press. First delivered as a paper read to UNESCO, Stockholm, 10 June 1970.

Dieter, Michael. 2014. "The Virtues of Critical Technical Practice." *Differences: A Journal of Feminist Cultural Studies* 25 (1): 216–30.

Impett, Jonathan. 2016. "Music, Thought and Technology." Orpheus Instituut. Accessed 2 April 2021. https://orpheusinstituut. be/en/projects/music-thought-and-technology.

Kerner, Hannah. 2020. "Too Many AI Researchers Think Real-World Problems Are Not Relevant." *MIT Technology Review*, 18 August 2020. https://www.technologyreview. com/2020/08/18/1007196/ai-research-machine-learning-applications-problems-opinion/.

Lexico. 2021a. Artificial, adjective, 1. Accessed 2 April 2021. https://lexico. com/definition/artificial.

———. 2021b. Intelligence, noun, 1. Accessed 2 April 2021. https://lexico. com/definition/intelligence.

———. 2021c. Knowledge, noun, 2. Accessed 2 April 2021. https://lexico.com/ definition/knowledge.

McDonald, Mark A., Sarah L. Mesnick, and John A. Hildebrand. 2006. "Biogeographic Characterisation of Blue Whale Song Worldwide: Using Song to Identify Populations." *Journal of Cetacean Research and Management* 8 (1): 55–65.

Merriam-Webster. 2021. Technology, noun, full definition 1b. Accessed 23 September 2021. https://www.merriam-webster.com/ dictionary/technology.

Oestreich, William K., James A. Fahlbusch, David E. Cade, John Calambokidis, Tetyana Margolina, John Joseph, Ari S. Friedlaender, et al. 2020. "Animal-Borne Metrics Enable Acoustic Detection of Blue Whale Migration." *Current Biology* 30 (23): 4773–79.

Peirce, Charles S. 1958. "Book 3; Chapter 4: Consciousness. §1. Categories of Experience." In *Collected Papers of Charles Sanders Peirce. Volume VII: Science and Philosophy*, edited by Arthur W. Burks, section 524–38. Cambridge, MA: Harvard University Press. Text from Section 2, "Some Logical Prolegomena," final section of the undated archival manuscript "On Topical Geometry, in General."

Rancière, Jacques. 2004. *The Politics of Aesthetics: The Distribution of the Sensible*. Translated by Gabriel Rockhill. London: Continuum. First published 2000 as *Le partage du sensible: Esthétique et politique* (Paris: La Fabrique).

———. 2010. *Dissensus: On Politics and Aesthetics*. Edited and translated by Steven Corcoran. London: Continuum.

Small, Christopher. 1998. *Musicking: The Meanings of Performing and Listening*. Middletown, CT: Wesleyan University Press.

Wagstaff, Kiri L. 2012. "Machine Learning That Matters." *Proceedings of the 29th International Conference on Machine*

Learning, ICML 2012, Edinburgh, Scotland, UK, 529–36. Accessed 2 April 2021. https://arxiv.org/ftp/arxiv/papers/1206/1206.4656.pdf.

Welby, Victoria. 1903. *What Is Meaning? Studies in the Development of Significance*. London: Macmillan & Co.

The Composer's Domain

Method and Material

Nicholas Brown
Trinity College Dublin

In this chapter, I explore the use of two kinds of computer technology—mobile phones and physical computing devices—in compositional practice, with particular reference to two of my recent works: *Vanishing Points* (2017) and *The Undulatory Theory of Light* (2018).[1] I focus on how the use of such computer technology raises two key issues. First, it may necessitate an understanding of technical concepts from computer science not typically addressed in formal musical training. Second, it issues a challenge to the standard model of music as a performing art. I am interested in how the use of certain computer technologies augments core aspects of compositional practice, namely the domain of skill and typical modalities for sharing new work. I take this augmentation as the premise for the creative deployment of the technologies under consideration, as well as the reason for reflecting upon issues that follow their use.

My interest in computer technology, more broadly, concerns the way in which its use may be practical.[2] By this I mean that it affords musical acts through which we may explore compositional ideas and their reification in the world. Further, there is a degree in which the technologies I use are appropriated for musical purposes. Some initial, technical research into their nature and capabilities is therefore required, combined with a process of adaptation. As composers, we may investigate certain technologies, have ideas about their compositional application and share their reifications, which we may or may not call "performances." This act of sharing is always practical, operative.

Given some degree of appropriation, there is perhaps reason to think of each of the technologies concerned as being in a state of tension as regards their primary purpose (a function of their design, say) and their musical deploy-

---

1 Both works were created as part of my association with the Music, Thought and Technology research cluster at the Orpheus Institute, Ghent. The first performance of *Vanishing Points* formed part of the inaugural Open Circuit event of live sound art at the Orpheus Institute on 3 September 2017. It was subsequently performed at Sonorities, Belfast, on 21 April 2018. *The Undulatory Theory of Light* was presented at Turner Contemporary, Margate, on 2 June 2018 as part of the Oscillate festival of experimental music and sound, a collaboration between Turner Contemporary and the CISA (Composition, Improvisation, and Sonic Art) Research Unit at Canterbury Christ Church University, in association with the Orpheus Institute. Further information and documentation concerning both works is available at https://www.nicholasbrown.co.uk.
2 Here I draw upon the philosophy of John Dewey. As Don Ihde writes, "It could be said that Dewey was the first to model *philosophy itself upon a technological model of inquiry* . . . [his philosophy] saw human inquiry, insofar as it focused upon knowledge, as a problem solving, expansive mode of inquiry very like all practical or *praxical* action" (1993, 43).

ment. The process of composing with new technological means is in part one of learning how to adapt and utilise that means. Any tension that derives from this repurposing, with reference to the original design function, is always significant. This is in accordance with the view that technologies can partially be understood as products of engineers trying to change the world in some way and their intended use primarily being consistent with that purpose ("technology is about what is to be or what ought to be rather than what is" [Franssen, Lokhorst, and van de Poel 2018]). Given any tension, therefore, between the purposeful design of some technology and its practical-exploratory usage as a compositional tool, I am particularly interested in this adaptation/deployment sequence. This is because of its effectiveness in revealing values embedded in existing paradigms of new music-making and, potentially, in permitting greater coherence between "art" as a product of creative practice and wider, aesthetic experience in our daily lives.

I begin by considering the transdisciplinarity of practice in computer-assisted composition. I consider issues in negotiating machine-based, computational processes, particularly heuristic matters concerning the control of algorithmic operations. And I offer some remarks on the relation between the mechanical and the digital in my own work. Next, I consider how the use of computer technology challenges musical culture as dealing in "performable works" and opens up alternative ontologies for the presentation of musical ideas. Finally, I consider the use of physical computing devices and address issues of materiality in the deployment of sensor technology. I consider how such devices allow composers to engage directly with the world of things and I consider the meaning and value that such embedded computer systems accord creative practice in relation to wider issues of society, culture, and ecology.

MACHINE WORK

Effective use of computational processes for musical purposes may necessitate an awareness and understanding of programming principles.[3] As Nick Collins notes, "programming's dire requirement for perfect syntax can still obstruct getting to the musical outcome" (2016, 9). Fluency in computer-aided composition may therefore require self-led learning, with successful problem-solving often depending on some working solution in some context (such as an online user forum) being effectively generalised and applied in a different context.

Even with understanding and experience, creative-computational work can still hamper creativity, such as in the need to keep pace with software updates. F. Richard Moore points out that software developments can be disruptive for practitioners, more so than any equivalent alteration of computer hardware,

---

3   I mean, for example, an understanding of such things as zero-based numbering, indexical storage of data/data storage techniques more widely (dictionaries, etc.), the concept of loop-based operations (and the need for exit conditions), and so on. These concepts transcend specific programming languages and are implicated in the use of software beyond DAWs (Max, Pure Data, Supercollider, JavaScript audio synthesis frameworks, etc.). Further, the possibilities for musical work offered by physical computing devices may require technical facility such as the navigation of directories via terminal software, the installation of dependencies, and so on.

because they are typically issued with considerable frequency (1993, 348). Indeed, novel reform of software capability may not necessarily lead to the amelioration of challenges. Batya Friedman notes that while new features in software development may enhance capability, they may increase complexity in a way that decreases usability (1996, 18). And so creative work with computer technology may lean on familiarity with principles from computer science and necessitate the practical integration of externally controlled, technical modification. In relation to the latter, there may be a need to resolve matters of functionality caused by updates issued to the operating system and/or software dependencies.

In an interview from 1987, Iannis Xenakis discussed some of the challenges for composers working with computers. "The fundamental problem," he states, "is that a musician is not necessarily a computer expert, an engineer or a mathematician" (Xenakis 1987, 25). Interestingly, he states the likelihood of this situation changing, "for a new category of musicians is appearing" (25). Xenakis's approach to technical work is grounded in experience: practice constitutes an evolving dialectic between the workings of the machine and human intervention. He advocates for active engagement with developments in science and technology ("theory"), provided that the object of such engagement is understood as a guide that stimulates a response. Theory therefore plays a structuring role that organises and reassures, "so that we can act, know how to act and what to do" (47). For Xenakis, it is in working in "the theoretical domain" that one guards against the regressivity of convention. Otherwise, the artist becomes "trapped by clichés, by inherited structures that we manipulate without knowing them perfectly" (42).

Theoretical, rational-algorithmic approaches thus act as safeguards for artistic practice. But this is problematic because in order to make "creative blunder[s]," which are desirable, artists must free themselves of supporting, "mental rails" (Xenakis 1987, 22). Technical work therefore requires a response from the artist—a kind of self-defence or readiness for overruling its control. For Xenakis, practice in music constitutes an opportunity to assert individual freedom. It presents a call to manipulate and shape concepts and materials. The response is in the confrontation between the human hand, which "stands between randomness and calculation," and machine (mathematical law) (23). Artistic practice emerges from frictive points of negotiation between mathematical rationalism and the embodied self.

It is interesting to reflect on Xenakis's view of technical work given the epistemological problems that may face the musician with limited knowledge of computational operations. "Computer science," he states, "is a product of simple rationality; as a composer, I unceasingly bring complexity, sometimes irrational, to this rationality" (Xenakis 1987, 27). This speaks to the function of mathematics, which "gives structures that are too regular and that are inferior to the demands of the ear and the intelligence" (23). To be sure, any deployment of computational means will inevitably necessitate technical understanding in order to develop fluency and efficiency in computer-aided creativity. But it would seem that technical facility does not forestall need for a critical relation with that means. In speaking to this necessity, Xenakis uses the metaphor of manual intervention. Algorithmic approaches to musical composition may present the composer with a quandary: whether and how to intervene in an unfolding process, by which material and formal layout is established. The composer is called to play a mitigating role in addressing the way in which technological means in computer-aided composition instantiates creativity.

An intervention of the hand

Vanishing Points, my 2017 work for clavichord, distributed (mobile phone) audio, and electronics, addresses the historical circumstances concerning the creation of C. P. E. Bach's *Abschied von meinem Silbermannischen Claviere in einem Rondo*, H.272 (1781).[4] It uses different forms of technology for the production and distribution of sound: (1) the mechanical construction of the clavichord; (2) computer-based, quadraphonic sound processing; (3) browser-based, mobile phone audio; and (4) the control of digital audio over a wireless network.

Bach's *Abschied* makes use of a performance technique known as *bebung*. Bebung is an expressive feature of clavichord design. It allows a player to vary the pitch of a note by varying the pressure of a finger on a key. This facility of the clavichord is unique among (acoustic) keyboard instruments as it permits the clavichordist to control the sounding string *after* the key has been depressed. Bebung might thus be interpreted as a curative method of prolongation, a way of modulating the bloom and decay of a tone before finally letting it go.

Bach composed his *Abschied* in honour of his beloved Silbermann clavichord, which he sold to Dietrich Ewald von Grotthuss in 1781 (Brauchli 2008, 161). Accordingly, the premise for *Vanishing Points* is the physical separation of musician and instrument, mediated through the expressivity of bebung: modulations of finger pressure protest against such disunion. My compositional strategy was one of thinking of the pitches in the *Abschied* that are allocated a bebung marking (dots above a note, beneath a curve) as "vanishing points"— musical moments when the player tries to retain the clavichord's sound.

Each bebung marking in Bach's *Rondo* allows the player to intervene in the vibrations of a string, to engage a mechanistic enveloping of an oscillating finger, establishing, I suggest, a "body-instrument." This intervention of the hand opens an uncommon, gestural expressivity in keyboard technique. Indeed, Mozart wrote about vocal vibrato ("the human voice trembles naturally") and observed how "people imitate it . . . even on the *clavier*" (quoted in Brauchli 1998, 274). Interestingly, for Mozart, the end-conditions for this technical operation are physiologically constructed: "the moment the proper limit is overstepped, it is no longer beautiful—because it is contrary to nature" (ibid.). And so I suggest that bebung momentarily aspires to a fusion of opposite means of sound-making: the action of a mechanical keyboard and the act of human voicing.[5]

---

4   See https://www.nicholasbrown.co.uk/vanishing-points.
5   Indeed, Trevor Wishart writes, in *On Sonic Art* (1996, 29), that "the voice and keyboard may be seen as occupying the two opposite ends of the musical spectrum. Voice, the immediate source of intellectual-physiological gesture. . . . The keyboard on the other hand represents the ultimate rationalisation of a lattice-based [i.e. pitch/duration-based] view of music."

My starting point in composing *Vanishing Points* involved a score-based analysis of Bach's *Abschied* with a particular focus on the notes marked with the bebung technique. Performatively, bebung shapes the already subdued and decaying clavichord sound by working the protruding tangent where it makes contact with the string. The action is perhaps reminiscent of sustaining a vocal sound against depleting breath support. This sonic decay seemed to warrant a technology for its prolongation that was coherent with the instrument's fragility, yet also supplanted it. My compositional "solution" was to activate digital sound samples on individual audience smartphones using the Nü framework project, which is based on Soundworks, a JavaScript framework for distributed WebAudio and multimedia applications.[6]

The mobile-mediated audio material is downloaded, temporarily, to a listener's mobile device (via the browser/web audio API). Its playback is triggered during the performance by a MIDI foot pedal, which the clavichordist controls according to indications in the score (see figure 5.1). This distribution of audio makes a "bebung" of a different sort. It creates a shift in listening modality, from the collective mode of the hi-fidelity, quadraphonic loudspeakers in the performance space to the individuated mode via the small speaker drivers of mobile devices, hand-held by audience members. This shift in technological mediation of a clavichord's sound is marked by a change in frequency response, from the relatively full audio range of the fixed, quadraphonic loudspeakers to the relatively limited range of a mobile device's speaker drivers.

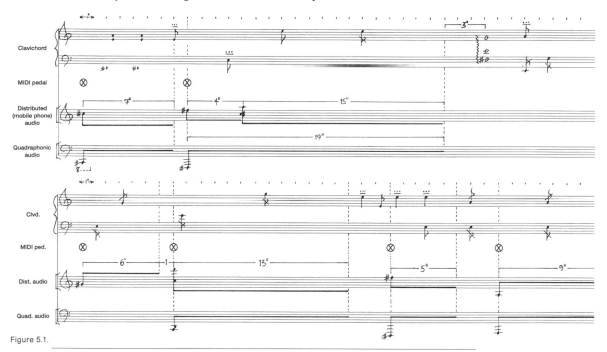

Figure 5.1.

---

6 Nü is controlled live, during the performance, via objects written for and implemented in Max software. The Nü framework has been developed at IRCAM-CNRS within the CoSiMa research project, supported by the French National Research Agency (ANR). See https://ircam-cosima.github.io/soundworks-nu/; https://github.com/collective-soundworks/soundworks; Schnell and Robaszkiewicz (2015).

Figure 5.1. Excerpt from the manuscript score of *Vanishing Points* (2017).

This qualitative change in sonic experience speaks to a correlative change in timbre: the sustaining of a voicing, given the depletion of breath. The distribution of sound, via mobile technology, also extends the work, as regards perceptual modality, towards a multisensory experience. The Nü framework project allows the composer to programme a change in the browser display on a user's phone, which can be triggered by a sonic event. Further, the act of holding the phone while the audio is triggered, remotely, activates a sense of "touching" the distributed sound material.[7]

Kirsten Boehner et al. (2004) note that technological systems are useful "for enhancing people's own awareness of context, affect and other complex experiences that are being augmented" ([1]). Working with them becomes a way of bringing attention to and critically appraising ways of doing and making things. For Boehner et al., a "questioning and highlighting" of values is within the gift of technology designers ([5]). The authors note that this process of analysing, of questioning and resetting embedded hierarchies—and of seeking alternatives that lead to the development of new technologies—constitutes a critical technical practice ([2]).

The use of networked, mobile technology in *Vanishing Points*, in distributing digital sound in a context of live performance, is intended to shift the listener's awareness to a technology that is ubiquitous in our everyday lives and to do this in a context wherein this technology is not normally visible or audible. In so doing I am interested in exploring and questioning values inherent in the social practices of concert-style electroacoustic performance, particularly the fixed listening spaces typically required by acousmatic traditions. Without the inclusion of these networked mobile technologies and the software-based instantiation of individual listening domains (and the possibility of establishing diversity in sonic experience by distributing sonic material to particular domains) the performance would remain a quadraphonic experience, with the clavichordist seated in the centre.

Vanishing Points attends to a historical work of music that is itself especially concerned with the technical affordances and organological values of a particular means of sound-making. The deployment of new technologies responds to the muted, terminal nature of the clavichord's sound and the possibility of extending it. The intermixing of live acoustic sound and its mobile individuation in the digital, networked domain seeks to query the ethos (technical, social) of each form of aesthetic experience. Given that Bach's *Abschied* marks the sale of a beloved instrument, *Vanishing Points* marks a narrative of player–instrument separation through a process of transduction—of mechanical sound as digital information, delivered to the ears, eyes, and hands of its audience.

---

7   In a recent book chapter, Georgina Born writes that sound "should be theorized as affording a particular kind of sensory or even haptic empathy, a type of resonant, vibration-imbued touching—a sonic touching that can double the 'mental touch' of affective empathy" (2019, 201).

ENCOUNTERING THE NEW

In his philosophical study of musical performance, Stan Godlovitch outlines "the traditional view of music as a performing art guided by the performer's craft" (1998, 2). Compositional practice that is invested in this view typically concerns the creation of musical scores and subsequently—as David Davies puts it—"the performance of a performable work" (2011, 24). Yet as Godlovitch observes, "the most significant alternatives to tradition have come from technology, especially the development of electronic and computer-based sound-processing machines" (1998, 2). Indeed, in writing about creative work with computer technology, Trevor Wishart has suggested that it might "be better if we referred to ourselves as *sonic designers* or *sonic engineers*, rather than as composers, as the word 'composer' has come to be strongly associated with the organisation of notes on paper" (1996, 5).

From a sociocultural perspective, this expanded realm of possibility concurs with the development of new modes of sharing compositional work more widely, regardless of technological deployment. It is often the case that new work necessitates an alt-presentational situation: an ambulatory encounter might be preferred to a static, focused act of concert-style listening and it might take place in a space circumscribed, ad hoc, for a unique event. But any non-standard requirements for the presentation of a new work may be at odds with a venue or institution's available resources. Consider, for instance, the ubiquity of "technical riders" from composers to venue managers that carry uncommon presentational conditions and financial implications.

Concert venues are not typically designed for fluid and immediate reworking of infrastructure, except perhaps where alternatives to main stages exist in the form of "black box" spaces. In *Gallery Sound*, for instance, Caleb Kelly notes that the fixed seating arrangements of concert halls "foster a specific listening experience" (2017, 122). He suggests that art galleries offer more flexibility in the arrangement of a performance space and that such spaces allow "events that rethink the proscenium arch" (ibid.). Contemporary musical experience thus finds its way to alternative places and spaces, including those intended for exhibitions of the plastic arts, theatrical productions, workshops, and community events as well as those unrelated in purpose to any artistic production.

A correlative challenge to conventional practice also inheres in a critical approach to musical education on the one hand and in the design of music software on the other. Educational institutions and their learning materials are typically informed by historically and culturally conditioned fundamentals of musical composition. Indeed, in an article on processes in musical composition, Horacio Vaggione claims that "every musical process contains 'primitives' which derive from a specific common practice" (2001, 59). In discussing conservatory training in music, he notes that the rules learned are "the result of a long historical effort of codification of evolving practices" (ibid.).

Music software design is equally likely to be founded upon the deployment of foundational music theory through operations that assume stylistic-formulaic creativity—arpeggiators and harmonisers that operate according to equal temperament, formal templates, and so on. Innovative software design may seek to challenge such codification, for as Boehner et al. write, "technologies reflect and perpetuate unconscious cultural assumptions" (2004, [2]). Working with technologies or reworking established pedagogies can thus mean being embroiled in—to use a phrase by Michel Foucault—"the art of not being governed or better, the art of not being governed like that and at that cost" (2007, 45). By such a phrase, as Michael Dieter (2014, 219) points out, Foucault refers to a definition of "critique."

In the remainder of this chapter, I address one way of building a critical, presentational paradigm through the use of an embedded computer system. I am particularly interested in the creative potential of the sensing/actuating capabilities of physical computing devices. Just as it is possible to take digital sensor readings of things in the world, it is equally possible to feed something back into the world, though processes of actuation. To conclude, I offer some remarks on my 2018 work, *The Undulatory Theory of Light*, the identity and meaning of which is strongly determined by the sensing capabilities of a physical computing device.

Embedded systems[8]

Physical computing technologies allow the composition of musical experiences that are founded upon direct engagement with real-world extra-musical phenomena. A composer working with such technology may set up an embedded system that is capable of sensing changes in the state of some physical thing via an appropriate sensor technology, connected to a computer processor. As Steven F. Barrett puts it, "The link between system inputs and outputs is provided by a coded algorithm stored within the processor's resident memory" (2013, 69–70). The encoded, sensor data may be used computationally, for digital operations and, potentially, for actualisation processes that cause changes in the physical state of a thing, via a transducer. Data from one form of energy (light, for instance) may be reified in another, given appropriate technology for realising the isomorphism of digital information.

The composer's task in working with sensors in embedded computer systems becomes one of dealing with how some thing "is" at any particular moment. The designated compositional experience relies on data drawn from some stream of digital information. Potentially, the detection of changes in the physical state of things affords greater coherence between compositional work, qua *art*, and the wider aesthetic experiences of our everyday lives. To work with sampled, abstracted information that is correlative with everyday perception and use that information in some compositional process points towards a melding of artistic creativity and the perception of things common to a non-artistic realm of living.

8　"An embedded system contains a microcontroller to accomplish its job of processing system inputs and generating system outputs" (Barrett 2013, 69).

Techniques from computer science thus open up alternate modes of aesthetic engagement with the real world. Composers otherwise engaged in the production of score-based, performable works may shape hybrid forms of sonic experience that are concerned with the autonomy of nonhuman objects. Sonic practices of this kind are informed by the physical-spatial circumstances of their presentation.[9] They furnish opportunities for augmenting the composer's domain of practice—ways of sharing compositional ideas and altering the nature of musical experience for percipients, potentially leading to the development of new audiences.

As stated in my introduction, it is this potential augmentation of practice that catalyses my use of such technical means. This "opening up" of a compositional work to encompass the digital "sensing" of physical objects (which can sometimes also be sensed in a physical manner, by any present observer) renders formal interest in how some physical thing is functioning at a particular moment, given the way any correlating data is handled computationally.[10] Indeed, a creative work that utilises embedded computer systems still permits a multiplicity of realisations, given that the blueprint for any particular realisation is encoded in a computer programme. The scope of a work's potential assembly, in any moment of encounter, however, depends not solely on the data, but the way in which that data is processed, which is a function of the work's compositional design.

Composition at a primary level of activity, digital or otherwise, involves the structuring of relations between events over time. Work with embedded systems—given their capacity for sensing sonic and non-sonic events—means that the composer may activate these structural relations by querying the state of things. What is critical is that a creative work that deploys such a system is computationally engaged with the particular state of some physical thing in relation to that work's design. This extension of compositional operations beyond the performances of works provides the composer with access to a kind of information repository, the polling of which allows engagement with matters beyond human art-making: issues of place, environment, and ecology, for instance.

REAL ELEMENTS

The process of creating my sound installation *The Undulatory Theory of Light* (2018) was informed by the appendix to a paper by Michael Faraday, delivered to the Royal Society of London in 1831.[11] Faraday's excursus describes the "crispations" that appear on the surface of fluids when contained within

---

9   In such cases where there is creative use of sensor technologies and the processing of correlative data leads to aesthetic experience, we have clearly moved beyond what David Davies (2011) calls "the classical paradigm" in the performing arts, that is, "the interpretation and rendering of a performable work" (24).

10 There may still be some way of intervening in the stream of information by waving one's hand over a light receptor, for instance. Any such intervention would be a function of the work's affordances of interactivity, themselves a function of the compositional design.

11 The appendix is titled, "On the Forms and States Assumed by Fluids in Contact with Vibrating Elastic Surfaces" (Faraday 1831, 319–40).

a vibrating receptacle. Accordingly, *The Undulatory Theory of Light* develops my interest in the formation of cymatic patterns as assumed by certain physical materials in response to sonic vibrations.[12] I mentioned above that the installation relies upon the sensing capabilities of a physical computing device, in this case, an Arduino platform.[13] Its compositional structure deploys some of the possibilities afforded by sensor technology in a quasi-scientific context where the properties of elements and materials are explored. Specifically, the work utilises a light sensor to take readings of the red, green, and blue components of ambient light and makes use of these readings to generate three frequencies in the audible range, which have the dual function of (1) constituting a musical triad; and (2) being used to create crispations on the surface of a small container of water. The work is intended to be installed in an environment that is illuminated, primarily, by natural light.[14] Given that the colour of natural light changes throughout the course of a day (and given any artificial light that is also present in the installation environment), the constituent pitches of the triad also fluctuate accordingly. Further, the installation is designed in such a way that the crispations on the water surface cast tiny shadows on the light sensor itself, thereby affecting the data readings, and, consequently, the sonic vibrations. The sound of the installation is thus in a constant state of flux, according to the slowly changing colour of daylight in the exhibition space and the activity of crispations on the surface of the water.

What interests me here is not only that the elements that comprise the sounding object are given to human perception—light, water, sound, and their interrelationships, in a compositional context—but also, that these elements partake in their own interrelationships, independent of any human perception, and are thus, in a sense, "beyond" the artistic context through which the work is presented. In *Art and Objects*, Graham Harman writes that for object-oriented philosophy, "the thing-in-itself does not just haunt human awareness of the world, but is found even in the causal relations of non-human things with each other" (2020, 12). Indeed, there is some sense in which a sounding object is more than that which is present to an onlooker. Its constituent elements interact in a way that is independent of human activity, its properties extend beyond our appreciation. My interest is in bringing these elements and properties forward to the senses, via the composition of the sounding object. And in this "bringing forward," of becoming aware of their "background" function.[15]

Georgina Born (2019, 190) points out that "Nonhuman sound, in the guise of environmental sound or noise, has . . . featured in a number of ways in the development of the fields now coalescing as sound studies" and particularly

---

12 My theatrical work on the psychology of voice, *As I Have Now Memoyre* (2008), for instance, uses Chladni patterns for the physical "inscription" of a voice recording on a vibrating plate of salt (see Brown 2011, 179).

13 See http://www.arduino.cc. The design of the installation also utilises the wireless transmission capabilities of an XBee system, on which see https://www.digi.com/xbee.

14 See MF5.1 in the online repository for this book at https://orpheusinstituut.be/en/sound-work-media-repository. Further details of the repository can be found in the appendix on p. 355.

15 These elements are, in a Heideggerian sense, invisible: "the phenomenal world . . . first arises for Heidegger from an invisible system of background entities" (Harman 2020, 17).

within a Cagean legacy of "working with the sonorities of everyday environments beyond the concert hall." Indeed, a key part of the purpose of developing *The Undulatory Theory of Light* was in exploring how sensor-based operations with physical computing permit a way of "enquiring" about nonhuman things in the world, though in this case, beyond a unisensory focus on sound. In this installation, I set about designing an experience that intentionally calls upon more than one form of perception and, therefore, the coordinated use of different senses—specifically, seeing and hearing.[16] Working in this multisensory domain relies upon harnessing the isomorphism of digital data, which is provided by an embedded computer system capable of sensing changes in the state of things.

In a conversation with Garnet Hertz, Natalie Jeremijenko discusses making as "fundamentally an intellectual activity" and claims that "the material reality of the world is where we integrate . . . social, political, ecological and intellectual ideas" (Jeremijenko and Hertz 2015, 26). And as Phoebe Sengers points out in a conversation on critical technical practice, "your understanding of what you're doing is deeply tied in with the material practices of making" (Sengers and Hertz 2015, 11). And so we may elicit an ethical dimension in our creative practices, one that can be addressed by considering the way we use technologies like physical computing platforms to reflect our values. We may seize the opportunity to adapt and use new technologies in ways that focus attention on anthropocenic conversation. For, as Sengers notes, critical technical practice and maker culture point to "the ties between the ways we organize our everyday lives and our sense of our moral place in the universe" (Sengers and Hertz 2015, 19). Computer-aided musical creativity that is concerned with materiality may therefore be a way of opening practice outwards, towards things in themselves—a way of reworking paradigms of performance that instantiate cultures of performable works and of seeking closer continuity between artistic work and the non-artistic, aesthetic experiences of our lives.

References

Barrett, Steven F. 2013. *Arduino Microcontroller Processing for Everyone!* 3rd ed. Synthesis Lectures on Digital Circuits and Systems. [San Rafael, CA]: Morgan and Claypool.

Boehner, Kirsten, Shay David, Joseph "Jofish" Kaye, and Phoebe Sengers. 2004. "Critical Technical Practice as a Methodology for Values in Design." Paper accepted for CHI 2005 workshop "Quality, Value(s) and Choice: Exploring Wider Implications of HCI Practice," April 2004. Accessed 16 March 2021. http://alumni.media.mit.edu/~jofish/writing/.

Born, Georgina. 2019. "On Nonhuman Sound—Sound as Relation." In *Sound Objects*, edited by James A. Steintrager and Rey Chow, 185–207. Durham, NC: Duke University Press.

Brauchli, Bernard. 1998. *The Clavichord*. Cambridge: Cambridge University Press.

Brown, Nicholas G. 2011. "Being Among the Living: On the Inter-Relations between Performers, Witnesses and Environment in *As I Have Now Memoyre*." *Organised Sound* 16 (2): 176–83.

Collins, Nick. 2016. "Live Coding and Teaching SuperCollider." *Journal of Music, Technology and Education* 9 (1): 5–16.

---

16   For an investigation of perceptual evidence being "distinctively multisensory," see O'Callaghan (2020).

Davies, David. 2011. *Philosophy of the Performing Arts*. Malden, MA: Wiley-Blackwell.

Dieter, Michael. 2014. "The Virtues of Critical Technical Practice." *Differences* 25 (1): 216–30.

Faraday, Michael. 1831. "On a Peculiar Class of Acoustical Figures; and on Certain Forms Assumed by Groups of Particles upon Vibrating Elastic Surfaces." *Philosophical Transactions of the Royal Society of London* 121: 299–340.

Foucault, Michel. 2007. "What Is Critique?" In *The Politics of Truth*, edited by Sylvère Lotringer, translated by Lysa Hochroth and Catherine Porter, 41–81. Los Angeles: Semiotext(e). Originally delivered as a lecture in 1978; first published 1990 as "Qu'est-ce que la critique?" *Bulletin de la Société française de la philosophie* 84 (2): 35–63.

Franssen, Maarten, Gert-Jan Lokhorst, and Ibo van de Poel. 2018. "Philosophy of Technology." In *Stanford Encyclopedia of Philosophy*, fall 2018 ed., edited by Edward N. Zalta. Accessed 15 March 2021. https://plato.stanford.edu/archives/fall2018/entries/technology/.

Friedman, Batya. 1996. "Value-Sensitive Design." *Interactions* 3 (6): 16–23.

Godlovitch, Stan. 1998. *Musical Performance: A Philosophical Study*. Abingdon, UK: Routledge.

Harman, Graham. 2020. *Art and Objects*. Cambridge: Polity Press.

Ihde, Don. 1993. *Philosophy of Technology: An Introduction*. New York: Paragon House.

Jeremijenko, Natalie, and Garnet Hertz. 2015. "Engineering Anti-Techno-Fetishism: Natalie Jeremijenko in Conversation with Garnet Hertz." In *Conversations in Critical Making*, edited by Garnet Hertz, 23–33. N.p.: CTheory Books.

Kelly, Caleb. 2017. *Gallery Sound*. New York: Bloomsbury Academic.

Moore, F. Richard. 1993. "A Technological Approach to Music." In *Companion to Contemporary Musical Thought*, edited by John Paynter, Tim Howell, Richard Orton, and Peter Seymour, 2 vols., 1:329–54. London: Routledge.

O'Callaghan, Casey. 2020. "Multisensory Evidence." *Philosophical Issues* 30 (1): 238–56.

Schnell, Norbert, and Sébastien Robaszkiewicz. 2015. "Soundworks—A Playground for Artists and Developers to Create Collaborative Mobile Web Performances." In *Proceedings of the Web Audio Conference (WAC'15)*, Paris. Accessed 2 February 2019. https://hal.archives-ouvertes.fr/hal-01580797.

Sengers, Phoebe, and Garnet Hertz. 2015. "Critical Technical Practice and Critical Making: Phoebe Sengers in Conversation with Garnet Hertz." In *Conversations in Critical Making*, edited by Garnet Hertz, 9–21. N.p.: CTheory Books.

Vaggione, Horacio. 2001. "Some Ontological Remarks about Music Composition Processes." *Computer Music Journal* 25 (1): 54–61.

Wishart, Trevor. 1996. *On Sonic Art*. Rev. ed. Edited by Simon Emmerson. Amsterdam: Harwood Academic.

Xenakis, Iannis. 1987. "Xenakis on Xenakis." Translated by Roberta Brown and John Rahn. *Perspectives of New Music* 25 (1–2): 16–63.

Dissociation and Interference in Composers' Stories about Music

The Renewal of Musical Discourse

Jonathan Impett

Orpheus Institute, Ghent

INTRODUCTION

The notion of composition, the role and figure of the composer, have retained significant cachet in a wider context of music in which hierarchies of genre, style, or practice have been substantially dissolved. The composer is afforded a unique place despite the various challenges of contemporary culture: challenges from music philosophy to the concept of work, from sound art and improvisation to the idea of pre-determining any aspect of musical phenomena or to the social hierarchy thus implied, or from the democratising of cultural values to the exceptional status of art music. This changes little if we broaden the category of composition to include the work of individual sound artists or solo improvisers, for example. We will therefore use the term *composer* here to refer to all such artists who take responsibility for conceiving and producing a musical phenomenon that has some degree of boundedness and identity, regardless of how reproducible it might be or at what remove composers stand from a listener's experience. On some level, at some point, they com-pose—they put together. *Creative* is used here as a shorthand term, a veil for a multitude of sins. It does not imply subscription to any Romantic notion of inspiration or genius, of "work" or sole authorship; it rather stands for a human, inventive, adaptive, situated, distributed, practised craft behaviour.

There is no shortage of detailed technical discussion within particular areas of creative musical practice, nor of reflection on their socio-aesthetic nature and implications. But otherwise, exchanges between artists and between genres, and the engagement of both musicology and criticism, seem to balk at passing beyond the immediate sonic surface—ironically, perhaps, a reification by omission of the work concept. Beyond very specific discourses (of style, genre, practice, technique, or technology) little attention is paid to the ways in which a musical phenomenon is constituted. Attention glances off into other aspects. Expert discourse tends to self-referentiality, public discourse to description and reportage. It is as if the growing awareness of the embodiment, materiality, individuality, and cultural specificity of musical experience has engendered a sort of skin-deepness in our understanding of composition.

This situation is compounded by a wider Western encouragement of individualism, a tendency that conditions the production, reception, and evaluation of both creative and intellectual work. When uniqueness and novelty are highly prized, there is little incentive for artist or critic to focus on the commonalities of the work of making art, as Badiou has observed (2006).[1] A further challenge to discourse has emerged with the imperative to substantiate art's claim to be a vital mode of human knowledge production, and to be able to do so in particular cases. Personal and critical accounts avoid the musically substantive, technical reports are just that, and both analytical and cognitive treatments separate the object from the context of its production. Technical, theoretical, personal, and social stories are told around the creation of music, but largely in ways that contribute to cultural fragmentation. A discourse gap has opened up around the topic of composition, in both public and expert spheres. In both areas, a critical discourse for music requires us to tell better stories about its generation: stories of creation that are more honest and situated in their particularity, and that at the same time afford constructive engagement and commonality.

By whatever pattern or sequence of decision or circumstance a musical experience comes about, the act of listening is performative—intentionally or otherwise—and its object is, at that point, determinate. And this act of listening is itself swept into other waves of narrative: personal, cultural, critical, technical, "factual." In each act of listening—acoustic or imaginative, in "real time" or compressed and reordered in the imagination—the listener shares in the process of construction, of emergence. The experiential phenomenon is fragmented and redistributed as soon as it takes place—indeed, as soon as it is anticipated. Creation and listening are both acts of imagination. They are united in sharing the experience of a time and place framed and inscribed. Neither are linear, neither are constituted only by the time and sonic phenomenon at hand. In the century following Cage and Beckett, perhaps we have learned to listen to the artist's act of listening, to share this emergence of the putting-together. It is a commonplace of art criticism that the paint on canvas embodies the moment of its application (Berger 1972, 31), and that the viewer's eye senses the movement of the brush in the artist's hand (T. J. Clark 2018, 197). Gesture in performance has been widely discussed (Gritten and King 2011), but in the case of score-based music, this is largely predicated on gesture as reflected in the notation—which is highly unlikely to be the result of the same gesture (let us leave to one side the particular case of keyboard composers, the predominance of which in the Western canon tends to obscure the general case). This points to a blindness to longer time frames in both visual art and music. The object in question embodies the actions of the artist over a much wider time span. The planning of Picasso's *Guernica* documented in Dora

---

1 See also Badiou (2001) on the distorting effects of over-valorising difference.

Maar's photographs is as sequential and contingent as the application of paint itself. Likewise, a musical phenomenon (a composition in our broader sense) bears the traces not only of its direct inscription but also of its conceptual and technical emergence. And it shares these traces with the listener—whether in a consciously almost-observable linear form (Bach's *Musical Offering*, the piano Études of Ligeti, for example) or in a more layered, complex manner that constantly challenges the ascription of formal narrative. The role of anticipation in the activity of musical sense-making is widely accepted (Huron 2006). Such predictive behaviour can only be predicated on a continuous modelling of how the music is constituted—an interpretation of the present musical surface in terms of a broad-ranging set of experience, knowledge, and understanding. Following Noë we might think of this as an act of human organisation in which the listener becomes a co-participant (2015). A useful discourse, then, might involve its interlocutors in such a continuous process, irrespective of style or technique.

I have argued elsewhere that we might understand composition, in its Western art-music context, as an iterative process of inscription (Impett 2016a). Inscription onto sound may have complex relationships with contributing inscriptions into notation, recording, or text, or the *idea* of any of these, and these relationships are multiply distributed across time. A generative thought is thus likewise an act of inscription, encoded or recoded in whatever terms constitute the framework for such a thought to articulate itself. The tools of this inscription—notation as an abstract convention, for example, but also the material modes of its instantiation—are best understood as technologies (Impett 2016b). The technological environment of any given moment determines not only the tools and modes of inscription but also the conceptual models and operations they afford. Such a technological milieu conditions the modes of inscription, the kinds of manipulation, that can be imagined (Impett 2021).

A generation ago, Philip Agre responded to a discourse-gap in his own area of artificial intelligence (AI) with an approach he termed critical technical practice (CTP) (Agre 1997b). I will show how composition (in the broad sense described above) has much in common with the computational design Agre was discussing, and that the CTP he proposed might provide important indications for the development of more common, constructive, and critical discourse in and around the creation of music.

COMPOSITION AND KNOWLEDGE

The notion that composition might be understood as a knowledge-producing activity has been much contested (Croft 2015). How has this perceived need for composition to explain itself come about? Briefly, the shape, terms, and dynamics of the Western knowledge economy have been transformed over the last half century. In science, the "objectivity" of empirically derived knowledge increasingly requires critical context. The range of loci and modes of manifestation of knowledge has expanded to incorporate notions of embodiment, situation, and distributedness (Chemero 2009; A. Clark 1997; Hutchins 1995).

And earlier cultural hierarchies and value systems have (justly) dissolved to the extent that implicit or explicit evaluation of artistic production is polarised, in general terms, to an account of popularity (using metrics of income generation, public engagement, or internet attention) or of something broadly understood as research. There is an odd contraflow here: as the sciences of brain and cognition observe the roles of modes of knowledge that resist verbalisation and quantification, art—at least in an academic context—is increasingly called upon to specify and quantify its contribution as knowledge production. A further challenge arises from the disjunction between knowledge as immanent experience and knowledge that allows for explicit and shared interrogation or use. What is lost between these poles is a public sphere of critical discourse, and it is perhaps to this that the reflection of composers might usefully contribute.

Wider understanding of the activity of composition has evolved beyond earlier caricatures of creativity as either instinctive, inspired poetic act, impenetrable to interrogation, or formal technical execution divorced from emotion or sonic imagination:

> We find his faculties working with such a glorious freedom as scarcely any other artist has ever attained. This is not to say that he was fluent. [The composer in question] was never that on paper; least of all in these later years, when he was increasingly bothered by inertia in beginning a new composition. But once the momentum was up he found himself stimulated, not hampered, by the formal, technical side of his art. He could freely utter his profound mind and pour out his great heart, because he was now at last an emancipated artist, in full command of his medium. (Schauffler 1929, 368)

> It will be relatively easy to show how his music is an admirable unity of predetermined elements....
> Construction is in the essence of [another composer's] nature. He distrusts "divine inspiration," for mysticism is foreign to his temperament. Composition means for him the controlling and placing of every smallest element in a musical design according to a pre-conceived plan. (Smith Brindle 1961, 248)

Such absurd mid-twentieth century perspectives (on Beethoven and Nono, respectively) have of course been superseded and nuanced in musicology, criticism, and the cultural imagination. A fundamental and potentially constructive tension remains at the heart of the composer's craft, however. The incapacitating vertigo of the composer faced with infinite possibility is described by Ferneyhough ([1982] 1995, 22). The sense of responsibility to make a decision that is "right" on some plane is persistent—a decision that is consistent with some essence of the musical object in question, in terms of an originating concept, an aesthetic or technical theory, a poetic image, a present situation, or Haydn's habitual "Laus Deo" at the conclusion of a score. We might see the practice of composition as a continuous deferral of the partially arbitrary. To paraphrase Agamben (2019, 28), the emerging musical object resists its own persistence (a timely warning to those inclined to assume "works" at this point: such emergence may take place over months or minutes). This resistance can be read into the object as a surplus; it contains the seeds, the potential of what the object is not, signs to the paths that the artist chose not to take. These will be an integral part of a CTP in music. Each decision, every encounter with a constraint, assumption, or attractor constrains certain dimensions of freedom and adds others. One "problem" is solved and another emerges. Matthias Gross (2010) describes the processes of science and technology analogously, as the production of provisional models that have some human salience in a given context, that must crucially remain open to the surprises they might bring forth or the new areas of ignorance they might circumscribe. The map of the total space of possibilities is drawn only as that space is explored. The turns of that trajectory remain inscribed in the "object" experienced by the listener. If this process of deferral ever seemed to be resolved in the shape of the score to be "interpreted" by performers, this was only by temporary cultural consensus that blinded us to the perpetual reinscription of music through acts of instantiation and imagination.

The path is nonlinear and polyphonic, its turns multiple, parallel, and potentially contradictory. They may be acts of physical, material inscription—notation, performance, coding, producing. They may be the acknowledgement of cultural assumption or practical constraint. Equally—and more often—they may be moments of emergent perception or imagination, acts of identification of figure, action, process, concept, relationship, or technique. The sequence of these turns, their particular context and parameters, map out the sonic, referential, and imaginative space that the performed experience will inhabit—the space some related version of which may form itself in the minds of performers or listeners (or even musicologists). Giorgio Agamben refers to the *potentiality* of the aesthetic object (1999), Manuel DeLanda to the *potential* energy and dynamics of physical or simulated systems (2011, 4). We might adopt their notions to conceive of the emerging map of compositional possibility as a "space of potential."

Such decisions are not only at the stage of inscribing a note in a score or of an improviser's action. Sketch studies tend to prioritise staff notation and coherent, contiguous, recognisable passages. Except where they can be mapped directly through to a final surface, graphical materials, matrices, numbers, and so on tend to be presented as the humus layer from which compositional material will grow. The very term *pre-compositional*—often used to refer to material not directly descriptive of the final musical surface—is misleading. It suggests that the act of composition proper begins with some kind of description of the musical outcome, however tentative; it implies a directional narrative, a linear trajectory from concept to performability. Boulez voices just this perspective in a late lecture: "Why erect, at whatever level of sophistication, a kind of array of coordinates? To make the birth of the idea possible, placing it in space and time, giving it the possibility of developing within a given *context*" (Boulez 2018, 565). Boulez's analysis of the situation is itself sophisticated, of course; the "array of coordinates"—numerical, in his example, and thus affording numerical operations—not only provides a matrix for the gestation of the "idea," but also stands as a "foreign body" to counteract "inbuilt automatisms" of material or musician. As he begins to discuss specific examples—Messiaen, Carter—

his tone changes slightly: "The network generates the idea . . ." (ibid., 566). Inscription and imagination are in an intimate dance.

The implication that this "idea" has assumed or will assume figural form has long roots in eighteenth- and nineteenth-century compositional theory. It receives a full treatment in Anton Reicha's encyclopaedic composition manual of 1826, but continues to haunt Schoenberg in his teaching over a century later: "The two-or-more-dimensional space in which musical ideas are presented is a unit" (Schoenberg [1995] 2006, 15). There appears to be a cultural assumption that the Cartesian space of figure is the state in which the actions or decisions of the composer are most readily apprehended as such. This is a crucial area in which sound practice of all kinds has moved ahead not only of public critical discourse but also of that of artists themselves. The space of figure, even with all its supplementary parameters, was never the whole story, but with recording media and computational tools of composition, modes of representation and manipulation have proliferated to challenge such persistent assumptions.

By having little trace of such abstractions—in the case of earlier music—or by linearising this mode as "pre"-compositional in more recent instances, we obscure the possibility that for music this situation has always obtained. Sketch studies tend to construct a goal-directed, linear narrative of increasing focus and detail. At what point in the compositional process any such descriptive or prescriptive thought might become externalised is, in terms of the conventional discourses of music, one of the key parameters of genre or style. What are these turns in the path, when does an idea become an idea? Precisely at these moments of inscription—external or internal, conscious or otherwise—each with their own context and motivation. Even in the case of score-based music, the path from intention to score is nonlinear and multimodal. Plans, ideas, materials, process, and constraints all exist in multiple modes and representations. Technical, theoretical, personal, and social stories are told around the creation of music, but largely in ways that contribute to cultural fragmentation. They intervene at multiple and parallel points in the iterative, recursive process of emergence of the "object." It is precisely the inevitable *incompleteness* of every representation that affords the plasticity necessary for this process. The nature of the nonlinearity, of the narrative, of the process is further conditioned by the media involved, and particularly with the role of computational elements.

Dalibor Vesely analyses the transformation of architectural practice brought about by the use of digital tools. He describes a situation of "divided representation," in which architects can operate on their project either from a traditional descriptive perspective or as process, as the product of multiple abstractions (Vesely 2004). They can work with a "recognisable" representation of the object in question—an inevitably reduced image from a particular perspective—or with the processes and data that might generate the design, which in many respects is a more complete representation, but one that affords less cognitive transparency. The practice of parametric design stands even farther back from the object itself. It builds a model of requirements, constraints, and affordances within which the brief can be satisfied; a solution is effectively induced (Schumacher 2009). Scaling presents an additional dimension of distance and mediation in music. Complex visual compositions retain some intelligibility when reduced to outline; storyboarding gives an impression of the development of a moving image. Reduced representation of musical form gives little indication of sound or temporal development. Of course, a creative practice may encompass many different approaches, many modes of inscription; this is what Agre's critical technical practice invites us to consider.

We might broaden the canvas on which we understand this process and refine our distinctions. Decisions—externalised or otherwise, explicit or implicit—are performative acts. They are also moments of inscription—inscription into common cultural experience and individual memory. Both have their own non-linear remediating effects as they contribute to the subsequent transmission of a particular performance moment. By the same token, moments of determination, decision, or inscription within what is normally understood to be the compositional process are also acts of performance. They are actions that transform the space within which the artist works. The distribution of decision-making through time and through modes of inscription is thus a key characteristic of any musical phenomenon. Distributed creativity is widely acknowledged as a vital component of contemporary practices (Clarke and Doffman 2018; Redhead and Glover 2018). We would rather suggest that distribution of decision, agency, and constraint is key to understanding *all* kinds of music practice. Edwin Hutchins's *Cognition in the Wild* (1995) remains a paradigmatic presentation of the distribution of action through technology, practice, social structure, and circumstantial affordance.

All such moments of inscription/performance are modulated by and embody aspects of their environment: the current state and concerns of the artist in question, constraints of time or resource, aspiration and expectation. Whatever moment or mode of inscription/performance we experience, therefore, is the product of multiple networks and dynamics. Which of these "belong" specifically to that experience and its direct history, which can be ascribed to the artist(s) and which to external forces? The boundaries cannot be drawn clearly. Whether composer in an opera house, improviser in a club, or artist-researcher at a conference, the context brings clear constraints and expectations, and the artist has a career he or she presumably wishes to advance. The act of listening is thus a further moment of inscription, through the nonlinear, infinitely complex mediation of the listener's own attention, motivation, and experience. This level of activity is perhaps the plane on which "creators" and "listeners" find common cause, the space in which useful critical discourse might emerge. But it requires creators to tell better, more honest stories.

Philip Agre and *critical technical practice*

Over nearly two decades of his writings, Agre takes issue with the unquestioned fundamental assumptions of AI and with the lack of acknowledgement of its socio-cultural context. He observes that AI researchers discuss their work as if it were the inevitable realisation of a particular theoretical or technical stance. Despite developments in the understanding of knowledge and invention as situated, embodied, distributed, and contingent, such work is presented shorn of narrative, taste, or contingency. In this way it is unable to fully reflect either on its own working or on the wider assumptions it may embody or effect it may have—whether technical-intellectual or social-political. He identifies the need for "a critical technical practice: a technical practice within which such reflection on language and history, ideas and institutions, is part and parcel of technical work itself" (Agre 2002, 131). In some ways, AI research has retreated into the situation first challenged by Agre in the late 1980s. Many instances of machine learning are prime examples of "black box" technologies; little is learned of their real-world context from investigating their inner workings, few researchers reinvent or reinvestigate the wheels and cogs with which they function, and access to and ownership of the ideas, computing power, and data is highly political.

The relationships of music creation with technology are many, complex, and distributed across multiple periods and various cultural structures—but they are inescapable. It is commonplace for people to say that they like music but don't "understand" it; there is a natural sense that some kind of technique is at work. To create a structure any more complex than simple repetition of rhythmic groove and melodic hook requires some kind of technical operation. The technologies of inscription—whether wax tablet (Owens 1997) or computer—are implicated in any such operation, material or conceptual. Agre refers to technical practice, not technological. The distinction is significant; the notion of technical practice implies the negotiation of a relationship with technologies. Critical technical practice emerges in relation to the development of *instances* of artificial intelligence. That is, these are artefacts, not merely the application of theory. They are bounded, have identity and some kind of cultural place. They pose new questions, produce new theory *in their making*.

Agre (1997b) distinguishes between two kinds of technology: those that "are employed in a specific site" and others "so ubiquitous . . . that we have no idea how to begin reckoning their effects upon society" (131). Both perspectives are relevant here. He refers to *borderlands*—areas in which relationships with technologies are fluid, dynamic, ambiguous, and evolving: "Each of the borderlands is a complicated place; everyone who resides in them is, at different times, both an object and an agent of technical representation, both a novice and an expert" (132). His particular context is the use of digital technologies—equally relevant to contemporary musicians—but the notion of borderlands affords a wider perspective encompassing musicians' relationships with notations, instruments, techniques, and formalisms of all kinds. Agre continues: "Above all, every resident of them is a translator between languages and worldviews: the formalisms of computing and the craft culture of the 'application domain'" (132). This process of translation is central to CTP. Ignoring for a moment the wider critical context, every process of music creation involves a continuous and complex shifting between different modes of conception and representation—symbolic, theoretical, physical, sonic—each with their own practices, habits, affordances, references, and implications. In the case of music, then, this is less a matter of translation than transduction—not just recoding, but the mapping of one kind of pattern of energy or behaviour onto another kind. Not every current technology figures in any given situation, of course; on the other hand, a technological milieu is a complex network constituted of all its components, real and imaginable.

MUSICAL AND DIGITAL OBJECTS

The artefacts of music—textual, media, sonic—have much in common with the artefacts of the digital world, with the virtual or digital objects we now seek to understand, and with our new world of augmented materiality (Massumi 2002). They exist in a unique state of materiality/immateriality: while they are intensely bound to direct experience, to technologies, techniques, and materials, this physicality can exist in multiple instantiations; they can be manipulated, engaged with, and acted upon as cultural abstractions. In cultural terms, music is the area of human activity in which we deal with the virtual, with the constructive relationship between human affect and abstract structures or formal systems.

The notion of *digital object* both challenges any residual assumed materiality of the tool and reminds us that digital artefacts as we make them and as we use them are not entirely abstract. Indeed, they are not at all abstract, even when used to invoke percepts that are quite separate from any associated physical "reality." Geoff Cox has shown how computer programming is both aesthetic and performative (Cox and MacLean 2012). Code is both script and performance, he says, and like the speech acts to which code is often compared, it is distributed and networked. The act is constituted in the interaction between subject and others, an interface that brings a high degree of indeterminacy. This suggests a critical, indeed a political dimension: "the act of coding is a deliberate action across cultural and technological fields" (ibid., 15). Sometimes—as Yuk Hui demonstrates with his analysis of the Facebook-style FOAF (friend-of-a-friend) code—a construct born in such a context can itself become part of a major cultural shift (Hui 2016, 2). Both musical and software constructs inhabit, contribute to, and potentially transform the social, technological, economic, and political milieu of their use. The conception, design, and construction of either kind of object is thus inherently a critical act, whether the designer chooses to recognise this or not.

Friedrich Kittler drew attention to the situated nature of the digital object in his provocative essay "There Is No Software": "All code operations . . . come down to absolutely local string manipulations, that is, I am afraid, *to signifiers of voltage differences*" (Kittler 1997, 150). Only code written directly in the lowest-level assembly language of a particular machine can have any claim to abstraction as software, he says; in the general case, code is written in a language that brings its own forms and affordances, translated for any given machine and operating system environment, and instantiated as action with a user by means of some kind of sense-engaging interface. Remoteness of the user in space or time from the software action does not change this situation. There is no access to or manipulation of the physical phenomena at the root of computing or music except through codes, languages, or models, however informal or unreflected.

Kittler observes that hardware development is in an eternal Sisyphean struggle to achieve the infinite precision and connectivity that is its implicit end goal. A more constructive path, he proposes, is not to pursue the ever-greater minimalisation of noise but to fully embrace it, performing computation on non-programmable machines, "a physical device working amidst physical devices" (Kittler 1997, 154). The operation of such physical computing depends entirely on its particular material properties; generalisation as in the conventional Turing/von Neumann machine model is no longer possible. "The inverse strategy of maximizing noise would not only find the way back from IBM to Shannon, it may well be the only way to enter that body of real numbers originally known as chaos" (Kittler 1997, 155). As a manifesto, this resonates strongly with aspects of sound art: the crucial importance of particular materiality, the impossibility of "pure" transmission of a message from sender to receiver, the irrelevance of generalised rules of form production.

Recent developments in AI bring another significant analogy with the condition of musical objects. The technology of machine learning allows particular instantiations of software to evolve their own "knowledge," their own set of behaviours with respect to certain kinds of data. Such digital objects can thus be understood from two perspectives: as the initial software construct with its non-specific, unrealised potential, or as the trained system that has constructed a model of its world and evolved an appropriate repertoire of responses. David Berry terms these as *compute-computed* and *compute-computing* (terms derived from Spinoza's *natura naturans* and *natura naturata*), which he describes as "constitutive" and "operational" states (Berry 2017). In its constitutive state, a musical object is complete within the terms, abstraction, and limits of a particular technology of inscription: a score, a textual instruction, a computational construct for sound processing or generation. By virtue of necessarily being shared, objects in this state themselves afford aesthetic contemplation and cultural currency. The mediating states of music—scores, specifically—may have less cultural currency than was once the case, just as the aesthetics of computer code are not universally accessible. Such public mediating inscriptions are less common in other arts; Michael Craig-Martin—mentor of two generations of British artists—articulates the situation in the visual arts thus:

> One should think of works of art as involving two fundamentally different ideas. The first is the idea that incentivizes the artist to act, that is, to make a particular work. I am using the term "idea" in a very broad sense here. I mean whatever mix of intention, instinct, thought, imagination, observation, curiosity, memory and bravado the artist needs in order to initiate the making of a work. . . .
>
> The second idea in art is that elicited by the finished work. It speaks for itself. Even the artist/maker has to respond to the reality of the finished work. People often think they will get closer to the work's true "meaning" the more they know about the artist's original idea. This is not true. . . . Works of art are not straightforward embodiments of their initiating ideas. They are themselves new ideas and their function is to act as primary objects, initiators of ideas, emotions, perceptions. (Craig-Martin 2015, 259)

"Works" may indeed not be straightforward embodiments of their initiating ideas, but active reception and critical response must be grounded in some kind of creative empathy. However autonomous the experienced phenomenon becomes, it inevitably bears some trace of the path of its separation. Whether through nature or culture, the process of creation is more instinctively reconstructible in visual art than in music. By and large, the mediating states of visual art afford visual representation; those of music are largely not sonic. A better understanding of this complex path must be part of a more useful discourse for music.

ELEMENTS OF A CRITICAL TECHNICAL PRACTICE

Intermediation and actor–network theory

What Agre proposes is certainly not a formal method, rather an informal methodology or perhaps an ethos. It is, he says, crucially different from introspection, which in most cases would tend to reinforce the boundaries of its own framing. He developed his own approach that he called "intermediation"— the recording of sequences of thought or action in both everyday life and more focussed work "that seemed relevant to some technical concern" (Agre 1997b, 146). The term derives from the fact that Agre found it most useful to identify such moments at an intermediate stage of abstraction. He was particularly interested in routines, in patterns of behaviour at all levels of time, detail, and awareness. This is crucially distinct from autoethnography, in that Agre's approach has no aspiration to autobiographical "truth" or balance; the objects and objectives of CTP still derive from the work in question. In this respect it might rather be considered a meta-creative process. This is not to deny that the many flavours of autoethnography have a key critical component in common with CTP. As Jones, Adams, and Ellis point out in their comprehensive survey, "One characteristic that binds all autoethnographies is the use of personal experience to examine and/or critique cultural experience. . . . autoethnographers intentionally *highlight* the relationship of their experiences and stories to culture and cultural practices, with many authors choosing to launch a critique of this relationship in their work" (Jones, Adams, and Ellis 2013, 22). "Fundamentally, autoethnographers aim to show 'people in the process of figuring out what to do, how to live, and the meaning of their struggles'" (Adams, Ellis, and Jones 2017, interpolating a quotation from Bochner and Ellis 2006, 111).

Lessons from autoethnography are relevant, therefore, but in most cases it is the author that remains at the centre of such reflection—not the emergence, the taking-form of his or her work. The worlds of visual art, sculpture, and architecture have been much better at acknowledging the materiality of the creative process, even if the very weight of this materiality sometimes blinds to the role of other elements. The history of musical modernism is replete with instances of composers explaining their technical innovation or their aesthetic stance on the basis of specific works. Some—from Schoenberg through Stockhausen,

Nono, Cage, and Boulez to Grisey, Ferneyhough, and Lachenmann—become indispensable documents of the craft and stand next to the major works to which they relate. Others retain continued currency because of their radical or prophetic nature. Many more are self-referential—the work justifies the theory or technique and vice versa—with little critical reflection on the real motivation, context, or implications of the process. Anecdotal accounts are of passing interest except to biographers. Coherent self-analysis of the actions and decisions of composition from a broader perspective is rare. Nico Muhly offers a valuable exception in a 2018 "Diary" column in the *London Review of Books*— that, tellingly, is not addressed to an expert readership. He begins: "When I talk to my colleagues, I am of course happy to hear about their sex dramas and squabbles with the landlord, but what I really want is shop talk: what kinds of pencil are you using? How do you find this particular piece of software? Do you watch the news while you work? I find these details telling" (Muhly 2018). Muhly continues to describe his way of responding to a commission, his processes for organising heterogeneous kinds of materials, and his practice of reconstructing a familiar physical working space in unfamiliar environments around the world. His article makes no claim to critical thoroughness or to comprehensively documenting a particular work, but such practical self-awareness must be fundamental to a new discourse of musical creativity.

A more thoroughgoing methodology might adopt a model such as actor–network theory (ANT) as a way of connecting what are conventionally presented as the "musical" aspects of composition with the myriad other factors that contribute to the process of creating music. Indeed, we might paraphrase Latour and describe this as a process of "reassembling the musical," suggesting that we should not start with the "musical" but end with it. Particularly resonant for the present project is Latour's assertion, "Dispersion, destruction, and deconstruction are not the goals to be achieved but what needs to be overcome. It's much more important to check what are the new institutions, procedures, and concepts able to collect and to reconnect the social" (2005, 11). On his view, ANT has constructive, generative potential, alongside its social-critical and analytical power. It would seem an ideal tool with which to contribute to the generation of new discourse.

ANT has many resonances with and important lessons for a critical technical practice. It traces associations, rather than looking for preconceived kinds of structure. It acknowledges the heterogeneity of actors: the roles of social structures, of patterns of behaviour, of ideas and of objects, including those that may be taken for granted, have become "invisible." Latour emphasises the role of physical environment:

> The first solution is to study *innovations* in the artisan's workshop, the engineer's design department, the scientist's laboratory, the marketer's trial panels, the user's home, and the many socio-technical controversies. In these sites objects live a clearly multiple and complex life through meetings, plans, sketches, regulations, and trials. Here, they appear fully mixed with other more traditional social agencies. It is only once in place that they disappear from view. (Latour 2005, 80)

The heterogeneity of elements is fundamental to ANT: "Objects too have agency" is Latour's assertion (2005, 63). An earlier explanation of his term *actant* is useful in this regard: "something that acts or to which activity is granted by others" (Latour 1996, 373). This reveals the asymmetry of networks, not only in the nature of agents but in the apparent—or projected—direction of influence. Actants might play a mediating role in a relationship, rather than acting directly. Distance—geographical or in time—is no measure of the effect of an encounter. To this we might add a notion of *conceptual* distance. There is no "truth" test; apparent *mis*understandings may be equally instrumental. Latour insists on the need to observe actions as much as stable connections. These need not be intentional or conscious; an apparently passive response to a given situation or an unreflected assumption becomes an action as it participates in the network. In this respect, Latour's actions might be considered equivalent to the moments of inscription discussed above; such networks are dynamical, evolving.

A critical technical practice certainly has much to learn from ANT therefore, but there are limitations. Two in particular are already problematised by Latour. First, he raises the issue of "context"—the catch-all for factors that appear too complex or trivial to trace. He recommends us to eliminate any apparent border between the initial area of interest and its wider environment—to proceed "by foot," to painstakingly pursue potentially relevant detail however distant physically or temporally. Here, the perspective and judgement of the viewer, the reporter—the sociologist, in Latour's case—come into play, if the map is not to be larger than the territory. Second, he acknowledges the challenges presented by the articulation of complex temporal relationships and sequences. Interactions take place between actants functioning across timescales from the momentaneous to the historical, and interactions themselves are neither synchronous nor synoptic (all visible for a single point) (Latour 2005, 201).

Both issues point to a necessary distinction between critical technical practice and ANT. Understanding or knowledge, however historical, obtains in the particular present, the situated moment in which it plays a role. A CTP traces the narrative of such moments as they relate to an instance of technical work, however mediated or indirect. Clarity as to the nature of the instance of practice in question is crucial to retain focus and to avoid perpetual relativising and proliferation: a score, a performance, a particular articulation of a concept or theory, a recording or an installation in its place. Independently of any residual notion of "work," a musical experience is particular and bounded. We might think of its emergence as a pattern of processes of "individuation" in Simondon's terms, to "seek to know the individual through individuation rather than individuation through the individual" (Simondon [1954–58] 2005, 24). Evolving relationships and understandings are at work across multiple parallel and interacting temporal planes; in CTP their traces are revealed at moments of consolidation, of decision, or inscription. Benjamin Piekut provides a perceptive survey of the potential of ANT for musicology (2014); but however radical the departure from convention, the musicologist's perspective remains closer to that of the sociologist. CTP demands a new voice—a first-person presence in discourse. In the case of CTP and composition, the composer is explicitly both subject and critic. Latour acknowledges this situation to an extent in ANT, but there as a challenge to overcome; here, this reflective nature defines the very voice of CTP.

But there is also an important reflexive component to composition that ANT is less equipped to address. Richard Sennett calls this the "material consciousness" of the craftsman—the response to materials modulated by particularity, contingency, or happenstance (2008, 119). Nurturing this consciousness is a large part of the training of musicians; maintaining and developing it is the mark of a mature musician. Sennett observes the way in which such personal actions lead to changes in cultural practice. He identifies the speciation of type-forms—of paradigms of cultural object—and domain-shift: how principles from one activity are applied to another (ibid., 125–27). Such transformations also happen continuously within individual practice, and from a CTP perspective these are of fundamental interest. The materiality of music creation is, in general terms, internalised to a greater extent than in, say, the plastic or visual arts. The mechanisms and habits a composer (still in our broadest of senses) develops to achieve critical distance from such internalised actions strongly characterise an artist's practice, as do the ways in which an artist chooses to reveal them to others or to him- or herself. They reflect models and paradigms that all have critical implications. The sources of these models are not mystical; they arise from the artist's perception or reception of his or her own environment. Reflection on such mechanisms and models is therefore integral to a notion of CTP in composition.

Dissociation and interference

Agre later refers to what he describes as "dissociation" in the way AI researchers speak about the oppositions implicit in their work. His examples include mind versus world, mental activity versus perception, and abstract ideals versus concrete things. "Dissociation has two moments: an overt distinction between the two terms and a covert conflation of them" (Agre 2002, 132). Agre's language reflects his reforming mission:

> dissociation is not consciously avowed. It must be sought in the internal tensions of texts and in the dynamics of technical work. Dissociation occurs in many ways, none of which is fixed or stable. To the contrary, much of the history of AI can be understood as attempts to comprehend and manage the signs of trouble that originate in dissociation and that AI practitioners can recognize within the conceptual system of the field. (Agre 2002, 132–33)

The notion of "covert theorising" reappears regularly through Agre's writing. The discourses of music creation may appear more diverse, more personal, than those of computer science, but this is an equally valid component of CTP in the context of composition. Sennett's "domain-shift" is one possible manifestation. In general, we are not looking for "signs of trouble" in bringing CTP to composition—although some Adornian criticism could be read in these terms—but rather the production of new concepts, of new kinds or instances of musical thought. Alertness to the implied negative connotations is a necessary corrective, and such clarity a vital part of reflection.

The phenomenon underlying Agre's dissociation also has an important productive role, one affording ontological generation as well as covert theorising. Michel Serres's early work explores the nature of both exact and human sciences by studying their evolution and interaction. He refers to the various assemblages of paradigms, theories, assumptions, and practices of any given moment as "models," and describes the wealth of often incommensurable models at play in the modern world as the "encyclopaedia." Their domains of study he calls "regions." Most often, he points out, the most recent model in any given region is accepted as the most "truthful," and its predecessors as curiosities of historical-cultural interest. Thought within a single region such as this, however coherent or complex, will remain self-referential: "every region has (is) its philosophy, blind in one sense and reflexive in another" (Serres 1972, 30). Within the world of the new encyclopaedia, new knowledge emerges from the intersection of regions—not from their synthesis or reconciliation but from their *interference*.

Why is this different to a Kuhnian paradigm shift—the emergence of a new model as its predecessor becomes increasingly unable to account for observed phenomena? Because here we are interested in the state of interference that produces that shift: in its texture, its dynamics, its inner rhythm. Interference is not an occasional phenomenon, one to be sought out in particular circumstances—it becomes the very mode of thought, of the perception of knowledge. Every encounter is inevitably an act of transfer, of transformation, of translation. They constitute a complex space to which there is no inherent linear or hierarchical order; the task of creative thought is to identify the potential of interference. The background to thought is therefore also constituted of interference; noise is the source of a new signal:

> Background noise is the ground of our perception. . . . No life without heat, no matter, neither; no warmth without air, no logos without noise, either. Noise is the basic element of the software of all our logic, or it is to the logos what matter used to be to form. Noise is the background of information, the material of that form. (Serres 1995, 7)

Serres considers the objects of science—of physics, specifically—and identifies three states of knowledge in historical sequence. First the geometric or "Cartesian" state of figure or shape, analogous to the two-dimensional musical idea described by Schoenberg. Then the physical state known through properties such as molecular structure or transmission of energy; here we might posit a parallel with the waveform, spectral, acoustic, or statistical representations of the computational manipulation of sound. The third, that appropriate for our present state of knowledge, he describes as a nexus of communication and information—a state that encompasses the previous two. The object not only affords description, has physical or energetic properties and behaviours, but also bears the traces of the forces and events that produced it, with which it has come into contact, that have transformed it. The locus of knowledge is "interegionality, meditation on interference" (Serres, 1972, 158, my translation).

Musical metaphors abound in Serres's writing, from his early essay on Xenakis to his late book on music. His emphasis on the role of noise—of the constant stimulus from inner and outer environment—and his concept of objects or materials as interfaces of informational transformation both offer useful tools for critical technical practice in music. Serres's notion of interference is particularly resonant if we take modulation in sound synthesis as an analogy: the emergence of a new artefact from the interference of other signals, an artefact with its own behaviour, its own affordances and properties that are not intuitively predictable from the source signals. If we interpret Agre's dissociation in the light of Serres's interference, acts of dissociation become the very stuff of composition; a critical technical practice might seek to trace and articulate them, to expose them to critical reflection.

CONCLUSION

To return to the analogy between musical and digital objects, we might consider the generation of music as a process of encoding a motivation. This seed of motivation has no form until it begins to be encoded, but there is no inherent inevitability as to the form it will take; that will be conditioned by the modes of encoding adopted or assumed, their sequence and relationships. The "note"—a fuzzy but highly plastic and useful notion—is a paradigmatic example of such a mode of encoding. The self-perception of the seed of motivation itself is likewise conditioned by other forms of encoding: social, professional, economic. Of course, these codes are living, evolving things, themselves reconceived with every instantiation. They afford various perspectives or ways of understanding: cultural, cognitive, music-theoretical. But they have in common the fact that they can be traced to technological-scientific-cosmological models. This is true for what appear to be music-psychological frameworks: from the blacksmith's hammers of Pythagoras or the monochord of theorists from Boethius to Rameau to the computer-calculated spectra of Grisey. But it is equally true of social contexts, for example: the court, the concert hall, the internet. These can all be regarded as technologies, as modes of inscription predicated on other technologies. Each "idea," each decision, every acknowledgement of or response to a circumstance or constraint, the embodiment of every cultural assumption, is an encoding. And each encoding is a subscription to a model, a paradigm of some kind.

Over a decade ago, Georgina Born (2010) called for a new, interdisciplinary "relational musicology," in response to the fragmentation of modes of music study and their aggregate incapacity to respond to the cultural-intellectual context of the twenty-first century. In that lecture, Born points to Stephen Feld's proposal of "a critical anthropology of music intended to overcome the music/social dualism by analysing 'sound structure as socially structured'"

(220). The present call for a critical technical practice requires precisely that the "musical," the "technical," the "aesthetic," and the "social" are considered as a single field. Born analyses different modes of interdisciplinarity to consider how the various modes of music study might work together: the "comforting" mode of integration, the "imperial" mode of subordination, and "the agonistic-antagonistic mode, which suggests that addressing music as immanently social and cultural requires a break—an epistemological and ontological shift in our understanding of all musics, an approach that is irreducible to the addition of the antecedent (sub)disciplines, since all will be changed in the process" (231).

The ethos of critical technical practice suggests that the creators of music have a vital part to play in generating this new discourse. As Agre proposed for computer scientists, this is now the task, the obligation of musicians. To act responsibly in terms of their own work, of course, but also to provide a bilateral path between their thought and act and public and expert discourse. Born identifies four topics that she suggests "may be generative for emergent redefinitions of the field [of relational musicology] . . . : questions of the social, technology, temporality and ontology" (2010, 231). The social, the technological, and the temporal have all figured importantly in this discussion; we might add topics such as distribution, inscription, and environment. Born suggests that "A non-relativist, relational musicology can proceed from the comparative study of distinct ontologies of music" (241). The fundamental understanding of critical technical practice in a musical context is that any musical creation embodies *multiple* ontologies: ontologies that are cultural, cognitive, historical, imagined, or appropriated, the ontologies of materials, circumstances, encodings, and technologies. Their bringing-together has narratives, conflicts and contradictions, context and contingency. The reconciliation, or rather the non-reconciliation of multiple ontologies, is a universal human challenge. One of the fundamental roles of music is to offer a space and experience in which to confront this, and the most useful contribution composers can make to discourse is to unfold their negotiation of this space as broadly and honestly as possible. Such an approach is necessary if the creators of music themselves are to play their vital part in the "fully relational and reflexive, social and material conception of all musics" called for by Georgina Born (2010, 242). Agre summarised his project thus: "Technology at present is covert philosophy; the point is to make it openly philosophical" (Agre 1997a, 240). Our point, then, is to make music openly philosophical by sharing the actants and agents, the noise and interferences that produce it, in order that it might find a place in shared discourse.

References

Adams, Tony E., Carolyn Ellis, and Stacy Holman Jones. 2017. "Autoethnography." In *The International Encyclopedia of Communication Research Methods*, edited by Jörg Matthes with Christine S. Davis and Robert F. Potter. https://doi.org/10.1002/9781118901731.iecrm0011.

Agamben, Giorgio. 1999. "On Potentiality." In *Potentialities: Collected Essays in Philosophy*, edited and translated by

Daniel Heller-Roazen, 177–84. Stanford, CA: Stanford University Press. Essay first given as a lecture (Lisbon, 1986).

———. 2019. *Creation and Anarchy: The Work of Art and the Religion of Capitalism*. Translated by Adam Kotsko. Stanford, CA: Stanford University Press. First published 2017 as *Creazione e anarchia: L'opera nell'età della religione capitalistica* (Vicenza: Neri Pozza).

Agre, Philip E. 1997a. *Computation and Human Experience*. Cambridge: Cambridge University Press.

———. 1997b. "Toward a Critical Technical Practice: Lessons Learned in Trying to Reform AI." In *Social Science, Technical Systems, and Cooperative Work: Beyond the Great Divide*, edited by Geoffrey C. Bowker, Susan Leigh Star, William Turner, and Les Gasser, 131–57. Mahwah, NJ: Erlbaum.

———. 2002. "The Practical Logic of Computer Work." In *Computationalism: New Directions*, edited by Matthias Scheutz, 129–42. Cambridge, MA: MIT Press.

Badiou, Alain. 2001. *Ethics: An Essay on the Understanding of Evil*. Translated by Peter Hallward. London: Verso. First published 1998 as *L'éthique: Essai sur la conscience du mal* (Paris: Hatier).

———. 2006. "Third Sketch of a Manifesto of Affirmationist Art." In *Polemics*, translated by Steve Corcoran, 133–48. London: Verso. Chapter first published 2004 as "Troisième esquisse d'un manifeste de l'affirmationnisme," in *Circonstances 2* (Paris: Léo Scheer: Lignes), 81–105.

Berger, John. 1972. *Ways of Seeing*. London: Penguin.

Berry, David M. 2017. "Prolegomenon to a Media Theory of Machine Learning: Compute-Computing and Compute-Computed." *Media Theory* 1 (1): 74–87.

Bochner, Arthur P., and Carolyn S. Ellis. 2006. "Communication as Autoethnography." In *Communication As . . . : Perspectives on Theory*, edited by Gregory J. Shepherd, Jeffrey St. John, and Ted Striphas, 110–22. Thousand Oaks, CA: Sage.

Born, Georgina. 2010. "For a Relational Musicology: Music and Interdisciplinarity, Beyond the Practice Turn; The 2007 Dent Medal Address." *Journal of the Royal Musical Association* 135 (2): 205–43.

Boulez, Pierre. 2018. "Writing and Idea (1992–93)." In *Music Lessons: The Collège de France Lectures*, edited and translated by Jonathan Dunsby, Jonathan Goldman, and Arnold Whittall, 560–91. London: Faber & Faber. Book first published 2005 as *Leçons de musique (Points de repère, III): Deux décennies d'enseignement au Collège de France (1976–1995)*, edited by Jean-Jacques Nattiez and Jonathan Goldman (Paris: Christian Bourgois).

Chemero, Anthony. 2009. *Radical Embodied Cognitive Science*. Cambridge, MA: MIT Press.

Clark, Andy. 1997. *Being There: Putting Brain, Body, and World Together Again*. Cambridge, MA: MIT Press.

Clark, T. J. 2018. *Heaven on Earth: Painting and the Life to Come*. London: Thames and Hudson.

Clarke, Eric F., and Mark Doffman, eds. 2018. *Distributed Creativity: Collaboration and Improvisation in Contemporary Music*. New York: Oxford University Press.

Cox, Geoff, and Alex MacLean. 2012. *Speaking Code: Coding as Aesthetic and Political Expression*. Cambridge, MA: MIT Press.

Craig-Martin, Michael. 2015. *On Being an Artist*. London: Art/Books.

Croft, John. 2015. "Composition Is Not Research." *Tempo* 69 (272): 6–11.

DeLanda, Manuel. 2011. *Philosophy and Simulation: The Emergence of Synthetic Reason*. London: Continuum.

Ferneyhough, Brian. (1982) 1995. "Form—Figure—Style: An Intermediate Assessment." In *Brian Ferneyhough: Collected Writings*, edited by James Boros and Richard Toop, 21–28. London: Routledge. Essay written 1982; first published 1984 in French translation (*Labrys* 10).

Gritten, Anthony, and Elaine King, eds. 2011. *New Perspectives on Music and Gesture*. London: Routledge.

Gross, Matthias. 2010. *Ignorance and Surprise: Science, Society, and Ecological Design*. Cambridge, MA: MIT Press.

Hui, Yuk. 2016. *On the Existence of Digital Objects*. Minneapolis: University of Minnesota Press.

Huron, David. 2006. *Sweet Anticipation: Music and the Psychology of Expectation*. Cambridge, MA: MIT Press.

Hutchins, Edwin. 1995. *Cognition in the Wild*. Cambridge, MA: MIT Press.

Impett, Jonathan. 2016a. "Making a Mark: The Psychology of Composition." In *The Oxford Handbook of Music Psychology*, edited by Susan Hallam, Ian Cross, and Michael Thaut, 2nd ed., 651–66. Oxford: Oxford University Press.

———. 2016b. "Notation as Technology." Presentation at IRCAM, Paris. Accessed 29 April 2021. https://medias.ircam.fr/x437e31.

———. 2021. "Discourse and Intuitive Technology." *AI and Society*. https://doi.org/10.1007/s00146-020-01126-4.

Jones, Stacy Holman, Tony E. Adams, and Carolyn Ellis. 2013. "Introduction: Coming to Know Autoethnography as More Than a Model." In *Handbook of Autoethnography*, edited by Stacy Holman Jones, Tony E. Adams, and Carolyn Ellis, 17–48. Abingdon, UK: Routledge.

Kittler, Friedrich A. 1997. "There Is No Software." In *Essays: Literature, Media, Information Systems*, edited by John Johnson, 147–55. Amsterdam: G+B Arts International.

Latour, Bruno. 1996. "On Actor-Network Theory: A Few Clarifications." *Soziale Welt* 47 (4): 369–81.

———. 2005. *Reassembling the Social: An Introduction to Actor-Network-Theory*. Oxford: Oxford University Press.

Massumi, Brian. 2002. *Parables for the Virtual: Movement, Affect, Sensation*. Durham, NC: Duke University Press.

Muhly, Nico. 2018. "Diary: How I Write Music." *London Review of Books*, 25 October 2018. Accessed 7 June 2021. https://www.lrb.co.uk/the-paper/v40/n20/nico-muhly/diary.

Nöe, Alva. 2015. *Strange Tools: Art and Human Nature*. New York: Hill and Wang.

Owens, Jessie Ann. 1997. *Composers at Work: The Craft of Musical Composition 1450–1600*. New York: Oxford University Press.

Piekut, Benjamin. 2014. "Actor-Networks in Music History: Clarifications and Critiques." *Twentieth-Century Music* 11 (2): 191–215.

Redhead, Lauren, and Richard Glover, eds. 2018. *Collaborative and Distributed Processes in Contemporary Music-Making*. Newcastle upon Tyne: Cambridge Scholars Publishing.

Schauffler, Robert Haven. 1929. *Beethoven: The Man Who Freed Music*. Garden City, NY: Doubleday, Doran & Co.

Schoenberg, Arnold. (1995) 2006. *The Musical Idea and the Logic, Technique, and Art of Its Presentation*. Edited and translated by Patricia Carpenter and Severine Neff. Bloomington: Indiana University Press. First published 1995 (New York: Columbia University Press).

Schumacher, Patrik. 2009. "Parametricism: A New Global Style for Architecture and Urban Design." In "Digital Cities," special issue, *Architectural Design* 79 (4): 14–23.

Sennett, Richard. 2008. *The Craftsman*. London: Penguin.

Serres, Michel. 1972. *Hermès II: L'Interférence*. Paris: Minuit.

———. 1995. *Genesis*. Translated by Geneviève James and James Nielson. Ann Arbor: University of Michigan Press. First published 1982 as *Genèse* (Paris: Grasset).

Simondon, Gilbert. (1954–58) 2013. *L'individuation à la lumière des notions de forme et d'information*. Grenoble: Jérôme Millon. Contains texts written 1954–58. This collection first published 2005 (Grenoble: Jérôme Millon).

Smith Brindle, Reginald. 1961. "Current Chronicle: Italy." *Musical Quarterly* 47 (2): 247–55.

Vesely, Dalibor. 2004. *Architecture in the Age of Divided Representation: The Question of Creativity in the Shadow of Production*. Cambridge, MA: MIT Press.

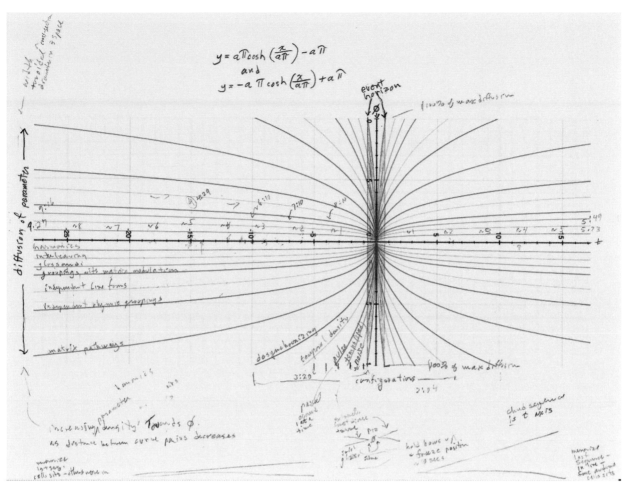

Plate 2.1.

Plate 2.1. Page from composer's sketches showing how rotated catenaries outline the diffuseness of compositional parameters, event horizons marked by silence and frozen motion, and the Ø point where one time ends and another begins.

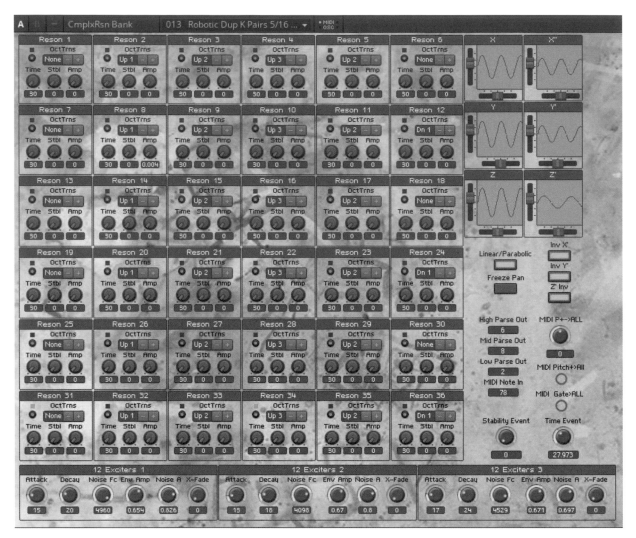

Plate 2.2.

Plate 2.2. Control surface for the complex resonator bank used in *Earth Encomium* and *Nothingness is Unstable*, programmed with Reaktor software.

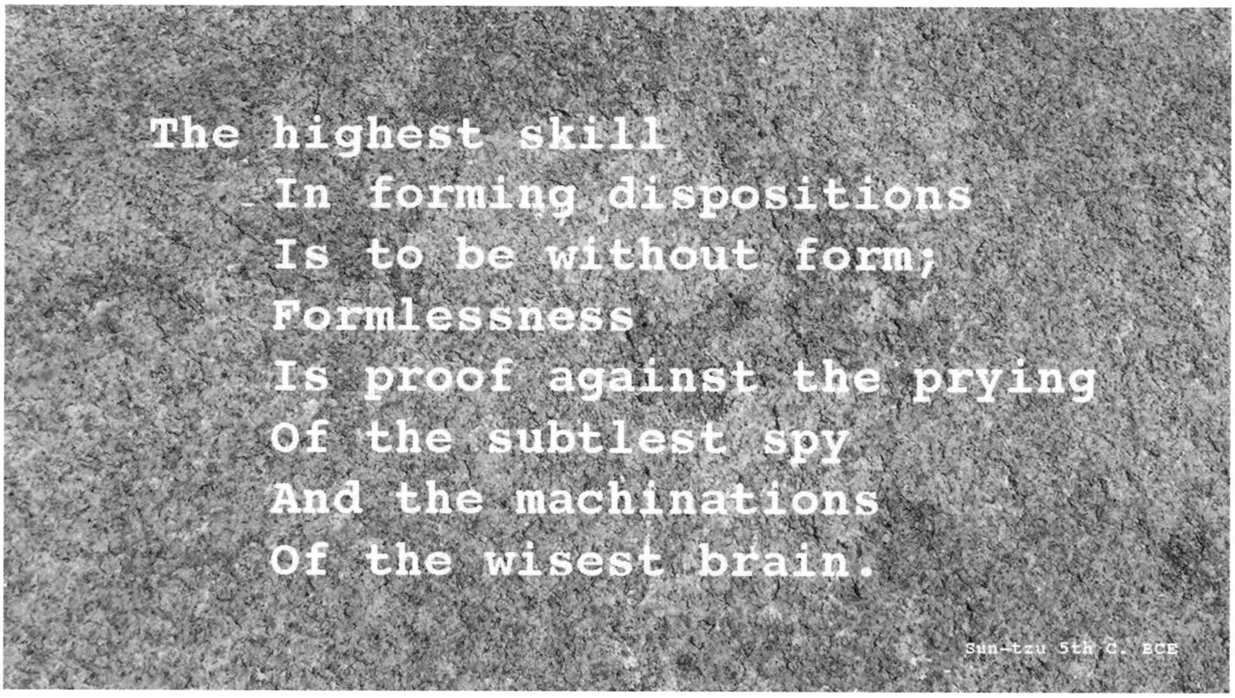

The highest skill
    In forming dispositions
    Is to be without form;
Formlessness
Is proof against the prying
Of the subtlest spy
And the machinations
Of the wisest brain.

Sun-tzu 5th C. BCE

Plate 2.3.

Plate 2.3. The penultimate projected during performances of *Earth Encomium* with *Nothingness is Unstable*.

Plate 2.4a.

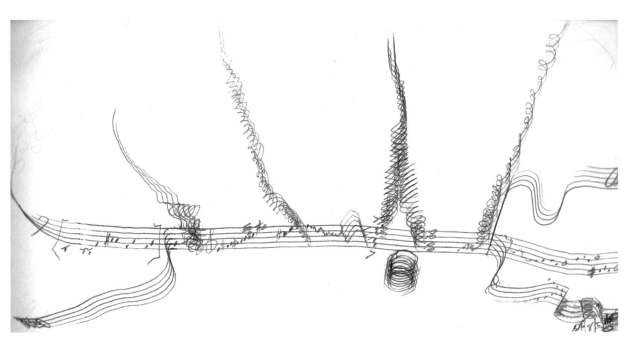

Plate 2.4b.

Plate 2.4a–c. Drawings from my book *Natural Scores* also used in *Choose Your Universe* performances.

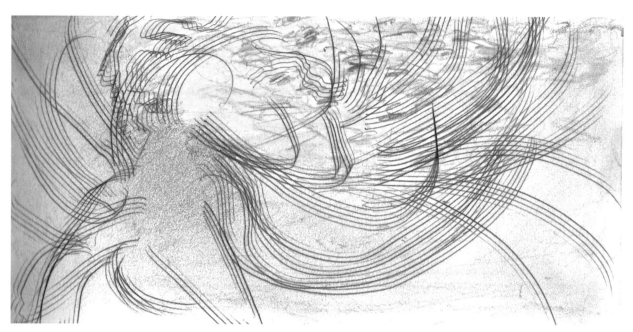

Plate 2.4c.

Plates

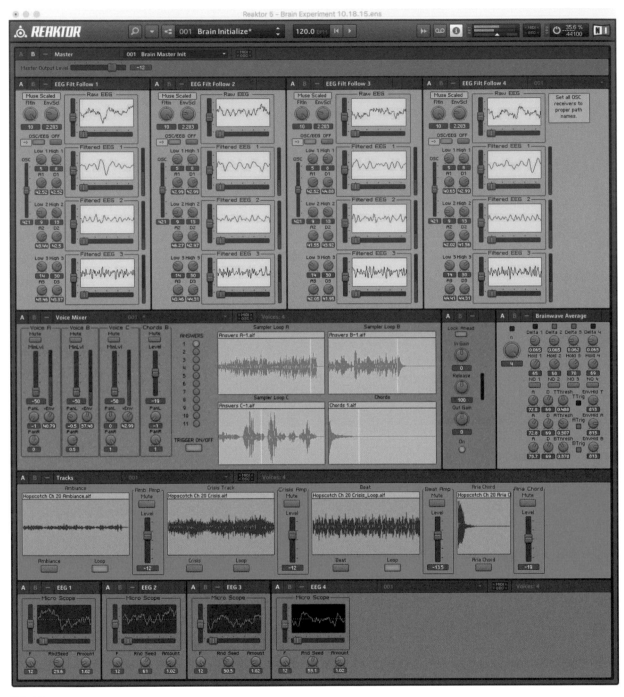

Plate 2.5.

142

Plate 2.5. Control surface for the software developed for performances of *The Experiment*, written in Reaktor. This version accommodates four audience members at one time, who were brought into a limousine where the performances took place. A separate concert version of *The Experiment* has also been created, which permits various kinds of expanded presentations.

Plates

Plate 2.6a.

Plate 2.6a–f. Images from *Swarming Intelligence Carnival*: preparations taking place in the Lotus Pond, participants getting ready, three performance snapshots from ground level, and a computer control and performance station.

Plate 2.6b.

Plate 2.6c.

Plate 2.6d.

Plate 2.6e.

Plate 2.6f.

Plates

Plate 16.1.

Plate 16.2a.

Plate 16.1. Set-up of *Rave Séance* with a circular arrangement of five tables and the laser projection in the middle (photo: Katja Goljat).

Plate 16.2a–b. Audience members interacting with the performance of *Rave Séance* via illuminated buttons (photos: Katja Goljat).

Plates

Plate 16.2b.

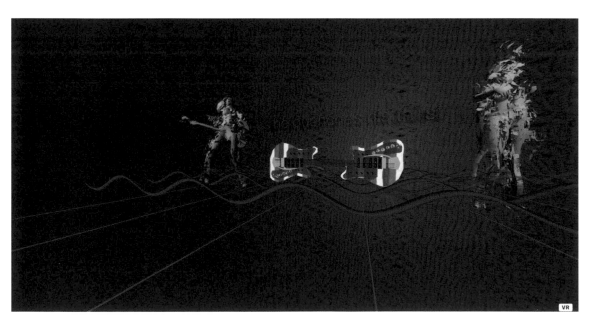

Plate 16.3.

150

Plate 16.3. View of the net-art part of *Why Frets?* (photo by the author).

Plates

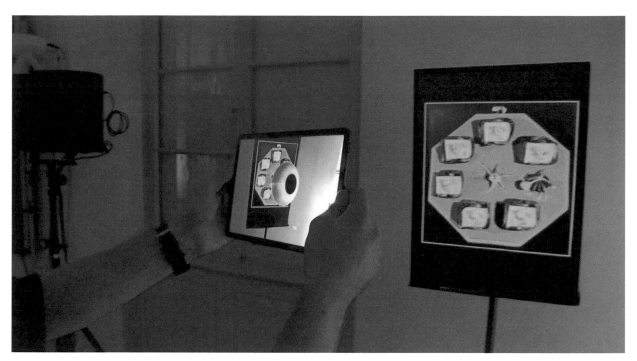

Plate 16.4.

Plate 16.5.

Plate 16.4. An audience member using a tablet to generate augmented reality (photo: nmzMedia).

Plate 16.5. Arrangement of the space of *Anna & Marie* with the violinists in playing positions and no audience members (photo: nmzMedia).

Plates

Plate 16.6.

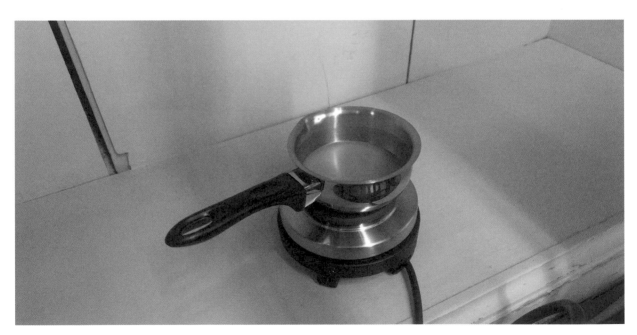

Plate 16.7.

Plate 16.6. Audience members listening to the narrative using earpieces during the installation phase (photo by the author).

Plate 16.7. Hot plates with beeswax were used in *Anna & Marie* in order to create a subtle
odour of melted wax throughout the venue (photo by the author).

The Impossibility of Material Foundations

Scott McLaughlin

University of Leeds, UK

My sound work is composing for the material indeterminacy of continuous sounds. These terms will come up a lot in this chapter, so an explanation will be useful. By *material* I mean the physicality of the instrument, the way it makes sound and the breadth of sounds that it makes; this assumes also avoiding traditional dichotomies between "musical" and "non-musical" sounds, and instead treating the instrument in a more ecological way where all sounds have validity and the relationship between sounds (how they change, how they stabilise and destabilise) is primary, though some may have priority in creating structure in musical pieces. By *indeterminacy* I'm aligning my work with the tradition of experimental music following John Cage. However, rather than using dice or the I Ching, I use the unstable and unpredictable elements of the instrument's materiality to suggest different paths as the piece unfolds. This allows the "material agency," the material preferences or "will" of the instrument, to have an impact on how the piece unfolds, and to guide the player. Because these pieces require the player to respond in real time to an unpredictable instrument, the term *contingent* will also feature as the situation of the player working-with and responding-to[1] the sometimes unpredictable instrument. Lastly, for materiality and indeterminacy to have time to act, and for the relationship between player and instrument to be a continuous feeding-back of actions and energy, the focus here is on continuous sounds—where energy continuously excites an object into vibration, such as bowed objects, blown instruments,[2] guitar/microphone feedback, and so on. Composing "for" material indeterminacy involves setting up musical material and scoring such that live performance involves the unfolding of decisions made through both human agency and material agency, and the emergence of structure in performance: because there are different ways the piece might unfold due to the unpredictable material agency of the instrument, the pieces are composed such that whatever emerges in performance can become the focus of the piece, creating an audible structure. The work here begins (and continues) with a very close relationship

---

1 These terms are deliberately hyphenated to reflect the conjoinedness of player and instrument in this reading.

2 Both blown and bowed instruments are not perfectly continuous because the continuity of the sound is broken (or at least seriously perturbed) when taking a breath or changing bow direction. However, within each breath or bow the system is continuous, and resonances may carry over to influence what comes after the breath/bow change, all of which is the focus of this practice. This is explicitly in opposition to the attack-based model of much music (and its notation) that takes the piano as the basic model of sound production, an attack-decay model where continuity of sound is functionally irrelevant.

with the instrument in order to learn its behaviours, especially those unstable zones of sound production that are contingent but not chaotic to the point of unmanageability. Once the right behaviours have been studied (usually by playing the instrument myself), the work is twofold: (1) building an open-form performance system (usually in text or diagrammatic form) where structure can emerge from the interaction of embodied techniques of performance, score-based rules/instructions/principles, and the indeterminate materiality of the instrument; and (2) working with an experienced performer to ensure that the piece is built on universal phenomena of the instrument, not simply by-products of my own untrained technique.

My concern with contingency found a touchstone in Philip Agre's proposal for critical technical practice (CTP) as not "seeking foundations" but instead "embrac[ing] the impossibility of foundations, guiding itself by a continually unfolding awareness of its own workings as a historically specific practice" (1997, 23). In my sound work, Agre's practice resonates strongly with the performance-based revealing of emergent forking paths and networked structures inherent in the materiality of the performer-instrument (which can treated as a single system, an "assemblage"). The culture of music and its instruments is a complex balance between rich and lively materials and the controlling technique of the performer—the entrenching of musical systems (notes, tunings, harmonies, rhythms, etc.) and capture of material liveliness in reified instrumental technique (how a player controls the instrument into producing culturally desired tone colours), but also the vibrant embodied skills and imagination of the player that pushes against received ideas. Perhaps a musical CTP can take materiality as its entry point to a continual unfolding where the imposed *logos* of Western musical systems become subsumed in Donna Haraway's "speculative fabulation of 'Terrapolis,'" an "*n*-dimensional niche space for multispecies becoming-with. . . . a chimera of materials, languages, histories. . . . mak[ing] space for unexpected companions" (2016, 11).

This chapter discusses my compositional practice in a mix of modes in an attempt not to disentangle but to further entwine the strands of compositional thought. Elements under discussion—both alone in sections of singular focus and composed and "composted" together (Haraway 2016, 32)—include: technical description of material and compositional elements; poetic and phenomenal description of engagement with materials; and the enrolling of concepts from philosophy both to permeate the "doing" and to drive practice-based enquiry. The first half of the chapter outlines the main ideas in relation to work for prepared bowed strings, while the remainder of the chapter unfolds the same ideas and methods in the context of works for clarinet.

First, some concepts should be outlined that are central to all this work.

Phase-space:[3] This term is borrowed from physics where it is used prominently in dynamical systems theory (chaos theory) to represent all possible states of a system, and usually visualised in relation to important parameters relative to their orders of freedom. Phase-space often includes features prominent in the dynamics of the space, known as attractors. Both simple and complex attractors delineate areas of attraction, including stable states (such as simple attractors like the final resting point of a pendulum), or in continuous systems it can also capture patterns and metastable states; that is, complex attractors that are only stable under highly specific conditions, and that might shift relative to the initial conditions of the system. This sound work thinks through the player-instrument assemblage in terms of phase-space, as a multidimensional topology of energy in a space of flows and resistances. The work happens mostly in the boundaries of this space, where the instrument becomes like a cybernetic black box: knowable only by parsing the inputs and outputs, the performative feedback and the phenomenal reading of productive paths as they emerge.

Recursivity: To make use of phase-space (all the possible behaviours of the instrument) and the contingencies of its unstable boundary spaces, this sound work recursively explores the same space to reveal the variety of different paths. The same musical phrases or gestures are repeated over and over, knowing that their instability will lead to different versions emerging. Often, the same things will result in many cases, but other less-likely things will also emerge, revealing a sense of the material's preferences and the stronger and weaker paths that emerge through these contingent repetitions. Over time, the performance becomes a structure of the interaction between the respective weight of paths through contingency, and the productive tensions encoded in the score that specify which paths are to be preferred by the player. In some pieces this recursive looping is strict; as in Alvin Lucier's "scanning" pieces, this allows the material phenomena to be foregrounded, limiting human agency in the process. In most of the pieces, though, the recursivity is loose, and often given to the player to enact when the performance offers rich spaces to explore. However, this is not simply a tool to maximise the richness of contingency; in the player-instrument assemblage the continuously updating knowledge is a mycelial thread that strengthens the connection between player and instrument, entwining them further in a singular performance instance of an open work. As Yuk Hui describes it: "Recursivity is not mere mechanical repetition; it is characterized by the looping movement of returning to itself in order to determine itself, while every movement is open to contingency, which in turn determines its singularity" (2019, 4).

---

3 While in physics this term is not normally hyphenated, I have chosen to hyphenate it here for ease of communication, and to avoid confusion with discussions of physical space.

How does composition happen?

First, prepare the cello. Take the preparation and place it on the string in an arbitrary place. Begin to bow, gliding, pushing, gently probing for boundaries, changes of state and hints of new terrain that may lie just out of hearing. Also, mirages, resonances that exist only as a consequence of where I am right now, coupled to this unfolding moment, and collapsing as soon as I try to move out of this space, to change. Action proceeds all at once in and out of focus: offering the cello the resources for change; listening to what the instrument says, in the foreground and the background; feeling with the bow and body and moving to support, to accommodate, or to thwart; learning the instrument's behaviours from within the feedback loop of cello-string-bow-body; categorising and classifying behaviours as features on an instrumental topology; filtering, selecting, and hierarchising to make a dynamic map of tensions and openings, stabilities and instabilities updated continuously through selective reinforcement inside the performative loop. As performance unfolds, the map becomes the territory of composition (for a while at least), and real material forces are abstracted into a mental model of relationships. The instrument is put down and tentative steps towards diagramming and score building begin.

Sometime years ago I absorbed an idea that lodged in my mind in a fundamental way. It was when I was reading lots about chaos theory and cellular automata (Conway's Game of Life, of course). I forget the detail, but what stuck was a description of a space that was largely sterile and predictable but for a single meandering thread of life running across it (life occurs in the cracks . . .). This thread meandered and forked its way across the space, unwilling to settle into the ultimate stability of zero or infinity. Instead it roiled with patterns and repetitions, spiralling off at times, splitting, rejoining, dying out, and starting again in a new way, a fizzing, splitting edge where the potential for change overwhelmed forces of constraint. At the core of the thread was a chasm, like the endless enfolding edges in a fractal, a space where repetition and variation furled and unfurled into each other to create . . . well, just to create. The chasm is not a void, though it may pragmatically become one at some point, its function is precisely not in emptiness but in vitality. Philip Agre's line about "embrac[ing] the impossibility of foundations" resonates vibrantly with this image as an injunction to follow the repetitions of the practice as they continuously reveal, not to untangle them but to become-with them, to "become humus," "not Homo, not Anthropos, we are compost" as Donna Haraway puts it (2016, 40, 55).

In my compositional practice, the instrument becomes the space where I seek such threads, and in this chapter I'll outline the form they take and how composition happens around them. The key idea is what I have come to call *material indeterminacy*, a compositional strategy of using the contingencies of an instrument to balance the agency of the performer and the agency of the instrument (see McLaughlin, forthcoming). Here, indeterminacy is an inherent property of the instrument, the lively space between the chasm of total unpredictability and the plateaus of stable sound—where the player can be, in anthropologist Tim Ingold's terms, a "wayfarer" (2007, 15) in the space of the instrument, where the possibility for forking paths is always present in the unfolding moment of performance, and where composition encourages following these paths while always searching for points to recognise and acknowledge recursion.

As I sit with the cello, I bow. Each time I begin again the bow movement, I'm listening for stability and also for potentials: resonance here and now, and resonances on the horizon. Each time the bow movement begins, there's a transience, a perturbance of the vibrational system that opens a door to change. The system may stay in place, or it may step over that boundary. Resonant systems are hysteretic. Like a metal that when bent returns to its shape, the resonance is materially entrained; it wants to stay in its groove as long as conditions are favourable. But the sudden transient movement of the bow changing direction is a perturbance that always wants to refigure.

Waves. Water sloshing and spilling over a boundary. I hold a bowl of water, gently swirling it, trying to find a balance where each swirl brings the water just up to the edge. On each swirl perhaps it will go just enough over the edge to break the meniscus, flow out, change its path. Perhaps the meniscus will hold. If it does break, a new path is opened up; then on the next swirl as the wave builds again, does it push over the edge again? Does the water remember? Will it push the same way or is the swirl's rhythmic sameness only an illusion that imperceptible differences of force define which path is taken. Do I have two states: one where the water stays in the bowl and one where it escapes? Or, do I have two families of states? In one family, water pushes over the bowl edge. Perhaps it dribbles down the side or perhaps it splashes out into the air. But those are extremes; more likely, the gentle movement of hands will give the swirl a stability that affords variation on only the smallest scale. The compositional art here is in finding and maintaining the balance point where material indeterminacy comes into play, where material agency can tack the system towards one course or the other. How small is the space in which my oscillations vary?

Moving with the bowl, I fix into a rhythm that both directs the water to this side of the boundary and is always slightly too much, always becoming. The water gently sloshes over the edge of the bowl, more or less the same way each time, pouring down the side to the ground, never demonstrative, but always with a rhythm that is both lively and predictable. My rhythm fixes on the impossibility of finding that perfect balance of fifty-fifty chance that any given cycle will break the meniscus, the truly aleatoric. But in aiming for this, I know that what I will actually reach is the chaotic, a tidal movement between motions of slightly-too-much and slightly-too-little, where each testing of the meniscus is decided by knife-edge materialities beyond my intentional control.

Composition here is an arrangement of forces and techniques to produce relationships in time. The forces are the intra-action[4] of player and instrument, and techniques are those relationships recast as forms of knowledge that allow productive engagement. When John Cage, late in his career, wrote his "music of contingency" pieces, he used the sloshing of water inside a conch shell as an instrument so that he could have improvisational activity without improvisational style, to avoid improvisers imposing their musical history on his piece by replacing their familiar instrument with an unfamiliar object. For Cage, this would allow the players to be purely responsive, free of the baggage of style. In my music, I need the players to know the contingencies of their instrument, precisely so they can find and sustain those metastabilities[5] where material indeterminacy can come to the fore. My water vignette is analogous to my instrumental compositions. The player knows the water and the bowl, he or she knows there is a meniscus and the feel of the water's weight in the bowl that guides the rhythm of movement. The player develops a technique of knowing the materiality of the instrument, knowing its behaviours and edges and how it communicates these, its thingliness. These techniques are in a constant state of becoming because the composition always pushes the player to the next level by asking him or her to find stabilities and instabilities. Each stability emerges from a former instability. The metastable is continuously turning over new possibilities both because the material is infinitely rich and because the material and the player and the environment are entwined and constantly changing.

The behaviours and affordances of liquid water provide a productive analogue for thinking about the materiality of instruments. On the cello, the bow moves back and forth, not unlike the water. Also like the water, the cycle of back and forth is not smooth, the transitions perturb the system. The cello departs from the water in several ways, but key to this is the training of the cellist,[6] a player with many years of embodied techniques and sedimented agency attuned to his or her instrument.[7] While the prepared cello will challenge traditional cello technique, it is not completely alien, requiring more a shift of expectation than treating it as a new instrument. The player builds on his or her existing techniques of bow control to work with the system so that the perturbation is productive. The cello preparation is a circular ring that connects two adjacent strings (without touching the

---

4 Intra-action is Karen Barad's term for "the mutual constitution of entangled agencies . . . the notion of intra-action recognizes that distinct agencies do not precede, but rather emerge through, their intra-actions" (2007, 33).

5 *Metastability* is a stable state that is not the ground state. For example, a spinning coin is a series of metastable states, held in place by the energy of spinning, which as the energy ebbs away will finally reach the ground state of complete stop. In rare cases the coin may stop spinning while still on its edge: arguably either a rare unstable ground-state, or another type of metastable state. In instruments, metastable sounds are often found by accident, sometimes they can be repeated or a technique developed to repeat them, or sometimes they remain elusive.

6 Tragically (perhaps), the practice of swirling water in a bowl is not something we have a cultural tradition of technical training for.

7 For more on *sedimented agency* see Spatz (2015, 50).

fingerboard),[8] coupling their vibrations into an interference pattern that varies from single pitches to noisy multiphonics. As the player's familiarity grows, he or she can quickly attune embodied skills to the tasks prescribed by the score: following behaviours, locating edges, surfing the contours of metastabilities, and being-with the instrument in what Donna Haraway calls "ongoingness," the continuity of things in relationship with one another and life.

As I move the bow and the transient subsides into stable periodic pitch, that resonance is a sonic version of what I describe above as the "slightly-under" of the moving water-in-bowl. Sound too has a meniscus, a surface tension pressed by resonance. Resonance is the hysteresis of the system, holding the just-now-previous pitch in the material vibration and smoothing the way for that same pitch to happen again, while impeding unrelated pitches.[9] That meniscus of resonance is where the system is, where it's stable, and where it wants to stay. But as the bow changes direction again there can be just enough energy in the transient to break that meniscus, to push it over the edge to something else, one of several possible elsewheres. The bow movement can be leaned towards just-too-much in different components of sound, all of which have boundaries open to exploration, such as: transitions within a harmonic series from one partial to another; transitions between voiced and unvoiced sound, across the boundary where the bow's stick-slip action is enough to produce periodic vibration; or transition between monophonic and multiphonic sounds.

In the fractal image, magnification at the boundary reveals different-but-the-same structures as the equation traverses scales of self-similarity. Here, Agre's "impossibility of foundations" maps across to the mantra of chaos theory where systems continuously diverge due to "sensitive dependence on initial conditions" (Weisstein 2021). Repetition in a metastable space is the impossibility of foundations: each boundary opens up space for new stabilities and instabilities, and each repetition both stabilises and opens another possibility for new instabilities to explore. The phase-space of the cello is incredibly complex, with many variables being coupled to one another in non-linear ways, and the player's embodied skills are the result of training that mostly seeks to avoid the unpredictable and metastable.

On the prepared cello, the left hand is rarely used (see below for exceptions) and due to the interference of the coupled strings, a wide variety of sound can be produced by bowing in different places and in different ways. Here is the way that I break down the cello behaviours, searching for boundaries and stabilities both in the string segment (the physical space between the bridge and the preparation) and through varied approaches to bow technique: the bow is the transducer of movement and the human is the site of feedback between sensing and acting. The following description proceeds from "first bowing,"

---

8   This is because touching the fingerboard would ground the vibration, stopping the string; essentially it is a double-stop at that point on the strings. By allowing the ring to float, the strings are coupled in such a way to create four string segments (two strings, each one partitioned in two by the ring) all of which are excited when any one of them is bowed.

9   That is, very close pitches and pitches low in the same harmonic series—and near to a favourable formant—tend to be strongly related and may be promoted by the resonance, with others being impeded.

when an experienced cellist is encountering the system initially, through levels of increasing familiarity.

- On first bowing, begin with the boundary between noise and pitch. This is a highly porous boundary where various forms of coloured "pitchy" noise can be produced, but it is characterised by a definite bump when the boundary is crossed from noise to pitch; as the resonance floods in there is a sudden appearance of pitch, which is sometimes very obtrusive. This boundary is not specific to the prepared cello, but the behaviour is amplified here by the unpredictable resonances arising from interferences.

- Once pitches start to emerge, notice that there are fundamentals[10] and non-fundamentals. The string segment can be divided into a mid-segment and two end segments. The mid-segment tends to produce fundamental pitches corresponding to the length of that segment, while the end segments also produce these but are easily pushed into producing harmonics. At the bridge end (sul ponticello playing), as expected these are usually harmonics of the fundamental; however, at the preparation end (sul tasto) these can be harmonics or also be subharmonics derived from string interference: when bowing on or very near to the preparation itself, subharmonics are almost unavoidable.

- Bow-direction: The mid-segment has an unusual boundary where up and down bow strokes produce two different fundamentals. This odd behaviour, once it is "found" by isolating the correct bow technique, is completely consistent in pitch terms; it produces the same two pitches, usually only a few semitones apart. The behaviour is unpredictable and difficult to isolate: once found it can usually be maintained for a while, but if lost it may be hard to retrieve. This behaviour seems to be suppressed by strong non-fundamentals in the end segments, and is less prevalent there.

- Bow-speed/pressure: The baseline speed and pressure for the prepared cello is slow and light; a *pp–ppp* technique works best for me. There is a loose boundary where faster bowing and greater pressure tends to produce harmonics (when playing towards the bridge), and multiphonics when playing in the mid-segment or towards the preparation.

- Monophonic and multiphonic: The general tendency (especially on shorter segments where the preparation is near the end of the fingerboard) is for a constant low-level multiphonic sound where one or more resonances sit behind the prominent monophonic percept; these resonances are perceived separately. With higher pressure this can fuse into a single multiphonic percept. As well as the obvious boundary of multiphonic fusion, there is a more productive boundary in trying to find states (in the phase-space) where single pitches can be isolated.

---

10 Of course with rigorous acoustic analysis it may turn out that these are in fact not fundamentals but actually partials of a low interference tone; but without recourse to that level of analysis I will use *fundamental* because that's what they sound like, and they mostly match the pitch of the equivalent fingered string segment.

· Modifying the system using the left hand: The preparation connects and intersects two adjacent strings to make four string segments coupled into a system. By bowing one string, energy travels through the system recursively to create a single vibration through complex mutual filtering across the four string segments. The left hand can then be applied to modify this system in a variety of ways: stopping a string will shorten one string segment and alter the resonance; stopping with a glissando acts like a subtle filter sweep of interference; harmonic pressure on a segment has a similar effect but interacts with light sul ponticello bowing more; and muting the segment completely removes a component of the overall sound that can allow for focusing on remaining components.

The behaviours above indicate the initial and subsequent levels of exploration of the system, and the basis for compositional thought; both thought-in-action and "offline" thought. Placing the preparation at different positions on the string produces the same behaviours generally but alters the specific performative response. Continued exploration of the system reproduces these boundaries at more fragile levels, but always with the possibility of phenomena emerging in metastable states: as an example, my 2015 piece for violin and electronics (*The Endless Mobility of Listening*) is based on a bowing technique that results in indeterminate harmonics emerging from a drone, these harmonics tended on the whole to be low-order partials (5th, 7th, 9th, maybe 11th or 13th) but at any moment in the performance there was always the possibility of statistically unlikely partials (17th, 19th, even a 23rd in one Canadian performance) emerging. To return briefly to water swirling in a bowl, the compositional questions are about phenomena that can be explored in performance through their emergence in relation to tightly defined contingencies. The score sets up edges and boundaries in relation to physical phenomena, which when explored can lead in various different directions.

This is the beginnings of a compositional material that can lead to multiple different pieces across an ontological spectrum from the representational (reifying the sound phenomena as fixed entities represented through notation and subsequently recreated in performance) to the performative (guiding the player into structured intra-action with instrumental materiality in open-ended performance).[11] My recent music has tended almost exclusively towards the performative, which focuses the compositional act less on the fixed sequencing of events and more on creating open networks of contingencies. This is not to propose a bare dichotomy of open versus closed (which would not stand up to much scrutiny), more to make the point that the site of composition is shifted into a different stratum. Here the compositional thought is primarily about where the contingency lies in the instrument's phase-space (an easy place to reach or a hard place?), how open it is (what is the range of likely and unlikely outcomes?), what the ratio of stable to unstable spaces is, how they are connected, and whether there are fixed beginning and end points.

---

11 A key influence on my thinking on performative ontology is from philosophy of science (see Pickering 1995).

All these questions are part of the construction of a labyrinth where decisions happen performatively across the combined agencies of the player-instrument assemblage.

This at least is the ideal: material things have their own limits. While a fractal is infinitely emergent, an instrument eventually reaches physical limits where the interaction of bow and string can go no further; thus, part of the compositional process is a question of the richness of the system, the possibilities for variation in recursion. This decision is tied in some ways to the technical question of whether the phenomena in question are of an order of contingency that is within the window of human perception and action—for example, avoiding phenomena that happen too quickly for a human to react to in performance, or that are too low or high-frequency to be meaningfully parsed as pitches.

As an example of one composition that has emerged so far as an instantiation of this technique, I turn to my piece *The whole is encountered by going further into the parts* (2019–20) for contrabass prepared with string-coupling rings, which was written for Christopher Williams. While my research was initially on prepared cello, the ideas transferred quite readily to bass, with Christopher as an ideal collaborator due to his experience as an improviser and with open forms and open notation in experimental music (see Williams 2016). The piece is a text score, outlining a performance technique (interaction with the behaviours of the prepared instrument) and an open formal scheme defined around the interaction of performance technique and the contingent materiality of the instrument. The piece also uses a physical meditation as part of the rehearsal process—more on this later. This is the opening of the score:

> This piece is built on cycles of repetition and change driven by feedback between player and instrument. An instrument made unstable by preparations that pass energy from one string into its neighbor, creating interference patterns that the player enters into.
>
> Cycles happen at many scales.
>
>> Event-level cycles of slowly bowing back and forth to reveal stable sounds; drones of single pitches or pitch-timbre-complexes, or repeating patterns of pitches that emerge from interference.
>>
>> Phrase-level cycles of stability and instability as drones and patterns are disrupted by small but constant change.
>>
>> Section-level cycles of changing environments. Moving between strings differently prepared, and living now in the consequences of a previous cycle's activity. (McLaughlin 2020)

Compositionally speaking, this sets up the different levels of player agency and contingency (as material agency) (see McLaughlin, forthcoming) as both points and strata of decision-making in performance. In the score, event-level cycles are mostly human-agentic as the player chooses materials to work with, while the material may specify exactly what happens in that space. The player, instead of controlling the instrument works "with" the particular instrumental state or behaviour that emerges, aiming for a state but being responsive to contingencies, the nature of which may influence the player to stay or move on. Here the player and the material can both make decisions about ongoingness. For example, will the player decide to step out of a material that is too stable (or too unstable, depending on what the score directs), or will the material refuse to be what the player wants, forcing a change? The score directs the player to find stabilities at this level, which are then put in tension at the next level. Above this, phrase-level cycles are largely material-agentic, with the player following a quasi-mechanistic process of making small incremental changes to find tipping points where the material breaks into a new state. The stable states of the phrase-level pattern are moved across the topology of the instrumental phase-space until they hit a boundary. Being-with and ongoingness are still active and present in the form of what Haraway calls response-ability (2016, 28), which, translated into this context, I posit as the player being aware of and responsive to where the instrument wants to go. The player is always present and attentive to the instrument for the aural and haptic cues that there may be other spaces to move to, snakes and ladders in the contrabass phase-space.

At the macro-structural section-level, the response-ability (Haraway's pun on "responsibility" that places the weight of the word on our actions, our response) outlined above steps a little back from "being-with" the instrument so that the player can make human decisions to sculpt the shape of interactions across the piece, to choose what aspects of the piece the player wishes to be "with." The score outlines options for "transitions" and "interventions" as structural gambits. Interventions are high-level variations in texture, such as adding pizzicato open strings as an internal accompaniment, or going against the main method of the piece by sustaining a single sound without change for a long time. Transitions are part of the main method of ongoingness of variation and repetition in the piece by starting again. Transitions begin the form of event and phrase cycles again in a new and different materiality, where the same initial conditions might produce different outcomes. Transitions mostly involve the player making changes that the instrument could not change on its own, such as crossfading (through a double-stop) to bowing a different string, or moving the preparation to a different point on the string. Unlike phrase-level movement across the phase-space, which is looking for a tipping point to respond to, transitions are a complete reset of the performative space where the player must re-enter being-with a new instrument. Of course, over both the micro-time of a single performance and the macro-time of a lifetime's practice, the player comes to know the instrument behaviours; but the compositional artifice that I strive to get right is that the piece will always offer new interactions, a richness where contingency and response-ability work in tandem. Like our relationships with animals and friends, we are always in a process of getting to know.

This takes my commentary on this piece full circle, back to the epistemology of practice and bringing the player into the world of the piece. The score contains instructions for technique and the application of that technique in structuring contingency. Additionally, there is a rehearsal technique described for engaging with the piece away from the instrument. The player is asked to engage in a simple practice of drawing:

> As part of the practice-regime, make drawings of cycles. On a large sheet of paper, draw a continuous line that moves in overlapping circles. Each new circle should pass through the first one at the same point. Now try again but crossing the first circle at two or more points. Keep drawing continuously until knots emerge, stable points in the wayfaring curves, responding to the constraints of rules and materiality unfolding in time. (McLaughlin 2020)

Figure 7.1.

Over many years of engaging with materiality, my notational practice has vacillated between approaches that place the weight of communication on different mediums. I think I am only now starting to find what works for me. Initially I often relied on instructional text to tell the player what to do (and what not to do), but this usually needed me to demonstrate to clear up misunderstanding that lay below the level of prescribed actions. Symbolic and graphic approaches offered more intuitive paths for the player but often at the expense of clarity. More recent pieces have been more successful by combining instructional and poetic text that afford both clarity and the sensuous connection to the materiality at the core of the piece. The inclusion of a separate-but-connected physical practice in this piece sets up an analogy for the piece in a different medium, an additional path to connecting the player, instrument, and score that roots the piece in a practice of doing, without closing down interpretations.

This approach is indebted to similar approaches, such as those of Jennifer Walshe and Cassandra Miller. Walshe's THIS IS WHY PEOPLE O.D. ON PILLS (2004) asks the player to "learn to skateboard, however primitively" in preparation for the piece; however, the piece itself does not involve skateboarding (quoted in d'Heudieres 2015). Performer Louis d'Heudieres describes this as a way of changing perception that resonates entirely with my line drawing:

Figure 7.1. Excerpt from *The whole is encountered by going further into the parts*, for contrabass prepared with string-coupling rings (McLaughlin 2020).

> the activity itself requires you to engage differently with the environment around
> you. An incline is no longer just an incline; it's an opportunity. A strip of smooth
> tarmac has a certain feel; a cobbled alley isn't going to be particularly pleasant;
> wood is fast, rubber is slow, grass is an injury-safe sanctuary for practising ollies. You
> go around spotting these different zones where different types of movement and
> behaviour are possible, earmarking that spot for speed, or that one for smoothness,
> or that one for attempting a trick. (d'Heudieres 2015)

This concept of "opportunity" is key in responsive performance where contingencies in the instrument become pathways not simply to new sounds, but new structural connections.

In Cassandra Miller's recent work she uses a form of embodied practice in her composition that she refers to as "automatic singing." The technique references Robert Ashley's "automatic writing" as a method of distancing and opening up intuition in a context of "mimicking and transformation" (Miller 2018, 38). Miller describes it as:

> listening (in headphones) to a recording while attempting to sing-along to that
> recording in real time, often while distracted by a mental task such as a body-scan
> meditation. The resulting audio is then recorded, holding the potential for further
> soundings and listenings. . . . I am making an utterance that is unique to myself on
> that day at that time, and with the new knowledge learned in each previous iteration.
> To sing "along" does not imply copying, quoting, or stealing, but instead implies
> a togetherness, an accord, an attunement; a listening, an empathetic physical
> response, and—originating from that response—a participating, an expressing
> alongside. (Miller 2018, 37–39)

Miller's technique, while superficially different to my own, is strongly connected as an embodied act that relies on the performer attuning him- or herself in a space of constraint and contingency to produce new knowledge by moving recursively, repeating the same movements in an unstable space—composition as a series of decision paths through a network of ideas and materialities that mutually constrain and constitute themselves.

The remainder of this chapter will transpose the ideas discussed above onto composition for clarinet, where the same concerns apply but unfold in a different way due to differences between the instruments.

String instruments are fairly predictable in that they produce a reliable harmonic series with indeterminacies largely relegated to extremes of sound production, to the extent that I needed to use preparations to make the instrument more inharmonic and increase the size and richness of the contingent space. Clarinets are in some ways the opposite of this since they are inherently inharmonic and contingent, with indeterminacies lurking just outside the edge of even the best player's technique. No preparations are needed for the clarinet,[12] but the shift in technical expectations for the clarinettist is arguably steeper than that of the cellist; since clarinet technique needs to work harder to avoid contingencies, working those contingencies back into performance

---

12 Though I have done some experiments in this area with clarinettist Heather Roche, the results of which
     will be disseminated as part of the Garden of Forking Paths project in 2021.

technique is more difficult. In terms of the compositional work outlined above, the two instruments are similar because they afford sound production that is continuous and also continuously alterable. Additionally, both afford multiple simultaneous resonances that can interact, but the instruments tend to produce a low number of simultaneous resonances, making them manageable and traversable yet still rich. The cello preparation couples across two strings to produce (usually) two strong resonances and related harmonics; it also produces the subharmonic, but this is mostly only active at one end of the segment and doesn't seem to interact strongly. Similarly, the clarinet tends to favour multiphonics where two strong resonances interact, and like the cello preparation there is a more-or-less traceable path between these resonances as separate but entwined, and as completely fused. My recent research on the Garden of Forking Paths project[13] aims to bring to light the technical mechanics underpinning these clarinet phenomena in ways that composers and performers can better understand the systems and their indeterminacies.

How does composition happen on the clarinet? In this case I will present two cases with different initial conditions.

Starting with the known: Play long and slow a standard monophonic fingering on the clarinet such as the chalumeau register C4 (transposed). Play the note long, and listen inside to its spectrum, bringing individual strong partials into perception: be "co-present" with the sound (Manning and Massumi 2014, 5). Using the standard techniques of overblowing, play through the available harmonics of the fingering. All the work here is done by the mouth as a complex interaction of variables in what I will call production technique—an umbrella term for the variable-system that includes embouchure position/pressure/bite, tongue position, breath speed/pressure/angle, throat-tuning, and so on—and the specific position of all these variables required to produce each harmonic is a point (of varying narrowness) on the phase-space of the clarinet. In learning these techniques, the clarinettist learns to separate these points to be confident in technique—performative security in knowing that you won't land between the points and make an error. **Now, as gently as possible, tack away from the stable point until something else emerges, and stabilise the two as a multiphonic. Explore between these points to find new points and strata of interaction, different levels of balance and imbalance.** Each new breath breaks the system and perturbs the delicate setting of the body's parameters; but equally, each new breath and resetting reinforces the technique of finding that point. Begin again on a stable tone, sustained and steady. **Gently slide a finger off any hole—as slightly as possible, and without altering any other parameters. Listen for change. Don't compensate pre-emptively. Allow resonances to slosh towards the edge of the spectrum; concentrate on the meniscus. Whether change is fast or slow, support where the instrument wants to go. Try again. Alter the movement of the finger and the focus of production. Where do stabilities and instabilities emerge?** What is the terrain of the phase-space here, and there, and between? What can be known and learned and sedimented, and what will always be contingent?

---

13 See https://forkingpaths.leeds.ac.uk/.

Starting with the unknown: Invent a fingering (or distort a known fingering) and excite the air column. There are compositional decisions here: to blow as though this was a chalumeau pitch or an altissimo? To apply a known bodily configuration of production technique to an unknown topology is to begin in alienation. **Listen and be with the instrument in sounding. Follow and support emerging resonances. Push into different corners of the phase-space with embodied techniques.** Move across the continua of the terrain, not teleporting from point to point. **Establish the stable points, the key features of the topology. Now start again with a change to the fingering, enter again a new world.**

The relationships here are the same as in the bass piece: materiality, agency, contingency, emergence, and structure all interact at different levels. Composition begins with understanding materiality as behaviours, structuring these as topological relationships, and scoring a schema for emergent structure by productive constraining and aligning of relationships. Macro-structural alterations, like the transitions in the bass piece and the change of fingerings—whether discrete or continuous—create new resonant topologies to explore, effectively resetting the piece. Phrase-level activities can include the process of slowly opening a hole, which can be controlled slowly over several breaths to explore that space. However, slow processes of change are much more difficult in the embouchure and airstream because (a) these mechanisms are internal, knowable only through feel and muscle memory (which requires extended time to build-up), and (b) retaking breath (or circular breathing) is difficult to do without perturbing the system in some way, so the exploration can only happen within a single breath in most cases. This difficulty is easily flipped into an opportunity for compositional structuring by continually parsing, over a sequence of breaths, the same approximate point in phase-space. Such a recursive process produces a range of emergent sounds but with a high probability of revealing many variations on a small set of different outputs; hence, structure is emergent from recursion.

At the event-level, the clarinettist learns the phase-space of the instrument through performative exploration moving between stabilities and instabilities, where the latter are a state of continuous becoming. The player's awareness of the self and the instrument as an assemblage is what Erin Manning and Brian Massumi (2014, 4) refer to as a "dance of attention": "the holding pattern of an immersive, almost unidentifiable set of forces that modulate the event in the immediateness of its coming to expression. Attention not to, but with and toward, in and around." They continue: "A dance of attention is not attentiveness of the human to the environment but attentiveness of the environment to its own flowering, at the very limit where experience and imagination, immediacy and cross-checking, overlap. It is the making-felt of a co-compositional force that does not yet seek to distinguish between human and nonhuman, subject and object, emphasising instead an immediacy of mutual action, an associated milieu of their emergent relation" (ibid., 6). Here, the clarinet and the player are themselves the environment, continuously attentive and immediate. The compositional act is in structuring the potentials and resistances that allow that "co-compositional force" to emerge.

The known fingerings of the clarinet—that is, the core set of fingerings commonly taught, and augmented by individual players' accreted knowledge—and their associated production techniques always offer stable outputs, while deviation from this limited set opens up unpredictable terrain. As previously mentioned, the known spaces of the clarinet are rigorously embedded techniques of the body, while unexplored spaces, lacking this rigorous embedding, are liable to rapid failure if resonances are paired with incompatible production techniques and vice versa. The clarinet is a good example of Deleuze and Guattari's "smooth" and "striated" spaces in action. The known fingerings are striated by the "state," the external system of tempered pitch and uniform timbre imposed by musical convention, and thus "limited by the order of that plane to preset paths between fixed and identifiable points" (Massumi 1987, xiii). The expansive network of not-known fingerings is the smooth space of nomadism, "projective" and "topological" (Deleuze and Guattari 1987, 361), where "space is occupied without being counted," without measurement or grid, only emergent relations (362).[14] This is Deleuze and Guattari's "problem" space, "affective and . . . inseparable from the metamorphoses, generations, and creations within [performance] itself" (362). Productive wayfaring by the player-instrument assemblage in this space requires both the striation of the score and the dance of attention. Composition here corrals forces to be "mutually constitutive"—what Andrew Pickering describes as the "quality of interplay between the state and the nomad" (2009, 160). "The nomad supplies a transformative dynamic, upsetting state formations, which are then reconstituted on a new basis, only to be nomadically disrupted again, and so on. The state adapts to the nomad" (ibid.).

To return to Agre, his "impossibility of foundations" is here transposed into the performative by composing for the player to continuously dig further into the contingent materiality of the instrument as a way of curating emergent structure. The sound work moves erratically between thinking with instruments to instrumentalising their territories as a State of states whose only purpose is to fall apart in unfolding becoming-with: an insistent tendency towards what Cornelius Cardew colourfully characterises as a commitment to "a music which is going wild again" (quoted in Piekut 2014, 774). By beginning with the material phenomena of the instrument, and asking the player to engage by recursively stretching his or her embodied techniques into pure *physis*, can critique be embedded in composition? My hope for this follows Andrew Pickering's performative ontology of the "mangle," that "the world becomes sufficiently full of explicitly and self-consciously decentered practices and their products that an ontology of becoming becomes the natural ontological attitude" (2008, 9).

---

14 [Deleuze and Guattari here paraphrase Boulez (1963, 95–107; 1971, 85–94); the phrase in quotation marks is Deleuze and Guattari's adjusted quotation of Boulez (1963, 107; 1971, 94).—Ed.]

REFERENCES

Agre, Philip E. 1997. *Computation and Human Experience*. Cambridge: Cambridge University Press.

Barad, Karen. 2007. *Meeting the Universe Halfway: Quantum Physics and the Entanglement of Matter and Meaning*. Durham, NC: Duke University Press.

Boulez, Pierre. 1963. *Penser la musique aujourd'hui*. Paris: Gonthier. Translated by Susan Bradshaw and Richard Rodney Bennett as Boulez 1971.

———. 1971. *Boulez on Music Today*. Translated by Susan Bradshaw and Richard Rodney Bennett. London: Faber and Faber. First published as Boulez 1963.

Deleuze, Gilles, and Félix Guattari. 1987. *A Thousand Plateaus: Capitalism and Schizophrenia*. Translated by Brian Massumi. Minneapolis: University of Minnesota Press. First published 1980 as *Mille plateaux: Capitalisme et schizophrénie* (Paris: Minuit).

d'Heudieres, Louis. 2015. "Better Know a Weisslich: Jennifer Walshe's THIS IS WHY PEOPLE O.D. ON PILLS/AND JUMP FROM THE GOLDEN GATE BRIDGE." Weisslich, 29 October 2015. Accessed 6 April 2021. https://weisslich.com/2015/10/29/better-know-a-weisslich-jennifer-walshes-this-is-why-people-o-d-on-pillsand-jump-from-the-golden-gate-bridge/.

Haraway, Donna J. 2016. *Staying with the Trouble: Making Kin in the Chthulucene*. Durham, NC: Duke University Press.

Hui, Yuk. 2019. *Recursivity and Contingency*. London: Rowman & Littlefield International.

Ingold, Tim. 2007. *Lines: A Brief History*. London: Routledge.

Manning, Erin, and Brian Massumi. 2014. *Thought in the Act: Passages in the Ecology of Experience*. Minneapolis: University of Minnesota Press.

Massumi, Brian. 1987. "Translator's Foreword: Pleasures of Philosophy." In Deleuze and Guattari 1987, ix–xv.

McLaughlin, Scott. 2020. *The whole is encountered by going further into the parts*, for contrabass prepared with string-coupling rings. Accessed 6 April 2021. http://lutins.co.uk/scores/mcLaughlin-wholeisencountered-prepared-bass-v1.pdf.

———. Forthcoming. "On Material Indeterminacy." In "Performing Indeterminacy: Experimental Music in Practice," edited by Emily Payne, Martin Iddon, and Philip Thomas, special issue, *Contemporary Music Review*.

Miller, Cassandra. 2018. "Transformative Mimicry: Composition as Embodied Practice in Recent Works." PhD thesis, University of Huddersfield. Accessed 6 April 2021. http://eprints.hud.ac.uk/id/eprint/34998/.

Pickering, Andrew. 1995. *The Mangle of Practice: Time, Agency, and Science*. Chicago: University of Chicago Press.

———. 2008. "New Ontologies." In *The Mangle in Practice: Science, Society, and Becoming*, edited by Andrew Pickering and Keith Guzik, 1–14. Durham, NC: Duke University Press.

———. 2009. "Cybernetics as Nomad Science." in *Deleuzian Intersections: Science, Technology, Anthropology*, edited by Casper Bruun Jensen and Kjetil Rödje, 155–62. Oxford: Berghahn Books.

Piekut, Benjamin. 2014. "Indeterminacy, Free Improvisation, and the Mixed Avant-Garde: Experimental Music in London, 1965–1975." *Journal of the American Musicological Society* 67 (3): 769–824.

Spatz, Ben. 2015. *What a Body Can Do: Technique as Knowledge, Practice as Research*. Abingdon, UK: Routledge.

Weisstein, Eric W. 2021. "Chaos." *Wolfram MathWorld*. Accessed 6 April 2021. https://mathworld.wolfram.com/Chaos.html.

Williams, Christopher. 2016. "Tactile Paths: On and Through Notation for Improvisers." PhD thesis, University of Leiden. Accessed 6 April 2021. http://www.tactilepaths.net/.

Thinking *Liveness* in Performance with Live Electronics

The Need for an Eco-systemic Notion of Agency

Agostino Di Scipio

Music Conservatory of L'Aquila, Italy; "Arts, écologies, transitions" Research Team, Paris

INTRODUCTION

Live performance practices with electroacoustic equipment and digital audio media have grown enormously in number and diversity, as documented by a large body of publications. Here I am concerned with the basic premise those publications seem to share and often leave aside: the alleged "liveness" of highly technologised and mediatised performance. The difficulty is twofold: on the one hand, any attempt to define *live electronic music* is today an increasingly problematic task (Bertolani and Sallis 2016), due to the variety of connotations that have arisen in different social and cultural contexts since the 1960s at least (Bernardini 1986, 61). On the other hand, the notion of *liveness* is itself "historically contingent" (Auslander 2008, 60). Further confusion may also arise from the informal usage of *live* and related terminology, in the ubiquitous and hegemonic discourse of the mass media (live set, live streaming, etc.). In short, by and large, "there is clearly a loss of certainty as to what *live* is any more" (Emmerson 2012a, 10).

In this chapter, I want to try a peculiar and hopefully fruitful approach: I ask, how is one to think *liveness* in live electronic music performance practices? What are these practices telling us about liveness as a topic of larger theoretical interest? (such as discussed in performance studies and media studies [Phelan 1993; Auslander 2008; Schechner 2002; Salter 2010; McCormick 2015]). These are probably just ways to rephrase the more fundamental question, what is *live* in live electronic music? (Emmerson 2012b, 152; Sanden 2013, 87). However, by leaning on various interdisciplinary research efforts and by broadening the range of creative endeavours deemed of direct pertinence, the rephrasing may eventually expand the purport of the subject and suggest new directions for further analysis.

We shall start with a few general remarks and the historical background. Next, we shall move to the main topic and discuss related theoretical implications. Overall, we discuss liveness as an experiential dimension of the agency that can be acknowledged to the techno-cultural assemblage involved in performance, inclusive of interdependent component resources, either human or non-human.

A biological metaphor turned into ecological and technological reality

The adjective *live* is typically used to denote real-time performance practices as different from studio production practices. But it also carries a clear and meaningful metaphorical value, suggestive of the opposition between biological phenomena *in vivo* (experienced by a living entity in real-world conditions) and *in vitro* (experimented on "in the lab," produced and observed in highly formalised, controlled, and protected working conditions). This semantics resonates in languages other than English (e.g., Italian *musica dal vivo*, Spanish *música en vivo*), while it disappears in others (French speakers regularly use the more generic *en direct*).

That metaphorical value is probably worth being recast in a more materially grounded view of the ecology of mediatised performance. It may be taken as referring less to the involvement of musicians or other performing artists, and more to the overall dynamics proper to a larger ensemble of several agents of a different kind, namely to the performance ecosystem (Waters 2007, 2011). The latter can be understood as a composite dispositif or assemblage consisting of mutually responsive components, whose network of interactions gives rise to a collective and hybrid form of agency. Later in this chapter, the notion of *eco-systemic agency* will be introduced, certainly not to provide yet another term of metaphorical value, but to characterise the complex interactional dynamics of the performance ecosystem and its "situatedness" in a material environment irreducible to an abstract or neutral container space. For a performance to be live, the real-space working conditions should be deemed no less crucial than real-time conditions.

The perspective elaborated in these pages is twofold. On the one hand, it approaches liveness with a conceptual framework drawn from studies in cognitive science, particularly as elaborated at the crossroad of cybernetics, biology, and related views in constructivist social science and media ecology (Maturana and Varela 1980; Varela 1979; Latour 1996; Maturana 2002; Hallowell 2009; Clarke and Hansen 2009; Froese 2011). That requires pondering issues of distributed agency in human–machine interaction (Agre 1995; Rammert 2008) and the interplay of situated and distributed action in common labour activities (Quéré 1997; Laville 2000).

On the other hand, I feel it appropriate and urgent to connect the discourse on liveness with broader questions concerning the environmentalisation of technology and the cybernetisation of the world (Hörl 2012, 2013). Live electronic practices are creative instances of contemporary media ecology. As such, they should be specially expressive of the current, widely shared conditions of individual and social life, that is, of the "technological condition" (Hörl 2015). At their best—provided they do not reduce themselves to fuelling the aggressive aestheticisation of mainstream communication media and the fetishisation of the latest "state-of-the-art" devices—live electronic performance practices may eventually define a domain of critical praxis where one asks, what is it like living in today's hyper-technologised world? How do we deal with and dwell in the techno-ecosystems we build for ourselves?[1]

In short, I suggest that live electronic performance practices are instances of artistic research in music (Impett 2016) that creatively explore—and return, in sonic shape—the conditions of the *living* in the face of the historical phenomenon of the becoming-environment of technology (Di Scipio, forthcoming). As such, they may enact forms of critical technical practice (Agre 1997) and "subversive rationalization" (Feenberg 1991; Di Scipio 1997, 1998) bearing on significant aspects of contemporary life, maybe in ways more peculiar and poignant than other forms of critical praxis can.

HISTORICAL BACKGROUND

Let's briefly recall that the rhetoric of liveness in the context of media communications was born in the 1930s, when it first seemed appropriate to distinguish the radio broadcasting of speech and music events ("live broadcast," equivalent to the French *émission en direct* and the German *Direktübertragung*) from the increasingly common practice of playing-back phonographic records ("canned music," typically used in a pejorative sense). In later decades, as new electronic media were integrated in artistic production, *live* eventually came to denote innumerable performative and communicative contexts. A widely accepted implication was that live music, made and heard "immediately," represents a more genuine experience than music played back from fixed audio media.

Yet, *live* has never really meant "immediate," with the sense "without technical mediations" (save in the rhetoric and the advertising of popular entertainment industries). On the contrary, this terminology has always referred to very specific technical and cultural mediations (Sanden 2013, 34), with multiple technological layers and related engineering competences. Today, in an age when common life appears by and large to be structured by and imbued with the immanent logic of electronic and telematic networks, it is reasonable to doubt whether there is really any ontological difference between *live* and *mediatised*: indeed, "live performance . . . itself is a product of media technologies" (Auslander 1999, 25).

---

1 *Techno-ecosystem* is a term borrowed from ecosystem design and engineering (Odum 2001; Prominski 2007).

Live electronic music, live electronics

It is usually agreed (e.g., Sallis et al. 2018, 1) that the expression *live electronic music* was coined by John Cage in 1962 (with reference to his *Cartridge Music*, 1960) and then adopted for the most radical strands of experimental music that emerged in subsequent years, both in North America[2] and Europe.[3] Later, the shorter *live electronics* was also to become frequent, at least among practitioners. The latter is indeed a very telling expression, in that it assigns *live* directly to the *electronics*, not to the music or the performers. The semantic shift can hardly be without reason.

Taking advantage of portable sound-synthesis and -processing equipment (ranging from small-sized analogue synthesisers to various cheaper or self-built circuitries), those earliest endeavours aimed to take electronically generated music "out of the studio" (Chadabe 1997, 81) and to "animate" (Pousseur 1976, 243)[4] creative designs that were otherwise limited to fixed audio media (tape music) and were perceived by many as laboratory experiments (however wrongly). They ended up "vitalizing the work/environment relationship" (Centore 2011, 63). Partly inspired by coeval trends in the visual arts, many musicians started exploring a more direct relationship to the place(s) where their work was presented, and eventually devised site-specific sound installations in spaces other than concert halls and auditoria (art galleries, industrial plants, archaeological sites, gardens, living rooms, etc.). One could say, with some caution, that sound installations and other sound art practices emerged out of the earliest live electronic endeavours, between the late 1960s and early 1970s (Di Scipio 2017; Saladin 2017). That is clear from the work of such representative figures as Max Neuhaus, David Tudor, and Alvin Lucier, which was often poised between music and sound installation in those years.

In later decades, as computer music systems and digital audio technologies were increasingly accessible and interactively manageable, the term *live electronics* has come to be used for an increasing number of trends in contemporary music and the sound arts. On the one hand, there are new forms of chamber music pairing musical instruments with real-time digital signal processors—a repertoire that has grown ever larger since the early 1980s.[5] On the other, there is the huge body of more informal, improvisational approaches, often using handmade or hacked hardware (Collins 2009) and free software.[6] In recent years, these two general orientations have regularly

---

2 As in the work of Gordon Mumma, David Tudor, David Behrman, the Sonic Arts Union, Composers Inside Electronics, and many others.

3 One may think of Karlheinz Stockhausen's *Mikrophonie I* (1964), of course; however, we should not forget other relevant yet less well-known proposals by Hugh Davies, Franco Evangelisti, Mario Bertoncini, MEV (Musica Elettronica Viva), Gentle Fire, and so on.

4 Unless otherwise indicated, translations are my own.

5 Well-known examples include Luigi Nono's late works (technical support from the Experimentalstudio, Freiburg) and a few of Pierre Boulez's late works (technical support from IRCAM, Paris).

6 Examples could be drawn from the work of composers and sound artists of different generations and different aesthetic horizons, such as David Behrman, Nicolas Collins, Ron Kuivila, John Bowers, Owen Green, Pedro Rebelo, Andrea Valle, and many others. Recent proposals include improvisational approaches using "audio commons" (Stolfi et al. 2018).

crossed and been mixed with extended playing techniques and "augmented" instruments.[7]

Overall, this makes for a wide territory of performance approaches. This territory becomes even wider when considering practices closer to more popular languages and communication contexts.

The techno-cultural quantum leap from instrument to environment

The expression *live electronic music* is sometimes used to also refer to certain bold musical efforts dating from the earlier decades of the twentieth century, particularly chamber music works scored for electronic instruments.[8] While this usage is widely accepted (Mumma 1975; Manning 1985; Bernardini 1986; Battier 1999), in the present chapter I consider it misleading. Not because of the overt anachronism, and certainly not because of a will to decrease the historical and aesthetic relevance of those early works, but in order to avoid infiltrating the discussion of the inherently mediated dimension of liveness with conventional views of technology implicated in music scored for and played with *instruments*, albeit electronic ones—namely, technical objects having a fixed, standard functional design that are meant to match well-established cultural expectations as to what music really is about.

Instrumental theories of technology have for a long time been of very limited use (Feenberg 1991). They can't help us, today, make a very necessary link between the material conditions of music-making and the hyper-technologised environments of individual and social life. A shift in focus from "composing for new instruments" (Appleton 1989) to "composing the instruments" (before also composing for and with them) (Davies 1981; Schnell and Battier 2002) is appropriate to secure a more substantivist view and bridge artistic praxis with critical theories of technologies (Di Scipio 1998; Impett 1998; Hamman 2002). But the shift needs to be stretched even farther, fostering novel views of "instrumentality" and "instrumental agency" (Magnusson 2019) and promoting an awareness that creative practices always take place in construed, artificial environments, structured by multiple technical and cultural mediators (Hennion and Latour 1993; Assis 2018, 2019).[9]

Therefore, of special relevance for a discussion of liveness are those live electronic practices where the artist's own appropriation and making of technological configurations forms a substantial part of the creative process. Such practices shape *dispositifs* that specify singular sound works (Baranski 2009;

---

7   As in the work of, among others, Jonathan Impett, Michelangelo Lupone, Simon Waters, Giovanni Verrando, and Giorgio Klauer.

8   Examples range from Paul Hindemith's *7 Triostücke* (for three trautoniums, 1930) to Darius Milhaud's Suite for ondes Martenot and piano (1933), from Percy Grainger's *Free Music 1* (version for four theremins, 1936) to Olivier Messiaen's *Fêtes des belles eaux* (for six ondes Martenots, 1937). The music of the Futurists' intonarumori can also be included.

9   Pre-Second World War examples consistent with a post-instrumentalist view of technology can be found in the appropriation and *detournement* of gramophonic devices, as in certain proposals by the very young Stefan Wolpe (Berlin, 1920s) and in John Cage's *Imaginary Landscape No. 1* (for two record players, large Chinese cymbal, and piano, 1939).

Panaccio-Letendre 2011) and that are inherent outcomes of music-making (Magnusson 2019, 57). They remind us that music is not just about creating sonic structures and auditory experiences of peculiar aesthetic interest, but also about creating the means by which those structures and experiences materialise (Di Scipio 1998).

The living *and the performance ecosystem*

Confronting the question of liveness, we ask, Under what conditions can a dynamical assemblage of different resources (including, among others, human, mechanical, electroacoustic, and software resources) operate so that it can be experienced as a living process and described as a live event? What is there, in its operation, that can ever be felt as *living*? We need to address the fragile and precarious coupling of multiple human and non-human agents,[10] and the dynamics born of their situated exchanges and interactions.

It is often assumed (Small 1998; Emmerson 2007; Sanden 2013) that the crucial factor of liveness is the physical involvement of humans (instrumentalists, vocalists, technical assistants, "electronic musicians," etc.) capable of acting in real time *upon*, *in between*, and *in control of* various technical objects (sound-making and sound-processing devices), with the postulate that they do not resort to previously recorded audio or control signals. This view is most valuable in that it clearly relates performance to direct bodily action and emotional experience, viewed in fact as essential factors of liveness in performance studies. There is a tacit and taken-for-granted implication that the involvement of human beings provides the performance ecosystem with a source of causal processes and agency.

However, for a performance—not a performer—to be *live*, human action is perhaps a necessary but not yet sufficient factor. More decisive seems to be the enactment of a more comprehensive interactional dynamics, inclusive of other-than-human agents. Music—as composed, performed, listened to, and commented upon—always entails techno-cultural assemblages of peculiar "epistemic complexity" (Assis 2014), where representations, information, and action are materially distributed (shared, spread, or deliberately relinquished) across different kinds of mediators. In live electronic performance, that epistemic complexity involves a possibly larger array of mediators, and gives rise to thoroughly technologised cause-and-effect chains where "interactive contingency" is a more critical dimension of performance than "instrumental causality" (Rammert 2008, 65). One may say that the "live" character of performance concerns a larger "ecology of action" (Morin 2007), with the "circular causality" (von Foerster 2003) or the "tangled causality" (Sève 2005, 62) engendered by the multiplicity of lines of causation actually involved.

---

10   To be clear, one can only speak of *non-human* agents by deliberately omitting (maybe provisionally) the culture-specific and thus genuinely human element proper to any technical system and to any built space.

Of central interest is that performance reveals human actions and machinic processes as dynamically coupled to and weighted against the spatial niche where the performance actually takes place. The resultant sound events bear audible traces of that coupling and that weighting. The liveness of performing—together with its liveliness and its livelihood—stems from the perceptible interdependency of heterogeneous agencies, affecting one another in ways *relative to real time and real space circumstances.*

The here and now, real space, and real time

In this regard, I should emphasise that *live* is not the same as *real time* (Emmerson 1994, 2012a). Computer music institutions have always customarily spoken of "real-time computers" rather than "live electronics," assuming the technologically-determined criterion of higher and higher computational speed in the description of performative resources.[11] However, the notion of *real time* is not in itself a sufficient criterion for liveness; rather, it needs to be integrated with a notion of *real space*, that is, with the audible presence of the material site of performance, including its physical, social, and cultural connotations (acoustics, logistics, various facilities, etc.).

Sanden (2013, 34) contrasts "temporal liveness" and "spatial liveness," noting that "they are not always considered interdependent [as they appeared to be in Walter Benjamin's concept of *aura*]." Still, for any action to literally take place, it takes time: the conceptual separation should not imply that the two can be split in phenomenological reality. It seems crucial to focus on the indivisibility of time-space coordinates in lived experience, in fact often evoked by the common language expression *the here and now*—moulded after the Latin *hic et nunc*. Clearly, "in the very heart" of a performance,[12] everything happens within and across a larger ecology of actions and perceptions that cannot be abstracted from a particular physical space of one's own material and cultural connotations.

When readying and testing sound equipment in preparation for a performance, it is customary to set it up in a way to block or at least minimise the side-effects of the local acoustics and to avoid, as much as possible, a number of technical artefacts (circuit noise, sonic halo, excessive audio feedback, interfering radio signals, etc.). This is of course necessary to correctly couple the electroacoustic infrastructure to the particular room acoustics. This is also like bending the given space to behave in a way closer to a studio (albeit a provisionally installed studio). The live character of performance, however, stems from a direct confrontation with the contingencies of the particular situation, from an attitude that deals in constructive ways with less-than-ideal circumstances and working conditions. Liveness testifies to the impossibility of perfectly

---

11   For example, at IRCAM (as well as in other French institutions) it has long been like that, from the early 1980s (Manoury 2007) to recent years (Cont 2012; Bonardi 2015). Tristan Murail is among the few composers, in his country, talking of "musique électronique *live*" (Murail 1991; Béranger 2009). On the semantics of *temps réel* and related connotations, see Barkati (2009).

12   The English "in the very heart" is equivalent to the French *dans le vif* and the Italian *nel vivo*.

integrating resources and disentangling intentional action from contingent (and contagious) factors: it springs from the ability of agents to maintain positive exchanges among themselves *qua* agents situated in—and therefore mediated by—the local environment. Note that this concerns not only *human* agents, but more heterogeneous resources and their interactional dynamics.

The *live* character thus implies that contingencies born of the real space are not perceived just as inevitable imperfections and annoyances one has to live with, but as opportunities for a productive coexistence and connivance (complicity). In a live performance, sound and music are born not simply *notwithstanding* real and thus less-than-ideal conditions, but also *thanks* to them.[13] Performance is when sound and music elude reification and can be finally perceived less "in themselves," independent of source and place (*objets sonores*, signal files, etc.), and more as "relational events," that is, belonging to the shared and interrelated conditions of lived experience (Di Scipio 2012, 2014).

Note that, during a performance, the sounding environment always includes both the sound delivered by performers and equipment, and a variety of incidental, random sonorities coming from different sources (including the audience). The latter are typically denoted as "noise" only to remark that they are not part of the intended sound fabric. Still, in real-time and real-space performance conditions, the local space is bound to vibrate from wanted as well as unwanted events, and it is not always fine to say that the latter are really foreign to the performance.

No matter how virtual the space evoked and represented by the performance of a particular work is, the very act of synthesising such a space takes place in real, material, and shared environments. In this regard, liveness certainly lies not in apparent cause-and-effect relationships, mimicked in sound and heard as realistic yet purely illusory (Emmerson 2007, 93), but in the cause-and-effect chains situated in the lived—not the represented—space. In any case, it can be argued that one learns more about liveness from practices where real-space conditions are not concealed or surrogated, or where strategies of virtual liveness—and "artificial life"—are deconstructed.

The emphasis on real-space working conditions implies a peculiar ethos: it demands ad hoc empirical arrangements that are bound to remain *relative* and even poor in technical efficiency, but are also meant to be *relational* in scope and purport. That is at odds, quite evidently, with the *absolute* reliability requested and expected of efficient and powerful engineering standards, and with a general view of modern electronic media as a technology empowering us to suspend or augment phenomenological reality. In its living dimension, performance stages and makes audible the relational and the relative even when it is pervasively structured by multiple technological layers, or perhaps exactly because of that.

To be clear, these annotations to the contingent and situated dimension of live performance should not be taken as tacitly referring to improvisational

---

13 Turning technical problems into opportunities is a recurrent *topos* in the history of (not only experimental) music (Di Scipio 2017).

musical approaches only. They should not be considered alien in the context of more deterministic approaches where music performing is score-centred and bound to follow precise musical notations. We are trying to think liveness as a topic of broader theoretical relevance, of course, independent of the discourse of specific musical aesthetics.

The performance ecosystem as operative unit

A more detailed illustration of the perspective taken here would need to include many other issues and would require too lengthy a detour into methodological and theoretical matters (a preliminary tour de force is attempted in Di Scipio [forthcoming, 9–84]). Anyway, within the limits of this chapter, the main direction should be clear: my observations point out that liveness in highly technologised performance contexts refers to the phenomenology of a composite and heterogeneous operative unit whose partial components reveal themselves interdependent (mutually dependent) in their operations. The operative unit includes

- an ensemble of different (human, mechanical, electroacoustic, and digital) resources, understood as a *system*;[14] and
- a site (room, hall, court, or other) where that ensemble is installed and made to work, understood as the *environment* for the system and its components.[15]

The unit is incomplete until the *system* and *site* are materially coupled with each other, that is, until the very moment of

- performance, understood as the process (time-wise) and situation (space-wise) through which *system* and *site* materialise a larger and autonomous dynamical system.

Performance is when *system* and *site* bring forth a greater operative unit whose peculiar *agency* is not reducible to its individual components. Because both *system* and *site* may include several components and subcomponents, their coupling will give rise to an intricate ecology of local and global interchanges, a meshwork of feedback lines across multiple cause-and-effect chains. To emphasise the interrelatedness and situatedness, this manifold but integrated operative unit is called here a *performance ecosystem*—a term elsewhere utilised with reference to a certain number of creative sound practices (Waters 2007; see also Di Scipio 2003, 2008; Waters 2013; Green 2013; and several contributions in Waters 2011).

---

14 In the etymological sense of *σύστημα*, that is, an ensemble or assemblage of parts working together in close functional connection—the same as the Latin *compositus*, a composite of several parts. A working definition of *system* in general system theory is "a complex of interacting elements" (von Bertalanffy 1968, 55). Living organisms are "open systems," that is, systems interacting with their environment (ibid., 32). The current state of any single element in a system is a function of the single element's earlier states, of the current state of any other element, and of the current state of the environment.

15 A working definition of *environment* is an ensemble of systems other than the particular systemic unit under consideration, but structurally coupled to it through energetic or informational exchanges, and acting as its medium. Not everything in the surrounding space is part of a system's environment, as in fact the latter constitutes the *milieu spécifique*—the medium specific to the particular system.

In its operation, the performance ecosystem is a *processual unit*: each single interaction among any two components or groups of components has, sooner or later, one or more effects (even missing effects could set the conditions for subsequent exchanges to take place). Furthermore, the performance ecosystem also defines a *spatial unit*: the effects of each single interactional event will spread across the ecosystem, thus affecting either concurrent or subsequent interactions to some lesser or greater degree. Multiple chains of causes and effects will eventually ensue, depending on component typology as well as on local and global feedback connections among components.

Furthermore, our operative unit will reveal itself *performant* inasmuch as it shows minimal and yet peculiar cognitive capacities: in a way perhaps reminiscent of a biological system (organism), the performance ecosystem as a whole can keep itself in operation and try to fulfil its goals only so far as it can somehow sense the environment and act upon it. This cognitive potential implies that it also construes for itself a body of observations about the environment, and about itself as an entity belonging to that environment. In which case, the performance ecosystem should be viewed as an "observing" and "self-observing" system (von Foerster 1960, 2003). The live or living character proper to its dynamics could be traced to its cognitive autonomy, that is, to its peculiar *agency*—the ability to take action in and with the environment.

The question is posed, where exactly are we to locate the very means by which an actual instance of a performance ecosystem can sense and act in the environment? Were one to connect liveness solely to the participant performers, the answer would be straightforward: the *locus* of cognition and agency lays in the involved human resources, constituting de facto an incredibly complex sensorial interface between machine and environment. However, in a composite, highly technologised performance ecosystem, it seems reasonable to say that agency is rather distributed across a number of distinct but interlaced component layers.

The performance ecosystem as bio-cognitive unit

We need now to reconnect our analysis to the biological metaphor implicit in talking of *live performance*. Assuming a constructivist epistemological perspective, we might finally take the metaphor more literally than figuratively, and try to work it out in the conceptual framework of neo-cybernetics (Clarke and Hansen 2009), where constructivist social science (Latour 1996; Mancilla 2011) meets system biology (Bich 2012; Bich and Arnellos 2012) and post-computational cognitive science (Varela, Thompson, and Rosch 1991; Barbaras 2002; Thompson 2009; Froese 2011). Common to those different research directions is an understanding of cognition as a biological phenomenon, and as a process of central interest for the phenomenology of embodied experience and enactive perception. The epistemological posture consists essentially in asking how information and knowledge about the surrounding world are construed by taking part in a shared world, rather than retrieved and analysed as symbolic representations of an objective, external world.

Interesting research work in the area has focused on modelling entities described as "minimally-cognitive systems" (Etxeberria, Merelo, and Moreno 1994; Barandiaran and Moreno 2006; van Duijn, Keijzer, and Franken 2006), where cognition is investigated as it happens at the level of the simplest and most negligible biological organisms (e.g., unicellular organisms such as bacteria, protozoans, some algae, some fungi, etc.). Even the most trifling, tiny living forms feature some kind of sensory-motor system. Or better, they *are* materially constituted as sensory-motor systems. They implement more or less intricate instances of the fundamental *action-perception loop* mechanism by which a cognitive system is able to perceive the environment in order to act upon it—being, at the same time, itself perceived and acted upon by the environment, that is, by other entities in the surroundings (Maturana and Varela 1980; Stewart 1992, 1993; Maturana 2002). The most trifling, tiny living entity senses changes happening in its contiguous space and acts accordingly. Or better, it takes action in order to sense the environment and senses in order to take action in it. Action and perception are looped through the environment. With a formula, *life = cognition* (Stewart 1992; Thompson 2009, 81). A living organism looks for food (energy) in order to get to know the environment, but it needs to explore and know the environment (information) in order to feed itself. The recursive dynamic is captured less well in terms of *interaction* than it is in terms of *structural coupling*, in the technical sense of a permanent, bidirectional connection providing the interface for the reciprocal determination of a system and the nearest environment (*oikos*).

The agency proper to a particular bio-cognitive unit is forged through a whole history of specific system-environment exchanges: it emerges in the co-evolution and the "concretion" (mutual creation) of system and environment (Jonas 1966). By bringing itself around, in fact, a bio-cognitive unit also transforms the surroundings into its specific vital space, into its "own" environment. With a formula, *life = cognition = building and maintenance of an environmental niche*. Therefore, however minimal and trivial, a bio-cognitive unit is an autonomous system. It is somehow capable of taking care of itself and of its spatial niche on the basis of a record of past system–environment exchanges, thereby developing a sense of self and, jointly, what we might call its *culture*. Such is, in overly short and rough terms, the overall process by which agency emerges in a living entity.[16]

Needless to say, any particular music performance ecosystem is, however simple and basic, a hugely complex kind of autonomous system. Nonetheless, in an operative sense, it is essentially a system able to sense the local (sonic) environment and cause changes in it.[17] This is because it has perceptual and cognitive mechanisms, coupled with the environment through sensors and effectors. In typical cases, it is performing artists who provide the ecosystem with such

16   In a different but related line of thinking, Gilbert Simondon (1958) coined the term *individuation*. In current social science research one may talk of a "situated process of subjectivation" (Rebughini 2014). One can say that "subjectivation"—the construction of an autonomous subject—is not an individual's affair but an intersubjective, social one, that is, "distributed" across multiple social relations.

17   Henceforth, by writing "local (sonic) environment," I suggest that *environment* is to be taken as *mainly* but not necessarily *only* related to sound.

mechanisms, being of course inherently equipped with highly trained motor systems coupled with highly sensible auditory systems via complex neural networks. As expert practitioners, performers are able to coordinate audition and bodily action in incredibly refined ways. (Listeners, too, seem to be able to do so, when their response to a music performance turns from neutral *attendance* to true *participation* in the performative act).

In mediatised performance, and certainly in many instances of live electronic music, technical resources are often themselves (made) able to change their real-time functional process, either adapting them to other performative agencies (e.g., instrumental gestures and/or the sounds they make) or otherwise driving their operations depending on other events in the environment. Audio devices sense (via microphones or other devices known as *sensors*) specific features of the surrounding environment (sonic or other), analyse them (e.g., with some form of data processing), and regulate their internal process accordingly, in their turn causing minor or major changes in the environment through special effectors (signal converters, loudspeakers—devices also known as *actuators*). Their operative autonomy has the effect of laying down the material conditions for further changes due to the actions of performers or other technical apparatus (and listeners, of course).[18]

Acknowledging the agency of technical systems is not at all surprising, today: it often appears reasonable and normal, as in references to complex and maybe "intelligent" algorithmic models of human agency or other fully automated technical procedures. However, it must be clear that I am not necessarily assuming any artificial intelligence in the present discussion. I only mean to value the agentive role of sound equipment and related devices, in virtue of the nonlinear, limiting, transformative effects of their electro-acoustic transductions and the ergonomics of their material design—and to emphasise the increasing recourse to adaptive and self-regulating control mechanisms in analogue and digital electronics, which are indeed susceptible to turning mere *objects* into *agents*. Be it purposely designed or implicitly inscribed in the technical code, a kind of collective machinic agency ensues as multiple devices are made to affect one another's functionality in a "multi-agent system" (Weiss 1999)—independent of whether they also include "artificial intelligences," internet bots, and the like.[19]

---

18 Needless to say, *autonomy* (self-regulating behaviour) is not to be mistaken for *automation*. Automata are devices that operate unsupervised thanks to deterministic controls, independent of real-time and real-space contingencies. Very complex automata (including pre-AI robots and innumerable mechanical automata dating back to ancient times and the Middle Ages [Losano 1991]) can mimic animal behaviour in their exterior appearances, maybe also reacting to external events, but can modify neither their process nor the environment on the basis of their interactions: they do not include the functional analogies that specify living systems as cognitive systems, and thus remain essentially *allonomic*—as opposed to *autonomic* or, indeed, autonomous.

19 Among the early instances of this machinic agency one could include Gordon Pask's *A Colloquy of Mobiles* (1968), a mixed-media installation where a small network of multiple electromechanical agents manifests a larger, collective kind of intelligent behaviour. For other recent and not-so-recent examples, see Bown, Gemeinboeck, and Saunders (2014).

The environment as the medium of the action-perception loop

The analogy with a generic biological-and-thus-cognitive system is only possible to the extent that we consider the performative resources as being inherently open to the local environment, in different forms and degrees. "Being open" to the environment happens through multiple cognitive mechanisms, that ultimately constitute a more encompassing and hybrid action-perception loop. As noted in the previous section, these cognitive mechanisms not only are those of women and men involved in the performance, but also include self-regulating mechanisms proper to a number of technical systems and subsystems, either dependent or independent of direct human control. As performers intervene in the medium (sound or else) through which they are mechanically coupled to the technical apparatus, the apparatus in turn intervenes in the same medium, to which it is in fact electro-acoustically coupled. The (sonic) environment is the very locus and indeed the medium of a composite action-perception loop, and the essential mediator of the structural coupling of human and machinic agents.

Mediation, however, is never a linear transfer of energy or information (Latour 1996). To a greater or lesser extent, the (sonic) environment transforms what it mediates. The environment implies multiple forms of agency, including the idle but crucial mechanical agency inherent to architectural shapes and other material designs, the inherent *affordance of the environment* (Gibson 1979) and the availability of objects to suggest (or hamper) convenient technical usages and physical arrangements (ergonomics). The emotional participation of the audience is itself a kind of collective agency, inasmuch as it reveals itself able to affect the proceedings of the performance, thereby increasing (or decreasing) its artistic significance. Various local facilities, too, may occasionally have an impact on the actual proceedings of a performance (e.g., lighting, heating systems, etc.).

The cognitive activities carried out by the performance ecosystem and its components are only carried out in and through the environment: they are instances of a situated cognitive dynamics, whose detailed processes are dispersed or distributed across the ecosystem components. They are crucial in order for the live character of the performance to signify a prompt and attentive interaction with the real-space and real-time working conditions. Reconsidered and analysed in systemic and operative terms, the biological metaphor implicit in talking of live performance seems now to be specially connected with organism–environment mutual relationships and co-determinations. Thus it takes on connotations closer to a more ecologically-oriented and indeed eco-systemic perspective.

ECO-SYSTEMIC AGENCY AND LIVENESS

The above discussion suggests that performance is live inasmuch as the composite ensemble involved in its process manifests a kind of eco-systemic dynamics (the latter is yet to be defined). It portrays liveness as a phenomenological character born of the open-ended and situated interplay of various types of agency: human (performers), technical (electroacoustic equipment, computer and digital audio devices), and environmental.

In ecosystem theory and engineering (Jørgensen and Müller 2000), an ecosystem is defined as a network of biotic and abiotic components sharing the same physical space. The design of artificial ecosystems is generally in agreement with that definition (Prominski 2007). The dynamics of the whole ecosystem emerges in the physical interconnectedness and interdependency of the component parts, as well as in the co-determination between the parts and the whole. This is crucial: each individual part is virtually an autonomous systemic unit in itself, but it can only pursue its potential autonomy (never fully achieving it) through a web of mutually affecting partners. The French sociologist and epistemologist Edgar Morin once spoke of "dependent autonomy" (1977, 204).

The main agents in the performance ecosystem are therefore to be seen as autonomous-but-dependent loci of action: they can only pursue their task through other agents involved, notably including the local (sound) environment. Each behaves itself through its individual action-perception loop, but the latter is tightly intertwined to all other loops through the common surrounding environment—which in turn mediates (transforms, directs, favours, or contrasts) each individual action and perception. Taken together, the multiple action-perception loops realise a more intricate control loop belonging to the performance ecosystem as a larger autonomous system: it indeed provides the latter with a hybrid and non-centralised cognitive apparatus. We can say, in short, that the agency in performance is inherently distributed across and among several different resources.

From distributed to eco-systemic agency

Distributed agency is not centralised in human actors and spreads across multiple resources, including technical ones (Laville 2000) and for many years now also hardware and software resources (Rammert 2008). Besides, we should not forget the environment, the role of which is simultaneously constitutive and dialectic: being *distributed* across the environment (Laville 2000), agency is in fact also *situated* (Quéré 1997; Biset 2012), that is, it is relative to the spatial niche offered as the performance space. This dialectics of *distributed* and *situated* is also a peculiar dimension of live performance. Even more so in consideration of the sheer technological complexity we meet today in most private and public spaces, including of course places where musical and sound-art works are presented. We "cannot ignore the agency that is wielded by the environment" (Hansen 2009, 114). Following a neo-cybernetic view, the performance ecosystem shall be considered a "system-environment hybrid" (Hansen 2009), and its agency described as a distributed agency of peculiar hybrid constitution.

It is today common among scholars to characterise such composite and dynamical assemblages as *multi-agent*—or, maybe more aptly, *inter-agent*—systems. These terms evoke artificial intelligence and related research, in a line of technological innovation inspiring, among others, various developments in interactive computer music and interactive sound art (Hamman 1997; Dahlstedt and McBurney 2006; Bown, Eldridge, and McCormack 2009; Bown and Martin 2012; Bown, Gemeinboeck, and Saunders 2014; Stapleton 2017; Tatar and Pasquier 2019; Sanfilippo 2019). However, multi-agent systems implemented in such developments typically involve multiple instances of the *same kind* of agency, often of a kind that has been called "algorithmic agency" (Rutz 2016). The agentive role of the physical performance space is very rarely overtly acknowledged (Di Scipio 2003; Waters 2007; Di Scipio 2008; Borgo and Kaiser 2010; Borgo 2016). A notion of *eco-systemic agency* is especially needed in order to include the site of performance, understood as the environment actively mediating between other resources, either human or technical (Di Scipio 2018; Di Scipio and Sanfilippo 2019; Di Scipio forthcoming, 77–80).

The threefold structure of eco-systemic agency

We can parse eco-systemic agency in three distinct agentive couples or inter-agencies:

performer $\leftrightarrow$ environment,
performer $\leftrightarrow$ equipment,
equipment $\leftrightarrow$ environment.

These are distinct subsets of recursive processes in the performative ecosystem (we are not concerned here with the agents possibly included in the subsets). The first can be loosely referred to as the experience—for example, essential to instrument playing—of "feeling one" with the room. The second concerns, of course, human–machine and human–computer interaction (for a long time the subject of a large body of research and theory). It also concerns the ergonomics and the "ergodynamics" (Magnusson 2019, 10–12) of instruments, controllers, and other tools handled by performers—their size, shape, and building materials.[20] The third seems instead to define an area never really theorised, and only researched by practitioners interested in designing site-specific and self-regulating sound generating systems, working unsupervised by human performers (Sanfilippo 2019; Di Scipio and Sanfilippo 2019).

Yet, only for the benefit of analysis can the three be discussed as distinct, separate subsets of the complete performance ecosystem. In the very moment of performance, they work as co-dependent agencies constituting a larger ecology of overlapping feedback loops (figure 8.1).

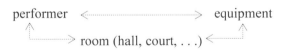

Figure 8.1.

---

20 The direct contact with objects of different materials opens up a scenario of physical and bodily involvement that has been nicely described as "dialectical materialism in action" (Keil 1995, 3). Here we see no reason why this should not include the direct manipulation of electroacoustic and digital resources, as instead claimed in Keil (1995).

Figure 8.1. The threefold loop structure of the performance ecology. Each of the three types of agency included here actually implies a network of subcomponent agents and loops.

Clearly, different approaches involve different priorities and differently nuanced blends of (several instances of) the three types of agency. In actual performance contexts, the dynamics of the performance ecology is determined by *how* and *how many* recursive subsets are really integrated and experienced as partners in the complete ecosystem process.

Strong and weak liveness

The notion of liveness elaborated here seems more directly related to creative sound practices where the mentioned three dimensions of eco-systemic agency are more fully integrated. They illustrate what we might call *a strong notion of liveness*: highly technologised performance is experienced as live inasmuch as it implements a rich entanglement of several different agencies and fosters a more global eco-systemic agency of possibly higher dynamical complexity. And that, *despite* but also *thanks to* the exposure to contingent real-time and real-space circumstances. A "strong notion of liveness" hence implies that the environment is experienced as an agentive factor and as the medium in which the coupling of human and machinic agents can be creatively manipulated.

In contrast, a *weak* notion of liveness seems proper to practices where only one out of the three dimensions of eco-systemic agency is involved, as is the case with approaches equating liveness with real-time human–computer interaction.

Quite evidently, the binary opposition *strong versus weak liveness* is overly simplistic, considering the variety of performance approaches. Each particular approach is likely to mark a different spot in between the two opposites. Each is likely to feature its own, unique blend of human, technical, and environmental agencies. In any case, no judgement criteria or aesthetic normative assessments are implicated. For lack of better terms, the terminology adopted here only aims to draw, on the basis of the above analysis, a clear conceptual framework for further inquiries into a spectrum of practices too often indistinctly qualified as *live* (Di Scipio forthcoming, 81–84). It might also be useful to convey the idea that, in their particular manners of coupling human machinic and environmental agencies, different live performance practices capture different ways of understanding the thorough mediatisation of individual and social life in today's world. As prompted in an earlier passage, live performance practices are willy-nilly expressive of what it means for an individual artist or group of artists to go through the historical phenomenon of the *becoming-environment* of technique and to confront the technological condition of (not only) human life. That perhaps defines "what *more* there is to [live electronic] music than sound" (Croft 2007, 65, my interpolation).

Summary and final annotations

This chapter has attempted first and foremost to provide a characterisation of liveness through the lens of the performance ecosystem, understood as a techno-cultural hybrid assemblage of its own cognitive and agentive capacities.

Second, it has attempted to locate the potential of live electronic music practices as relative to that notion of liveness.

I have connected the live character of performance with the emergence of a kind of eco-systemic agency, insisting that the material environment be included as a crucial agent in the assemblage of human and non-human resources. To that aim, I have elaborated a functional analogy with living systems qua biological-and-thus-cognitive systems: the agency of a living system is one and the same with its exposure to (and dependence on) the surrounding physical space plus related contextual, contingent factors. Performance is live inasmuch as the performance ecosystem shows an operative autonomy born in the structural and yet fragile joining of human, machine, and environment. That requires that the achievable autonomy, by definition, can never be without some level of heteronomy.

In such a neo-cybernetically oriented view of liveness, it is not inappropriate to hear echoes of broader questions in the politics of knowledge (Feenberg and Hannay 1995): albeit never fully achievable, autonomy (freedom of choice and action) always requires competent appropriation of one's own means of action, plus an awareness that ones' own means of actions are distributed in (and sometimes relinquished to) the shared social and physical environment. In fact, the recursive structure of what we have called *eco-systemic agency* (figure 8.1) seems nothing but a particular case in a much broader scenario of huge political relevance (figure 8.2).

Figure 8.2.

This threefold loop constitutes a genuinely complex relationship central to thinking the contemporary world, as preliminarily illustrated by ethno-technologist Gilbert Simondon (1958) and discussed again and again in more recent decades, from multiple perspectives (Morin 1977, 2007; Guattari 1989; Bogue 2009; Clarke and Hansen 2009; Hörl 2012, 2015; Barthélémy 2015). Asking what and where the live character of highly technologised performance is may be equivalent to turning the question of performance liveness into a question of bio-political relevance (Di Scipio 2014, 2015).

Living (in) machine environments

Live electronic practices create vivid sonic images of that broader, "bio-political" scenario. They can do so, in virtue of a constitutive but frail coupling of humans and machines under real-time and real-space working conditions—in situated, *in vivo* conditions. Independent of specific aesthetic orientations and technological contexts, they ultimately seem to acknowledge and make sonically perceptible that, at a general level, the threefold relationship

Figure 8.2. The complexity of performance ecology today maps directly onto broader issues of political relevance.

"human–machine–environment" that structures the dwelling of humans on earth is not only a peculiar phenomenon of modern, postmodern, and contemporary societies, but also a more fundamental phenomenon constitutive of what it means to be human.[21] And that, at a more particular level, the array of technologies today structuring the shared spaces where people live and meet act less as extensions or augmentations of the physical space, and more as constituents of a different, hybrid environment. Creative artistic elaboration of this hybrid constitution testifies, in perceivable form, to the fundamental awareness that *technique* and *nature* are both social constructions.

The plurality of live electronic practices surely mirrors various aesthetics and historically contingent views of art- and music-making, yet today it seems especially to mirror different manners of *living in electronic environments*. Such practices ask, how is life that is lived through actions and perceptions profoundly mediated by, or even relinquished to, interconnected technical layers and codes? In several different ways, ever since their inception in the 1960s, live electronic practices have ultimately had this to claim: "we are natural-born *cyborgs*."[22] Today such practices also show that artistic research commitment can be a territory where the nexus of "continuity between technique and nature" (Simondon 1958, 244) can be tangibly experienced and imaginatively worked out.

Finally, when deliberately appropriating, designing, and shaping up the performance ecosystem, live electronics not only emphasise the human constitution of the utterly technologised environments we live and dwell in, but also show very well that the naturalisation of technical mediators ends up making these mediators invisible and obscures their actual impact in individual and social life. That conveys a powerful dialectical meaning. By way of turning the hybrid constitution of techno-ecosystems into phenomenologically shared auditory events, these mediators audibly expose the human, all-too-human reality of our pervasive technological condition.

REFERENCES

Agamben, Giorgio. 2002. *L'aperto: L'uomo e l'animale*. Turin: Bollati Boringhieri. Translated by Kevin Attell as *The Open: Man and Animal* (Stanford, CA: Stanford University Press, 2004).

Agre, Philip E. 1995. "Computational Research on Interaction and Agency." *Artificial Intelligence* 72 (1–2): 1–52.

———. 1997. "Toward a Critical Technical Practice: Lessons Learned in Trying to Reform AI." In *Social Science, Technical Systems, and Cooperative Work: Beyond the Great Divide*, edited by Geoffrey C. Bowker, Susan Leigh Star, William Turner, and Les Gasser, 131–58. Mahwah, NJ: Erlbaum.

Appleton, Jon. 1989. "Composing for New Instruments." In *21st-Century Musical Instruments: Hardware and Software*, 1–13. New York: Institute for Studies in American Music.

---

21 This implies the well-known theory of *exteriorisation*, developed by various authors over the decades—among them Leroi-Gourhan (1945), Simondon (1958), Stiegler (1994), and Agamben (2002). In this view, technical means are designed, implemented, and placed by human beings in their environs, exteriorising cognitive functions initially situated only in the body.

22 "Natural-born cyborgs" is of course a well-known title (Clark 2003).

Assis, Paulo de. 2014. "Epistemic Complexity and Experimental Systems in Music Performance." In *Artistic Experimentation in Music: an Anthology*, edited by Darla Crispin and Bob Gilmore, 41–54. Orpheus Institute Series. Leuven: Leuven University Press.

———. 2018. *Logic of Experimentation: Rethinking Music Performance through Artistic Research*. Orpheus Institute Series. Leuven: Leuven University Press.

———. 2019. "Musical Works as Assemblages." *La Deleuziana: Online Journal of Philosophy*, no. 10. Accessed 6 February 2021. http://www.ladeleuziana. org/wp-content/uploads/2020/01/De-Assis.pdf.

Auslander, Philip. 2008. *Liveness: Performance in a Mediatized Culture*. 2nd ed. Abingdon, UK: Routledge.

Barandiaran, Xabier, and Alvaro Moreno. 2006. "On What Makes Certain Dynamical Systems Cognitive: A Minimally Cognitive Organization Program." *Adaptive Behavior* 14 (2): 171–85.

Baranski, Sandrine. 2009. "Manières de créer des sons: L'œuvre musicale *versus* le dispositif musical (expérimental, cybernétique ou complexe)." *Démèter*, November 2009. Accessed 6 February 2021. http://demeter.revue.univ-lille3.fr/lodel9/index.php?id=260.

Barbaras, Renaud. 2002. "Francisco Varela: A New Idea of Perception and Life." *Phenomenology and the Cognitive Sciences* 1 (2): 127–32.

Barkati, Karim. 2009. "Entre temps réel et temps différé: Pratiques, techniques et enjeux de l'informatique dans la musique contemporaine." PhD thesis, Université Paris 8.

Barthélémy, Jean-Hugues. 2015. *Life and Technology: An Inquiry Into and Beyond Simondon*. Translated by Barnaby Norman. Lüneburg, Germany: Meson Press.

Battier, Marc, ed. 1999. "Aesthetics of Live Electronic Music." Special issue, *Contemporary Music Review* 18 (3).

Béranger, Sébastien. 2009. "Réflexions partisanes sur l'usage du 'live-electronic' dans nos musiques savants." In *Actes des Journées d'Informatique Musicale, Grenoble, 1er–3 Avril 2009*, 35–39. Accessed 23 March 2021. http://jim.afim-asso.org/jim09/downloads/actes/JIM09_Beranger.pdf.

Bernardini, Nicola. 1986. "Live Electronics." In *Nuova Atlantide: Il continente della musica elettronica 1900–1986*, edited by Roberto Doati and Alvise Vidolin, 61–78. Venice: La Biennale di Venezia.

Bertolani, Valentina, and Friedmann Sallis. 2016. "Live Electronic Music." In *Routledge Encyclopaedia of Modernism*. Accessed 6 February 2021. https://www.rem.routledge.com/articles/live-electronic-music.

Bich, Leonardo. 2012. *L'ordine invisibile: Organizzazione, autonomia e complessità del vivente*. Soveria Mannelli, Italy: Rubbettino Editore.

Bich, Leonardo, and Argyris Arnellos. 2012. "Autopoiesis, Autonomy, and Organizational Biology: Critical Remarks on *Life After Ashby*." *Cybernetics and Human Knowing* 19 (4): 75–103.

Biset, Sébastien. 2012. "Une praxis radicale: Éprouver la situation (de la 'radicalité' des musique 'expérimentales')." In "L'art de la performance," special issue, *Ligeia* nos. 117–20, 214–20.

Bogue, Ronald. 2009. "A Thousand Ecologies." In *Deleuze/Guattari & Ecology*, edited by Bernd Herzogenrath, 42 56. Basingstoke, UK: Palgrave MacMillan.

Bonardi, Alain. 2015. "Rejouer une œuvre avec l'électronique temps réel: enjeux informatiques et musicologiques." In *Genéses musicales*, edited by Nicolas Donin, Almuth Grésillon, and Jean-Louis Lebrave, 239–54. Paris: Presses de l'Université Paris-Sorbonne.

Borgo, David. 2016. "The Ghost in the Music, or the Perspective of an Improvising Ant." In *The Oxford Handbook of Critical Improvisation Studies, Volume 1*, edited by George E. Lewis and Benjamin Piekut, 91–113. New York: Oxford University Press.

Borgo, David, and Jeff Kaiser. 2010. "Configurin(g) KaiBorg: Interactivity, Ideology, and Agency in Electro-acoustic Improvised Music." In *Beyond the Centres: Musical Avant-Gardes Since 1950 Conference Proceedings, Thessaloniki*. Accessed 6 February 2021. http://btc.web.auth.gr/_assets/_papers/BORGO-KAISER.pdf.

Bown, Oliver, Alice Eldridge, and Jon McCormack. 2009. "Understanding Interaction in Contemporary Digital Music: From Instruments to Behavioural

Objects." *Organised Sound* 14 (2): 188–96.

Bown, Oliver, Petra Gemeinboeck, and Rob Saunders. 2014. "The Machine as Autonomous Performer." In *Interactive Experience in the Digital Age: Evaluating New Art Practice*, edited by Linda Candy and Sam Ferguson, 75–90. Cham, Switzerland: Springer.

Bown, Oliver, and Aengus Martin. 2012. "Autonomy in Music-Generating Systems." In *Proceedings of the 1st International Workshop on Music Metacreation (MUME2012), Held at the Eighth AAAI Conference on Artificial Intelligence and Interactive Digital Entertainment (AIDE'12), Stanford University, Palo Alto, California, October 9th 2012*. Accessed 6 February 2021. https://iat-metacr-org.dcr.sfu.ca/mume2012/content/proceedings/Autonomy%20in%20Music-Generating%20Systems.pdf.

Centore, Leandro. 2011. "Du processus dans l'art contemporain: Une tentative de définition." [MA?] dissertation, École Nationale Supérieure des Arts Visuels "La Cambre" et Université libre de Bruxelles.

Chadabe, Joel. 1997. *Electric Sound: The Past and Promise of Electronic Music*. Upper Saddle River, NJ: Prentice-Hall.

Clark, Andy. 2003. *Natural-Born Cyborgs: Minds, Technologies, and the Future of Human Intelligence*. New York: Oxford University Press.

Clarke, Bruce, and Mark B. N. Hansen, eds. 2009. *Emergence and Embodiment: New Essays on Second-Order Systems Theory*. Durham, NC: Duke University Press.

Collins, Nicolas. 2009. *Handmade Electronic Music: The Art of Hardware Hacking*. 2nd ed. New York: Routledge.

Cont, Arshia. 2012. "Synchronisme musical et musiques mixtes: Du temps écrit au temps produit." *Circuit* 22 (1): 9–24.

Croft, John. 2007. "Theses on Liveness." *Organised Sound* 12 (1): 59–66.

Dahlstedt, Palle, and Peter McBurney. 2006. "Musical Agents: Toward Computer-Aided Music Composition Using Autonomous Software Agents." *Leonardo* 39 (5): 469–70.

Davies, Hugh. 1981. "Making and Performing Simple Electroacoustic Instruments." In *Electronic Music for Schools*, edited by Richard Orton, 152–74. Cambridge: Cambridge University Press.

Di Scipio, Agostino. 1997. "Interpreting Music Technology: From Heidegger to Subversive Rationalization." *Sonus (A Journal of Investigations into Global Musical Possibilities)* 18 (1): 63–80.

———. 1998. "Questions Concerning Music Technology." *Angelaki: Journal of the Theoretical Humanities* 3 (2): 31–40.

———. 2003. "Sound is the Interface: From *Interactive* to *Ecosystemic* Signal Processing." *Organised Sound* 8 (3): 269–77.

———. 2008. "Émergence du son, son d'émergence: Essai d'épistémologie expérimentale par un compositeur." In "Musique et cognition," edited by Anne Sedes, special issue, *Intellectica: Revue de l'Association pour la Recherche Cognitive*, nos. 48–49, 221–49.

———. 2012. "Ascoltare l'evento del suono: Note per una biopolitica della musica." In *Musica e Architettura*, edited by Alessandra Capanna, Fabio Cifariello Ciardi, Anna Irene Del Monaco, Maurizio Gabrieli, Luca Ribichini, and Gianni Trovalusci, 63–70. Rome: Edizioni Nuova Cultura.

———. 2014. "Sound Object? Sound Event! Ideologies of Sound and the Biopolitics of Music." *Soundscape: The Journal of Acoustic Ecology* 13 (1): 10–14.

———. 2015. "The Politics of Sound and the Biopolitics of Music: Weaving Together Sound-Making, Irreducible Listening, and the Physical and Cultural Environment." *Organised Sound* 20 (3): 278–89.

———. 2017. "Storia *della* musica e storia *nella* musica: Alcune riflessioni sulle pratiche elettroacustiche." *Musica/Realtà*, no. 114, 25–57.

———. 2018. "Dwelling in a Field of Sonic Relationships: 'Instrument' and 'Listening' in an Ecosystemic View of Live Electronics Performance." In *Live Electronic Music: Composition, Performance, Study*, edited by Friedemann Sallis, Valentina Bertolani, Jan Burle, and Laura Zattra, 17–45. Abingdon, UK: Routledge.

———. Forthcoming. *Qu'est-ce qui est "vivant" dans la performance live electronics? Une perspective écosystémique des pratiques musicales et d'art sonore*. Paris: L'Harmattan.

Di Scipio, Agostino, and Dario Sanfilippo. 2019. "Defining EcoSystemic Agency in Live Performance: The Machine Milieu Project as Practice-Based Research." In

"Agency," edited by Miriam Akkerman and Rama Gottfried, special issue, *Array*. Accessed 6 February 2021. https://journals.qucosa.de/array/article/view/2655.

Emmerson, Simon. 1994. "'Live' versus 'Real-Time.'" *Contemporary Music Review* 10 (2): 95–101.

———. 2007. *Living Electronic Music*. Aldershot, UK: Ashgate.

———. 2012a. "Location, Dislocation, Relocation (Where Is Live Electronic Music?)." *Seminário Música Ciência Tecnologia*, no. 4, 7–16. Accessed 6 February 2021. http://www2.eca.usp.br/smct/ojs/index.php/smct/article/view/48. Page numbers refer to PDF version.

———. 2012b. "Live Electronic Music or Living Electronic Music?" In *Bodily Expression in Electronic Music: Perspectives on Reclaiming Performativity*, edited by Deniz Peters, Gerhard Eckel, and Andreas Dorschel, 152–62. New York: Routledge.

Etxeberria, Arantza, Juan Juliano Merelo, and Alvaro Moreno. 1994. "Studying Organisms with Basic Cognitive Capacities in Artificial Worlds." *Intellectica* 18 (1): 45–69.

Feenberg, Andrew. 1991. *Critical Theory of Technology*. New York: Oxford University Press.

Feenberg, Andrew, and Alastair Hannay. 1995. *Technology and the Politics of Knowledge*. Bloomington: Indiana University Press.

Froese, Tom. 2011. "From Second-Order Cybernetics to Enactive Cognitive Science: Varela's Turn from Epistemology to Phenomenology." *Systems Research and Behavioral Science* 28 (6): 631–45

Gibson, James J. 1979. *The Ecological Approach to Visual Perception*. Boston: Houghton Mifflin.

Green, Owen. 2013. "User Serviceable Parts: Practice, Technology, Sociality and Method in Live Electronic Musicking." PhD thesis, City University London. Accessed 23 March 2021. https://openaccess.city.ac.uk/id/eprint/2730/.

Guattari, Félix. 1989. *Les trois écologies*. Paris: Galilée. Translated by Ian Pindar and Paul Sutton as *The Three Ecologies* (London: Athlone Press, 2000).

Hallowell, Ronan. 2009. "Humberto Maturana and Francisco Varela's Contribution to Media Ecology: Autopoiesis, the Santiago School of Cognition, and Enactive Cognitive Science." In *Proceedings of the Media Ecology Association* 10. Accessed 6 February 2021. http://www.media-ecology.net/publications/MEA_proceedings/v10/13_varela_maturanda.pdf.

Hamman, Micheal. 1997. "Computer Music Composition and the Dialectics of Interaction." PhD thesis, University of Illinois at Urbana-Champaign.

———. 2002. "From Technical to Technological: The Imperative of Technology in Experimental Music Composition." *Perspectives of New Music* 40 (1): 92–120.

Hansen, Mark B. N. 2009. "System-Environment Hybrids." In Clarke and Hansen 2009, 113–42.

Hennion, Antoine, and Bruno Latour. 1993. "Objet d'art, objet de science: Note sur les limites de l'anti-fétichisme" *Sociologie de l'art*, no. 6, 7–24.

Hörl, Erich. 2012. "Le nouveau paradigme écologique: Pour une écologie générale des médias et des techniques." *Multitudes* 51 (4): 74–85.

———. 2013. "A Thousand Ecologies: The Process of Cyberneticization and General Ecology." Translated by James Burton, Jeffrey Kirkwood, and Maria Vlotides. In *The Whole Earth: California and the Disappearance of the Outside*, edited by Diedrich Diederichsen and Anselm Franke, 121–30. Berlin: Sternberg Press.

———. 2015. "The Technological Condition." Translated by Anthony Enns. *Parrhesia*, no. 22, 1–15. First published 2011 as part of the introduction to *Die technologische Bedingung: Beiträge zur Beschreibung der technischen Welt*, edited by Erich Hörl (Berlin: Suhrkamp), 7–53.

Impett, Jonathan. 1998. "The Identification and Transposition of Authentic Instruments: Musical Practice and Technology." *Leonardo Music Journal* 8: 21–26.

———. 2016. "The Contemporary Musician and the Production of Knowledge: Practice, Research, and Responsibility." In *Artistic Research in Music: Discipline and Resistance; Artists and Researchers at the Orpheus Institute, edited by Jonathan Impett, 221–38. Orpheus Institute Series. Leuven: Leuven University Press.

Jonas, Hans. 1966. The Phenomenon of Life: Toward a Philosophical Biology. New York: Harper and Row.

Jørgensen, Sven E., and Felix Müller, eds. 2000. Handbook of Ecosystem Theories and Management. Boca Ratan, FL: Lewis Publishers.

Keil, Charles. 1995. "The Theory of Participatory Discrepancies: A Progress Report." Ethnomusicology 39 (1): 1–19.

Latour, Bruno. 1996. "On Actor-Network Theory: A Few Clarifications." Soziale Welt 47 (4): 369–81.

Laville, Frédéric. 2000. "La cognition située: Une nouvelle approche de la rationalité limitée." Revue économique 51 (6): 1301–31.

Leroi-Gourhan, André. 1945. Milieu et techniques. Paris: Albin Michel.

Losano, Mario. 1991. Storie di automi: Dalla Grecia classica alla belle époque. Turin: Einaudi.

Magnusson, Thor. 2019. Sonic Writing: Technologies of Material, Symbolic, and Signal Inscriptions. London: Bloomsbury Academic.

Mancilla, Roberto Gustavo. 2011. "Introduction to Sociocybernetics (Part 1): Third Order Cybernetics and a Basic Framework for Society." Journal of Sociocybernetics 9 (1–2): 35–56.

Manning, Peter. 1985. Electronic and Computer Music. Oxford: Clarendon Press.

Manoury, Philippe. 2007. "Considérations (toujours actuelles) sur l'état de la musique en temps réel." L'étincelle, no. 3. Accessed 6 February 2021. http://etincelle.ircam.fr/733.html.

Maturana, Humberto. 2002. "Autopoiesis, Structural Coupling and Cognition: A History of These and Other Notions in the Biology of Cognition." Cybernetics and Human Knowing 9 (3–4): 5–34.

Maturana, Humberto, and Francisco J. Varela. 1980. Autopoiesis and Cognition: The Realization of the Living. Dodrecht: Reidel.

McCormick, Lisa. 2015. "Performance Perspectives." In The Routledge Reader on the Sociology of Music, edited by John Shepherd and Kyle Devine, 117–26. New York: Routledge.

Morin, Edgar. 1977. La méthode. 1: La nature de la nature. Paris: Seuil.

———. 2007. "Complexité retreinte, complexité générale." In Intelligence de la complexité: Épistémologie et pragmatique, edited by Jean-Louis Le Moigne and Edgard Morin, 28–50. La Tour-d'Aigues: Éditions de l'Aube.

Mumma, Gordon. 1975. "Live-Electronic Music." In The Development and Practice of Electronic Music, edited by Jon H. Appleton and Ronald C. Perera, 286–335. Englewood Cliffs, NJ: Prentice-Hall.

Murail, Tristan. 1991. "Écrire avec le live-electronic," La Revue Musicale, nos. 421–24, 93–103.

Odum, Eugene P. 2001. "The 'Techno-Ecosystem.'" Bulletin of the Ecological Society of America 82 (2): 137–38.

Panaccio-Letendre, Charlotte. 2011. "L'œuvre d'art comme dispositif: Hétérogénéité et réévaluation de la notion de public." MA dissertation, Université du Québec à Montréal. Accessed 6 February 2021. https://archipel.uqam.ca/4688/1/M11993.pdf.

Phelan, Peggy. 1993. Unmarked: The Politics of Performance. London: Routledge.

Pousseur, Henri. 1976. Introduction to "Parte quinta: Animazione." In La musica elettronica: Testi scelti e commentati, edited by Henri Pousseur, 241–47. Milan: Feltrinelli.

Prominski, Martin. 2007. "Ökosysteme entwerfen." In Landschaft in einer Kultur der Nachhaltigkeit, edited by Ulrich Eisel and Stefan Körner, 3 vols., 2:146–57. Kassel: Universität Kassel.

Quéré, Louis. 1997. "La situation toujours négligée?" Réseaux 85 (5): 163–92.

Rammert, Werner. 2008. "Where the Action Is: Distributed Agency between Humans, Machines, and Programs." In Paradoxes of Interactivity: Perspectives for Media Theory, Human-Computer Interaction, and Artistic Investigations, edited by Uwe Swifert, Jin Hyun Kim, and Anthony Moore, 62–91. Bielefeld, Germany: Transcript Verlag.

Rebughini, Paola. 2014. "Subject, Subjectivity, Subjectivation." Sociopedia. ISA. Accessed 6 February 2021. https://www.isaportal.org/resources/resource/subject-subjectivity-subjectivation/.

Rutz, Hanns Holger. 2016. "Agency and Algorithms." CITAR: Journal of Science and Technology of the Arts 8 (1). Accessed 6

February 2021. https://doi.org/10.7559/citarj.v8i1.223.

Saladin, Mathieu. 2017. "Electroacoustic Feedback and the Emergence of Sound Installation: Remarks on a Line of Flight in the Live Electronic Music by Alvin Lucier and Max Neuhaus." *Organised Sound* 22 (2): 268–75.

Sallis, Friedemann, Valentina Bartolani, Jan Burle, and Laura Zattra. 2018. Introduction to *Live Electronic Music: Composition, Performance and Study*, edited by Friedemann Sallis, Valentina Bartolani, Jan Burle, and Laura Zattra, 1–14. Abingdon, UK: Routledge.

Salter, Chris. 2010. *Entangled: Technology and the Transformation of Performance*. Cambridge, MA: MIT Press.

Sanden, Paul. 2013. *Liveness in Modern Music: Musicians, Technology, and the Perception of Performance*. New York: Routledge.

Sanfilippo, Dario. 2019. "Complex Musical Behaviours via Time-Variant Audio Feedback Networks and Distributed Adaptation: A Study of Autopoietic Infrastructures for Real-Time Performance Systems." PhD thesis, University of Edinburgh.

Schechner, Richard. 2002. *Performance Studies: An Introduction*. New York: Routledge.

Schnell, Norbert, and Marc Battier. 2002. "Introducing Composed Instruments, Technical and Musicological Implications." In *NIME '02: Proceedings of the 2002 Conference on New Instruments for Musical Expression*. Accessed 6 February 2021. https://dl.acm.org/doi/10.5555/1085171.1085205.

Sève, Lucien. 2005. "De quelle culture logico-philosophique la pensée du non-linéaire a-t-elle besoin?" In *Émergence, complexité et dialectique: Sur les systèmes dynamiques non linéaires*, by Lucien Sève, with Roland Charlionet, Philippe Gascuel, François Gaudin, José Gayoso, Janine Guespin-Michel, and Camille Ripoll, edited by Janine Guespin-Michel, 49–210. Paris: Odile Jacob.

Simondon, Gilbert. 1958. *Du mode d'existence des objets techniques*. Paris: Aubier Montaigne. Translated by Cécile Malaspina and John Rogove as *On the Mode of Existence of Technical Objects* (Minneapolis, MN: Univocal, 2017).

Small, Christopher. 1998. *Musicking: The Meanings of Performing and Listening*. Middletown, CT: Wesleyan University Press.

Stapleton, Paul. 2017. "Beyond Control: Improvisation, Listening and Distributed Agency in Human-Machine Musical Ecosystems." Human Algorithmic Listening Network, 29 May. Accessed 6 February 2021. http://www.algorithmiclistening.org/introductions/PS_beyondcontrol/.

Stewart, John. 1992. "Life = Cognition: The Epistemological and Ontological Significance of Artificial Life." In *Toward a Practice of Autonomous Systems*, edited by Francisco J. Varela and Paul Bourgine, 475–83. Cambridge, MA: MIT Press.

———. 1993. "Cognition without Neurones: Adaptation, Learning and Memory in the Immune System." *Cognitiva* 5 (2): 187–202.

Stiegler, Bernard. 1994. *La technique et le temps, 1: La faute d'Epiméthée*. Paris: Galilée. Translated by Richard Beardsworth and George Collins as *Technics and Time, 1: The Fault of Epimetheus* (Stanford, CA: Stanford University Press, 1998).

Stolfi, Ariane de Souza, Luca Turchet, Miguel Ceriani, and Mathieu Barthet. 2018. "Playsound.space: Inclusive Free Music Improvisations Using Audio Commons." In *Proceedings of the New Musical Interface Conference (NIME2018), Blacksburg, VA*, 228–33. Accessed 6 February 2021. https://www.nime.org/proceedings/2018/nime2018_paper0050.pdf.

Tatar, Kıvanç, and Philippe Pasquier. 2019. "Musical Agents: A Typology and State of the Art towards Musical Metacreation." *Journal of New Music Research* 48 (1): 56–105.

Thompson, Evan. 2009. "Life and Mind: From Autopoicsis to Neurophenomenology." In Clarke and Hansen 2009, 77–93.

van Duijn, Marc, Fred Keijzer, and Daan Franken. 2006. "Principles of Minimal Cognition: Casting Cognition as Sensorimotor Coordination." *Adaptive Behaviour* 14 (2): 157–70.

Varela, Francisco J. 1979. *Principles of Biological Autonomy*. New York: North Holland.

Varela, Francisco J., Evan Thompson, and Eleanor Rosch. 1991. *The Embodied Mind: Cognitive Science and Human Experience*. Cambridge, MA: MIT Press.

von Bertalanffy, Ludwig. 1969. *General System Theory: Foundations, Developments, Applications*. New York: Braziller.

von Foerster, Heinz. 1960. "On Self-Organizing Systems and Their Environments." In *Self-Organizing Systems: Proceedings of an Interdisciplinary Conference; 5 and 6 May, 1959*, edited by Marshall C. Yovits and Scott Cameron, 31–50. Oxford: Pergamon Press.

———. 2003. *Understanding Understanding: Essays on Cybernetics and Cognition*. New York: Springer.

Waters, Simon. 2007. "Performance Ecosystems: Ecological Approaches to Musical Interaction." In *EMS07: The "Languages" of Electroacoustic Music. Proceedings of the Electroacoustic Music Studies Network, De Montfort University, Leicester, 2007*. Accessed 6 February 2021. http://www.ems-network.org/spip.php?article278.

———, ed. 2011. "Performance Ecosystems." Special issue, *Organised Sound* 16 (2).

———. 2013. "Touching at a Distance: Resistance, Tactility, Proxemics and the Development of a Hybrid Virtual/Physical Performance System." *Contemporary Music Review* 32 (2–3): 119–34.

Weiss, Gerhard, ed. 1999. *Multiagent Systems: A Modern Approach to Distributed Artificial Intelligence*. Cambridge, MA: MIT Press.

Experiment and Experience

Compositional Practice
as Critique

Lula Romero

Composer, Berlin

INTRODUCTION

During my formative years as a composer, I always felt uncomfortable with the ideal of "mastery" inherent in the figure of the composer. I was against its reactionary character and the hierarchy of powers that it implies. However, I have had conflicted feelings because as a person identified as a woman and as a migrant I need to exercise my agency in order to be heard. My research towards a compositional practice that fosters my agency outside the frame of the master composer is based on this conflict.

This figure of the master composer has been criticised by experimental practices embracing openness. Since then, experimentation has been assimilated in institutional composition; however, in composition schools and in some contemporary music practices there is an ongoing uncritical consensus that still understands composition as the "mastery" of skills and sound materials. Composition is thus understood as the manipulation and transformation of a material in accordance with a composer's structure or idea—in other words, the imposition of a form onto formless material. This understanding implies a hierarchical division between a passive material and an active subject, the composer. Under this premise, art is the elevation of raw material by the abstract thinking of the subject. The material world is an object to be exploited and used by human thinking. The ideological aspects of this hylomorphism have been discussed by composers and theorists and have been continuously criticised by sound art, improvisation, performance art, and practices that embrace embodiment.

John Cage's rejection of the subjective manipulation of sounds by composers is well known: let the sounds be "themselves." This solution, also followed by some practices of sound art, implies the removal of the composer's agency to varying degrees. In this understanding, the activity of the artist is that of presenting "raw" sounds before the listener. This approach has been artistically productive and successful in demonstrating the necessity of a critique in composition and in revealing the possibility of the agency of the material itself. However, the process of presenting things, of re-presenting reality, is not free of ideology and subjective influence. A presentation of things implies a selection and a judgement of what is worthy of being presented. On the other hand, a re-presentation of things means an understanding or a translation of a reality into another code, which implies decisions, generalisations, and subjectivity.[1] Hence, the impossibility of eradicating some form of control by the artist and the inexistence of a non-representational sound in itself constitute the limitations of this position. Moreover, an external law is imposed on art here, which is thus limited to being the frame that exposes a sound phenomenon to be heard. In addition, a different hierarchical relation is built, a relation between an observant subject and a passively observed object.

Another practice that criticises the figure of the composer opens the agency of the musical event to others, such as in collaborative and improvisational practices. The critical potentiality of such practices has proved to be prolific and is well established in the figure of the composer-performer and the work of collectives. Although the question is far from being exhausted, I consciously centre my practice, and therefore the topics of this text, on the less-researched question of openness and its critical potential in the compositional process and in the relation between material and composer.

In light of social movements of reclaiming agency by members of excluded collectives, current changes in the conception of subjectivity, and new conceptions of non-hierarchical ways of interacting with the world, I find it necessary to rethink the category of the composer and its critique. In this current context, the solution proposed by Cage of rejecting the subject is not enough. A member of an excluded collective—woman, queer, non-white, marginalised, migrant—gains agency by acting. To negate the agency of the composer when she is a member of those collectives is to negate her agency once more. Still, this new agency of the composer is not to be gained by mastering the material and reproducing the same power relations. Therefore, I consider it essential to reformulate the critique of the figure of the composer and, in light of feminist theories, the nature of her agency.

Yet, what would the nature of this composer be and how can her agency be exercised? I try to answer this question in my compositional practice by fostering openness in the compositional process. In what follows, I discuss how a practice oriented towards openness in the process of composition and experimentation could represent a critical practice. I do so through the description of two main case studies from my compositional work. The critical aspects of my practice are related to my understanding of experimental composition and can be articulated along three different axes: the figure of the composer and her relation with material in the compositional experiment; the experience of the listener and the creation of new knowledge; and the place of experimental art in society and its critical potential. In so doing, I relate my practice to

---

1 Even in experiences of field recording that claim to be devoid of any subjective influence there are decisions—microphone positioning, recording technology, and the performance situation, just to mention a few—that influence the presentation and perception of the thing itself.

conceptualisations of material and experimentation in the arts and the sciences, as well as with feminist theories and practices. My method resonates with Philip Agre's critical technical practice, in the sense in which the critique relies on my own practice. The theoretical and aesthetic frames are understood as tools to understand and explain my practice; they should not be seen as a justification of my work or as guidelines to be translated into sound. The first part of this text is concerned with the possibility of establishing a non-hierarchical relation between material and composer in compositional practice. This section contains case studies of *Parallax* (2019–20) for symphonic orchestra and the fixed-media piece *MTRAK* (מטרקא) (2018). In the second part, I discuss how an experimental practice that fosters openness and multiple understandings offers knowledge different from that created by language. By doing so, my practice aims to contribute to the ongoing discussion about the possibility of knowledge generated in art. The third part involves a discussion of the role of music and art in society, its position as well as the nature of its critique.

EXPERIMENTS

Intra-actions between subject and material

To describe an alternative relation between composer and sound material with regard to my notion of the compositional experiment, I refer to Karen Barad's concept of the scientific experiment. In *Meeting the Universe Halfway: Quantum Physics and the Entanglement of Matter and Meaning* (2007), Barad, a quantum physicist and theorist, develops the concept of diffraction as a method and metaphor for the creation of scientific knowledge. Diffraction is a type of wave behaviour (figure 9.1). It is the interference[2] between two waves of water, light, or sound. Diffraction describes how two waves combine when the waves encounter an obstruction. In their interaction, a new pattern is created, which is called an interference or diffraction pattern. Barad sees diffraction as a possible way to research nature, in which observer and nature create patterns and interfere with each other. Following Donna Haraway, Barad proposes diffraction as an alternative to the metaphor of reflection conventionally used to describe the scientific method. The reflection method mirrors our knowledge—or image—of the world into the world, and understands the identity between our image and nature as true knowledge. In contrast, the diffraction method searches for differences and patterns of difference. The new knowledge emerges in the intra-action of waves and forces, in the intra-action of material and subject.

---

2 Karen Barad understands and uses the terms *diffraction* and *interference* interchangeably.

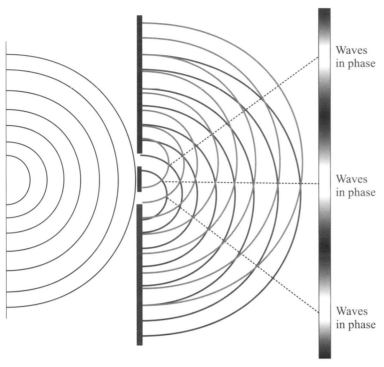

Waves
in phase

Waves
in phase

Waves
in phase

Figure 9.1.

I understand the notion of the compositional experiment as the interference between composer and material. The experiment is not produced when the composer imposes an idea or form onto a raw material, nor does it prove or disprove a previously existing theory or concept. On the contrary, it takes place in the encounter between the material and the composer and in the contingent patterns of diffraction created in this encounter. This type of experimental practice poses a critique of the "master composer," while proposing a different relation in which the composer is not devoid of her agency. Hence, a critical experimental practice searches for the possibilities of the material and renders them audible in the musical work. In the intra-action between composer and material a new situation emerges, a musical event.

This intra-action between composer and material is not easy to identify. It happens in the composition process and is not always self-evident in the final result. However, I regard Alvin Lucier's 1975 piece *Bird and Person Dyning* as a remarkably clear example of openness in composition. An experimental approach oriented towards something that is discovered in the process and the intra-action between material and composer manifest themselves audibly in this piece.

Figure 9.1. Diffraction patterns between two waves.

Bird and Person Dyning is based on the phenomenon of heterodyning, in which two waves are combined in a non-linear system resulting in two new waves, which are the sum and difference frequencies of the first pair. During the performance of *Bird and Person Dyning*, the composer searches for the emergence of this phenomenon between two sources: the recording of an electronic bird call and the feedback created by a binaural microphone and a stereo loudspeaker system. Feedback and heterodyning phenomena depend on the movement and position of the performer and on the characteristics of the space in which the piece is performed. The sound result thus depends on the contingencies of the performance. The sound is not designed a priori but emerges in the piece, as a result of the composer/performer exploring the performance space. The musical work is the discovering, research, and creation of the piece by the composer and the material. It is the result of their interference, of the—not only metaphorical but in this case also literal—diffraction between two waves, the recording of the electronic bird and feedback, as well as the diffraction between the agencies of material and composer.

In *Bird and Person Dyning*, the process of composition happens during the performance. Still, the achievement of openness and intra-action between composer and material are not self-evident if the composition takes place prior to the performance. Several strategies have been proposed in the past to embrace openness in the process and to foster the agency of the material, as in stochastic and aleatory music or open scores. More recently, there have been compositional experiences oriented towards openness sometimes in relation to conceptions from New Materialism. These practices explore the physicality of instruments and performance and the concept of parametric decoupling, as in the work of Simon Steen-Andersen and Aaron Cassidy, and the sounds produced by the interaction between different frequencies, as in the work of Chiyoko Szlavnics, or concepts of material agency, as in the case of Ashley Fure's and Liza Lim's pieces.

Against this background, I will discuss two case studies that depict strategies oriented towards openness in my composition process.

MTRAK *and* Parallax

The phenomenon of heterodyning in Lucier's *Bird and Person Dyning* is the result of a non-linear system. In opposition to a non-linear system, the output of a linear system is proportional to its input. Linear systems can be analysed by examining their parts and constituent relations and their results are predictable. In this sense, linear systems as idealisations are important tools to represent reality and emulate behaviours. Still, nature does not always behave in a linear way. On the other hand, a non-linear system is difficult to analyse, its parts collide and intra-act with each other. Its results are not always proportional to its inputs and therefore it cannot be completely foreseen. In classical scientific conceptions of the experiment, linear systems are used to confirm theories. While linear systems are a means of translating ideas into music, non-linear systems do not necessarily prove or translate ideas into sound matter.

Non-linear systems can be used as the means to allow openness in the composition process and to enable a search for the unknown, as well as to intra-act with sound and to discover the musical work while creating it. In the diverse interactions of its parts, a non-linear system allows the material to have agency in the creation of the musical work.

The piece *MTRAK (מטרקא)* (2018)[3] was created through a process in which its parts intra-act with each other. First, I create an audio file in the non-standard sound synthesis program SEGMOD,[4] whose resultant synthesised sounds are the concatenation of simple periodic waveforms. This audio file becomes the basis for a granular synthesis process with two-channel output. The parameters of both channels are equal by default; however, the parameters of the second channel can be scaled with a factor. The granular synthesis process starts with given initial values for each parameter. Later on, the output of the granular synthesis controls some of its own parameters in a feedback process (figure 9.2). The transformed signal thus affects itself and this process is repeated recursively. In addition, I can modify other parameters of the granular synthesis process by using a MIDI controller, thereby also changing the feedback (figure 9.3). The sound result is an ever-changing, unexpected, highly dense, fluid sound that is partly controlled by me and partly controlled by itself. The influence of the feedback and of the actions that modify the feedback has immediate effects and affects subsequent transformations. The sound is influenced by the nature of the SEGMOD non-standard synthesis system and by previous changes and actions. The material and its development affect each other. Moreover, instead of being the translation of the composer's idea forced onto sound, *MTRAK* is an encounter between the material produced by the system and the composer. This encounter manifests itself in different unexpected appearances and transformations. The diverse iterations retain a coherence that is based on the tracing of relations between the different reappearances of the material. In doing so, the musical work maintains cohesion while advancing in continuous unexpected drifts.[5] A musical experiment that fosters openness creates unexpected outcomes but can also display multiple results, multiple behaviours, relations, and activities, allowing for the emergence of different understandings of itself.

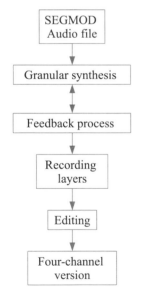

Figure 9.2.

---

3   The piece was created for the CD *SEGMOD* (Dumpf Edition #12, 2019). See, https://dumpfedition.bandcamp.com/album/segmod.

4   By Luc Döbereiner and Martin Lorenz. See https://github.com/lucdoebereiner/segmod.

5   A stereo version of *MTRAK* can be heard at https://dumpfedition.bandcamp.com/track/mtrak.

Figure 9.2. *MTRAK (מטרקא)*, chain of processes.

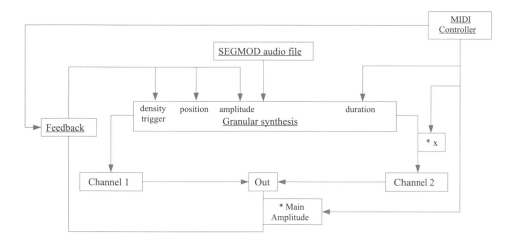

Figure 9.3.

Well-known strategies to achieve multiple results include the use of open scores—as in approaches from the 1960s—the use of different degrees of improvisation, and the blurring of the performer-composer distinction. In such works, the result differs between each iteration of the piece and each performance. In my compositional practice, I seek another strategy to achieve a multiplicity of results. I work towards the creation of different simultaneous results and understandings of the same sound event, which can be described as open and coherent, through the spatialisation of sound sources. A sound event, while retaining its identity, is differently understood by the listener depending on her position in space and in relation to the sound sources. Multiple understandings are thus possible depending on the space. In doing so, I switch the focus from time to space, from the shared agency with the performer to the shared agency with the material and the listener.

In order to create these synchronous multiple understandings, I formulate a network of relations localised in space that is open to be traced and retraced by the audience. Parameters, such as frequency, duration, density, timbre, and the amount of distortion or noise, are arranged according to scales and categories, which are inherently connected to a spatial dimension.[6] These categories are generalisations that I use as tools in order to enable the production of concrete sound materials, which are conceived as processes rather than as static objects. Still, the resultant materials are not the mere summation of the different parameters,[7] they are rather the result of the intra-action and encounter between different layers of parametric organisation. In this way, sonic identities

6　An interesting project on the use of parametric spatialisation is the one developed by Nyström (2018).

7　A multiphonic is a clear sound example of a result not being equal to the sum of its part. Although a multiphonic on a clarinet is the result of the interaction of a number of partials, dividing up these partials so each is played by a different instrument will not result in a multiphonic. In this sense, the clarinet can be described as a non-linear system.

Figure 9.3. *MTRAK (מטרקא)*, flow chart.

emerge as sorts of "phenotypes" that are always more than their "genotypical" parametric description. The audible commonality of these sound materials can be described phenomenologically in terms of family resemblances. Since such family resemblances are perceptual categories, they create a connection between my imaginative listening in the composition process and the listeners' experience of the performance. The creation of meaning is thus always distributed among perception, composition, performance, and space. Semantic functioning, such as causation, contrast, and continuation, remains ambiguous and is activated by the perception of a situated listener in a concrete space.

The latest formulation of the idea of the network of behaviour and parametric spatialisation can be found in my recent piece for symphonic orchestra *Parallax* (2019–20).[8] The whole piece is a continuous development of different non-resolving processes, an ambiguous sound mass, which is the product of different networks and parametric organisations. As an example, I will focus on a passage towards the end of the piece—bars 132 to 213. This passage is the sonification of the paths of reflection of an imagined sound moving between six points in space using an acoustic raytracing algorithm. These points are localised among the instruments of the orchestra. The orchestra is divided up asymmetrically into three groups. The disposition is based on the Donaueschingen Baar-Sporthalle (figure 9.4). The first group is situated in a gallery above the audience to its left side. The second group is on the stage, subdivided into three subgroups. The third group is behind the audience. The points are distributed in space and time in the following connected trajectories: (1) from group 1 to group 2 right, (2) from group 2 right to group 2 left, (3) from group 2 left to group 2 centre, (4) from group 2 centre to group 3, (5) from group 3 to group 2 left, and (6) from group 2 left to group 1 (figure 9.5 shows trajectories in time; figure 9.6 shows trajectories in space). There are twenty paths of reflections connecting the start and end points of each of the six trajectories. Figure 9.7 shows the paths in the first trajectory between a point in group 1 and a point in group 2 right.[9] A path is characterised by its number of reflections (zero to three) and its total duration. The number of reflections of the generated paths is mapped to instrumentation and dynamics. Since each of the twenty paths connecting two points has a different duration, the sum of these paths creates a unique rhythmic pattern. These durations typically last a number of milliseconds. In order to use them musically, I scaled them by a factor of 420 to map them to processes at the macrolevel and by 15, 20, and 30 for the microlevel (figure 9.8 shows mapping to rhythm, instrumentation, and dynamic of the first array of paths).

---

8 *Parallax* (2019–2020) for symphonic orchestra, commissioned by Südwestrundfunk for the Donaueschinger Musiktage 2020.

9 Calculations of the reflections in a space with the dimensions of the Donaueschingen Baar-Sporthalle and the map of the reflections are calculated with the tool Amray. See https://amcoustics.com/tools/amray.

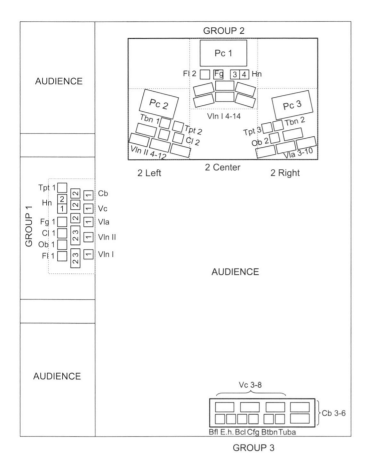

Figure 9.4.

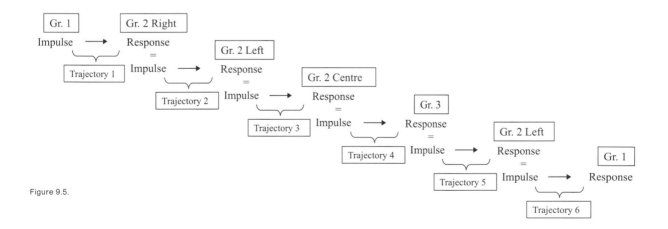

Figure 9.5.

Figure 9.4. *Parallax*, orchestra disposition.

Figure 9.5. *Parallax*, temporal sequence of trajectories between the different groups.

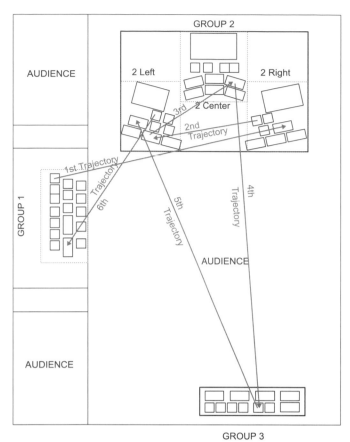

Figure 9.6.

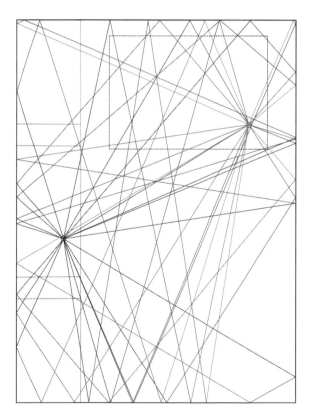

Figure 9.7.

Figure 9.6. *Parallax*, trajectories between the different groups in the performance space.

Figure 9.7. *Parallax*, paths in the first trajectory between a point in group 1 and a point in group 2 right.

Experiment and Experience

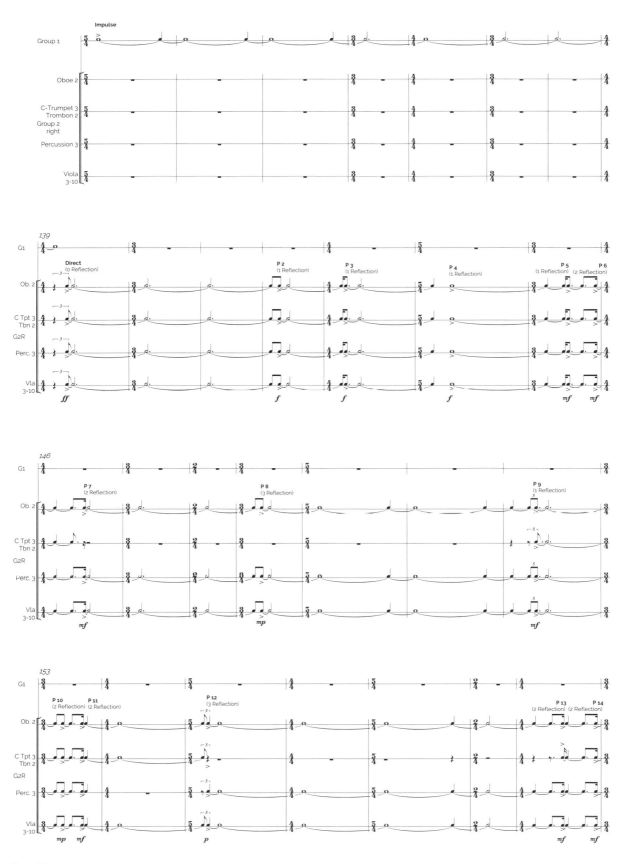

Figure 9.8.

Figure 9.8. Mapping of trajectory 1, *Parallax*, from group 1 to group 2 right.

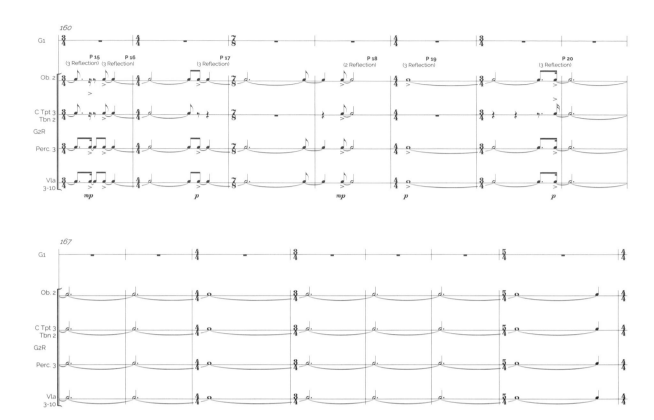

The passage can be described as follows: An impulse emitted in group 1 creates differently delayed responses in a point in group 2 right. These responses correspond to the rhythmic pattern, instrumentation, and dynamic level generated by the mapping of the paths. The first response in group 2 right occurs at the same time as the impulse of the second trajectory and generates responses in group 2 left. The process is repeated throughout the six trajectories (figure 9.5). While one array of paths is still sounding, another array starts, which results in a simultaneity and the interrelation of different spatial activities. In addition, within each response, "inner reflections"—a sort of feedback inside each group—can take place. In doing so, a chain of reactions and feedbacks is produced. Furthermore, each orchestral group uses a different aggregate of frequencies derived from the room modes[10] of the space that each group occupies (figure 9.9). The aggregates are presented in the course of the process in different degrees of distortion, oscillation, and density (figure 9.10).

Group 1

Subgroups 2
right, centre and left

Group 2

Group 3

Figure 9.6.

---

10 The different room modes for this piece have been calculated with the Amcoustics tool Amroc. See https://amcoustics.com/tools/amroc.

Figure 9.6. *Parallax*, sound aggregates.

Lula Romero

Figure 9.10.

Figure 9.10. *Parallax* score, pp. 19–21.

Parallax

The passage is the result of the encounters and intra-actions of all these different layers of activities—reflection, pathway, and feedback patterns, sound aggregates, instrumentation, and distortion—that develop in space in a continuous movement and process. The result of these encounters is consciously ambiguous, being open to interpretation in the listening.[11]

A new situation emerges in the described practice: a musical event that is not the reflection or material realisation of a composer's idea, but rather the intra-action between the composer and the characteristics and potentialities of a concrete material. In the case studies, material and form are not prior to the work; rather, they emerge in the composition process. In *MTRAK*, they are the result of a chain of non-linear systems consisting of SEGMOD, feedback, and granular synthesis. In the case of *Parallax*, material and piece are the result of a network of relations localised in space. In both cases, the outcome is the continuous transformation of a material that is being formed but is at the same time transforming subsequent developments. This new situation proposes a different relation between composer and material in which both share agency; thus, it criticises the binary hierarchical relation of subject and object. I regard it as fundamental to reconsider the category of composer along these lines. A different subject emerges when the composer searches for the potentialities of sound material and reinforces their emergence in the musical work.

RETHINKING THE COMPOSER: A NOMADIC SUBJECT

In the practice described in the case studies, neither composer nor material are prior to the piece. Composition starts in a *tabula rasa* state, similar to what the philosopher Christoph Menke defined as "ästhetischer Nullzustand" (an aesthetic zero state) (2013, 82, my translation). That does not mean that there is nothing before the compositional process, or that it starts *ex nihilo*. It rather refers to a conceptual shift, a different initial approach in practice and in the understanding of material and composer. In this *tabula rasa* state, material is not a passive object waiting for the action of the composer; rather, it appears in the process of composition, in its development and transformation, while at the same time material sets the conditions for its own development. In *MTRAK*, composition is not the development of a raw seed material; instead, the material emerges from the set of possible combinations that system and composer explore. By means of its own structure, the emergent material influences its subsequent development and transformation in the piece. *Parallax* is the result of researching a material that emerges from a set of conditions established by the network of behaviours localised in space. Systems, tools,

---

11   At the time of writing this chapter, *Parallax* was programmed to be premiered in October 2020 at the Donaueschinger Musiktage festival. Before the chapter's finalisation during the 2020 Covid-19 crisis, the premiere of *Parallax* was postponed to 2022. Instead, a miniature for chamber orchestra, *displaced* (2020), was planned to be premiered in 2020 in which I used the strategy of networks of behaviours explained in this chapter. With the second wave of the Covid-19 crisis, the festival and the performance of *displaced* were sadly cancelled. A recording of the piece was still broadcast on SWR2 in October 2020 and can be heard in the online repository for this book (MF9.1). For further details of the online repository, see p. 355.

instrumentation, spatialisation, and parameters set up conditions for the material to emerge and facilitate its agency.

On the other hand, a composer becomes subject by intra-acting with an object, the piece, which is not yet extant, but in the process of formation. In this "zero state," the composer is not a fully all-knowing master with total control over the sound matter. This refusal of total control does not mean a lack of expertise or a renouncing of the composer's agency, but rather an open mindset embracing experimentation. The composer in this critical practice does not mould sound matter to explain the world to a passive listener. She rather uncovers in the practice of composition a new entity, the piece, by intra-acting with material, and by doing so she regains her agency. Piece and material, but also the composer, are in a continuous process of *becoming*. In this sense, we can relate the composer as subject with the *feminist nomadic figuration* described by Rosi Braidotti in *Nomadic Subjects: Embodiment and Sexual Difference in Contemporary Feminist Theory* (1994). Braidotti describes *figuration* as a method of thinking, as a way to conceptualise something that is in fluctuation and in movement. It is opposed to the principle of identity in which what is described is identical to the concept that describes it. It is opposed to generalisation and is a means of approaching difference.

> The quest for multiple connections—or conjunctions—can also be rendered methodologically in terms of Donna Haraway's *figurations* (1991). The term refers to ways of expressing feminist forms of knowledge that are not caught in a mimetic relationship to dominant scientific discourse. The "nomadic" style is the best suited to the quest for feminist figurations, in the sense of adequate representations of female experience as that which cannot easily be fitted within the parameters of phallogocentric language. (Braidotti 1994, 75–76)

A figuration is a tool that attempts to grasp what difference, "the other," the female, the queer, the non-white are, what is left out by the category of the male and conceptual generalisation. The nomadic figuration is in continuous formulation herself. She does not impose her mimetic reflection onto the world but rather explores the world in her nomadic *dérive* and in the fluctuations of the world itself. By doing so, the nomadic figuration creates a knowledge of herself and of the concrete. In the same way, the composer proposed in my compositional practice explores concreteness and difference in the material and exercises her own difference and agency. This figuration-composer does not exercise her agency by displaying her authority nor by shaping the sound material into an "expression of the self"—which would be a form of reflection. Rather, she is shaped by her encounter with the material and by the concrete knowledge unveiled in the compositional practice. In her practice, this composer explores the possibility of a subject that does not need to comply with generalisation and with control mechanisms but rather finds in her nomadic movement a way of claiming and making perceptible her difference.

EXPERIENCE: OPENNESS AND MULTIPLICITY.
NEW KNOWLEDGE

A critical practice oriented towards openness in the compositional process suggests a different relationship between material and composer while reformulating the composer as a feminist subject. In the same way, such critical practice can pose a different relationship between a listener and a musical work, by allowing openness in its experience and understanding. Such openness poses a critique of the exclusivity of knowledge based on language and permits the generation of a form of knowledge specific to art.

Still, what is the open experience that a musical practice can offer? The openness in the experience of music can be understood in at least three non-conflicting ways: (1) The result of a musical experiment is not known in advance and it emerges in the process. (2) The musical experiment provides a different result in each iteration—as in the aleatory experimental music of the 1960s. (3) Openness depends on each listener's own subjective interpretation, as in Umberto Eco's semiotic understanding of the artwork (1989). A multiplicity of understandings is the result of different readings by listeners.

I would like to propose a fourth possibility of openness, which does not reject the previous ones: a multiplicity of experiences inherent to the result of the experiment rather than derived exclusively from the divergent semantic interpretations of each listener. In my practice, this openness is due to the relationships and family resemblances that the materials and the composer create. The experience of the piece, its knowledge, is the presentation of an ever-changing network of materials and their behaviours. This network of relations remains open in the contingency of its different appearances but still retains coherence by means of these very same relations. An openness inherent to the work goes beyond semiotic openness. In Eco's *opera aperta*, openness ultimately relies on the listener, presupposing that the work of art is an object projected by the listener's expectations or a symbol for her to interpret. That does not mean that any form of semiotic interpretation is excluded in my practice. Still, the work, due to its multiple nature, resists being reduced to be merely a carrier of meaning and rejects the status of a passive object. Therefore, the work forces the listener to actively encounter it, to intra-act with it, and to follow its continuous meandering. The work is ambiguous and inherently open, its understanding is activated in listening by the encounter with the listener. By doing so, the compositional practice again questions the hierarchical binary subject–object relation, now from the perspective of the listener and the piece, and subverts the consumer–commodity relation.

Parallax is a compositional attempt to subvert expectations and generalisations. The piece neither presents a narrative teleological form upon which the listener can rely in order to follow it nor displays a static situation in which one can be immersed in calm contemplation. On the contrary, the musical work asks the listener to encounter it by presenting different deliberately ambiguous manifestations of a reduced network in continuous movement through space and in its unfolding flux through time.

In my practice, space plays an important role by creating a multiplicity of experiences. Parameters and networks of relations have a spatial dimension and materials are the results of combinations of spatial processes instead of merely being distributed in space. This implies a relational conception of space. Although I use geometrical space as a tool to represent reality, and for the construction of models and systems, I understand space as a relativistic dynamic system of interactions between objects, structures, social relations, and actions (Löw 2016). Therefore, material and space itself emerge in the diffractive encounter between the network of relations, listeners, performers, and the performance space.

It can be argued that pieces that use localisation of sound sources and even any piece played in a concrete space are differently perceived depending on one's spatial position. However, this is not always compositionally explored. Pieces that make use of ambisonics—and also instrumental works that create a specific area or "sweet spot" in which an ideal sound image can be experienced equally by every member of the audience—do not favour a multiplicity of experiences. On the other hand, there are pieces that do offer multiple experiences but do not promote multiple understandings. These musical works display teleological forms in which ambiguity of understanding is not taken into account. Spatialisation in these pieces is always used to communicate a single unequivocal meaning and is understood as the imposition of a spatial position onto an otherwise non-spatial sound object. The listener will have different acoustic perceptions depending on her position, even different semantic interpretations of the piece. Still, the piece offers one possible understanding, the one intended by the composer. This is not problematic in itself but it is contrary to the aim of my compositional practice.[12]

MTRAK and *Parallax* promote different understandings of the relations and transformations of the material depending on the listener's position.[13] In the online repository for this book, there are three recordings created with a spatial model programmed in SuperCollider that render the piece *MTRAK* in three different listening positions.[14] In these simulations, it is apparent how the different appearances of material in continuous transformation uncovers the piece's intrinsic openness and how the use of space could contribute to enhance a multiplicity of understandings of the musical work.[15]

---

12 There are many well-known pieces that generate different experiences for the listener, but whose aim is not to create ambiguity, for example, Isabel Mundry's *Penelopes Atem* (2003) for orchestra, Beat Furrer's *FAMA* (2005), or Mark André's . . . *auf III* . . . (2007) for orchestra and electronics.

13 Listeners to *Parallax* are advised not to move. Movements of both sound and receptor annihilate the perception of movement.

14 Three binaural recordings that reproduce a quadraphonic version of *MTRAK* in three different listening positions can be heard in the online repository for this book (MF9.2, MF9.3, MF9.4).

15 If we compare the first forty seconds of the beginning of *MTRAK* in the three listening positions we will clearly hear the different understandings that spatialisation can provide. In the first listening position—the listener at the front in the middle—the appearance of a third voice is perceived as a rhythmical shifting of the first two. However, the second position—the listener towards the back left—shows the third layer clearly as independent and in rhythmic contrast with the other two. In the third position this layer is understood as a stronger and different rhythmic shift than in the one from the first listening position, while a high pitch results from the sum of the low frequencies.

The idea of openness in understanding and the role of space in musical listening lead to questions about the epistemology of aesthetic experience and artistic practice. It can be argued that art displays a specific form of knowledge different from language-based knowledge (Borgdorff 2012; Holert 2020). This form of knowledge is more experiential and embodied, and cannot be grasped by language, which deals with generalisation rather than with difference and concreteness. Language reduces the particular to general statements, and in doing so it segregates and hides particular realities, that is, that which does not fit the principle of identity. Nonetheless, artistic knowledge does not disregard or pretend to substitute the knowledge produced by language. Language represents a valuable tool to organise and create systems and in its generalisation it may unfold an artistically productive field of openness. This aspect is explored in poetry and compositional practice dealing with language as material. Still, artistic knowledge proposes an alternative to language-based knowledge by showing experiences that escape discursive enclosure and objectivisation. Far from being a delusional belief in the ideology of "sound music"—as would be claimed by some postmodern advocates of conceptual and semantic referentiality—this approach is a conscious critical practice, which focuses on the realm of sound and generates another kind of knowledge different from the knowledge of (using Jacques Derrida's terminology) *phallogocentric language*, a knowledge of what is left over by language.

OPENNESS AS CRITIQUE

Achieving openness in compositional practice is a difficult task for the composer, also implying an element of self-critique. A practice that fosters openness, forces the composer to go beyond herself and to share her agency with the material. A critique and a detachment of learned clichés are necessary in order to allow the emergence of material in its transformations. However, self-critique is an ongoing and challenging goal—never entirely achieved—of detaching oneself not only from hierarchical thinking, generalisations, and power relations, but also from expectations of what compositional practice is supposed to be. Different strategies can aid in pursuing this goal. As we saw previously, these strategies include different approaches and conceptualisations oriented towards material and composer and the use of different systems: a network of different layers of spatial activities—in *Parallax*—or the use of non-linear sound synthesis systems in *MTRAK*. The construction of systems is an important part of my compositional practice. They are not a way to achieve a pretended "scientific" objectivity, nor a means to avoid creative decisions—the choice of the system is a creative decision itself. Systems are rather a way to overcome myself, to lose unconsciously assumed stereotypes as well as to allow the agency of the material to unfold, and by doing so, to co-create the conditions for the piece to emerge.

Furthermore, openness implies a risk of failure: a risk is taken when the outcome of the compositional practice is unknown. This risk of failure is not related to its public performance, but to the fragility of the artistic experiment on the basis of its own premises. The success of a compositional practice is not the confirmation of an a priori idea—reflection of a theory—but rather the existence of the experiment under its own conditions. The success of Lucier's *Bird and Person Dyning* does not rely on the empirical demonstration of the heterodyning phenomenon but on the aesthetic experience produced in the encounter between recording, feedback, performance space, and the actions and movements of the composer-performer. It relies not only on its own existence but also on the fragility of its existence, on the possibility that it may not "work." As Menke (2013) points out, the fragility of art, this risk of failure of its own existence, is what constitutes the experimentality and openness of art.

In this sense, due to its experimental character and its precarious existence and by taking risks, compositional practice affirms its position in the world. It criticises society by proving its own existence and by displaying an alternative form of knowledge and practice. A compositional practice oriented towards openness exercises a different relation—one of intra-action—between composer and material and poses a concrete knowledge based on experience (*Erfahrung*) different from the one of language. In this sense, it criticises social assumptions, hierarchies and power relations, one's knowledge, and the power structures inscribed into it. *Parallax* and *MTRAK* offer a multiplicity of concrete experiences, meanings, and understandings. Their ambiguity hinders their categorisation and prevents them from being turned into commodities. They pose a critique of the myths of composer and composition. The critique inherent to my practice is not a didactic one; however, it does not show on a semantic level what is "wrong" with composition, but rather displays a possible alternative in practice. Far from being a moralising rebuke, this critique poses a "withdrawal of art to conform to the more violent violence of a society in which the art necessarily exists and to which it therefore responds" as described by Lydia Goehr ([2008] 2015, 36). This withdrawal of art is also its refusal to be complicit, which can also be a silent refusal to communicate, a withdrawal from structures of meaning, and it is therefore fragile. The compositional practice refuses to capitulate under the social and formal powers of administration and criticises the violence of social institutions and ideologies such as language, and generalisation imposed onto difference.

By proposing a relation of open encounter between material, composer, and listener, musical practice criticises hierarchical relations of subject and object, and the relations of exploitation by humans of their surroundings and of each other. In addition, it poses a new form of knowledge, a multifaceted event that is open to be experienced and understood by the listener, not necessarily in a semantic way but as an aesthetic experience. This more subtle critique immanent to the practice of composition and outside language locates itself in a fragile, subtle, almost silent place because it makes visible the invisible. Art shows what escapes language, what is repressed and hidden. It creates a sensory experience of what is ungraspable (invisible) by symbolisation, of what is different. Art becomes critical by aesthetically displacing its own borders and thus by contributing to "a new landscape of the visible, the sayable and the doable" (Rancière 2010, 149).

References

Barad, Karen. 2007. *Meeting the Universe Halfway: Quantum Physics and the Entanglement of Matter and Meaning.* Durham, NC: Duke University Press.

Borgdorff, Henk. 2012. *The Conflict of the Faculties: Perspectives on Artistic Research and Academia.* Leiden: Leiden University Press.

Braidotti, Rosi. 1994. *Nomadic Subjects: Embodiment and Sexual Difference in Contemporary Feminist Theory.* New York: Columbia University Press.

Eco, Umberto. 1989. *The Open Work.* Translated by Anna Cancogni. Cambridge, MA: Harvard University Press. First published 1962 as *Opera aperta* (Milan: Bompiani).

Goehr, Lydia. (2008) 2015. "Explosive Experiments and the Fragility of the Experimental." In *Experimental Affinities in Music*, edited by Paulo de Assis, 15–41. Orpheus Institute Series. Leuven: Leuven University Press. Chapter first published 2006 as "Explosive Experimente und die Fragilität des Experimentelle: Adorno, Bacon und Cage," in *Spektakuläre Experimente: Praktiken des Evidenzproduktion im 17. Jahrhundert*, edited by Helmar Schramm, Ludger Schwarte, and Jan Lazardzig (Berlin: de Gruyter), 477–506;

first published in English 2008 in Lydia Goehr, *Elective Affinities: Musical Essays on the History of Aesthetic Theory* (New York: Columbia University Press), 108–35.

Haraway, Donna J. 1991. "'Gender' for a Marxist Dictionary: The Sexual Politics of a Word." In *Simians, Cyborgs, and Women: The Reinvention of Nature*, 127–48. London: Free Association Books.

Holert, Tom. 2020. *Knowledge beside Itself: Contemporary Art's Epistemic Politics.* Berlin: Sternberg Press.

Löw, Martina. 2016. *The Sociology of Space: Materiality, Social Structures, and Action.* Translated by Donald Goodwin. New York: Palgrave Macmillan. First published 2000 as *Raumsoziologie* (Frankfurt am Main: Suhrkamp).

Menke, Christoph. 2013. *Die Kraft der Kunst.* Berlin: Suhrkamp.

Nyström, Erik. 2018. "Topographic Synthesis: Parameter Distribution in Spatial Texture." Unpublished paper. Accessed 8 April 2021. http://www.academia. edu/37191903/Topographic_Synthesis_ Parameter_Distribution_in_Spatial_ Texture.

Rancière, Jacques. 2010. *Dissensus: On Politics and Aesthetics.* Edited and translated by Steven Corcoran. London: Continuum.

Designing the Threnoscope or, How I Wrote One of My Pieces

Thor Magnusson

University of Sussex, UK; Iceland University of the Arts

INTRODUCTION

To Albert Einstein is attributed the statement that if we knew what we were doing, we wouldn't call it research. No reliable sources back this up and indeed it is most likely to be an academic joke that took on a life of its own on the internet. Nevertheless, there is much truth in jest and any examination of scientific practices will demonstrate that creativity and originality in science are often the result of serendipitous events, accidents, and coincidences, but most importantly emerging from play with materials and ideas, using instruments of thinking such as pen and paper, models, prototypes, simulations, specimens, and samples. Mathematicians extend their mind's power through the prosthesis of pen and paper, engineers build prototypes or models to test their ideas, and the example of biologists Watson and Crick discovering the structure of DNA using physical models of balls and sticks is well known (Baird 2004, 32). The mental capacity to realise a "truth" emerging accidentally, during a work process seeking to achieve something else, should not be underestimated. While we might be trained in the scientific practice of having a hypothesis, expressed in a clear set of research questions with appropriate methods of answering them, all laid out and articulated, we have to acknowledge that a large portion of original thinking in the natural and social sciences, as well as in the arts and humanities, does not happen this way.

Artistic research is typically practice-based, where a wide typology of expressions and their effects on human society are studied from a range of perspectives, whether material, formal, or cultural. The material of expression can be of any sort, ranging from written words or notes, through dance, theatre, sculpture, and architecture to landscape art or microorganism research. What characterises the practice is the emergence of new knowledge from the study and manipulation of these materials, not necessarily grounded in a theoretical framework, but arriving from actual doing, making, and evaluating. But what is the nature of such epistemological practice? This is different from the well-established scientific principles mentioned above, idealised as a process that goes from hypothesis to experimentation to formal knowledge published in academic settings after peer reviews, with findings that are reproducible by other scientists.[1] One metaphor of such practice might be the territorial map, where landmarks are clear, the field is given, but what needs to be explored are distinct routes and connections between points on that landscape. This metaphor covers what Boden calls combinatorial and explorative creativity (2011). Another metaphor might be that of a person, standing before thick fog that blankets swampy terrain rising into hills and mountains, who has a strong intuition that something interesting is to be found if the fog is entered. It is not clear what exactly that might be, but past experience and grounded knowledge of other similar journeys gives the artist-researcher confidence that something worth pursuing lies therein. Here, creativity is like a discovery, but often one that has to be hermeneutically contextualised within the language of the particular field in order for it to be accepted.

This chapter describes the artistic research and development of a live coding system, called *Threnoscope*, as an example of an artistic research process. The Threnoscope (Magnusson 2014a) is a graphic score system notated by code, which affords long durational drones of a microtonal nature, expressed in a multichannel speaker system. It has been released online[2] and other musicians have started using it in their work. But the final outcome of this completed system (or *nearly* completed, I should say, as software is never finished) was never one that I drew up, conceived, planned. It emerged from traversing swamps, with wet feet roaming the hills, and finally reaching the top of a mountain, where a sunny view was gained when the fog cleared, and I asked myself "what did I find here?"

THE THRENOSCOPE

The Threnoscope is a system for live coding spatial microtonal music. Or, at least, that is what it affords most people composing and performing with it. What typically happens when you release software out in the wild is that someone somewhere rejects the script of the technology, as is well theorised by actor–network theory (Akrich 1992), and makes something completely different with it. Ignoring such antics, for example where the system has been used to create a sixteen-step drum machine, the Threnoscope is a system that splits the screen into two views: a graphic visual representation of the microtonal sounds and their spatial locations, and a live coding interface that enables the live coder to compose microtonal music, spreading the sounds across a multichannel space.

There are two visual representations of the Threnoscope: a harmonic view and a scale view. Figure 10.1 shows the harmonic view, where the innermost circle represents a fundamental frequency, for example 55 Hz, the standardised A, and the concentric circles outwards are the harmonics of that frequency,

---

1   It should be noted that both the natural and the social sciences are currently undergoing what is called the "reproduction crisis" where a considerable bulk of peer-reviewed and published research cannot reproduce the same findings when experiments are rerun. This calls for a different methodology for research and the publication of findings, with solutions ranging from funding experiments rather than researchers to the pre-registration and peer review of experiments before they are conducted.

2   http://thormagnusson.github.io/threnoscope.

110Hz, 165Hz, 220Hz, and so on. The fundamental can be set to any desired frequency, which is important when performing with instruments of a specific key, like the clarinet or the horn, or simply to rest the ears from listening to specific frequencies for longer durations. Thin lines cross the circles, and these represent the speakers, whether they are stereo (left and right), quadraphonic (left, front, right, back or left-front, right-front, right-back, left-back), quintaphonic (5.1), septaphonic (7.1), or octophonic surround. The wedges represent the sound forms as they move through the space; the thickness of the wedge corresponds to the cut-off frequency of the low pass filter applied to the wave. All the parameters of the drone—waveform, frequency, amplitude, cut-off filter frequency, resonance frequency, speed, and length—can be set on initiation and controlled in real time.

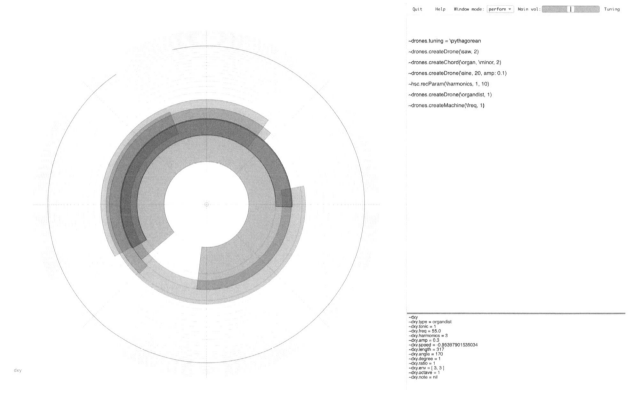

Figure 10.1.

The scale view can be seen in figure 10.2. Here the innermost circle is the fundamental frequency, but what follows are the degrees of the particular scale, set to a particular tuning. Octaves are represented with a red circle. The circles are rearranged when a new scale is chosen or when a new tuning is selected (the scale could be minor, but the circle ratios are adjusted when moving from, say, a twelve-tone equal-tempered tuning to a just intonation. Likewise, the circles change location when changing from, for example, a minor to a

Figure 10.1. The Threnoscope harmonics view. The concentric circles represent the harmonics of a set fundamental frequency. The crosshairs represent the speakers. The wedges are the "drones" (long-duration notes) and when they overlap a speaker line, they come out of that speaker. The interface is interactive, but most of the performance happens in the coding window.

mixolydian scale). The drones can be initialised on any of the degrees of the scale and they can be moved between degrees. This can also happen in the harmonic view; the only difference is that we don't see which degrees the drones are on. Additionally, chords can be initialised, new chords created, and drones grouped into clusters that can be controlled with central commands. These can be saved for later use.

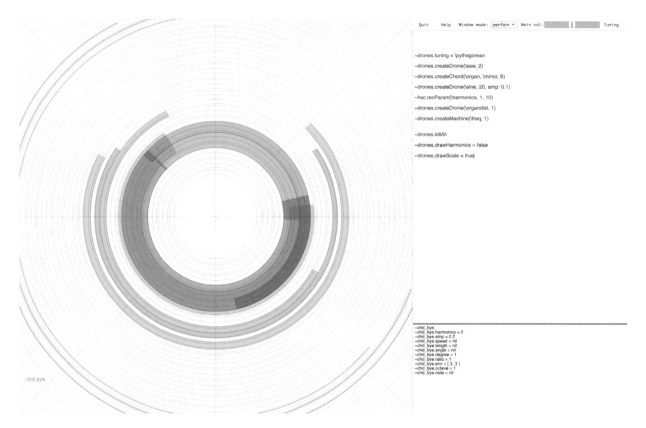

Figure 10.2.

The Threnoscope has a plethora of other functionalities, such as creating satellites, where a multitude of smaller drones appear on the stage according to the parameters set at initiation. There are various types of machines that can be made to appear at the middle of the interface to manipulate the drones (shifting their frequencies, timbre, amplitude, etc.). A score system was implemented in order to compose more set pieces, and this code score can be both deterministic and generative, depending on the code it contains. The score system can also be used to compose short "riffs" that can be initiated at any point in time in a performance. Finally, the state of the Threnoscope can be stored and recalled at any point and it is possible to move from one state to another over a specified timeframe.

Figure 10.2. The Threnoscope scale view. Here we see another representation of the pitch space. The red circles are octaves from the fundamental frequency. The other circles are the notes in the selected scale. A scale could be in various tunings, for example a Lydian scale in just intonation tuning.

The system is in many ways complete, although there are some features that would be good to work on further. My hope is that by releasing it as open source software, other users will contribute to the system or fork its development in other directions. I wrote the Threnoscope over a number of years, during free time from work. Unlike ixi lang (Magnusson 2011), I did not want to release the system nor the code as open source early, as I didn't want interruptions to my way of thinking and experimenting. In my experience, user requests can drastically change the way one thinks about the development of software, and in this case I wanted to take time with my own pace of development, and explore the system through performance and audience feedback. In the next section, I will explain how I developed this system, from initial experimentation to its completion.

Developing the Threnoscope

I began working on the Threnoscope sitting in the middle of an eight-channel surround sound studio in Brighton. With the audio programming language SuperCollider in front of me—my favourite way of thinking out loud about sound—I experimented with sending waves of different frequencies to the speakers around me, moving them from one speaker to another while changing them in pitch, amplitude, and texture. The code might have looked something like this:

{PanAz.ar(8, SinOsc.ar(110, 0, XLine.kr(1, 0.4, 10, doneAction:2), Line.kr(0, 1, 10))}.play

// [here a sine wave is panned across eight speakers in ten seconds. The wave is 110Hz, and its amplitude goes from 1 to 0.4 in ten seconds, then the synth disappears].

Or

{PanAz.ar(8, LPF.ar(Saw.ar(XLine.kr(55, 110, 10, doneAction:2)), XLine.kr(880, 440, 10, doneAction:2), Line.kr(1, pi, 10)) }.play

// [here a saw wave is panned across eight speakers. The frequency goes from 55Hz to 110Hz, and the cut-off frequency of the low-pass filter (LPF) moves from 880Hz to 440Hz, all in ten seconds].

In addition, series of variations containing different waveforms and filters were applied, morphing the sound in time, moving it in space.

Previously, I had developed the ixi lang live coding system, which affords a simple interface for creating beat-based music, supporting polyrhythm, polymetre, and a large range of tunings and scales, but primarily aimed at working with patterns of samples in a live coding setting (Magnusson and McLean 2018). Playing in this eight-channel surround sound studio, I didn't really have any strong intention other than to explore the movement of sound waves in frequency and space, and I was more interested in long durational notes, exploring further the drone music that I'd been listening to since I was a teenager, for example Indian music, the Velvet Underground, Terry Riley, La Monte

Young, and Phill Niblock. Much of this music, of course, is in complex microtonal tunings, and I was interested in studying their effect on the human listener. Although I had read much about the world's diverse tuning systems and musical scales, I had never properly explored their effect systematically and comparatively in my own musical experience and practice. Moreover, I had the intuitive idea that it might be interesting to explore the relationship between tuning and spatiality.

Thus, I began working on a musical piece that I could perform in different tunings, with waveforms ranging from the purest sine wave, through synthesised waveforms rich with partials, to more complex organ sounds, xylophones, or reed instruments. I implemented a system for circular looping of sampled sounds so I could use the output of real instruments as waveforms, leaving out the attack and the decay of the sound, but looping its sustaining part. I then wrote a SuperCollider class that would read the thousands of scales of the Scala library[3] and feed them as frequency data into my waveforms. This was exciting! Swapping the tuning of a cluster of drones in real time would completely change the feeling of the sound heard, and the sounds travelling through the surround system created an effect of movement, shape morphing, and liveliness.

Visual representation of sound and interaction design in music software has been a long-term interest of mine, so it was natural to think about how to visualise and control these drones through a graphical user interface. I wanted to "see" the sound as well as hear it. The context of sitting in the middle of eight speakers made it natural to start by drawing a double cross (a mix of an "x" and a "+") on the screen and somehow represent the drones on those speaker lines. Since I was studying alternative tuning systems, I subsequently drew circles of harmonics where the lowest harmonic was the innermost circle, and the next ones circling that one outward. I decided to represent this on a linear scale pattern (as opposed to an exponential one) as I wanted the octaves to appear at regular intervals, but also because the visual screen space would not easily (from a usability perspective) give room for the exponential drawing of harmonics.

With this visual system I had the physical speaker space and the sonic frequency space represented. The drones themselves would get a representation on their set frequency and a thickness depending on their frequency range before the low-pass filter cut-off and could be placed on any of the speakers depending on their length (in degrees, around the circle). The next step was to implement time, where the drones could move around the circular space (or increase in length, crossing more and more speakers). I experimented with using vector-based amplitude panning (VBAP) and Ambisonics for fading in and out of the speakers, but eventually I became more interested in conceiving of the eight speaker lines as static timelines through which the musical "notes" would pass. Here, I had suddenly arrived at a very peculiar system of representing circular musical time, and one that was certainly not decided on a drawing board before beginning to program the piece. This is an example of a satisfying artistic and technical solution emerging from iterative

---

3 http://www.huygens-fokker.org/scala.

experimentations and testing, with many failed ideas abandoned on the roadside, with others implemented and developed further.

Code can be good for many things, and for some it is a much better control interface than any graphical user interface. For example, in a few lines of code I can create one hundred drones, placed on every third degree of a particular scale, with a reducing number of harmonics and a random amplitude in each drone. Later, I might write another line and make these drones move around the space, following each other by 20 degrees.[4] It simply does not make sense to create a user interface for such a one-off random idea; but with code, practically anything can be expressed that fits within the parameters of the piece. However, looking beyond the power of code, since there was already a graphic representation of the sounds, this representation could easily become a control interface too. I thus implemented the capability of moving drones around with the mouse, and created a control mechanism to adjust the parameters of the sound, such as pitch, texture, or amplitude. I also implemented the functionality of recording the movements of those parameters in time, as it is often easier to demonstrate a trajectory in time and space intuitively with the hand than to write it as an algorithm in code. This direct interfacing with the drones after they have been created, both through code and the graphical interface, was important for the live performance of the piece and I subsequently supported both MIDI and OSC control to interface with the system.

An audiovisual collaboration with a colleague, Jüri Kermik, on an animated film prompted me to come up with a score system for precise timing (Magnusson 2014b). This was easy to design: simply a two-dimensional array with the first element being the time, and the code to be triggered at that point, all run by a dedicated clock. Of course, such functionality becomes interesting when one begins to explore the stretching or compressing of time, or to run multiple timelines or multiple scores at once—and here the spirit of experimentation has resulted in some design decisions that are uncommon in conventional software, probably for a good reason.

A PIECE OR A SYSTEM?

I have described the development process of the Threnoscope: how one idea led to another, following research interests, and working with the affordances of the sound equipment as well as the screen, physical interfaces, and the SuperCollider audio programming language. This was a bottom-up process, working with the materials at hand as they emerge or appear on the ideological horizon, as opposed to the top-down process of designing first, then implementing, for example using UML diagrams for a fully developed systems design. Shelly Turkle and Seymour Papert have described the distinction between these two types of programmers, terming one a bricoleur, the other a planner (Turkle and Papert 1990).

---

4 Note that the degrees of a scale are not the same as degrees (°) in the mathematics of a circle, measuring an angle.

The Threnoscope was given a name, as a system, very late in the process, for the simple reason that I only intended to write some music in my preferred notational format: code. The initial idea was to compose a piece that I would perform live through the method of live coding—only later did I realise that I had invented a compositional system. Now, the boundaries here are not clear and I have elsewhere described how contemporary music is moving from a definition of *composing a work* towards the idea of *inventing a system*. In a recent book, *Sonic Writing* (Magnusson 2019b), I analyse the tendency to invent systems to be navigated by performers (often themselves) rather than composing musical works in the manner we are accustomed to, like those that emerged with Romanticism and are so well analysed by Goehr (1992). Although musical works are still being composed—and common musical notation is not going anywhere—contemporary music is now eagerly exploring new instruments (Holland et al. 2013), new notations (Vear 2019), and new types of musical expression in new media formats (Magnusson 2019b).

This "new systematicity," or the shift from composing a work to inventing a system, is characteristic of twenty-first century music. In an article from 2000, Jonathan Impett investigates the concept of *invention* in his practice of interactive music: "In my work, I needed a name for a particular software construct: a unit of musical behaviour which encapsulates materials and behaviours from multiple sources which is formed by the interaction of several dynamical systems. . . . The *invention* in this context is the locus of materials, behaviour and relationships" (Impett 2000, 29). Impett applies the concept to describe a construct that is perhaps a musical piece, but not really. While he applies it to his own practice in a narrow sense, I wish to view it in the context of classical rhetoric, where invention was one of the key tropes, alongside arrangement, style, memory, and delivery. Invention was the *discovery* (and note that we make a distinction between these two words in modern English that did not exist in Latin) of a new version from a template or a set of rules. See Bach's *Inventions*, described by Dreyfus as "more than a static, well-crafted object, but instead like a mechanism that triggers further elaborative thought from which a whole piece of music is shaped" (1996, 2). In my book, I define the invention of a system as

> something that has been put together, not discovered, but actively created through combinatorics or out of nothing (as in *poiesis*). Examples include generative compositions, new musical instruments, audio games, live coding systems, animated notation pieces, unit generators in audio programming languages, verbal scores, virtual worlds, and so on. These are theoretical systems that "contain" the music through their affordances and constraints—objects, in other words, that generate actions through their ergodynamic potential. The contemporary act of composition and performance in these new media is therefore a search, a *ricercare*, where we explore the ergodynamics of the instrument, its playability, sound, and musical structures. Thus, the questions often asked, in twentieth-century language, whether the work is the instrument or the musical piece, or whether the live coding language is a system or a composition, become irrelevant. By applying the concept of *invention*, we transcend the work-concept and the conceptual problems that have lingered as

linguistic remains of a musical culture we have now surpassed. (Magnusson 2019b, 183)[5]

The Threnoscope has been released, and other people are using it. They are making *their* music with it. Yet, this is music based on a very strong personal vision that has been inscribed into this instrument, this system, this composition. And here is the problem: the language we have traditionally used to describe our musical practices—such as composer, performer, audience, score, work, composition, instrument, interpretation, space, sound system, producer, engineer—is not descriptive of how current work patterns and roles are evolving in contemporary music. Equally grounded in new philosophical theories of creativity and originality, as well as new computational media, new artistic practices transcend the interrelated twentieth-century discourses of research and creativity.

CONCLUSION

The Threnoscope has served as a testbed for experimentation. Through the research process, I have explored ideas of microtonal composition through applying and creating new tunings and scales. I have studied the psychoacoustics of microtonal sound in space, and relationships between waves as they are placed in speakers surrounding us. The interface has become the score, the instrument, the system, and I have learned a lot from audience feedback telling me what they learned from observing the system in operation. But most importantly, I feel I have been able to study ideas of authorship, creativity, authenticity, originality, and co-operation in music, as the system has become a connective device, a focus for discussion about the above-mentioned notions that are necessarily changing in today's music. I also feel that I have not only studied these changed notions through the work, but also actively contributed to their redefinitions, no matter how small that contribution might be.

The Orpheus Institute has organised exemplary symposia and published important work on practice-based research. This is a wide and complex field: what is practice-based research? How is it different from other research? There are innumerable points of view and distinct ideologies and methodologies, as can be seen in the institute's previous publications. Personally, I can say that without being able to make things, compose, program, perform, listen, talk, and present, I would not have been able to gather and formulate new knowledge of the role of the score, of microtonal tunings, of designing scales, of the spatiality of sound and related psychoacoustics, or partake in innumerable cases of collaboration with other musicians that have taught me so much. I have sought to present that knowledge in the form of the system itself, as an object resulting from the research: an epistemic tool pregnant with music theory of all kinds, including tuning and instrument design. The Threnoscope can be

---

5   For a further discussion on the notion of *ergodynamics*, *ergomimesis*, and *ergophor*, see Magnusson (2019a).

studied through use, through exploring its affordances and constraints (or better *ergodynamics*, see Magnusson 2019a), as a way of understanding the new knowledge imbued in it. It can be studied in performance by the audience whose interpretations bring new insights. The Threnoscope's source code can also be studied, reading the design decisions, line by line, analysing the actual theoretical constructs it encapsulates. Finally, I have presented the system at music festivals and academic conferences. I have written about the system and sought to communicate its qualities as an objective proposal for music-making, an intervention into the state of musical instruments, improvisation, live coding, notational practices, and musical collaboration.

In this chapter I have described my working methods in developing the Threnoscope. I explained how it moved from a musical piece to a compositional system, and I pointed out the problems in such dichotomies, as our new musical practices transcend our past language. But I should admit that I rarely work this way nowadays, and that I consider working in this way, as a bottom-up bricoleur, a privilege when operating in the academic context. The fact is that the structure of artistic practice-based research in university grant-proposal, evaluation, and quality-control systems, and for arts and humanities research funding bodies, is moulded to fit that of hypothesis-based scientific research. Here, the general assumption is that artistic work can be well defined as an idea before entering the studio or the workshop. That the work can be expressed as a set of research questions that will be answered through a well-defined research methodology. And that the final piece is simply the result of this process, an outcome. Most creative artists know this is not how it works: the materials we work with are not neutral: they speak, resist, protest, and at times go with the flow of our ideas as they emerge in a conversation with the materials. It is easy to mass-produce new work when a method has been reached, but this is *the result* of a research process, not research on its own. This is the character of artistic research (and indeed much research outside the arts): we serendipitously arrive at new visions or knowledge through forking paths that bend or recurse back; in a dialogue with the materials we work with, whether it is clay, canvas and brush, instruments, or code. And it is here that "Einstein's joke" begins to ring true, in that if we knew what we were doing, we wouldn't call it research.

REFERENCES

Akrich, Madeleine. 1992. "The De-scription of Technical Objects." In *Shaping Technology/Building Society: Studies in Sociotechnical Change*, edited by Wiebe E. Bijker and John Law, 205–24. Cambridge, MA: MIT Press.

Baird, Davis. 2004. *Thing Knowledge: A Philosophy of Scientific Instruments*. Berkeley: University of California Press.

Boden, Margaret A. 2011. *Creativity and Art: Three Roads to Surprise*. Oxford: Oxford University Press.

Dreyfus, Laurence. 1996. *Bach and the Patterns of Invention*. Cambridge, MA: Harvard University Press.

Goehr, Lydia. 1992. *The Imaginary Museum of Musical Works: An Essay in the Philosophy of Music*. Oxford: Oxford University Press.

Holland, Simon, Katie Wilkie, Paul Mulholland, and Allan Seago, eds. 2013. *Music and Human-Computer Interaction*. London: Springer.

Impett, Jonathan. 2000. "Situating the *Invention* in Interactive Music." In

Organised Sound 5 (1): 27–34.

Magnusson, Thor. 2011. "The ixi lang: A SuperCollider Parasite for Live Coding." In *Proceedings of the International Computer Music Conference 2011*, University of Huddersfield, 503–6. Accessed 9 April 2021. https://quod.lib.umich.edu/cgi/p/pod/dod-idx/ixi-lang-a-supercollider-parasite-for-live-coding.pdf?c=icmc;idno=bbp2372.2011.101;format=pdf.

———. 2014a. "Improvising with the Threnoscope: Integrating Code, Hardware, GUI, Network, and Graphic Scores." In *Proceedings of the International Conference on New Interfaces for Musical Expression 2014*, Goldsmiths, University of London, 19–22. http://doi.org/10.5281/zenodo.1178857.

———. 2014b. "Scoring with Code: Composing with Algorithmic Notation." In *Organised Sound* 19 (3): 268–75.

———. 2019a. "Ergodynamics and a Semiotics of Instrumental Composition." *Tempo* 73 (287): 41–51.

———. 2019b. *Sonic Writing: Technologies of Material, Symbolic, and Signal Inscriptions.* New York: Bloomsbury Academic.

Magnusson, Thor, and Alex McLean. 2018. "Performing with Patterns of Time." In *The Oxford Handbook of Algorithmic Music*, edited by Alex McLean and Roger T. Dean, 245–66. New York: Oxford University Press.

Turkle, Sherry, and Seymour Papert. 1990. "Epistemological Pluralism: Styles and Voices within the Computer Culture." *Signs* 16 (1): 128–57.

Vear, Craig. 2019. *The Digital Score: Musicianship, Creativity and Innovation.* New York: Routledge.

A Few Reflections about Compositional Practice through a Personal Narrative

Daniela Fantechi

Orpheus Institute, Ghent; University of Antwerp

1. Introduction

The notion of *critical technical practice* proposed by Philip Agre provides a perspective that can be fruitfully applied to the discourse on composition. The author of *Computation and Human Experience* aims to create a critical technical practice in which "rigorous reflection upon technical ideas and practices becomes an integral part of day-to-day technical work itself" (Agre 1997, 3). Agre expresses the need to reorient research in artificial intelligence (AI), shifting the focus from abstract cognitive processes towards a closer observation of daily activity. This need lies primarily in the contingent qualities of the material research processes of AI.

> Activity is fundamentally improvised; contingency is the central phenomenon. People conduct their activity by continually redeciding what to do. (7)

> "Improvisation," as I will employ the term, might involve ideas about the future and it might employ plans, but it is always a matter of deciding what to do *now*. (8)

> The . . . view of human activity that I have sketched here contains a seeming tension: how can activity be both improvised and routine? The answer is that the routine of everyday life is not a matter of performing precisely the same actions every day, as if one were a clockwork device executing a plan. Instead, the routine of everyday life is an emergent phenomenon of moment-to-moment interactions that work out in much the same way from day to day because of the relative stability of our relationships with our environments. (7)

Composition shares with the discipline of AI a certain degree of contingency and improvisation. During the routine of each compositional process, several factors intervene in the decision-making process, and composers are not always fully aware of their weight. Therefore, as Agre outlines, what matters most from both critical and disciplinary perspectives is not the analysis of the work itself—respectively, computer programs or musical compositions—but the observation of the process behind the technical work. Moreover, similarly to AI, composition can be considered as a technical practice, since its development relies on the use of many different technologies, such as notation, musical instruments, software, and so on. These technologies are means of realisation, as well as agents of the system, in which the practice of composition takes place. Each composer engages with all these different technologies in a very personal relationship, which seems to be stable even if—due to its interactive quality—it is constantly renewed during the process. Indeed, the whole experience of any compositional activity has an embodied, situated, and perceptual nature. Therefore, a more honest form of knowledge could emerge from the observation of daily routines, incorporating, at the same time, a reflexive activity that relates the personal experience to other disciplines such as philosophy, neuroscience, aesthetics, and so on.

Such a perspective has guided me in the adoption of a personal narrative, through which I will share a few considerations about my work and some aspects related to the routine of the compositional process, intended as a technical practice. This becomes a strategy to gain a more specific and detailed understanding of that practice. A common resistance to the adoption of a personal narrative concerns the fear of seeming too self-referential, or too cryptic in delivering some form of shareable knowledge. But it is also true that composers often make the mistake of using a too vague vocabulary to describe their strategies and methods, in order to make them seem broadly applicable, even when their adoption is the consequence of some unconscious and unrationalised assumptions, which remain, therefore, unexplained. Hence, I am going to honestly present a few observations about my personal work, trying to broaden the reflection while including meaningful perspectives from other thinkers and practitioners.

2. MY PERSONAL NARRATIVE: CONSIDERING CONTEXTUAL CONTINGENCIES

To show concretely how different contingencies have produced practical consequences in the development of my compositional work, I will refer to three pieces that represent my latest works within the project Composing with Piezoelectric Microphones. This is a research project concerning the composition of instrumental music implemented with specific use of piezoelectric contact microphones (simply *piezos*, from now on). A particular use of this low-cost and low-fidelity technology is explored not only to disclose and amplify instrumental sound but also to produce new sounds, through a reinterpretation of some instrumental gestures—glissando, tapping, scraping, and so on—produced by playing with the piezo directly on the instrument. The low-fidelity quality of these microphones presents limits and different degrees of controllability and predictability. These lead to reflection on the nature of the sound matter and on the different possibilities of controlling it within the compositional process. The pieces I will refer to are:

— *Hidden Traces* (2019), for guitar and electronics:[1]

This is an open-form piece, twelve to fifteen minutes in duration, in which overall control is left to the performer, who has however to follow a certain set of indications, also regarding the formal structure. Two transducers are placed on the soundboard of the guitar, to amplify both the instrumental and live-processed sound through the body of the guitar. Two piezos are, instead, employed with two different functions. The performer uses the first piezo to play on the strings and on various points of the surface of the guitar, while the second piezo has to be fixed on the soundboard to act as a "listener," providing information for the electronics. *Hidden Traces* was premiered in Belgium by myself and in the UK and Germany by the guitar player Seth Josel.

— *PianoMusicBox_1* (2019), for piano and electronics (written for Chiara Saccone):[2]

A few technical solutions explored within *Hidden Traces* were adopted in *PianoMusicBox_1*, turning the guitar piece into a sort of preparatory study for the piano piece. As in *Hidden Traces*, two piezos are used—one for the production of sounds and one providing information to the electronics— as well as two transducers. The latter are placed inside the stringboard of the piano to create a closed system, in which both the acoustic instrumental and live-processed sound are amplified through the body of the instrument. Moreover, many electronic processes have been derived from those used in the guitar piece, as well as the general structure of the piece. The piece starts with a few noisy sounds, produced by exploring with a piezo the inner part of the instrument—the soundboard and the strings—and it gradually moves towards the more familiar piano sound world when the pianist reaches the keyboard. The piece was premiered during the festival Collaborations are More Refreshing than New Socks, at the Royal Conservatoire Antwerp, on 4 December 2019.

— *Residual* (2019), for ensemble and electronics (commissioned by Hermes Ensemble):[3]

With this work I explored the possibility of working on two different layers of sound: in the foreground, the cello and the percussion, acting almost as soloists, in the background, the rest of the ensemble. To emphasise the perception of these two different layers, cello and percussion play with piezos, giving their sounds an intimate proximity; moreover, they are amplified through their own loudspeakers, placed next to them. The piece articulates a catalogue of actions and gestures that explore different degrees from almost pitchless to more pitched sounds; a quite unstable and unpredictable materiality of sound emerges from the gestures played with piezos.

---

1 A video recording of *Hidden Traces* (MF11.1) can be watched in the online repository for this book at https://orpheusinstituut.be/en/sound-work-media-repository. Further details of the repository can be found in the appendix to this book on p. 355.

2 Audio and video documentation of *PianoMusicBox_1* (MF11.2a, MF11.2b) can be found in the online repository.

3 Audio documentation of *Residual* (MF11.3) can be found in the online repository.

Residual was premiered by Hermes Ensemble at the Concertgebouw in Bruges on 21 November 2019.

Significant contingent circumstances are often related to social and institutional implications. I am thinking, for example, of the common case of a commissioned piece that determines a certain set of variables: what is the given instrumentation? Is there a given duration? Is there an established context for the premiere that calls for specific (technical) requirements? When is the deadline? (i.e., how much time is foreseen for the composition of the new piece?) Is it possible for the composer to collaborate with performers during the compositional process?

Hidden Traces, for example, was initially written for an exhibition in the Belgian art gallery Be-Part in Warengem. I was asked to propose a piece that I would perform. As composer, I am usually more concerned with writing pieces for someone else. Thus, this was quite an uncommon request, which led me to adopt what is for me an unusual solution, that is, the realisation of an open-form piece—which I formalised in a set of instructions only later, when I had the occasion to collaborate with the guitarist Seth Josel. The initial choice of instrument instead was due to very pragmatic reasons: the guitar is an easy instrument to borrow and transport around. Since I am not a guitarist, I took this occasion to look at the guitar from a different perspective, concentrating on a few technical issues, focusing on the use of two piezos, combined with two transducers, working as loudspeakers. So I exploited the guitar primarily as a resonant surface, experimenting with a few electronic solutions that I had never used before. This experimentation proved useful for *PianoMusicBox_1*, in which I reused several processes and solutions tested in the guitar piece. From the perspective of social and relational implications, the composition of the piano piece benefited from the close collaboration with Chiara Saccone, pianist and friend, who was available to work with me throughout almost the whole compositional process. Especially from the instrumental perspective, daily progress in the writing process went hand in hand with the schedule of our meetings; together we made many useful tests and recordings. Chiara became familiar with the use of piezos as means of sound production—trying them out also on different pianos—while providing me with helpful feedback. *Residual*, instead, was commissioned by Hermes Ensemble, which provided me with details of its available instrumentation to choose from, and a very well-structured schedule for rehearsals and delivery of the score. Moreover, I was informed from the beginning that the premiere of the new piece was planned for the big concert hall of the Concertgebouw in Bruges. Thus, it was clear that the number of rehearsals would be limited, as would access to the concert venue—which was actually planned only for the very last general rehearsal. During the compositional work, these factors influenced many choices, not only limiting them but also stimulating solutions that I would probably not have taken into consideration, such as focusing on the creation of a foreground and a background layer of sound. This idea originated from a very pragmatic reason: providing piezos to each member of the ensemble, and expecting to be able to test them with everyone, was unthinkable. Therefore I thought that it would have been simpler to choose two soloists—who were available to work with me individually—and to provide them in advance with piezos to play with, while using a more common and transparent amplification for the rest of the ensemble. In this way, I turned the consequences of using different means of amplification within the same ensemble into a creative idea.

3. My personal narrative: starting from the material, considering its mode of production

Different contextual circumstances naturally influence—reinforcing or questioning—the starting premises of new compositional works. But besides all external contingencies, the composer is first of all influenced by her or his own assumptions and recurring models, which are, nevertheless, constantly questioned by the emergence of personal and technical contingencies.

As a general and basic premise I tend to understand composition as a discipline of "organising sound," as was suggested by Varèse[4] and Cage.[5] But the term *sound* is very general, as well as being controversial, so I should try to provide at least one possible way to conceive it. I would start by considering several interesting understandings by Joanna Demers. In her book *Listening through the Noise*, she structures a vast discourse about electronic music since 1980, considering how it has changed the way we listen not only to music but also to sound itself, outlining her perspective on *sound* as material.

> What I mean by material here amounts to the objectified, audible phenomena in electronic music, from notes and rhythms to sound grains, clicks, timbres, even silence; it is, as Adorno puts it, "what artists work with" (1997, 148). (Demers 2010, 43)

Interestingly, she indicates heterogeneity as an important feature, considering how any kind of "objectified, audible phenomena," from pre-existing to newly created sounds, could be seen as material (ibid.). As Curtis Roads (2004, 327) observes, referring to Varèse, "the philosophy of organized sound extended the boundaries of accepted musical material, and hence the scope of composition, to a wider range of acoustic phenomena."

Nowadays, in fact, the idea that any sound can gain the status of musical material is completely accepted. Composers are used to dealing with a wide range of sound possibilities, and, in a compositional practice of organising sound, sound itself is intended as the raw material the composer chooses to work with.

A few questions arise from this first observation: how do composers choose their own sound material? How do they understand its properties? And how do these properties lend themselves to different kinds of manipulation, transformation, and organisation?

---

4 "I decided to call my music 'organized sound' and myself, not a musician, but 'a worker in rhythms, frequencies, and intensities'" (Varèse 1966, 18).

5 "If this word 'music' is sacred and reserved for eighteenth- and nineteenth-century instruments, we can substitute a more meaningful term: organization of sound" (Cage [1937] 1961, 3).

Most compositional work starts from the creation or selection of sound material, but then follows a process of definition and organisation. Hence, composers need to find strategies to understand a wide range of heterogeneous acoustic phenomena, that present different temporalities, different morphologies, and different properties. Demers observes that most of the time the discourse about material needs to converge on the activities—construction, reproduction, or deconstruction—that generate it: "As a concept, *material* may encapsulate the dual concerns of sound itself and sound generation, concerns that . . . are traits held in common among many electronica genres" (Demers 2010, 43). So, on one hand, Demers takes into consideration the sound material as the "sound itself," the "objectified, audible phenomen[on]," detached from any external semantic content. On the other hand, she considers the sound material from the perspective of its mode of generation, as the product of processes of construction, reproduction, or destruction. She sees it as a malleable material that, in opposition to Schaeffer's formulation of the sound-object (1966), can hardly be separated from its modes of production or from the media on which it is affixed: "material necessarily refers back to its own generation, and so any discussion of material must include the actions and devices involved in its creation" (Demers 2010, 43). Any information about sources, actions, and devices involved in the mode of production of a specific sound provides knowledge about its potentialities and about the different possibilities to work on it, as well as its relationship with other sounds.

This double perspective on sound material resonates particularly with my own compositional practice. In most of my works, I tend to start collecting raw sound material from the exploration of the instrument I am going to write for. In my experience, it is fundamental to get a full comprehension of modes of generation and production of what can be the raw sound material I will start from. This is why in the first stages of the compositional process, when writing for acoustic instruments, I try to play with the instrument myself, in order to gain a personal experience of its possible affordances. Borrowing Gibson's ecological perspective (1979), *affordances* should be understood as the action possibilities offered by the instrument to the performer. As a technological object, any instrument comes with its own design, and its physical and material features. But to overcome the subject/object duality that reduces the instrument to a physical object operated by a human subject, the instrument has to be understood from an ecological perspective, which takes into account the complexity of a network of different feedbacks, as well as practices, repertoires, institutions, social discourse, and so on. The instrument has to be seen as "something which comes attached with actions—we must understand the *instrument-as-played*, not *the instrument-as-constructed* or *-observed*" (Habbestad 2017, 317, italics original). In fact, the instrument comes to the musician with a set of operations or actions that can be performed on it, but without immediately informing the performer about their full use. A certain degree of experience and a huge amount of time are required to uncover, absorb, and, finally, master all the affordances of the instrument. Beginners usually interrogate more experienced performers on their playing techniques. Consequently, the musical instrument is never completely neutral to the performer because it comes with layers of embodied practices and idiomatic gestures, present in different repertoires, genres, historical practices, and traditions. Often what the instrument suggests is then studied by listening, learning, imitating, and innovating within specific historical and social contexts. And while becoming more and more sensitive to the multiple affordances of the instrument, the performer develops her or his own specific relationship with it. The performers' own agency is thus expressed and manifested in what is often defined as *expressivity* and *individual touch*. As Waters (2007, 2) suggests, those features result "not only from the physiology of the player, but the complex feedback into that player's body of vibrating materials, air, room, and the physiological adaptations and adjustments in that body and its 'software' which themselves feed back into the vibrating complex of instrument and room."

Aware of all these multiple layers of embodied instrumental practices, idiomatic gestures, and traditions, but devoid of the expertise of a real performer, I provisionally assume the performer's role, in order to empirically experience the physicality of the instrument, placing myself within the complex feedback relationships described by Waters. In doing so, I allow myself an exploration of the instrument that aims to go beyond the sound possibilities that the instrument has been designed for. My personal attempts to distance myself from established instrumental practice have to be understood as a practice that is shared among a larger community of musicians and performers. At any particular historical moment, the adoption of transgressive behaviours has stimulated the creativity of different generations of artists. And in the context of contemporary music, this mode of searching has become almost constant: many musicians, composers as well as improvisers, tend to extend or to operate at the edges of the sonic possibilities offered by the instrument, changing or forcing its original design features, looking for other means of expressivity.

Referring again to the three above-mentioned pieces, I can confirm a similar approach: at the very beginning of the three compositional works, I managed to get access respectively to a guitar, a piano, a cello, and a set of percussion. On each instrument, I experimented with the different uses of piezos, representing an external element, through which I aim to challenge the usual affordances of the instrument. My experiments consisted of using piezos as means of sound production, through the reinterpretation of a few instrumental gestures, such as glissando, tapping, scraping, hitting, and so on. Consequently, I found a way to enrich my vocabulary, testing how different modes of sound generation can be activated on various points on the instrument: on the strings, on frets, on the soundboard, and so on, producing more or less resonant sounds; and also through experimenting with different electronic elaborations, part of the exploration process on sound material.

It is worth noting that the introduction of the piezo determines a big change in the auditory perspective, entering the physical space of action of the performer and introducing interferences and elements of disruption in the usual performer–instrument feedback relationship. All contact with the instrument, even the smallest accidental movements, becomes audible. Hence, the extension of the instrument back into the body of the performer is strongly perceptible, and demands from the performer another kind of awareness and negotiation with respect to her or his own physicality. That is the reason why, after these first moments of personal exploration, the possibility to collaborate with performers becomes very important. First of all, because the performer needs to get familiar with the peculiar technology of piezos, becoming aware of their different usage possibilities and their way of hyper-amplifying the instrument; second, because the performer, with her or his own expertise and engagement, can usually add great value to the results of the experimental moments of improvisation, as I experienced before. Through rehearsals and moments of discussion, different performers have provided me with useful feedback about the collected sound material, enhancing the definition of playing techniques and notation of single gestures.

4. My personal narrative: how to understand the sound material?

At a certain moment, the creative act of experimentation through improvisation and exploration needs to converge on a clear understanding of its object of research: the sound material. Grasping and achieving control over sound material is a fundamental task for the composer, in order to proceed with the organisation of sounds within the frame of the compositional work.

In my personal experience, at the beginning of the compositional process, some kinds of sonic images tend to emerge from the exploration of the instrument. These mental sonic images are perceived as completely out of focus but at the same time as extremely significant, although their meaning eludes any attempt at definition. To give a few practical examples, in *Hidden Traces* I started the whole process focusing on three main elements: a set of noisy sounds produced by scratching the piezo at different points of the strings, and electronically processed through various granulators; a set of sinewaves; and a set of radio fragments. I have been fascinated by the way all these sounds, played through the transducers, make the surface and the strings of the guitar resonate. Therefore, during the process, I focused on further possibilities to expand these sounds, in order to develop the piece around them. Concerning *Residual*, instead, I started the process focusing on two main sonic images. The first referred to the long low sounds of the marimba, produced with the bow, recorded through the piezo, and then processed through the use of different filters. The second concerned various airy sounds from the cello, produced with the bow, "fingering" the string with the piezo. Both sonic images shared a certain degree of instability and spectral richness, which afforded me further development. Finally, concerning *PianoMusicBox_1*, the first sonic image that stuck in my mind was the one I called the "low guïro sound" because of its similarity to the sound produced by a guïro. The "low guïro sound" results from running the edge of a piezo along one of the piano's low strings. Curiously, during the process, I abandoned this first sonic image, focusing instead on its evolution through its "transposition" in two other similar sounds, one produced by running the edge of the piezo horizontally on a few strings of the middle register of the stringboard, and a comparable one produced in the narrowest space behind the bridge. The reason I abandoned the original form of this sonic image lies most probably in my initial difficulty in understanding the potentialities of the first sound material.

In fact, the process of gaining a clearer idea of these sonic images is often quite slow and usually difficult to grasp, so it may be worth questioning how the composer's mind works in elaborating and storing these unfamiliar images. I have slowly begun to realise that this mental process tends to be recursive, rather than linear, and that its recursivity is manifested on different layers. Principally, this recursivity is manifested in the constant shift between what can be called the "inside time" of the performance and the "outside time" of the composition process. While a picture can be observed for a long time, a sound permits its contemplation just for the duration of its happening. But, within a "real-time" phenomenon, effects of memory and anticipation are nevertheless at play. So, how does the imagination work outside time?

Among the strategies that I have identified in my practice, there is not only that of gaining a personal experience of sound by provisionally assuming the role of the performer, but also that of rehearsing this experience over and over. Therefore, I have developed a routine that consists of recording moments of improvisation and exploration, as well as rehearsals with performers, at different stages of the process. For each project or piece, I have started to store and catalogue in digital folders and subfolders different recordings, text files with their description, patches for the processing of sounds, notes, sketches, and so on. This material becomes then part of a sort of personal archive in which I organise the material that I am working with. During the process, this archive is constantly reshaped and updated. This act of cataloguing supports a non-linear approach to the compositional process, permitting multiple accesses to the empirical experience of sound material, as well as to the different ideas about its possible definition, transformation, and manipulation. The possibility to access different information at various stages of the process, and to rehearse as many times as needed the empirical experience of sound, permits a better understanding of the acoustic features of the sound material that I am working on, and for a constant redefinition of its auditory memory.

The role of auditory memory in our musical experience is described very well by Bob Snyder in his book *Music and Memory* (2001). Here the author addresses the abilities and limits of our memory in the organisation, recognition, and recollection of sound events. Snyder suggests that our memory is organised on a model consisting of three processes: an "early-processing echoic memory," a "short-term memory," and a "long-term memory." Each of these three memories differently processes information that comes to our ears. Each one functions on a different time scale, which for Snyder loosely relates to different time levels of music organisation, called respectively "level of event fusion," "melodic and rhythmic level," and "formal level." Within these processes, acoustic features are extracted from the continuous data of the echoic memory and then bound together and organised into groupings based on similarity and proximity in perceptual categories, which later become conceptual, in the long-term memory. These different memory processes do not function completely independently of one another, and the actual consolidation of long-term memories consists of a recursive process, which can occur either unconsciously and spontaneously, or as a result of conscious effort. The distinction between three processes of memory based on three different time levels reinforces the need for iterative listening in order for the aural memory of the related sound material to achieve definition.

The time levels of music organisation indicated by Snyder seem to correspond to the time scales inhabited by the sound material, described by Curtis Roads in *Microsounds* (2004). Here, the author outlines nine different time scales, specifying for each of them a temporal range. For example, the "sound object time scale" goes from a fraction of a second to several seconds, the "meso time scale" is usually measured in minutes or seconds, while the "macro time scale" is measured in minutes, or hours, or, in really extreme cases, days. Both the "meso" and the "macro" time scales refer, from the composer's perspective, to what concerns the organisation of the sound material. The "meso time scale" represents the local time in which musical ideas unfold, and processes of development, progression, and juxtaposition of different sound objects take place; while the "macro time scale" concerns the notion of form, the architecture of the composition. The "sound-object time scale" is instead the time scale of the material itself. Due to the wide heterogeneity of sound material, the "sound-object time scale" can be quite variable, and the internal trajectory of each sonic image can cover different temporalities. Hence, internal trajectories have to be related to an external temporality:

> In order to be recognized, audible figures require a nested temporality. On the one hand, the identification of a figure supposes that the figure itself is placed in the context of a temporality that is "external" to the figure. But on the other side, the figure itself is still an object to be appreciated "in real time," an intrinsically temporal figure which reveals (or at least, can reveal) an "internal" temporality. This aspect has been discussed by Schaeffer in the form of a recursive relationship between a sound object and a structure to which the former refers. (Valle 2015, 76–77)

Hence, the work of the composer can be seen as a continuous negotiation within this recursive relationship between the internal temporality of the audible figure or sound object, and the external one, that is, the structure to which the former refers. In my experience, the recognition of specific audible figures corresponds to the gradual focusing of those unclear sonic images that appeared at the beginning of the compositional process. Through the possibility of understanding and shaping their internal trajectory, sonic images acquire definition, so that they can be collected and represented through more specific sound events. This process includes a clearer definition of the sonic gesture through which the performer will produce a specific sound, or, more generally, of the mode of production of sound, which—as we saw earlier—provides empirical knowledge of the sound material through a series of information about sources, actions, and devices involved. From this perspective, I find it useful to refer to Denis Smalley and his spectromorphological theory, which considers spectral and morphological change over time as the consequence of the activity that generates the sound material, linking this activity to the notion of gesture.

> Sound-making gesture is concerned with human, physical activity which has spectromorphological consequences: a chain of activity links a cause to a source. A human *agent* produces spectromorphologies via the motion of gesture, using the sense of touch or an implement to apply *energy* to a *sounding body*. A gesture is therefore an *energy–motion trajectory* which excites the sounding body, creating spectromorphological life. (Smalley 1997, 111)

> In electroacoustic music the scale of gestural impetus is also variable, from the smallest attack-morphology to the broad sweep of a much longer gesture, continuous in its motion and flexible in its pacing. The notion of gesture as a forming principle is concerned with propelling time forwards, with moving away from one goal towards the next goal in the structure—the energy of motion expressed through spectral and morphological change. (113)

5. My personal narrative: process of the definition of sound material

The way Smalley speaks of the energy of motion can be linked to the distinction that Trevor Wishart (1986) makes between the "intrinsic" and the "imposed" morphologies of sound. The intrinsic morphology concerns the properties of the sounding system, while the imposed morphology relates to the energy input into the system. As examples, he proposes three sounds from the category of continuous sounds: the sustained sound of a violin, of a synthesiser, and of a bell. According to their physical properties, the first two sounding systems—the violin and the synthesiser—require a constant input of energy in order to produce a long sound, whereas the bell needs just a single input of energy to resonate for a long time. Hence, the input of energy is linked to the action that produces sound, and any sounding system can be considered as gesturally responsive. Consequently, the definition of the sound material depends both on the physical properties of the system and on the definition of the gesture that shapes its imposed morphology.

At different stages of the compositional process, the composer defines the imposed morphology of the sound material she or he is working on, taking into account what kinds of manipulation, intervention, or transformation the intrinsic properties of the material afford or suggest. While the material is shaped in different gestures, the initial abstraction of sonic images becomes clearer, and the necessity to notate the aural memory of these gestures starts to emerge, in order to find a way to bring each sonic image from its "inside" time to the "outside" time of composition. The visual translation of a sonic image becomes part of the process of comprehension and acquisition of the sonic material. Notation comes into play. Auditory imagination is helped to recall different sounds by visual cues, graphically represented with a symbol or a set of symbols, and notation becomes a means for the composer, as has been the case for the last few centuries of Western composed music. We can observe with Impett (2016, 661): "Symbol-manipulation lies at the heart of Western composition. The symbolic representation and manipulation afforded by technologies from wax tablet to computer constitute a form of conceptual prosthesis. Virtual, mental quasi-external representations are both more ephemeral and more plastic than their material counterparts. The points at which a current state is externalized constitute a unique signature in the compositional process."

The uniqueness of this signature lies in the personal set of choices made by the composer her- or himself. This decision-making process requires constant negotiation between the understanding of the mental representation of each sonic idea and the physical one in its visual form. In deciding how to translate the sonic image into a visual one, the composer has to choose what features of the sonic image she or he needs to graphically represent and how. Negotiation within the limits of the visual representation is required to define the amount of information that could be delivered by the notation, in order to define and make clearer specific features of a certain sound event. In my compositional practice, I am usually concerned to define and indicate the following aspects:

- the temporality of the sonic image, intended as the internal duration of the sound event or its rhythmic contour;
- the physical action, namely the movement that has to be done within the physical space of the instrument in order to produce the related sonic idea;
- the space of the instrument where the action takes place, as well as the material/tool through which the sound is produced—such as plectrum/ fingers/nails, piezos, string, wood, and so on;
- the quantity of energy—the dynamics—that has to be put into the action.

Through notation, the gestural structure in which the sounding matter is inscribed comes to constitute the starting material of my work, and, once I get a better understanding of the sound material I want to work on, that material tends to reveal its potentialities more easily. Around each sonic image, others come into being, by analogy, symmetry, or opposition, through an interplay between the aural memory and the aural imagination. From now on, the work can more easily progress within other time levels: namely, within the meso time level in which musical ideas unfold, and the macro time level of the structural form of the piece. Architecture-wise, a piece is usually built by various sonic images differently organised in time, which interweave to produce multiple stratifications or successions of varying temporal dimensions. Many decisions are taken simultaneously, constantly zooming in and out between different time-scales of music organisation. Compared with the retrospective perception of listening, the composer works in *prospect*, imagining sounds and their succession and combination though a complex set of operations. As outlined by Impett:

> Composition is a reflexive, iterative process of inscription. The work, once named as such and externalizable to some degree, passes circularly between inner and outer states. It passes through internal and external representations—mostly partial or compressed, some projected in mental rather than physical space, not all necessarily conscious or observable—and phenomenological experience real or imagined. At each state-change the work is re-mediated by the composer, whose decision-making process is conditioned by the full complexity of human experience. This entire activity informs the simultaneous development of the composer's understanding of the particular work in its autonomy, of their own creativity and of music more broadly. Environment (culture, technology) and agents (composer, work) coevolve at different rates. (Impett 2016, 661)

In my daily practice, again, I rely on notation as a tool to control each "state-change" of the work. I got used to constructing on paper a spatial representation of time, to visually represent the macro time level of the formal and architectural structure of the composition. My drafts are usually sketched on paper, following a timeline, placed on top of the score. Timelines are tools that enable me to visualise the disposition and the development of different sound-events in time, the possible relationships between them, and to get an overview of the global form of the piece. The adoption of a timeline reveals a "left-to-right" reading habit, which comes from the assimilation of traditional notation, as well as from frequent use of sound-editing software, in which the waveform is usually represented in the time domain.

The compositional practice that I have tried to outline corresponds quite precisely to the routine of my way of working, as well as to the compositional path followed for *PianoMusicBox_1* and *Residual*. Regarding *Hidden Traces*, I can instead observe a few deviations. For this piece, I never went through the usual process of notating gestures that I had been experimenting with during the process; rather, I focused more on getting control of different electronic processes, which allowed me to improvise with a certain set of pre-determined materials. As long as I was the only performer of the piece, I relied on my gestural memory to improvise, using just a draft as a reference point, with an approximate timeline for the general structure of events, and some reminders about how the MIDI controller was programmed. Only when the occasion arose to have the piece performed by the guitarist Seth Josel did I sketch out a more precise set of instructions, realising that the actual score was, for a large part, already embedded in the code of the software that controls all the electronics processes. During the whole compositional process, in fact, I relied mostly on the software as the "composing environment," rather than on more familiar tools such as pencil and paper. The whole process of externalisation of sonic images through their inscription on paper has been somehow condensed in the programming of the code. Consequently, the final score has turned out to be a set of textual instructions for the performer, who is asked to be fully aware of all the different electronic processes that she or he has to control, in order to move freely within an open structure, which has, nevertheless, a few fixed points regarding the succession of different events. In this particular case, I have observed that, more than ever, preliminary work with the performer has been fundamental; in the "score," a large set of information about possible playing techniques—which are in part left to the expertise and personal creativity of the performer—is missing, while the functioning of the system made of piezos, transducers, and various electronic processes requires certain skills that the performer might have to learn.

6. Conclusions

A close observation of daily activity during compositional work reveals the complex network of agencies and contingencies that come into play during the decision-making process. Composition is understood as a practice situated in a specific environment that constantly needs to be rediscussed in the light of emergent variables, contextual or personal. Musical instruments and notation, as well as electronic devices, software, and computers in general, are a complex set of diverse and broad technologies, all involved in compositional practice, as a ubiquitous part of the composer's environment. Technologies are in constant evolution, offering solutions and opportunities, demanding from composers constant updating, and any engagement with them heightens the sense of instability of the emergent contingencies. Through the observation of their daily practice, composers can achieve a better understanding regarding all interactions with the other agents of the technological and social environment in which they operate. They can, moreover, gain a deeper awareness of what kind of assumptions are more recurrent in their working modality.

While observing the general routine through which I tend to re-enact similar processes in the selection and definition of my sound material, as well as in its organisation in a certain time frame, I have started to understand the importance of different time dimensions in the recursive process of externalisation and decision-making that happen outside the real time of the composition.

> Composition is itself a supratemporal activity. Its results last only a fraction of the time required for its creation. . . . The electronic music composer may spend considerable time in creating the sound materials of the work. . . . Virtually all composers spend time experimenting, playing with material in different combinations. Some of these experiments may result in fragments that are edited or discarded, to be replaced with new fragments. Thus it is inevitable that composers invest time pursuing dead ends, composing fragments that no one else will hear. This backtracking is not necessarily time wasted; it is part of an important feedback loop in which the composer refines the work. (Roads 2004, 10)

In the temporal dimension dedicated to the activity of composition, aural memory and imagination come into play. Composers need to anticipate the structural relationships between different sound objects that they keep in memory while reconceptualising their definition. A varied selection of personal modes of representation allow them to keep track of the whole process, supporting the ability to create a robust memory of the sound material, and enhancing the role of intuition in the everyday practice made up of moment-to-moment interactions. To conclude with Agre, principles behind the technical practice can "explain something about human nature start-ing from basic facts: that we have bodies, that our environment is extensively adapted to our culture's ways of doing things, and that everyday life contains a great deal that is cyclical, repetitive, and routine" (Agre 1997, 20).

REFERENCES

Adorno, Theodor W. 1997. *Aesthetic Theory*. Translated and edited by Robert Hullot-Kentor. Minneapolis: University of Minnesota Press. First published 1970 as *Ästhetische Theorie*, edited by Gretel Adorno and Rolf Tiedemann (Frankfurt am Main: Suhrkamp).

Agre, Philip E. 1997. *Computation and Human Experience*. Cambridge: Cambridge University Press.

Cage, John (1937) 1961. "The Future of Music: Credo." In *Silence: Lectures and Writings*, 3–6. Middletown, CT: Wesleyan University Press. First delivered as a talk 1937 (Seattle).

Demers, Joanna. 2010. *Listening through the Noise: The Aesthetics of Experimental Electronic Music*. New York: Oxford University Press.

Gibson, James J. 1979. *The Ecological Approach to Visual Perception*. Boston: Houghton Mifflin.

Habbestad, Bjørnar. 2017. "No Flute Is an Island, Entire of Itself. Transgressing Performers, Instruments and Instrumentality in Contemporary Music." In *Musical Instruments in the 21st Century: Identities, Configurations, Practices*, edited by Till Bovermann, Alberto de Campo, Hauke Egermann, Sarah-Indriyati Hardjowirogo, and Stefan Weinzierl, 315–26. Singapore: Springer.

Impett, Jonathan. 2016. "Making a Mark: The Psychology of Composition." In *The Oxford Handbook of Music Psychology*, edited by Susan Hallam, Ian Cross, and Michael Thaut, 2nd ed., 651–66. Oxford: Oxford University Press.

Roads, Curtis. 2004. *Microsound*. Cambridge, MA: MIT Press.

Schaeffer, Pierre. 1966. *Traité des objets musicaux: Essai interdisciplines*. Paris: Seuil. Translated by Christine North and John Dack as *Treatise on Musical Objects: An Essay across Disciplines* (Oakland: University of California Press, 2017).

Smalley, Denis. 1997. "Spectromorphology: Explaining Sound-Shapes." *Organised Sound* 2 (2): 107–26.

Snyder, Bob. 2000. *Music and Memory: An Introduction*. Cambridge, MA: MIT Press.

Valle, Andrea. 2015. "Towards a Semiotic of the Audible." In "Sémiotique de la musique / Music and Meaning," edited by Aage Brandt and José Roberto do Carmo Jr., special issue, *Signata: Annales des Sémiotique / Annals of Semiotics*, no. 6, 65–89.

Varèse, Edgard. 1966. "The Liberation of Sound." Edited by Chou Wen-chung. *Perspectives of New Music* 5 (1): 11–19.

Waters, Simon. 2007. "Performance Ecosystems: Ecological Approaches to Musical Interaction." In *EMS07: The "Languages" of Electroacoustic Music—Leicester*. Electroacoustic Music Studies Network. Accessed 14 April 2021. http://www.ems-network.org/IMG/pdf_WatersEMS07.pdf.

Wishart, Trevor. 1986. "Sound Symbols and Landscapes." In *The Language of Electroacoustic Music*, edited by Simon Emmerson, 41–60. Basingstoke, UK: Palgrave Macmillan.

Temporal Poetics as a Critical Technical Practice

Karim Haddad

IRCAM—Centre Georges Pompidou, Paris

"In a manifold sense, music uses time. It uses my time, it uses your time, it uses its own time. It would be most annoying if it did not aim to say the most important things in the most concentrated manner in every fraction of this time" (Schoenberg 1975, 40). Schoenberg's statement underlines the importance of time as a founding principle in the art of composing. Beyond any hierarchical consideration of pitch, dynamics, and formal organisation, musical time in concept and perception is to be considered the most decisive factor of all.

This matter implies that a first imperative—duration, rhythm, musical time—takes precedence over all other musical components (parameters). When considering a musical object in terms of a temporal event, it is its own temporality that determines it as such. The other essential "components" of its identity remain important when it comes to the specificity of this object, discerning it by differentiating it in the event of a possible synchronicity of several concomitant time objects. The musical event is considered as a temporal unit inseparable from its own temporality perceived as a form (also temporal). It should be subject to certain criteria (or laws) that in their essence dissociate what it should be from any other sound event, that is, an object characterised by a musical sense. The first reason or principle that should be pursued, in my opinion, and that of Schoenberg, is *intelligibility*.[1] While Schoenberg comprehends intelligibility as a mode in a diachronic succession of events, I see it as a multidimensional form in relation to an essentially temporal discursiveness. By this, I mean a generalisation of a temporal intelligibility without any primacy granted to any given sound component, as in, for instance, the succession of a complex of chords, gestures, or rhythmic figures, but with a time-organised formal totality. For Schoenberg and most particularly for Webern, the necessary condition of intelligibility is *coherence*. Coherence may be found on any level: the choice of material, the process of deduction, but above all, in the coherence of musical form. In this chapter I present the development of a critical approach to the fundamental compositional-technical question of structuring time. Computational environments for composition afford new ways of conceiving and working with musical time, and they require new modes of encoding, notating, and formalising it. This situation challenges us to question received assumptions about musical time, and to seek enhancements to its description and thus our own understanding.

---

1 "Form in the arts, and especially in music, aims primarily at comprehensibility" (Schoenberg 1950, 103).

1. Time and form

In *Sculpting in Time*, Andrei Tarkovsky states:

> How does time make itself felt in a shot? It becomes tangible when you sense something significant, truthful, going on beyond the events on the screen; when you realise, quite consciously, that what you see in the frame is not limited to its visual depiction, but is a pointer to something stretching out beyond the frame and to infinity; a pointer to life. (Tarkovsky 1996, 117–18)

Tarkovsky's comment is just as apt applied to the art of composition, most particularly to the formal construct of a musical work, as time is essentially related to it. However, whether in the field of film-making or of musical composition, the formal conception of the work should not rely on a stream of arbitrary patchworked and collaged event sequences pasted without reasoning, without coherence, which would jeopardise the work's intelligibility. The structural order is to be found in the coherent organisation of time.

> Rhythm, then, is not the metrical sequence of pieces; what makes it is the time-thrust within the frames. And I am convinced that it is rhythm, and not editing, as people tend to think, that is the main formative element of cinema. (Tarkovsky 1996, 119)

On the other hand, coherence does not necessarily imply a monolithic exclusive organisation, a complete semantic compliance with the material, but could also include a wide span of various different objects—provided that the articulation between each different material in time is considered and structured following a temporal logic that transcends the work itself:

> This is . . . the highest poetry, in which even the unpoetic, because it is said at the right time and in the right place in the whole of the work of art, becomes poetic. . . . How can you employ the thing in the right place if you are still shyly tarrying over it and do not know how much is in it, how much or how little to make of it. That is eternal bliss, is the joy of the gods, that one sets every individual thing into the place in the whole where it belongs; hence without understanding, or without thoroughly organized feeling, no excellence, no life. (Hölderlin 2009, 240–41)

In order to illustrate the use of temporal poetics in a compositional context, I will start with a brief presentation of the *temporal unit* principle I have developed through my compositional practice, followed by some applications of this same principle.

2. Temporal units, a brief presentation

A temporal unit[2] is a symbolic expression of duration, metre, and tempo represented as a time vector. A temporal unit can be absolute or relative. In the first case, the temporal unit doesn't have any determined duration nor any tempo indication. In the second case, the temporal unit has a duration "relative" to the tempo assigned to it.

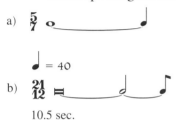

10.5 sec.

Figure 12.1.

A temporal unit is represented by a *tempus* (its time signature), and by the *prolationis* consisting of the proportions of the subdivisions.

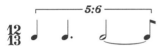

Figure 12.2.

The temporal unit in figure 12.2 can be notated in a condensed style like so:

$$\left(\frac{12}{13}\right)_{(2\ 3\ 5)}$$

2.1. Properties of temporal units

The most important properties of temporal units are tempo and metrical modulations. These properties have the ability to modify and create new temporal units that start from others.

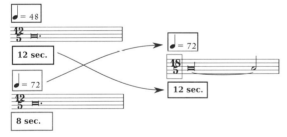

Figure 12.3.

Another property, autogenerativity, is based on such properties as subdivision, decomposition, concatenation, and reduction. An example of this process is shown in figure 12.4.

---

2 For a complete study on this subject, see Haddad (2020).

Figure 12.1. (a) Absolute and (b) relative temporal units.
Figure 12.2. A temporal unit with a *tempus* of (We) and a *prolationis* of (2 3 5).
Figure 12.3. Tempo modulation of two different temporal units.

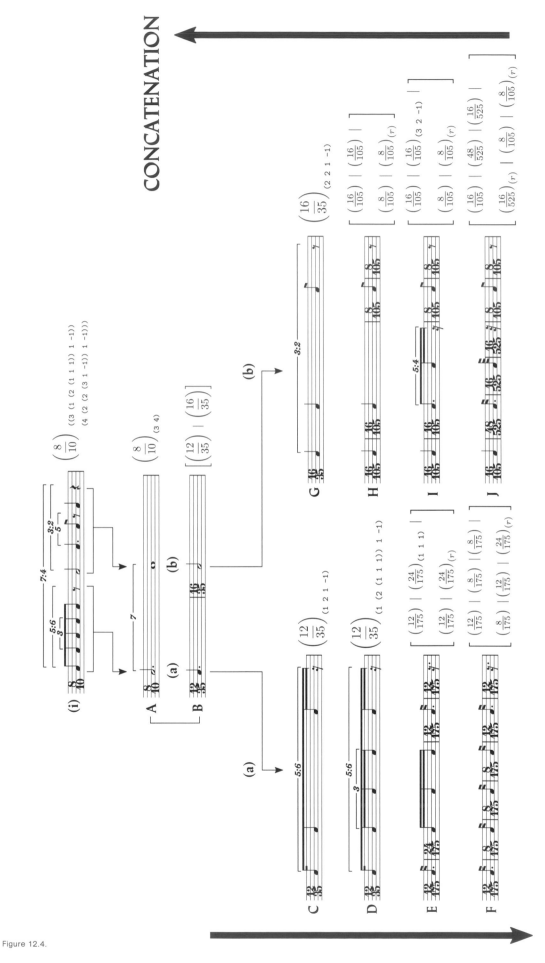

Figure 12.4.

Figure 12.4. Decomposition and concatenation operations on a complex temporal unit.

2.2. *Operations on temporal units*

A rich corpus of operations are available that can be applied to temporal units, such as algebraic operations (addition, subtraction, and scaling), prolational operations (augmentation, insertion, diminution, and extraction), and magnitude operations (expansion, contraction, stretching, compression, and segmentation). It is also possible to apply any mathematical or physical operation to temporal units, such as convolutions or even Fourrier transforms.

All these operations can be sequentially, recursively, or iteratively applied.

Figure 12.5.

$$\left(\frac{12}{5}\right)_{((4\ (1\ -1\ 1))\ 5\ -3\ 1\ 2)} \times \left\{2\,,\tfrac{1}{5},\,\tfrac{3}{2},\,\tfrac{2}{3}\right\}$$

$$\Rightarrow \left\{\begin{array}{c} \left[\left(\frac{24}{5}\right)_{((4\ (1\ -1\ 1))\ 5\ -3\ 1\ 2)}\right] \\[2em] \left[\left(\frac{12}{25}\right)_{((4\ (1\ -1\ 1))\ 5\ -3\ 1\ 2)}\right] \\[2em] \left[\left(\frac{18}{5}\right)_{((4\ (1\ -1\ 1))\ 5\ -3\ 1\ 2)}\right] \\[2em] \left[\left(\frac{8}{5}\right)_{((4\ (1\ -1\ 1))\ 5\ -3\ 1\ 2)}\right] \end{array}\right\}$$

Figure 12.6.

Figure 12.5. Iterative scaling operations on a temporal unit.

Figure 12.6. Condensed notation of figure 12.5.

3. The logic of time structures

One cannot expect a low-resolution material, whether pitch, duration, or dynamics, to express subtle ideas. The higher the definition, the more expressive the resulting composition will be. Nevertheless, using limited or constrained material may be interesting on one condition: that one follows the logical principle of the material itself. Therefore, the choice of starting material is utterly critical with regard to the resulting musical construct.

3.1. Time envelopes

Starting with temporal units, let us consider using their magnitude (*tempus*) as a time span containing functions of the type $y = f(x)$ represented by multiple envelopes[3] of different categories. The first category of envelope is based on piecewise linear functions.

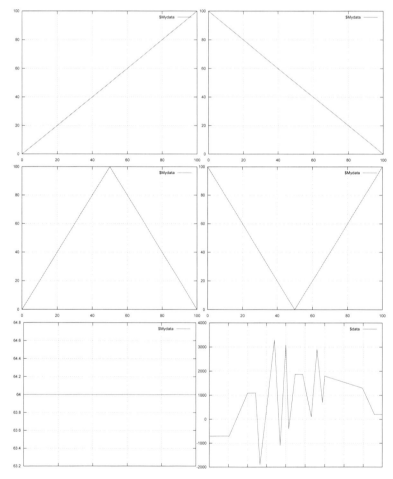

Figure 12.7.

---

3   The envelope concept should be understood as it is described by Pierre Boulez (1986).

Figure 12.7. Different piecewise linear functions.

The second category is based on staircase functions.

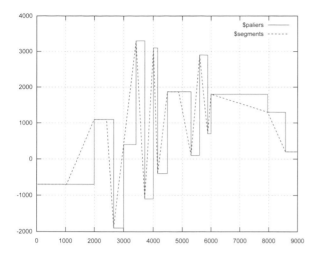

Figure 12.8.

The final category is non-linear envelopes, represented by smooth functions, as shown in figure 12.9.

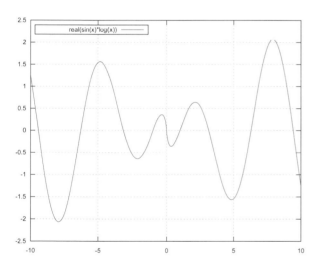

Figure 12.9.

The envelopes will be integrated in the temporal units' domain, the x axis, and their given data will be interpreted following the nature and content of the required field, which will be allocated to the y axis.

For instance, we could consider the following temporal unit:

$$\left(\frac{12}{5}\right)_{(5\ 6\ 3\ 2\ 4\ 1)}$$

Figure 12.8. Staircase function.

Figure 12.9. Non-linear envelope of the smooth function $y = Re(sin(x) \times log(x))$.

And we could consider a function in figure 12.9 where the (x, y) dimensions represent respectively the temporal axis and some data in the y axis that could be allocated to any parameter in the domain of pitch, dynamic, timbre, register, and so on. Once these are associated synchronously with a temporal unit, the *tempus* of this "floating" unit will conform to the *tempus* of the first. This flexibility between absolute time and relative time is one of the main characteristics of interpretation concerning the time scaling of the given data, which can be read discretely or continuously. The y axis is given different parameters for scaling depending upon the type of space we are using (pitch, dynamics, timbre, etc.), so that the original temporal unit can contain any kind of data associated with transformational operators according to the chosen field. In order to achieve this, two operations are necessary:

·   The first operation consists of the quantification of relative time, which will be scaled according to the given temporal unit following the y axis.
·   The second operation will sample the useful data following the nature of the given space and, if desired, will transpose these data to different possible spaces (for example, from pitch to dynamics, from dynamics to register, etc.).

The resulting action of these two operations will be a data transfer of time on the x axis and formatted data on the y axis.

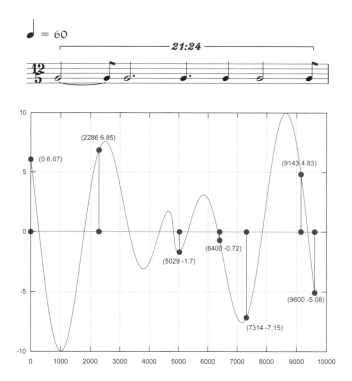

Figure 12.10.

254

This complex construct of a temporal unit and an envelope can be considered under the rubric of computational and combinatorial transformations starting from temporal data. This will result in an intrinsic formal potential, resulting from these same operations. Assuming that this procedure also operates on dynamics, let us consider a temporal unit composed of nineteen *prolationa* (proportions) with a pitch content and a set of levelled linear envelopes generated from the circular permutations corresponding to the pitch matrix of our temporal unit, as shown in table 12.1.

1	2	3	4	5	6	7	8	9	10	11	12	13	14	15	16	17	18	19
5	4	16	10	7	19	3	9	17	8	13	6	18	15	2	12	14	1	11
7	10	12	8	3	11	16	17	14	9	18	19	1	2	4	6	15	5	13
3	8	6	9	16	13	12	14	15	17	1	11	5	4	10	19	2	7	18
16	9	19	17	12	18	6	15	2	14	5	13	7	10	8	11	4	3	1
12	17	11	14	6	1	19	2	4	15	7	18	3	8	9	13	10	16	5
6	14	13	15	19	5	11	4	10	2	3	1	16	9	17	18	8	12	7
19	15	18	2	11	7	13	10	8	4	16	5	12	17	14	1	9	6	3
11	2	1	4	13	3	18	8	9	10	12	7	6	14	15	5	17	19	16
13	4	5	10	18	16	1	9	17	8	6	3	19	15	2	7	14	11	12
18	10	7	8	1	12	5	17	14	9	19	16	11	2	4	3	15	13	6
1	8	3	9	5	6	7	14	15	17	11	12	13	4	10	16	2	18	19
5	9	16	17	7	19	3	15	2	14	13	6	18	10	8	12	4	1	11
7	17	12	14	3	11	16	2	4	15	18	19	1	8	9	6	10	5	13
3	14	6	15	16	13	12	4	10	2	1	11	5	9	17	19	8	7	18
16	15	19	2	12	18	6	10	8	4	5	13	7	17	14	11	9	3	1
12	2	11	4	6	1	19	8	9	10	7	18	3	14	15	13	17	16	5
6	4	13	10	19	5	11	9	17	8	3	1	16	15	2	18	14	12	7
19	10	18	8	11	7	13	17	14	9	16	5	12	2	4	1	15	6	3

Table 12.1.

The first envelope's profile corresponds to that of the pitch of the associated temporal unit (see figure 12.11).

Table 12.1. Pitch set circular permutation matrix of the temporal unit of figure 12.11.

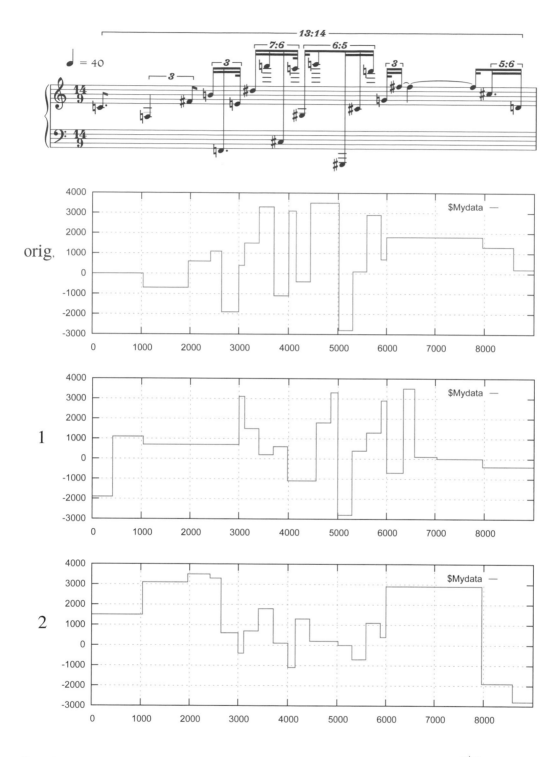

orig.

1

2

etc.

Figure 12.11.

Figure 12.11. A temporal unit and its corresponding envelope based on its pitch profile
(orig.) followed by the first two envelopes (1 2) of the first two permutations from
table 12.1.

If we apply the envelope related to the original profile of pitches scaled from pianissimo to fortissimo, this will comply with the logical pitch set profile, in which the lowest note is dynamically the softest and the highest the loudest. However, if we use other permutations with the same temporal unit's pitch order, the logical order will be less obvious concerning the register/dynamic correlation, resulting in singular and highly interesting dynamic profiles.

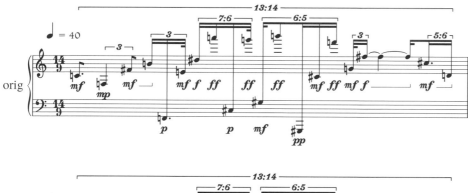

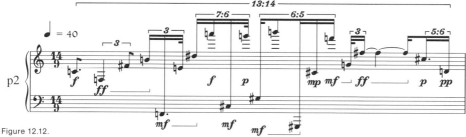

Figure 12.12.

From a larger-scale perspective, the generalisation of this process will provide a set of gesture material covering a wide range of different spaces, the referent space being duration in the form of temporal units guarantying relative control over the form in progress.

3.2. Matrices and arrays: a transformational space

Other strategies are available for reorganisation and redistribution that can be thought of as a development and proliferation of the material and ideas on a local level or more widely on the scale of musical form. These can be described thus:

> The virtual object has its own dimension containing concepts of permutation, interpolation, random structure, sieves, recursion, mapping and rules of writing, all suggesting the open ground of development. This dimension is seen in elements,

Figure 12.12. The original profile (envelope 0) applied to dynamics, followed by the second permutation envelope (see figure 12.1).

the informal, as much as in their combination. (Boulez 2018, 340)

In this example, we will start from a complex of temporal units generated from a DNA chain. Each deoxyribonucleotide composing this chain will determine the nature of the given temporal unit:

- · A for a simple temporal unit (one proportion)
- · C for a pulsed temporal unit (the number of pulsations is equal to the temporal unit's numerator)
- · T for a "mute" temporal unit filled with a rest
- · G for a "composed" temporal unit from two *prolationis* related to the temporal unit's *tempus* in the form of:

$$S = (numerator\ demoninator)$$

The main structure is built around twelve voices composed of temporal units. The *tempora* are derived from two Pisano periods:

$$P(5\ 7)\ mod\ 8 = (5\ 7\ 4\ 3\ 7\ 2\ 1\ 3\ 4\ 7\ 3\ 2)$$

for twelve elements assigned to the numerators and,

$$P(4\ 7)\ mod\ 13 = (4\ 7\ 11\ 5\ 3\ 8\ 11\ 6\ 4\ 10\ 1\ 11\ 12$$
$$10\ 9\ 6\ 2\ 8\ 10\ 5\ 2\ 7\ 9\ 3\ 12\ 2\ 1\ 3)$$

for twenty-eight elements assigned to the denominators. Using circular permutations, this will produce twelve sequences of twelve temporal units per voice.

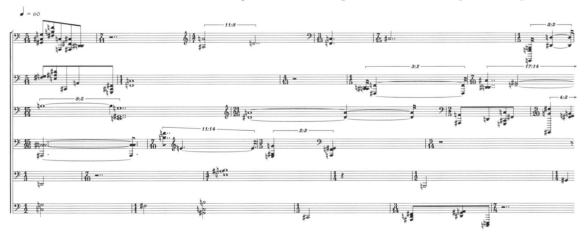

Figure 12.13.

I will construct an array with a dimension of 12 × 12 temporal units. Two envelopes and one row of integers will be associated with each temporal unit of the array. These will be used, respectively, to control the pitch register distribution, the dynamics,[4] and instrumentation.

---

4 Let us bear in mind that although this sort of array embeds temporal elements such as temporal units it is in no way a temporal representation itself. It is a transformational potential that is set to be quanti-

Figure 12.13. Main structure (first six voices).

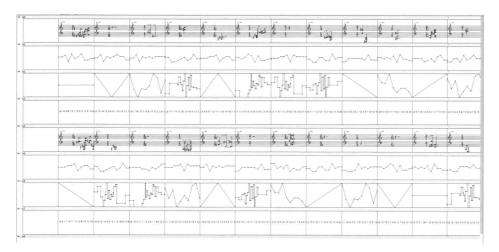

Figure 12.14.

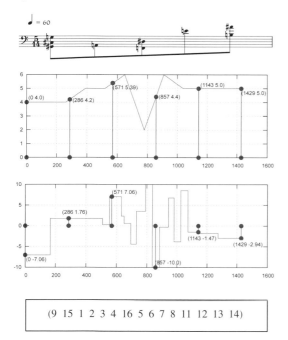

Figure 12.15.

I use an identical serial transformational matrix from the type found in example 4 in Pierre Boulez's *Penser la musique aujourd'hui* (1963, 41; 1971, 40), described by its author as follows:[5]

---

fied in time.

5   This transformational process was used in the first part of "Antiphonie" (Formant 1) in Pierre Boulez's Third Piano Sonata. An excellent analysis of this process can be found in O'Hagan (2006).

Figure 12.14. The first two rows of the array containing temporal units and their corresponding envelopes.

Figure 12.15. A cell from the array in figure 12.14 with its four components: temporal unit, registration envelope, dynamic envelope, and instrumentational sieve.

> Take the case of a non-homogenous complex comprising pitch and duration; if the pitches are accorded durations directly (or inversely) proportional to the intervals which seperate them, another form of generation will result from the order of the size of the interval being brought to bear on the order of succession. (Ibid.)

In our case, the order of succession is determined by the order of magnitude of the temporal units' time intervals for each voice in the array, which creates a matrix of non-permutational order (table 12.2).

8	11	10	4	9	3	1	5	6	12	2	7
9	12	5	2	11	4	1	3	10	7	8	6
10	9	5	6	11	2	1	7	3	12	8	4
6	9	7	8	11	2	1	3	10	12	5	4
5	11	9	3	8	4	1	7	10	12	6	2
7	12	6	4	11	1	3	8	9	10	5	2
12	10	4	6	8	5	1	7	9	11	2	3
8	10	11	2	12	5	1	6	7	9	4	3
7	11	3	9	12	4	1	5	6	10	8	2
10	7	9	8	11	4	1	3	6	12	5	2
5	12	10	7	11	2	1	6	8	9	4	3
11	12	9	6	10	2	1	7	5	8	4	3

Table 12.2.

This matrix is applied not to the pitch/duration pair but to temporal units. The first translational matrix generated from the first order is shown in table 12.3.

8	11	10	4	9	3	1	5	6	12	2	7
11-7		6	8-3-2					10-4-5		9-1	12
	10	8-4-5	7	6-12-2		11	3	9			1
4-9		7		5	1-12		10-2	8-3	6		11
	8-9	3		4	11-10	2	1	12-7	5	6	
1-2	6-7		11	3	4		8-9-12		10	5	
6	1-5-12				8-2		11-7		9-3	10	4
5	4	9		10-1	7	6-12		11	8	3	2
12	3	11	9-1			10-4-5			2-7	8	6
3	2			8-11	6	9	4		1	12-7	10 5
10		1-12-2	6	7	9-5	8-3			11	4	
			10-5-12			7	6	1-2	4	11	8 9 3

Table 12.3.

The matrix used in Boulez's "Antiphonie" (Formant 1 of the Third Piano Sonata) articulates pitch and durations; however, in this context I will use temporal units in the transformational matrix, which will provide reservoirs of a complex of gestures.[6] Computer-assisted composition will allow us to explore this rich material through several decisional combinatory processes.[7]

---

6 Gestures are to be understood here as an articulate grouping of all necessary parameters integrated in a temporal unit as a polyphony.

7 I have implemented most of my processes and compositional strategies in an OpenMusic environment (see Agon 1998; Haddad 2008).

Table 12.2. Matrix of non-permutational order.

Table 12.3. First translational matrix generated from the first order.

Having a matrix and an array at hand (I will use the terms of matrix *A* for the transformational matrix in table 12.3 and the array *TU* for the one integrating the temporal units in figure 12.14), we can map them both and "read" and "browse" them in different ways, as illustrated below.

Let us start with the array *TU* and apply an associative reading of matrix *A* through the permutational transfer from column to row. One will be used to sort the other. Let us take for instance the third row of matrix *A*, which will be used for the "reordering" of the reservoirs of the array *TU* using indexation (table 12.4).

1	2	3	4	5	6	7	8	9	10	11	12
4-9		7		5	1-12		10-2	8-3	6		11

Table 12.4.

We will interpret row *A* starting from column 1 of *TU* by collecting the fourth and ninth element of this same array. As the second column is empty, we will then move to column 3 and select the temporal unit of row 7, and so on. Through this matrix-to-array "transfer," we can build a polyphonic synchronous complex, such as is shown in figure 12.16.

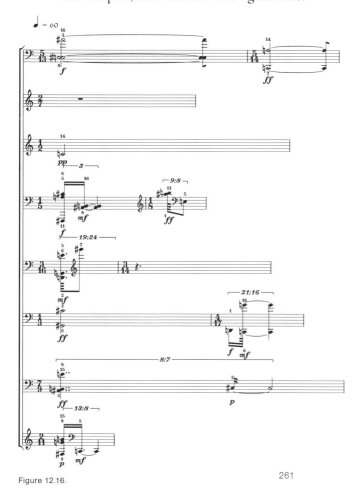

Figure 12.16.

261

Table 12.4. Third row of matrix *A*.

Figure 12.16. Reading of row 3 starting from matrix *A* in table 12.3.

After removing the voices entirely filled with rests, we can now transform the resulting "temporal reservoir" by ordering it following a temporal-block-type category (figure 12.17).[8]

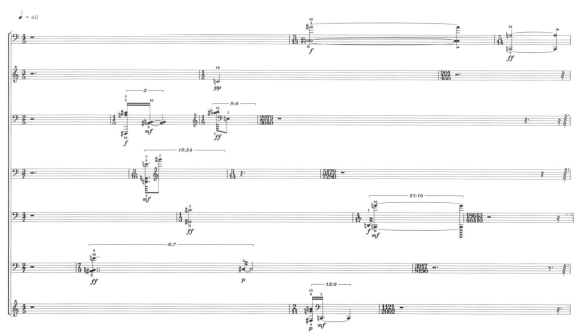

Figure 12.17.

For temporal blocks of an asymmetrical type I use the circular concatenation of temporal units (of the rest type) appended to the beginning of each voice in figure 12.16. These temporal units are the following:

$$\left[\left(-\frac{4}{5}\right),\left(-\frac{3}{5}\right),\left(-\frac{2}{5}\right),\left(-\frac{3}{7}\right),\left(-\frac{4}{7}\right)\left(-\frac{2}{7}\right)\right]$$

So far we have "interpreted" the *TU* array through the *A* matrix in a "synchronous" way. With the same interpretation of matrix *A* to the array *TU*, (*A* → *TU*) it is also possible to map this reading horizontally by omitting empty cells. Figure 12.18 shows a simultaneous and diachronic "reading" of rows 2 and 3 of matrix *A* mapped onto *TU*.

---

8 A temporal block is a geometrical grouping of a "field" of durations following three types of distributions—symmetrical, asymmetrical, and the combination of both fields—as described by Pierre Boulez in *Penser la musique aujourd'hui* (1963, 59–60; 1971, 55–57).

Figure 12.17. Distribution of temporal units in figure 12.16 following the configuration of an asymmetrical temporal block.

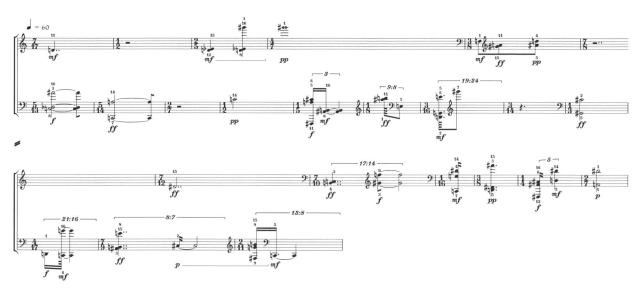

Figure 12.18.

3.3. Composition—decomposition—recomposition

Of course, vertical and horizontal (synchronous and diachronic) mapping can be alternated with a multiple choice of cells "read" or omitted (filtered) following a free and/or deliberate choice based on a given criteria. We can construct a free indexation as in the following example, where we have selected coordinates directly on the *TU* array in the form of (row column).[9]

```
(((2 2) (2 3) (2 4) (2 5) (2 6) (2 7) (2 8) (2 9))
 ((4 3) (4 4) (4 5) (4 6) (4 7) (4 8))
 ((5 4) (5 5) (5 6) (5 7))
 ((7 5) (7 6)))
```

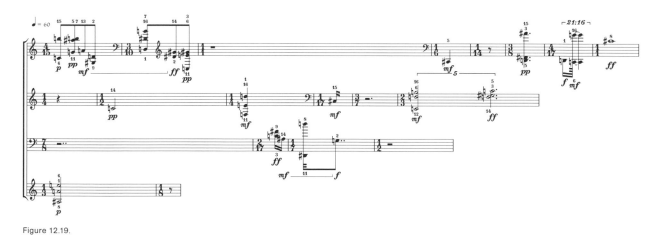

Figure 12.19.

9 Indexes starting at 0.

Figure 12.18. Horizontal reading of row 3 starting from matrix *A* of table 12.3.

Figure 12.19. The ordering of cells following a free selection of coordinates starting from Table 12.3.

Karim Haddad

After redistributing the voices in figure 12.19 from the longest to the shortest duration, we will "reorganise" them following a central symmetrical axis of a temporal-block form of type *a*:

Figure 12.20.

Once our complex is set in this temporal block, we can apply "global" envelopes (figure 12.21).

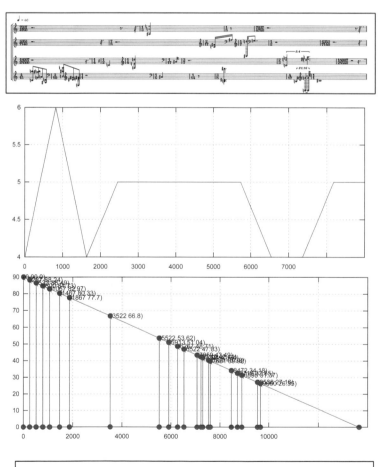

(15 4 1 2 3 9 5 6 14 16 7 11 8 12 13 14 3 15 1 2 4 9 5 13 6 16 7 11 8 12 8 13 14 2 15 1 3 4 9 12 5 16
6 7 11 7 12 8 13 1 14 15 2 3 4 9 11 16 5 6 6 11 16 7 12 15 13 14 1 2 3 4 9 8 5 5 6 11 16 8 12 13 14 15
9 1 2 3 7 4 5 14 7 11 16 8 12 13 15 1 2 9 6 3 4 13 6 7 11 16 8 12 14 15 1 5 9 2 3 4 4 12 5 6 7 11 8 13
14 15 1 9 2 3 16 3 11 5 6 16 7 12 8 13 14 4 15 1 9 2 2 4 9 8 5 6 11 16 7 12 13 14 3 15 1 1 3 4 9 7 5 6
11 16 8 12 13 2 14 15 2 3 4 6 9 5 7 11 16 8 12 1 13 14 1 2 3 5 4 9 6 7 11 16 8 15 12 13 14)

Figure 12.21.

Figure 12.20. Rearrangement of the complex in figure 12.19 into a symmetrical temporal block.

Figure 12.21. Global envelopes applied to the whole polyphonic structure.

In doing so, we have *redefined* the dynamic, register, and timbre envelopes (figure 12.22).

Figure 12.22.

Applying envelopes to a whole block will result in a rigid gesture that could seem mostly obvious, particularly on the pitch-registration level. However, it could be a very practical and profitable procedure to apply in order to obtain a global dynamic gesture, which, in this case, is a linear decrescendo.

The ordering of each cell inside a sequence of different or identical temporal blocks following specific sequence will result in coherently structured formal data. The numerous possibilities generated by this corpus of material based on these procedures offer a great freedom to reflect on the musical form. Obviously, we will not use simple editing techniques, such as "cutting and pasting" the chosen temporal-block sequences; on the contrary, we will use a formal and logical ordering based on a serial combinatorial process to choose or reject elements on the basis of a chosen temporal density. On freedom of choice, and more specifically, the freedom of choice of the composer, Pierre Boulez says:

> We might . . . regard a piece of music as a series of rejections among many probabilities; a choice has to be made and that is precisely the difficulty so easily wished away by the express desire for "objectivity." It is just this matter of choice, renewing itself at every stage of composition, which constitutes the work; the act of composing will never be the same thing as arranging thousands of points of contact statistically. Let us preserve this inalienable freedom: the continuously longed-for joy of the irrational. (Boulez 1991, 157)

Once we have established consistency through all these relational networks, some issues raised by the combinatorial processes directly related to the instrumental domain remain to be addressed, as the agnostic process leads sometimes to inconsistencies, impossibilities, and "absurd results"[10] in several domains:

---

10   "The composer was writing at the behest of a combinatorial power, ultimately intervening only to ascertain that the realisation was accurate, that the machine did not get carried away and produce nonsensical results" (Boulez 2018, 334).

Figure 12.22. The redefinition of envelopes (register, dynamics, and instrumentation) to the whole polyphonic structure of figure 12.17.

- Registration (instrumental range) can beget non-valid ranges for certain instruments, which could also happen with dynamics, leading to incompatibilities with respect to the pitch range
- Conflicting dynamic combinations, like for instance fortissimo against pianissisimo
- Vertical pitch combinations leading to octaves or tonal connotations

Depending on the case, there are two strategies that can be used: locally correcting point by point contentious or unwanted issues; or radically changing the envelopes used on the totality of the temporal block as was done in figure 12.21 to "retransform" dynamically either the pitch range or the timbral distribution of the whole block. This requires a supplementary structure on the hierarchical level of the system of envelopes.

4. ON TECHNOLOGY

Employing different instances, such as functions, envelopes, or any other musical contextual domain, should not lead to a hazardous collage or to "wild" editing; on the contrary, it should proceed from a deductive well-thought-out combinatorial process that chiefly implies the coherence and intelligibility of the work, leading to an expressive and singular unique style. In general, choosing the material before the transformation and deduction of elements regarding its totality is crucial to the cohesion and logical understanding of the work.

In order to put all these elements into a viable workflow, computer-assisted composition seems to me the most efficient environment, in particular, the OpenMusic CommonLisp-based visual programming language.

4.1. OpenMusic: the language

In order to consider a tool dedicated to composition, where most musical objects, computational strategies, and temporal procedures will be manipulated, it is necessary to assume there is a specific "language" that should be mastered before any prior musical orientation. It assumes a functional grammar and a symbolic representation of all musical components, such as rhythm, pitch, dynamics, and form, will be available. This environment should therefore be seen as a tool for building starting from a language and dedicated to a language—musical composition.

> Due to their particular audience, the music programming languages share the necessity to deal and balance between efficiency, expressive power on the one hand, and user accessibility and creativity issues on the other hand. Functional programming languages, and particularly Lisp dialects, were often used for these purposes. The interpreted characteristic of Lisp allows an interactive use and an incremental development of compositional processes, and its relatively simple syntax, its expressivity and general capacity for the manipulation of symbolic structures allow to perform advanced operations on symbolic musical material. (Bresson, Agon, and Assayag 2009, 81)

4.2. Etüde No. 6 ". . . où ton âme en le somme gît cachée, . . ."

Focusing on my own composition in progress *Etüde No. 6 ". . . où ton âme en le somme gît cachée, . . ."* for string quartet and orchestra, we shall use relatively concise examples to explore the potentialities of temporal units combined with a visual programing language in a compositional context. The piece is based on a string continuo and distributed fragments orchestrated using temporal blocs of time organised under a cantus firmus. I will describe how they are articulated and achieved using the OpenMusic programming language.

4.2.1. The string quartet

The rhythmic material of the quartet is derived from iterative circular permutations from four groups of four integers representing proportions of durations and is computed using the loop macro (see 1 in figure 12.23).

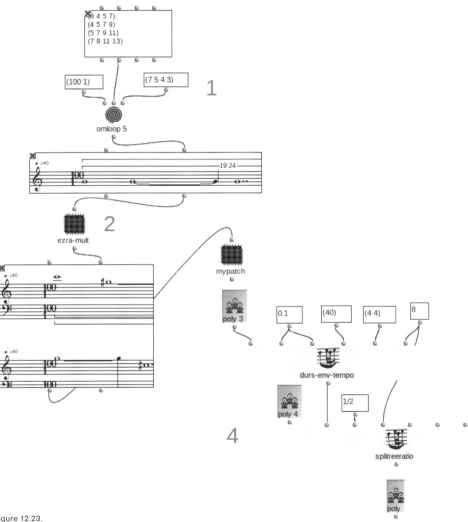

Figure 12.23.

267

Figure 12.23. OpenMusic patch for rhythm- and pitch-generated structures for the string quartet continuo.

The condensed expression for the first voice (violin) is as follows:

$$\left(\frac{100}{1}\right)_{\overline{\begin{array}{c} (3\;4\;5\;7) \\ i=1,4 \\ j\;in\;s \\ s:=(\;j\;(\sigma)\,)\,\| \end{array}}} \Rightarrow \left(\frac{100}{1}\right)_{\begin{array}{l} ((3\;(4\;5\;7\;3)) \\ (4\;(5\;7\;3\;4)) \\ (5\;(7\;3\;4\;5)) \\ (7\;(3\;4\;5\;7))) \end{array}}$$

The pitch is derived from duration/interval proportions (see 2 in figure 12.23) inspired by Ezra Pound's *Antheil: And the Treatise on Harmony* ([1924] 1968). Because all the proportions for each instrument are different, and are rounded to a quarter tone, the resulting harmony is non-tonal, as shown in figure 12.24.

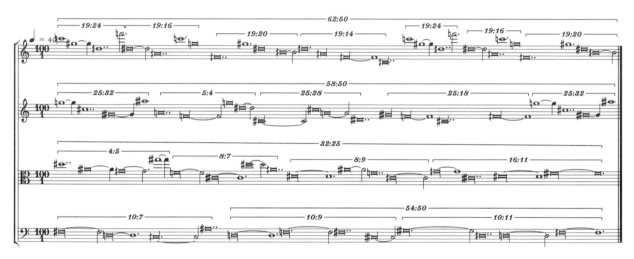

Figure 12.24.

4.2.2. Temporal "orchestral" blocks

The temporal units in the orchestral part are generated starting from two Pisano periods[11] (see 1 in figure 12.26). In 2 in figure 12.26, a string of DNA is used to set the types of temporal units following the following given order:

- For an *A* item, a fundamental temporal unit
- For a *C* item, a pulsed temporal unit
- For a *T* item, a temporal unit with a rest
- For a *G* item, a composed temporal unit using the proportions of its *tempus*

---

11 A Pisano period is a Fibonacci suite calculated with a given *modulo*.

Figure 12.24. Polyphonic temporal units representing the main structure of the string quartet's continuo.

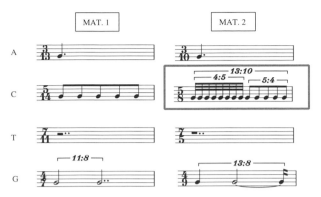

Figure 12.25.

As shown in figure 12.25, there are two types of material (mat. 1 and mat. 2), which differ in their relative complexity. If we examine the C and G types of both materials, we observe a construct of *prolationis* relative to the *TU* tempus. The material 2 C type has double-layered pulse subdivisions according to this construct.

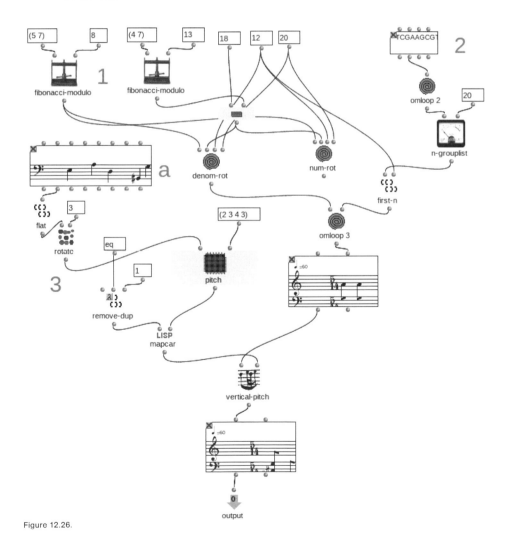

Figure 12.26.

Figure 12.25. DNA-derived temporal units.

Figure 12.26. Patch-generating temporal units starting from a DNA chain (2).

Once the temporal units are placed in a matrix with a dimension of 12 × 12 (see 5 in figure 12.27), they are coupled with dynamic and registration envelopes associated with lists of instrumental timbres (2, 3, 4 in figure 12.27).

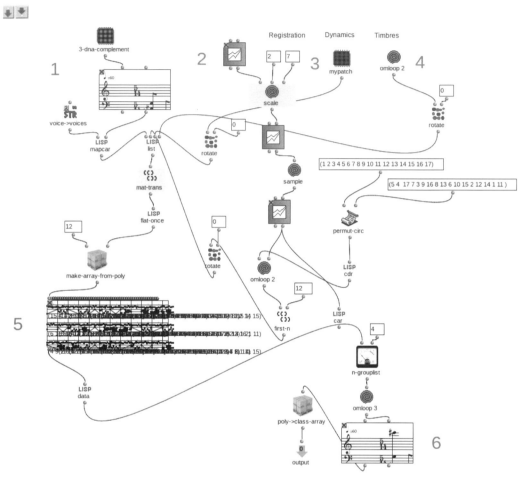

Figure 12.27.

The array will then be read starting from a transitional matrix such as described already in 3 in figure 12.28. Starting from here, we will derive temporal blocks (cf. figure 12.16) that will be used as distributed material on top of the string quartet continuo.

Figure 12.27. Temporal units (1) and envelopes (2, 3, and 4) placed in a matrix (5).

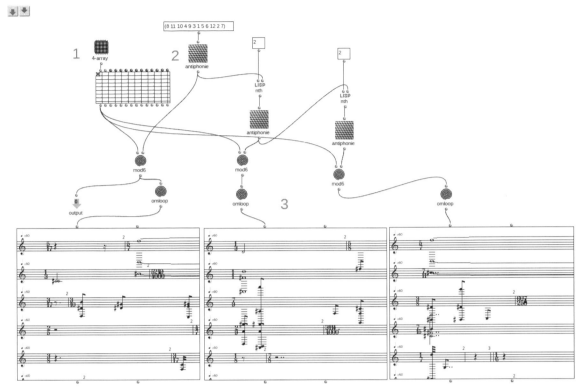

Figure 12.28.

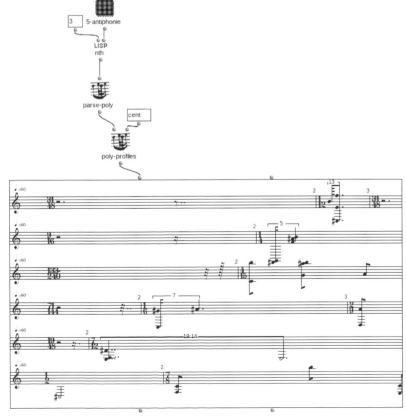

Figure 12.29.

Figure 12.28. Derivational method used for reordering the temporal units in new matrices.

Figure 12.29. A temporal block with a centred distribution of temporal units.

4.2.3. The "form"

The patch in figure 12.33 shows the part of the form dealing with organisational choice and materials. After a small introductory section ("Praeludium") played by the orchestra section, the string quartet starts with a $\frac{100}{1}$ *tempus* that is also the span of a cantus firmus (see figure 12.21), which distributes the temporal blocks accordingly. The cantus is generated again by iterative circular permutation in the same manner as the quartet but with one extra iteration (see 1 in figure 12.30). It is then filtered according to the chosen points of onsets (see 2 in figure 12.30). Temporal blocks from different derivational matrices are freely chosen starting from the two sets of types of temporal units (simple and more complex, as already mentioned and shown in figure 12.25). Each temporal block will then be organised with diverse ordering of distribution (straight, reverted, centred, axial, and asymmetrical, see figure 12.29).

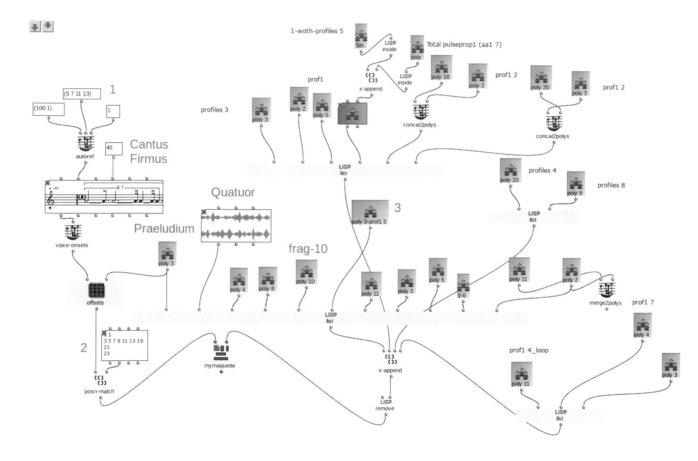

Figure 12.30.

272

Figure 12.30. OM patch showing the formal structure.

Temporal Poetics as a Critical Technical Practice

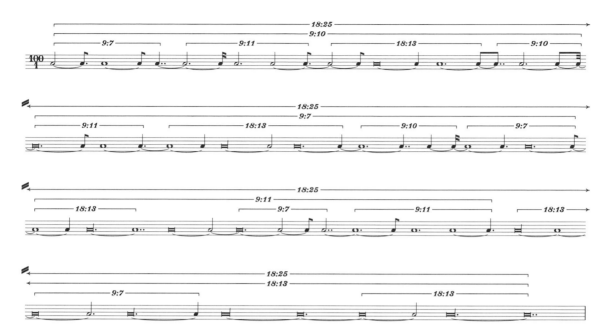

Figure 12.31.

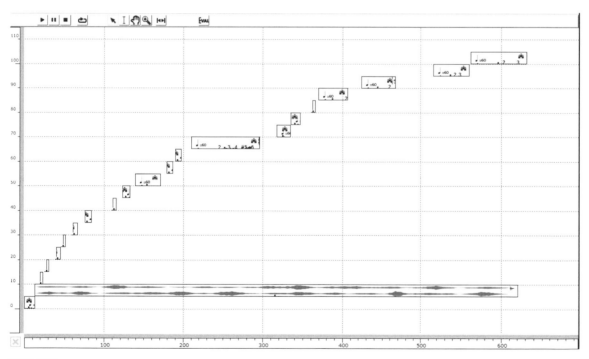

Figure 12.32.

Figure 12.31. Filtered cantus firmus setting the start of each temporal block.

Figure 12.32. The whole formal organisation as it is displayed in OpenMusic Maquette.

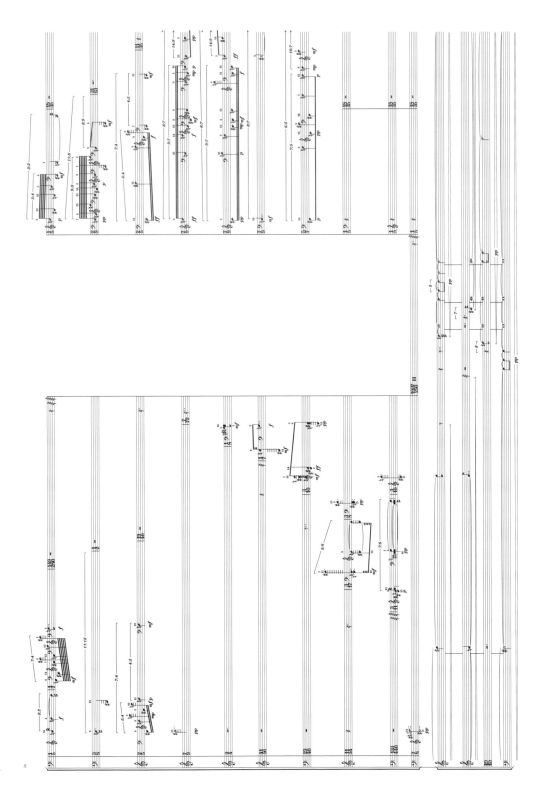

Figure 12.33.

Figure 12.33. Excerpt (p. 26) from the sketch of *Etüde No. 6* "*. . . où ton âme en le somme gît cachée, . . .*"

5. Conclusion

If serial and post-serial techniques are assumed to be a continuation of polyphony and a legacy of the Ars Nova, the approach detailed in this chapter seems to me necessary, for it leads us towards new and innovative possibilities, new combinatory practices revealing musical inner matter in itself,[12] rich in potentiality and "obliges us, in fact, to reflect on the mechanisms of composition" (Boulez 1989, 104, my translation). Moreover, "any situation of development . . . forces us onto a different route, to consider events from a different angle, which results in disturbing our habits forged by both education and practice" (ibid.). However, this raises questions over language as a technique and the nature of its operating mode as tools—notation, computation, and invention—the fundamental question being the one concerning technology itself and its relation with musical production, which can only be revealed by the work itself.

In thus questioning, we bear witness to the crisis that due to our sheer preoccupation with technology we do not yet experience the coming to presence of technology, that in our sheer aesthetic-mindedness we no longer guard and preserve the coming to the presence of art. Yet the more questioningly we ponder the essence of technology, the more mysterious the essence of art becomes.

> The closer we come to the danger, the more brightly do the ways into the saving power begin to shine and the more questioning we become. For questioning is the piety of thought. (Heidegger 1977, 35)

References

Agon, Carlos. 1998. "OpenMusic: Un langage visuel pour la composition musicale assistée par ordinateur." PhD thesis, IRCAM, Université Paris 6.

Boulez, Pierre. 1963. *Penser la musique aujourd'hui*. Paris: Gonthier. Translated by Susan Bradshaw and Richard Rodney Bennett as Boulez 1971.

———. 1971. *Boulez on Music Today*. Translated by Susan Bradshaw and Richard Rodney Bennett. London: Faber and Faber. First published as Boulez 1963.

———. 1986. "Le système et l'idée." In "Le temps des mutations," special issue, *InHarmoniques*, no. 1, 62–105. Later expanded version translated by Jonathan Dunsby, Jonathan Goldman, and Arnold Whittall as Boulez 2018.

———. 1989. *Jalons (Pour une décennie): Dix ans d'enseignement au Collège de France (1978–1988)*. Edited by Jean-Jacques Nattiez. Paris: Christian Bourgois.

———. 1991. ". . . Near and Far." In *Stocktakings from an Apprenticeship*, edited by Paule Thévenin, translated by Stephen Walsh, 141–57. Oxford: Clarendon Press. Book first published 1966 as *Relevés d'apprenti* (Paris: Seuil). Essay first published 1954 as ". . . Auprès et au loin" (*Cahiers de la Compagnie Madeleine Renaud–Jean-Louis Barrault* 2 [3]: 7–24).

———. 2018. "The System and the Idea." In *Music Lessons: The Collège de France Lectures*, edited and translated by Jonathan Dunsby, Jonathan Goldman, and Arnold Whittall, 281–356. London: Faber & Faber. Book first published 2005 as *Leçons de musique (Points de repère, III): Deux décennies d'enseignement au Collège de France (1976–1995)*, edited by Jean-Jacques

---

12 "'Technique' is not, in fact, a dead weight to be dragged around as a guarantee of immortality. It is an exalting mirror which the imagination forges for itself, and in which its discoveries are reflected" (Boulez 1971, 143).

Nattiez and Jonathan Goldman (Paris: Christian Bourgois). Essay first published in shorter form as Boulez 1986.

Bresson, Jean, Carlos Agon, and Gérard Assayag. 2009. "Visual Lisp/CLOS Programming in OpenMusic." In *Higher-Order and Symbolic Computation* 22 (1): 81–111.

Haddad, Karim. 2008. "*Livre Premier de Motets*: The Time-Block Concept in OpenMusic." In *The OM Composer's Book 2*, edited by Jean Bresson, Carlos Agon, and Gérard Assayag, 21–53. Paris: Delatour.

———. 2020. "L'unité temporelle: Une approche pour l'écriture de la durée et de sa quantification." PhD thesis, IRCAM—Sorbonne Université.

Heidegger, Martin. 1977. "The Question Concerning Technology." In *The Question Concerning Technology and Other Essays*, translated by William Lovitt, 3–35. New York: Harper & Row. Essay first published 1954 as "Die Frage nach der Technik," in *Vorträge und Aufsätze* (Pfullingen: G. Neske), 13–44.

Hölderlin, Friedrich. 2009. "Seven Maxims." In *Essays and Letters*, edited and translated by Jeremy Adler and Charlie Louth, 240–43. London: Penguin. Fair copy written 1799. Published in German as "Reflexion" (ed. Friedrich Beissner) and "Frankurter Aphorismen" (ed. Michael Knaupp).

O'Hagan, Peter. 2006. "'Antiphonie': Une étude du processus de composition." In *Pierre Boulez: Techniques d'écriture et enjeux esthetiques*, edited by Jean-Louis Leleu and Pascal Decroupet, 109–31. Geneva: Contrechamps.

Pound, Ezra. (1924) 1968. *Antheil: And the Treatise on Harmony*. New York: Da Capo Press. First published 1924 (Paris: Three Mountains Press).

Schoenberg, Arnold. 1950. *Style and Idea*. Edited by Dika Newlin. New York: Philosophical Library.

Tarkovsky, Andrey. 1996. *Sculpting in Time: Reflections on the Cinema; The Great Russian Filmmaker Discusses His Art*. Translated by Kitty Hunter-Blair. New ed. Austin: University of Texas Press. First published 1986 as *Die versiegelte Zeit* (Berlin: Ullstein).

Collaborative Creation in Electroacoustic Music

Practices and Self-Awareness in the Work of Musical Assistants Marino Zuccheri, Alvise Vidolin, and Carl Faia

Laura Zattra

IRCAM, Paris; Bologna, Castelfranco Veneto, and Rovigo Conservatories of Music, Italy

1. What is a musical assistant?

"Music, broadly defined, is a collaborative art form. Perhaps, even, the ultimate collaborative art form. The interdependence of the various actors within the field is manifestly clear" (Faia 2014, 15). This statement, by musical assistant and computer music designer Carl Faia, introduces us to the double theme of this chapter. If music is the ultimate collaborative art form, the art of organised sound with analogue or digital technology (sonic art or sound-based art, particularly as practised in electroacoustic music)[1] is collaboration at its best. In this chapter I will portray collaboration as it is viewed by those actors (one of whom is in fact Faia) who work closely with composers, and the traces remaining from this collaboration—a habitually wordless communication.

Unlike "traditional" acoustic music, where the actors are composers, performers, and directors (and where there is still a persistent myth or illusion that composers are the lone creators responsible for everything within the creative

---

1 I refer, here, to the definition of sound-based art given by Leigh Landy in "But Is It (Also) Music?" (2017): "both note-based and sound-based works" (17) that were created "over the last century catalyzing an ongoing need for a broader definition of music" (19). For those interested in the important issue of terminology (sonic art, sounding art, sound-based art, sound art, electroacoustic music, electronic music, etc.), Landy's article is essential reading. In this chapter I will oscillate indistinctly between the use of *sound-based art* as an umbrella term, and *electroacoustic music*, historically a more often used term, as for example in the "bible" (for musicologists) *The New Grove Dictionary of Music and Musicians*. Electroacoustic music indicates "[m]usic in which electronic technology, now primarily computer-based, is used to access, generate, explore and configure sound materials, and in which loudspeakers are the prime medium of transmission" (Emmerson and Smalley 2001, quoted in Landy 2017, 19). Historically we consider the period to start with musique concrète in 1948 and Elektronische Musik in 1950, with computer music starting in 1957.

chain of musical production),[2] sound-based art and particularly electroacoustic music are characterised from the start by a high level of teamwork. The revolution in sound recording, synthesis, and transformation from the late 1940s has involved the presence of different individuals with varied roles, who regrettably have often been concealed from the official literature. My research (Zattra 2013, 2018a; 2018b; 2018c; Zattra and Donin 2016) has tried to unveil these "invisible collaborators" (to quote Shapin's famous 1989 article), as also did Jennifer Iverson (2019) in her brilliant investigation of the Cologne WDR Studio.

The general framework of my chapter considers the practice of musical assistants in electroacoustic music.[3] His or her part in the creative process is to manage the technical set-up of a new musical piece, to help the composer cope with technologies and scientific knowledge, to translate the composer's aesthetic world into programming languages, and to take part in the performance of the piece (Zattra and Donin 2016, 437). The musical assistant acts as an "interface" between composer and technology, creation and research. His or her name has been loosely applied or even changed over the years. I will here use the term *musical assistant* most often, but historically the expressions technician, tutor, computer music designer, music mediator (Zattra 2013), Klangregisseur, live electronics musician, and digital audio processing performer (Plessas and Boutard 2015) have also been used. Analogue or digital instruments—depending on the historical period we are considering—may serve to develop compositional ideas and material, explore musical ideas, and perform a musical piece. Still, while traditional instrumental music has developed quite standardised systems for writing acoustic instrumental or orchestral music, in the electronic world it is unrealistic to think this equally possible and to imagine composers as perfect connoisseurs of those techniques. There are some composers who are also performers and professional electronic instrument experts. But they are the exception, because electroacoustic music requires highly specialised skills. In fact, until recently only a few composers

---

2   This is not the place to discuss the ontology of music in much detail. It seems, however, important to remember that this myth remains, at least among music listeners, despite the efforts of scholars from different disciplines who have tried to dismantle this rhetoric over the decades. The dualism works-composers introduced by the father of musicology Guido Adler in 1885 has been undermined, for example, in the seminal work by Lydia Goehr whose social history of music revised the strong work-concept "composer-score-performance" and the resulting "imaginary museum of musical works" (Goehr 1992). The approach of STS studies (science, technology, and society studies) is analogous (Pinch and Trocco 2004), as are studies that investigate musical organology: examples of which include the history of the Wagner tuba (Melton 2008), or the philosophical theory that music begins with the handling of musical instruments and the physicality of musicians (Sève 2013). On the other hand, twentieth-century music and creativity have gradually become more cooperative in breaking down this myth, for example, graphic, aleatoric, and Fluxus scores and improvisations or certain interesting cases of music co-creation and co-composition in works by Luigi Nono and his collaborators.

3   We must not forget that the term *musical assistant* has also been loosely applied over the course of music history, to a musician, translator, or interpreter of musical ideas (copyist, amanuensis, transcriber, etc.) who works alongside the composer to transcribe working documents, arrange musical pieces, develop rough ideas provided by the composer, and assist in the direction of a performance. Among many examples, I could cite the working relationships of Joseph Joachim Raff and Franz Liszt, Imogen Holst and Benjamin Britten, Alex Weston and Philip Glass, or even more complex relationships such as Ernst Krenek and Paul Bekker, Robert Craft and Igor Stravinsky, and Joseph Joachim and Johannes Brahms. To assist means to "help (someone), typically by doing a share of the work," "from Latin assistere 'take one's stand by,' from ad- 'to, at' + sistere: 'take one's stand'" (Lexico 2021).

had been able to generate electroacoustic music pieces autonomously, from the first conception and synthesis to the diffusion of sound.[4]

More specifically, while in the past I have investigated the socio-professional status, profile, practices, and expertise of musical assistants in electroacoustic music (see my aforementioned articles), here I concentrate on comparing specific examples of collaboration and focus in particular on three musical assistants, their strategies in action, and their self-consciousness issues. The musical assistants I am considering are Marino Zuccheri (who was active primarily during the 1950s and 1960s), Alvise Vidolin (active from the end of the 1970s to the present day), and Carl Faia (whose activity began during the 1990s and still continues). The choice is motivated by the significance of their work with composers such as Luciano Berio and John Cage (Zuccheri), Luigi Nono and Salvatore Sciarrino (Vidolin), and Philippe Leroux and Jonathan Harvey (Faia). The main reason for presenting these three cases is their focus on constructing a narrative of their collaborations, which is reflected in the archiving, conservation, technological migration of their outputs, and maintenance of their writings, sketches, diaries, and documentation (especially Vidolin and Faia), as well as their willingness to give interviews.

Thanks to their openness and awareness of the importance of documentation, it is possible to trace analogies and differences in their time management, areas of expertise, problems, communication, coordination, and modes of thought, which are also motivated by historical and technological circumstances. In examining this collaborative framework, I propose that collaboration in electroacoustic music continually prompts both composers and musical assistants to perform typical actions that are required in design and design thinking, as described by Nigel Cross (2006): context analysis, tension between "problem goals" and "solution criteria," establishing "problem frames" in order to find solutions, creative thinking, sketching and prototyping, testing, evaluating, and delivering (ibid., 74). In fact, on the one hand, musical assistants need to imagine what composers have in mind when they communicate their musical aesthetic vision, or their ideas about timbre, interaction, and musical form ("the mind set of computer music designers is different from the mind set and vision of composers" says Alvise Vidolin [pers. comm., 27 July 1999])—the translating process into sounds, codes, data, and algorithms needs to negotiate the possibilities and constraints of the technologies, running the risk of diminishing or changing ideas. On the other hand, composers ought to understand the technological framework and decide whether to remain within those possibilities and constraints or to cross those limits, developing at the same time their mastery of the compositional disciplinary and aesthetic vision.

In order to study collaboration in electroacoustic music, I propose a unified methodology at the intersection of (1) music analysis based on electronic and digital sources and instruments; (2) ethnographic research, as it is a collaboration based also on oral traditions and activities; (3) philology of

---

4   Of earlier practitioners, we could cite John Chowning, Jean-Claude Risset, and James Tenney, who were simultaneously composers, researchers, and computer programmers (Kahn 2012, 131–46).

music and source criticism. I report findings based on archival research—published and unpublished sources (written, oral, and video) and administrative documents—conserved at different archives: the archive of the Studio di Fonologia della RAI in Milan (now digitised and held at the Archivio dello Studio di Fonologia, Associazione NoMus, Milan), IRCAM (Institut Recherche et Coordination Acoustique/Musique) in Paris, and CSC (Centro di Sonologia Computazionale) in Padova; and the private archives of Alvise Vidolin and Carl Faia. Heterogeneous sources help reconstruct Marino Zuccheri's, Alvise Vidolin's, and Carl Faia's approaches to collaboration (sections 2–4). Their comparison (section 5), brings out new information on the way collaboration takes place in electroacoustic music.

2. MARINO ZUCCHERI

Marino Zuccheri (1923–2005) was the sound engineer, chief sound technician, and musical assistant at the Milan RAI (Italian Broadcasting Company) Studio di Fonologia.[5] He helped Luciano Berio, Bruno Maderna, Luigi Nono, Henri Pousseur, and John Cage, among others, in giving birth to their musical works (Novati, Pronestì, and Vaccarini 2018). To understand the importance of Zuccheri's contribution, I will cite semiotician and cultural critic Umberto Eco, who actively participated in the studio's activities. Eco suggested in 2008 that Zuccheri's contribution was so important that in some cases electronic pieces credited to other people were really his. As he recalled:

> all the protagonists of Neue Musik used to pass by there and it is fair to recall that, since many of them were in Milan to study with scholarships and had to present a complete composition at the end of their term, and the period was not long enough to master all nine oscillators' secrets, the great Marino Zuccheri would put together an acceptable composition with a couple of manoeuvres, thus many electronic music incunabula are his and not from those authors who signed them. (Eco 2008, my translation)[6]

Without questioning the place or authorship of avant-garde music composers, it is interesting to stress that we learn from this quotation that composers certainly came to the studio with their own visions, musical backgrounds, and aesthetic peculiarities; however, without Zuccheri's dexterity (and the machines created by physicist Alfredo Lietti, the first technical director and designer at the studio), there would be no musical outcomes. "Technicians from the first analogue era of electroacoustic music . . . , like Marino Zuccheri at the Studio di

---

5 Zuccheri worked first as a telegraphist for the Fascist-era radio network EIAR (Ente Italiano per le Audizioni Radiofoniche, the public service broadcaster in Fascist Italy) in Bologna in 1942, then as a wireless radio operator for the Italian military; he participated in the partisan resistance and in 1950 was appointed at RAI until his retirement in 1983 (Helms 2020, 141).

6 "Passavano di lì tutti i protagonisti della Neue Musik e sarà giustizia ricordare che, siccome molti avevano delle specie di borse per un periodo di studio a Milano, ma alla fine del periodo dovevano presentare una composizione finita, e il periodo non era stato sufficiente per impadronirsi di tutti i segreti dei nove oscillatori, il grande Marino Zuccheri manovrando di qua e di là metteva insieme una composizione accettabile, sì che molti incunaboli della musica elettronica sono dovuti a lui e non agli autori che li hanno firmati."

Fonologia . . . , can be seen more as cinematographers or directors of photography," Alvise Vidolin said; "these technicians had a crucial role to play, just as technicians did in . . . film production" (pers. comm., 12 April 2013; quoted in Zattra 2018b, 86). However, collaboration at the studio differed from case to case. Zuccheri later recalled that

> Bruno [Maderna] was the most enthusiastic, perhaps also the most instinctive, nothing stopped him; he was more of an "artist," he invented and . . . go ahead. Berio knew precisely where he was going, and he had a perfect knowledge of the machines. Gigi [Luigi Nono] was the most serious. . . . Three different attitudes, three different artists, three people of great value. I must admit that I had a great time . . . and such jokes! (Zuccheri and De Benedictis 2000, 178)

Zuccheri emphasises that "we got on very well in the respect of our different competences: the musicians 'ruled' the machines, and I made the machine work. It was great for me to work which such people: to be where you discussed art" (ibid.).[7] Zuccheri's role, as he perceived it, was not marginal. Alongside Zuccheri, physicist Alfredo Lietti understood the musical requirements of composition and, helped by the other technicians at RAI, designed and translated those needs into electrical circuits. Writing in 1956, one year after the opening of the studio, Lietti was well aware of those difficulties: "The musician may have a clear idea of the sound he wants to create, but this is obviously a musical idea. On the other hand, if the sound is to be created electronically, the technician is interested in its physical characteristics. It is clear that this difficulty can only be overcome if they make an effort to understand one another" (Lietti 1956, quoted in Vidolin 2012, 20).[8] Lietti was the skilled designer; Marino Zuccheri (and Luciano Berio, founder of the studio and its first director) listened and decided whether the new instruments were good enough to create interesting sounds. If not, they started all over again. Once ultimately approved by Zuccheri, each device was controlled by the capable hands of Zuccheri himself (Lietti 1959, 41, cited in Rodà 2012, 34).

While the technical equipment was set up by Lietti, Zuccheri was the link between the technical and musical worlds. Luigi Nono, who worked at the studio, was the first composer, to the best of my knowledge, to try to define the musical assistant's status. Nono wrote that Zuccheri was a "true musician-technician-theorist-practical-teacher-interpreter-performer of uncommon virtuosity, extremely humane in his desire to understand and participate" (Nono 1986, 176; also quoted in Vidolin 2012, 20). Marino Zuccheri invented

---

7 "The traditional approach of early electronic music studios was to assemble electronic devices already available in broadcasting companies, such as oscillators, ring modulators, tape recorders. This approach required a lot of tweaking and adaptations from the original aim for which these devices were designed, and induced severe constraints on the possible musical use. Instead, the Studio di Fonologia Musicale di Milano was conceived since the beginning as *a new musical instrument for a new musical practice*. The far-sighted and creative intuitions of composers such as Luciano Berio and Bruno Maderna met the technical skills and attention to musical needs of physicist Alfredo Lietti and technician Marino Zuccheri" (De Poli 2012, ix).

8 On a historical note, at the Studio di Fonologia, the WDR studio in Cologne and the GRM studio in Paris, machines and personnel were the same as they had been during the Second World War. Lietti was employed at RAI during the war as a military officer of telecommunications (Rodà 2012, 33).

this profession for himself, since he had no predecessors (as is stressed also by Vidolin [2012, 21]). He was a tutor, a teacher, a psychologist, and a performer. "My job, other than that of sound engineer, was to be a go-between between the equipment and the musician, to try and understand as much as possible what was needed in order to realize the material sound to begin with and to indicate the briefest technical route, thus collaborating indiscriminately for the success of that composition or musical experiment" (Zuccheri 1998, 1; [1998] 2018, 54).

Of course, not all composers worked in the same way. Therefore, as mentioned before, Zuccheri's involvement varied from case to case. If we consider the creative process in analogue electronic music, consisting of synthesising, recording, splicing, and editing, we can trace different approaches to composition. According to Zuccheri, John Cage in 1958 was autonomous: Cage worked alone setting up the sound fragments and cutting and reassembling them for *Fontana Mix* (Zuccheri 1962). Describing Cage's arrival at the studio in October 1958, Zuccheri recalls: "he follows my explanations with the maximum attention and takes notes. He asks for some graphic paper, and on this he designs with great precision all the central panel containing the electronic instruments, omitting not even one of the screws! I await in silence his next decisions for the preparation of the electronic material, as usually occurs with all other composers" (Zuccheri 1962–63, 45). Instead, Cage asked him to accompany him to the zoo and other places to record city and nature sounds, and was later completely autonomous in the mixing of the tapes for *Fontana Mix*. "I insist on asking Mister J. Cage if I can start up the machines in the Studio for eventual use, but he continues unperturbed his job of cutting up tapes, talcum powder etc." (ibid, 46.). Luciano Berio had a different method of work and collaborated closely with Zuccheri on the creation of *Thema (Omaggio a Joyce)* and other pieces (Zuccheri and De Benedictis 2000, 187). Luigi Nono, who worked in the studio in the 1960s and 70s also collaborated closely with Marino Zuccheri; they accumulated a vast collection of sounds, and in the process Nono discovered "compositional principles that were innate to the material itself" (Nono 1986, 175; also quoted in Vidolin 2012, 28–29).[9] In *Notturno* (1956) by Bruno Maderna, composer and technician worked together at night.[10]

---

9   They started with the sound material, said Luigi Nono in 1986 recalling his work with Zuccheri in the 1960s and 1970s: "we would listen, analyse, discuss and then decide how to proceed. / It was all put together on another four-track tape, adding further variation and modifications on each track. / The result was the 'sum' of 16 tracks. / Then again on another four-track tape = 64 tracks all of which were different. / We tried different tempi—synchronous or asynchronous starts, different intensities different pitch modulations (micro-macro intervals)" (Nono 1986, 175). The first work to use spatialisation at the studio was *Intolleranza 1960* by Nono (realised 1961), created with the help of Marino Zuccheri and Bruno Maderna, and recorded on four-channel tapes. The last sound materials to be realised by Nono at the studio, with the help of Marino Zuccheri, were recordings of flutist Roberto Fabbriciani, later used for the final bass-flute section of *Das Atmende Klarsein* (1981).

10 As Maderna recalls in a handwritten note from around 1957 now in the Paul Sacher Stiftung, *Notturno* "was realized mainly at night and in secrecy with the help of the technician [Marino Zuccheri], who had already then become a very good friend of mine, because I only had very little time—officially, I had to be finished within a week—, but also because it was impossible to use the devices during normal daytime operations, when they were used for realizing smaller and larger pieces [for broadcast programmes] on short notice. When we had finished towards four o'clock and were completely exhausted, the technician and I jokingly decided to call the piece *Notturno*, commemorating the lost hours of sleep" (quoted in De Benedictis 2018, 37).

As we can see, Zuccheri left sufficient traces of the workflow and strategies of these collaborations (the NoMus archive also holds charts of the scheduling and availability of the equipment during regular working hours). I was also able to see several letters between Maderna, Nono, and Zuccheri. These are particularly interesting in order to understand the atmosphere prevailing at the studio in its first and second decades. All the letters are in Venetian, the dialect spoken within Venice and by Maderna and Nono (both born in Venice). Venetian was, according to Zuccheri (1998), the "official" language of the studio (Zuccheri [1976–77] 1986). These letters were jotted down at the end of the day, or on leaving a session, and contain comments, annotations, reminders, jokes, greetings. Some letters, especially the ones written by Nono, also contain swearing and cursing! Such words stress the intimate confidence between Zuccheri and these composers. What follows is an example of an undated memo from Nono to Zuccheri (my translation).

> Sir Marino [Sior: Venetian for "Mister"] Vualtri [your Excellency]
> [in Venetian] Please make sure that this piece does not last 2'25"—!!! [continues in Venetian] (The inspiration of Penderecki strikes me—or [unclear] Pollini), instead it lasts [?] [?unclear] until the end ...

In the note, Nono is clearly asking Zuccheri to expand an idea of just 2:25 into a longer piece, or passage, through reference to Krzysztof Penderecki's music (we cannot know which work Nono is referring to). The close cooperation and trust between the two is clear and strong.[11]

3. Alvise Vidolin

Alvise Vidolin (b. 1949) is a co-founder (in 1979) of, member of, and researcher at the Centro di Sonologia Computazionale (CSC—University of Padova). He is a sound engineer, a live electronics performer, and a researcher. He has worked with composers including Luigi Nono, Salvatore Sciarrino, Giorgio Battistelli, Luciano Berio, Aldo Clementi, Franco Donatoni, and Adriano Guarnieri, assisting them during the creative process, and working as a performer in the first and in subsequent performances of the compositions. He has consistently taken care to preserve information pertaining to his work and the upgrading of technology. His concern for archival and conservation issues, as well as metacognition, is astonishing. I have already presented his modes of collaborations (in Zattra 2018b, forthcoming) and I compiled a bibliography of his writings (in Zattra 2009). In his texts, Vidolin discusses his role and

---

11 Here is another example from a letter from Nono to Zuccheri, concerning *La fabbrica illuminata* (first performance in Venice, September 1964), about a new performance in Paris (probably the one in November 1964): "Dear Marino, I say hello 'cause I have to go. BENISSIMO! (Great!). O***a [the communion wafer, typical Venetian blasphemy]. Ragasssssi ["boys," but with Venetian pronunciation]. Towards November 10th, in Paris there will be a performance of 'the Unenlightened Factory' [a pun on Nono's work's title in Venetian], etc." The letter continues with three pages of details (always in Venetian, sometimes hard to decipher) about the piece and the organisation of the performance (manuscript held at the NoMus Archive, Milan, my translation).

collaborations, issues pertaining to electroacoustic music notation, spatialisation, listening, sound synthesis/processing and analysis, live electronics and performance, archiving, and audio restoration, and the history and musicology of electroacoustic music. So far, he has written hundreds of books, handbooks, book chapters, articles, conference presentations, interviews, and concert programs, for practitioners and researchers, but also for more general audiences.

Here, I will only mention a few examples of his self-awareness, which reflects his commitment not only to his work but also to the definition of his and his peers' mission. He describes himself as an "interpreter of electronic music instruments," a professional capable of combining musical skills with sonological and signal processing know-how. This kind of musical performer "not only 'plays' during a concert but also designs the *performance environment* for the piece and acts as an interface between the composer's musical idea and its transformation into sound" (Vidolin 1997, 439). He or she "does not simply translate a score into a sound, but transforms the composer's abstract musical project into an operative fact, making use of digital technology and new developments in the synthesis and signal processing" (ibid., 440).

For Vidolin, it is necessary for a musical assistant to have a series of mandatory skills, abilities, and areas of knowledge:

> In my experience, a great work of oral communication and planning is the key to a successful collaboration. In my work, I feel I have two basic tasks: the first is to understand the composer's vision. This is possible only through dialogue, empathy and even imagination: as in any relationship, it is not always easy to decipher others' mind and intentions. Planning is the second important tool and the key to a positive experience. By planning, I mean taking the time to organize, reflect after meetings, submit my ideas, solutions, creations. After that, I leave composers the time to evaluate and discuss again and again every step of the creative process, in order to deliver on time something that really satisfies them, represents them, but still is something I am happy about. (Vidolin, pers. comm., 12 April 2013; also published in Zattra 2018b, 87–88)

Dialogue, empathy, planning, and time are the keys to collaboration. This also applies to Vidolin's role as an interpreter, because he is in a position to perform the musical work in the correct way, following the composer's intentions. For example, looking closely at Vidolin's collaboration with Luigi Nono, which culminated in the creation of *Prometeo: Tragedia dell'ascolto* (1981–84), we understand that they met several times, both in Padova and in Venice, during the period referred to as "Verso Prometeo" (towards Prometeo). Because Nono was not fully satisfied with the MUSIC 5 program used at that time at CSC, he decided with Vidolin to design a real-time digital sound processor. The result was the 4i system (Zattra 2018b, 89–90). Nono and Vidolin also met in Venice, the city in which the composer lived, where they listened to typical Venetian sounds. "I kept a diary of those meetings. He made me listen to some sounds with glass bells" (Vidolin, pers. comm., 1 June 2009; Zattra 2018b, 90). Vidolin's journal (unpublished), written during the creation of *Prometeo*, is rich in information. One of the first pages marks their first meeting. "*Prometeo*, incontro con Gigi, Aprile 1984 [meeting with Gigi (a nickname, short for Luigi)], April 1984." The notebook contains a series of comments, suggestions, diagrams, and computer printouts, which show discussions and decisions but also changes of course (discarded sounds, technical impossibilities) in the synthesis of the musical material that led to the definitive computer part of *Prometeo* (Vidolin and Nono's collaboration is discussed in Zattra, forthcoming). Vidolin was closely involved with all Nono's last productions and many works by Sciarrino and other composers. He has become their philological interpreter. His experience has made him a much-invited speaker to promote the conservation and performance practice of these works.

4. Carl Faia

Carl Faia (b. 1962) is an American French computer music designer, composer, and performer. Since 1995, he has been active at IRCAM in Paris and at the CIRM in Nice. He has collaborated with numerous composers including James Dillon, Jonathan Harvey, Harrison Birtwistle, Fausto Romitelli, Luca Francesconi, Alejandro Viñao, and Philippe Leroux. He has also worked towards preserving and performing several pieces using updated technology. Faia is an important case study for many reasons. On his website, he lists over sixty collaborations, providing a list organised according to the type of project: R = real-time project, S = studio project, C = combined project, P = portage (the porting of one piece with updated technology). This separation is to say that the activity of a musical assistant is multifaceted, but also clearly defined.

To date, besides Vidolin, Faia is the only musical assistant who discusses in his writings the theoretical and conceptual framework of his profession. In 2014, he defended his doctoral dissertation, "Collaborative Computer Music Composition and the Emergence of the Computer Music Designer" (Faia 2014). This source is particularly useful for two reasons: (1) it summarises Faia's activity through the consideration of a series of collaborations with composers over an eighteen-year period; (2) it indicates that self-awareness of this activity as an independent métier has reached a point where these professionals are validated within the realm of music creation.

Faia's dissertation is a goldmine because it includes the logbook of his collaborations with Philippe Leroux, James Dillon, and Jonathan Harvey, among others.[12] In the following quotation, Faia discusses the first phases of his work with Philippe Leroux on the piece *M* (1997), for two percussion, two pianos, and electronics (dedicated to Carl Faia):

> As this was the first time I collaborated with a composer at IRCAM, I learned that the typical steps in a collaboration would be meeting the composer and discussing in detail the work. These early meetings would involve technical discussions, as well as a certain social aspect that is not definable. Working out the technical and practical understanding the composer has for electronics, understanding the wants of the composer and already trying to build a glossary of usable definitions for

---

12   It also illuminates historical facts related to technology and the use of technology at IRCAM.

descriptions of sound that are non-technical (like saying "really soft" for pp): what does blue metal sound like? (Faia 2014, 22).

This passage emphasises three concepts that typify a composer–musical assistant collaboration. The first one is technical discussion: the musical assistant explains the latest developments in technology or psychoacoustics, he or she creates examples to hear and explore. This prompts Faia to say: "sometimes this might seem a little like showing off your trick pony while the buyer decides if he wants that one or not" (ibid.). The second point is the composer's level of technical know-how—a crucial aspect that influences the composer–musical assistant collaboration towards one side or the other. The third point is terminology, or, more generally, communication aspects between the musical and technical worlds. Both actors need to create a mutual language that is clear enough to find common ground between the composer's musical/aesthetic needs, on one hand, and the specific technological terms used by the musical assistant.

In his PhD thesis, Carl Faia is also honest about the problems and difficulties they encountered during the creation of this piece. When working with Philippe Leroux in 1997,

> I was doing the bulk of this [analysis of data][13] on the mainframe computer [at IRCAM] which meant that during my processing, any other user on the system was reduced to a fraction of a percentage of the computer processor and checking email could take several minutes instead of seconds. This is where my ignorance showed and I was quickly corrected and just as quickly learned how to program the necessary analysis during the late night hours when I would not bother other users.
> (Faia 2014, 24)

This technical problem is also important from a historical viewpoint, because it reflects the practical conditions of the time. Hardware capacity was smaller and slower than now, and big data analysis could affect the work of other people at the institute.

5. ANALYSIS AND COMPARISON

Through a comparison of the sources, stories, and behaviour of Marino Zuccheri, Alvise Vidolin, and Carl Faia, I was able to understand the collaborative process from different perspectives: division of labour, workflow, expertise/specialisation, synchronicity or diachronicity, psychology, preservation, and authorship.

5.1. Division of labour and expertise

Composer–musical assistant collaboration can be based on a highly structured relationship or a looser connection. Vera John-Steiner (2000) proposes degrees

---

13 Data were created in the form of dynamic partials of single sampled low piano notes. They were subsequently morphed from one sound segment to another (Faia 2014, 24).

of collaboration. At one end of the spectrum, in distributed collaboration, participants work on informal shared interests; at the other end, we find integrative collaboration where participants work in intense, committed partnership, so closely that they transform each other's practices, "the most common form, complementary collaboration, sits between and is characterized by clearly defined roles, distributed expertise, discipline-specific working methods, and, while all parties strive for the same goal, varying levels of commitment amongst collaborators. Rather than match each other, parties' values overlap" (Love and Barrett 2014, 52).

I suggest that musical assistants and composers, who share a common goal, are engaging in a form of integrative or complementary collaboration, depending on the particular case. Actors can work in intense partnership, so close that they transform one another (Zuccheri); but they can also have defined roles, and various levels of commitment. In the ideal collaboration, there is a process of mutual learning shared in each project. However, as I already stated in section 1, composers of electroacoustic music can be divided into two general groups depending on their relationship to technology. The first group would be those (although rare) who are or were capable of creating for themselves works using technology. The second group consists of composers who are or "were more or less incapable of creating on their own anything with technology (in whatever form), much like Philippe Leroux" (Faia 2014, 53).

When composers want to work with highly technical innovations or their projects are very complex, or when they want to work with specific environments or technology (such as is developed at IRCAM), a collaborator becomes necessary. From this exchange arises new knowledge on both sides. On the one hand, composers cannot learn all the specificities of the electronic instruments (except in rare cases of autonomous composers); on the other hand, musical assistants must have a certain level of musical training, though they are unlikely to have attained a professional level of expertise in music composition. Nonetheless, this dichotomy has varied over the years. During the analogue era at the Milan studio, the technologies that were used required real manual labour (twisting knobs and potentiometers, cutting and splicing . . .), and the process of creation/composition was very manual, requiring several "hands." For this reason, composers could attain a certain level of dexterity during the process of mutual learning, which was the case in the collaboration between Marino Zuccheri and Luciano Berio.

The computer music period is much more specialised. Composers are effectively forced (at least they were in the early computer music era, until the 1990s and the development of software such as Max/MSP) to collaborate with a highly specialised professional. The study of Carl Faia's activity (particularly his collaboration with Jonathan Harvey) reveals that there is also a lack of tools that could simplify the machinery used for composers. Faia, for example, is always working to create "meta-tools" to help composers get closer to complex technology. This does not necessarily mean that composers depend on musical assistants. As stressed before, it is a mutual learning process. "I am also part of the creative process that is, mostly, private and part of the composer's process. I will sit with a composer as he composes," said Faia (2014, 19). Musical assistants have the privilege of entering the composer's world. "I will experiment with ideas, [theirs] or mine or ours, that may be important in the final work . . . or not. There is time, effort, discussion, research, creation and finally, more time as essential ingredients to the collaborative process" (ibid., 19–20).

The general workflow process, according to my findings, usually develops in the manner shown in figure 13.1. The continually recursive actions are combinations of practical and more reflective moments that in design thinking (Cross 2007) range from context analysis to goals and solution criteria, from creative thinking, sketching, and prototyping to delivering and performing and reperforming in concerts.

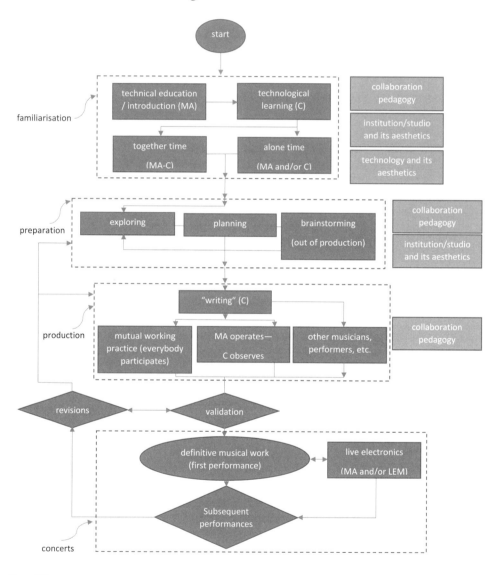

Figure 13.1.

Figure 13.1. The composer–musical assistant collaboration in electroacoustic music: typical workflow (MA: musical assistant; C: composer; LEM: live electronic musician).

5.2. Diachronicity versus synchronicity in collaboration

Keith Sawyer differentiates between two types of temporal pattern in music collaboration: (1) Diachronic collaboration occurs when each participant's contribution occurs at a different moment in time (and/or in different physical places); the creative contribution could be separated by days or weeks. (2) Synchronic collaboration occurs when the actors occupy the same place at the same time. They continuously monitor each other, and interact immediately (Sawyer 2014, 274–75). Marino Zuccheri's collaborations were mostly synchronic, because of the manual analogue equipment, at least according to most sources. Yet, the unpublished memo Nono left for Zuccheri asking him to prolong the sounds to last over two minutes and twenty-five seconds is proof that occasionally there could be diachronicity as well. Vidolin's and Faia's collaborations, conversely, are always both diachronic and synchronic. They meet with composers and work at the studio, but they also work on their own after the meetings.

5.3. Psychology

The activity of the musical assistant is not only a series of tasks and competences, it also involves social and psychological skills. "We got on very well in . . . respect of our different competences," Zuccheri told De Benedictis (Zuccheri and De Benedictis 2000, 178). Carl Faia emphasises that "the process of collaboration is never completely natural and requires effort from all parties. While my experience as composer allowed me a sense of empathy and understanding, there would be differences in age, background social standing, education and gender that would all play a role in the work itself" (Faia 2014, 20). Collaboration also creates special bonds. This is clear in the quotations from Marino Zuccheri's and Carl Faia's writings; the latter reveals (recalling his collaboration with Philippe Leroux) that

> there existed a certain complicity that is difficult to imagine and even harder to explain to outsiders. It is a privileged complicity and has allowed me from this piece onward [M] throughout my career to work with many composers and artists to create something unique, something that could exist only because there was this complicity and these two particular people working together in the studio in total confidence with each other. . . . I do see how the relationship changes once this creative period is over and we return to our respective spaces and social/professional "norms" take over. (Faia 2014, 35)

For Alvise Vidolin, it is a matter of empathy, as recalled in section 3.

5.4. Communication and tools for communication

Another important topic is communication. How composers and musical assistants interact, how they explain each other's competencies, is an issue inevitably linked with psychological aspects. Carl Faia is the most open on the subject.

There is also a certain metaphoric starkness that inevitably appears when assumption meets reality and we start working on the details of a project. Our respective ignorances become evident and we need to have confidence in the other to reveal what we don't know or know incompletely. In any event, this is an important aspect of collaboration, as is the psychological interaction that might be important in certain projects. (Faia 2014, 20–21)

As Faia puts it, "it is impossible to advance if there is not a common language. There is, by necessity, a give and take that is different but very real for every project as we work towards this common language" (ibid., 35). Finding a common language means going beyond technicalities and specific terms. Faia works to create meta-tools, patches that are easier to use. When collaborating with Jonathan Harvey, he developed Max patches for the composer to "play" with, based on their discussions and the artistic project they had in mind, and with which Harvey could also record the outcome. Faia calls these patches "composing tools" (ibid., 71).

When collaborating with Salvatore Sciarrino on the creation of *Perseo e Andromeda* (1991), Vidolin explained to the composer the possible effects (mainly filtered white noise) and they found a way to notate those sounds in diagrams. This became their way to communicate. Sciarrino made those diagrams after his period of training at the CSC in Padova, and they were then able to transform each diagram in sound and even write them in traditional notation (Zattra 2018b, 95).

5.5. Archiving, preservation, and technological migration

In recent years, more and more musical assistants are preserving their work through archives, articles, databases, and genetic documentation of their work with composers. Marino Zuccheri's sources—tapes, correspondence, sketches—were kept by him at the studio until his retirement (and were later preserved by Maria Maddalena Novati, founder of the NoMus association). However, there was no method in their preservation, since the profession was in its infancy. Still, Zuccheri recalled that he "tended to keep everything, even fragments of tape, because sometimes years later a producer would come and ask us for some effect that we already had (this tended to happen quite often for example after Bruno [Maderna] and Berio had gone)" (Zuccheri and De Benedictis 2000, 197).

Alvise Vidolin was one of the first to pay special attention to this part of his work through his writing of a large and continuing series of articles. Carl Faia has written a PhD thesis on his work and pays special attention to preservation and porting. This growing awareness is the result of the developing literature dedicated to collaborative environments in general, and in electroacoustic music in particular, and also the growing self-confidence of this profession. However, as demonstrated during an online questionnaire (in Zattra and Donin 2016, 449), there is no norm in the preservation of the output of musical assistants' work. Some archive, some candidly admit they never do so. Some conceive their archives as private, others share them. Not all musical assistants are aware of the importance of these issues.

5.6. Authorship

Generally, definitions of collaboration stress that, in addition to dialogue and extended time working together, it is characterised by equality and shared ownership (John-Steiner 2000; Love and Barrett 2014, 52). The last two issues are problematic in the musical assistant–composer collaboration. Equality is multifaceted: it depends on the relationship. Authorship remains in the hand of the composer, according to copyright law. "The musicians 'ruled' the machines, and I made the machine work," Marino Zuccheri said, recognising the composers' status (Zuccheri and De Benedictis 2000, 178). Carl Faia, however, takes a more forward-thinking position:

> I am not challenging the place of the serious music composer or the working methods here. . . . My observations have led me to believe, however, that there is a real place for Computer Music Designers at the side of serious music composers. In the same way that it is unrealistic to imagine a composer to be an expert performer in every instrument (bar the rare Hindemithesque composer), I believe it is unrealistic to expect every serious music composer to be an expert in technology. (Faia 2014, 16)

Faia also writes that at IRCAM, under Laurent Bayle's direction (1987–2001), he took part in meetings to discuss the status of assistants:

> I went from just listening to my colleagues complain about the lack of recognition received for the work done, the amount of salary versus the number of hours worked, and the increasing demands to do more with less and do it faster, to becoming vocal and demanding as I became more experienced and understood the importance of the role we played in the structure of the institution. Briefly, these demands included a better and clearer name of our role (at that time we were called musical assistants [later they became RIM (réalisateurs en informatique musicale) or CMD (computer music designers)]), to have our names always associated with the works on which we collaborated (this would mean, in some cases, that it would be a contractual stipulation for composers or publishers), to have our biography in the back of the program along with the composer or performer, and to have a salary more in line with the role and the time that this role demanded. (Faia 2014, 53)

Whereas more and more composers are recognising, in statements, texts, articles, or interviews, the important role of assistants, there are still issues in this regard from a legal and financial position, or simply in terms of recognition. In a longitudinal study made in 2016, musical assistants responding to a questionnaire confirmed that there is no clear statutory legal definition of their profession, which results in various conditions when being hired and a deficit of administrative recognition. Payment arrangements are generally of one of three different types: for a specific project, a percentage of rights or patents, or a steady paycheque (Zattra and Donin 2016, 450). What is interesting to stress is that although musical assistants agree when they say they expect greater recognition for their artistic contribution, it seems that they do not consider their technological contribution in the same way, and have not arrived at a point of consensus (ibid., 445–46).

6. CONCLUSIONS

The purpose of this study was to explore how musical assistants perceive their profession in the art of organised sound using analogue or digital technology and, through analysis of the sources produced by Marino Zuccheri, Alvise Vidolin, and Carl Faia, and of these musical assistants' stories and behaviours, to trace an understanding of their collaborative environment, their interactions with composers, division of labour, workflow, psychology, preservation issues, and authorship. As demonstrated in a previous article (Zattra and Donin 2016, 449–50), musical assistants share a number of similarities; however, at the same time, their experiences and skills are distinctive and individualistic. Particularly in the case of the three professionals presented here, this is of course related not only to the differences between technological epochs and the different composers with whom they collaborate or have collaborated, but also to an increasing self-awareness and to an interest in documenting their profession (the archiving, technological migration, and maintenance of their writings), which is particularly clear in Vidolin's and Faia's cases. This reverberates in a developing identity, I think, in which the distinction between occupation and full profession is changing—a typical feature of emerging professions according to the sociology of work. This emerging identity is forged from a multifaceted background in music, sound technology, music performance, and programming that shapes the musical assistant's uniqueness.

REFERENCES

Cross, Nigel. 2006. *Designerly Ways of Knowing*. London: Springer.

De Benedictis, Angela Ida. 2018. "The Beginnings of the Studio di Fonologia Musicale and Bruno Maderna's *Notturno*." In *The Performance Practice of Electroacoustic Music: The Studio di Fonologia Years*, edited by Germán Toro Pérez and Lucas Bennett, 47–53. Bern: Peter Lang.

De Poli, Giovanni. "Forward #2." In Novati and Dack 2012, ix–x.

Eco, Umberto. 2008. "Musica." *La Repubblica*, 29 October 2008, 43 (culture section).

Emmerson, Simon, and Denis Smalley. 2001. "Electroacoustic Music." In *The New Grove Dictionary of Music and Musicians*, edited by Stanley Sadie, 2nd ed., 29 vols., 8:59–67. London: Macmillan.

Faia, Carl. 2014. "Collaborative Computer Music Composition and the Emergence of the Computer Music Designer." PhD thesis, Brunel University London. Accessed 15 April 2021. https://core. ac.uk/download/pdf/30340104.pdf.

Goehr, Lydia. 1992. *The Imaginary Museum of Musical Works: An Essay in the Philosophy of Music*. Oxford: Clarendon Press.

Helms, Johanna Evelyn. 2020. "Electronic Music History through the Everyday: The RAI Studio di Fonologia (1954–83)." PhD thesis, University of North Carolina at Chapel Hill. Accessed 28 April 2021. https://cdr.lib.unc.edu/downloads/ qn59q951r.

Iverson, Jennifer. 2019. *Electronic Inspirations: Technologies of the Cold War Musical Avant-Garde*. New York: Oxford University Press.

John-Steiner, Vera. 2000. *Creative Collaboration*. New York: Oxford University Press.

Kahn, Douglas. 2012. "James Tenney at Bell Labs." In *Mainframe Experimentalism: Early Computing and the Foundations of the Digital Arts*, edited by Hannah B. Higgins and Douglas Kahn, 131–46. Berkeley: University of California Press.

Landy, Leigh. 2017. "But Is It (Also) Music?" In *The Routledge Companion to Sounding Art*, edited by Marcel Cobussen, Vincent Meelberg, and Barry Truax, 17–26. New York: Routledge.

Lexico. 2021. "Assist, verb 1" and "Origin." Accessed 15 April 2021. https://www.lexico.com/definition/assist.

Lietti, Alfredo. 1956. "Gli impianti tecnici dello Studio di Fonologia Musicale di Radio Milano." *Elettronica* 5 (3): 116–21.

———. 1959. "Évolution des moyens techniques de la musique électronique." *Revue belge de musicologie / Belgisch Tijdschrift voor Muziekwetenschap* 13 (1–4): 40–43.

Love, Karlin, and Margaret S. Barrett. 2014. "Learning to Collaborate in Code: Negotiating the Score in a Symphony Orchestra Composers' School." In *Collaborative Creative Thought and Practice in Music*, edited by Margaret S. Barrett, 49–64. Abingdon, UK: Routledge.

Melton, William. 2008. *The Wagner Tuba: A History*. Aachen, Germany: Ebenos.

Nono, Luigi. 1986. "Per Marino Zuccheri." In *Nuova Atlantide: Il continente della musica elettronica 1900–1986*, 174–76. Venice: La Biennale-ERI

Novati, Maria Maddalena, and John Dack, eds. 2012. *The Studio di Fonologia: A Musical Journey 1954–1983; Update 2008–2012*. Milan: Ricordi.

Novati, Maria Maddalena, Laura Pronestì, and Marina Vaccarini, eds. 2018. *Marino Zuccheri and Friends*. Milan: Die Schachtel.

Pinch, Trevor, and Frank Trocco. 2004. *Analog Days: The Invention and Impact of the Moog Synthesizer*. Cambridge, MA: Harvard University Press.

Plessas, Peter, and Guillaume Boutard. 2015. "Transmission et interprétation de l'instrument électronique composé." In *Actes / Proceedings Journées d'Informatique Musicale (JIM2015)*. Accessed 15 April 2021. http://jim2015.oicrm.org/actes/JIM15_Plessas_P_et_al.pdf.

Rodà, Antonio. 2012. "Evolution of the Technical Means of the Studio di Fonologia Musicale." In Novati and Dack 2012, 33–81.

Sawyer, Keith. 2014. "Musical Performance as Collaborative Practice." In *Collaborative Creative Thought and Practice in Music*, edited by Margaret S. Barrett, 271–86. Abingdon, UK: Routledge.

Sève, Bernard. 2013. *L'Instrument de musique: Une étude philosophique*. Paris, Seuil.

Shapin, Steven. 1989. "The Invisible Technician." *American Scientist* 77 (6): 554–63.

Vidolin, Alvise. 1997. "Musical Interpretation and Signal Processing." In *Musical Signal Processing*, edited by Curtis Roads, Stephen Travis Pope, Aldo Piccialli, and Giovanni De Poli, 439–59. Lisse, Netherlands: Swets & Zeitlinger.

———. 2012. "The School of Fonologia." In Novati and Dack 2012, 19–31.

Zattra, Laura. 2009. "Introduzione alla bibliografia di Alvise Vidolin." In *60 dB: La scuola veneziana di musica elettronica; Omaggio ad Alvise Vidolin*, edited by Paolo Zavagna, 163–80. Firenze: Olschki editore.

———. 2013. "Les origines du nom de RIM (Réalisateur en Informatique Musicale)." In *Actes / Proceedings Journées d'Informatique Musicale (JIM2013)*, edited by Anne Sèdes and Alain Bonardi, 113–120. Accessed 28 April 2021. http://jim.afim-asso.org/JIM2013/actes/jim2013_actes.pdf.

———. 2018a. "Collaborating on Composition: The Role of the Musical Assistant at IRCAM, CCRMA and CSC." In *Live Electronic Music: Composition, Performance, Study*, edited by Friedemann Sallis, Valentina Bertolani, Jan Burle, and Laura Zattra, 59–80. Abingdon, UK: Routledge.

———. 2018b. "Alvise Vidolin Interviewed by Laura Zattra: The Role of the Computer Music Designers in Composition and Performance." In *Live Electronic Music: Composition, Performance, Study*, edited by Friedemann Sallis, Valentina Bertolani, Jan Burle, and Laura Zattra, 83–100. Abingdon, UK: Routledge.

———. 2018c. "Symmetrical Collaborations: Jonathan Harvey and His Computer Music Designers." *Nuove Musiche* 4: 29–57.

———. Forthcoming. "The Use of Technology in Revolutionary Perspective: Computer Music Research in Luigi

Nono's *Prometeo. Tragedia dell'Ascolto* (1984–85)." *Rivista di Analisi e Teoria Musicale (RATM).*

Zattra, Laura, and Nicolas Donin. 2016. "A Questionnaire-Based Investigation of the Skills and Roles of Computer Music Designers." *Musicae Scientiae* 20 (3): 436–56.

Zuccheri, Marino. 1962–63. "Hur *Fontana Mix* kom till." *Nutida Musik* 6 (6): 19–20. Republished in Novati, Pronestì, and Vaccarini 2018, 45–49.

———. (1976–77) 1986. "Remembering Bruno." In *Nuova Atlantide: Il continente della musica elettronica 1900–1986*, edited by Roberto Doati and Alvise Vidolin, 173. Venice: La Biennale di Venezia. First published 1976–77 as "Working with Bruno" in the programme for the series *Musica nel Nostro Tempo* [Music in our time] (on which see Novati, Pronestì, and Vaccarini 2018, 56–57).

———. 1998. Typescript of oral presentation for a round table with Jean-Claude Risset, Hans Tutschku, Gérard Pape, Rudolf Frisius, Marino Zuccheri, York Höller, Giuseppe Di Giugno, et al., held 28 November 1998 at XXXV Festival Nuova Consonanza "1948–98 Elettroshock: Cinquant'anni di musica elettroacustica," Palazzo delle Esposizioni, Rome, 27–28 November 1998. Zuccheri collection, NoMus Archive, Milan. Published as Zuccheri (1998) 2018, 54–55.

———. (1998) 2018. "Relazione X [sic] esperienze ed incontri = [sic] Nuova Consonanza 98 Roma novembre." In Novati, Pronestì, and Vaccarini 2018, 54–55. For further details see Zuccheri 1998.

Zuccheri, Marino, and Angela De Benedictis. 2000. ". . . all'epoca delle valvole . . . Incontro con Marino Zuccheri" / ". . . at the Time of the Tubes . . . A Conversation with Marino Zuccheri." In *Nuova musica alla radio / New Music on the Radio: Esperienze allo studio di fonologia della RAI di Milano, 1954–1959*, edited by Veniero Rizzardi and Angela Ida De Benedictis, 176–212. Turin: CIDIM/RAI-ERI.

Parlour Sounds

A Critical Compositional Process towards a Cyberfeminist Theory of Music Technology

Patricia Alessandrini and Julie Zhu

Stanford University, CA, Center for Computer Research in Music and Acoustics (CCRMA)

1. Introduction: Judy Wajcman and cyberfeminism

> It is impossible to divorce the gender relations which are expressed in, and shape technologies from, the wider social structures that create and maintain them.
>
> —Judy Wajcman, *Feminism Confronts Technology* (1991, 25)[1]

Technologies do not merely shape society, but are themselves socially constituted by the individuals and institutions that bring them into being. While the bias built into some technologies may manifest through strongly evident negative consequences (O'Neil 2016, 87–88), no technology is neutral in this regard, including music technology. Social dynamics, including gender, class, race, and ability, inform the design, development, and implementation of technologies in music performance, improvisation, and composition. In this chapter, we propose an experimental compositional practice grounded in both the recognition and inclusive enactment of these social dynamics. Taking the feminist multimedia monodrama *Parlour Sounds*[2] and its collaborative developmental processes as a point of departure, we speculate on future creative manifestations of its theoretical frameworks and methodologies.

Parlour Sounds is informed by feminist/cyberfeminist/technofeminist[3] theory, and in particular, Judy Wajcman's feminist analysis of the development of

---

1 The full passage reads, "It is impossible to divorce the gender relations which are expressed in, and shape technologies from, the wider social structures that create and maintain them. In developing a theory of the gendered character of technology, we are inevitably in danger of either adopting an essentialist position that sees technology as inherently patriarchal, or losing sight of the structure of gender relations through an overemphasis on the historical variability of the categories of 'women' and 'technology.'"

2 A video trailer for *Parlour Sounds* (MF14.1) can be viewed in the online repository for this book at https://orpheusinstituut.be/en/sound-work-media-repository. Further details of the repository can be found in the appendix to this book on p. 355.

3 From this point on, *cyberfeminism* will be the all-embracing term for feminist/cyberfeminist/technofeminist theory.

technological paradigms. In *Feminism Confronts Technology*, Wajcman performs detailed analyses on technologies concerning manufacturing, human reproduction, domestic space, and technologies from the built environment in relation to gender dynamics. She, in the tradition of Foucauldian-feminist analyses of power (Allen 2016), posits that development in these domains would be fundamentally different if these dynamics were fundamentally transformed (Butler 1990), and more work must be done to critique the structures of power in technology that recursively determine even the boundaries of criticism.

Strategies to increase women's participation are anyway limited by the extent to which power relations are inscribed in the technologies themselves. Women's reluctance "to enter" cannot be seen as irrational given that so much technological development is devoted to war-mongering and making a profit at the expense of human beings and the environment. . . . This points to the need for a more radical critique of technology itself. Certain kinds of technology are inextricably linked to particular institutionalised patterns of power and authority (Wajcman 1991, 164).

Wajcman's aforementioned radicality is at the nascence of the term *cyberfeminism*, which arose from ideas in Donna Haraway's "Cyborg Manifesto," a revolt against gender-essentialism in technology. Haraway calls on feminists to code a new "cyborg" self that disassembles and reassembles the systems of myth and meanings structuring our imaginations with regard to "theory and practice addressed to the social relations of science and technology" (Haraway [1985] 1991, 163). The manifesto inspired the term *cyberfeminism*, wherein the concept of cybernetics (feedback-controlled) systems illustrate and call out technologies as instruments that enforce the otherwise fluid social interactions constituting them. Contemporary collectives continue the legacy of cyberfeminism (Old Boys Network 1997; Reiche and Kuni 2004) by foregrounding social justice in the domains of gender and technology (Goh and Thompson 2021a; Thompson 2018).

Haraway describes a boundary, which is at the centre of both the dramatic content and collaborative process of *Parlour Sounds*, a boundary that is "permeable between tool and myth, instrument and concept, historical systems of social relations and historical anatomies of possible bodies, including objects of knowledge" (Haraway [1985] 1991, 164). From *Parlour Sounds*, a key proposition emerged that will be a thread running through this chapter: the idea that subverting predominant practices of music technology, displacing technological applications for sound and music from their habitual contexts, and undermining or reversing existing power structures allow for underexplored or marginalised paradigms to come to the fore; and with these paradigm shifts, fertile ground is secured for the emergence of innovative techniques, technologies, and applications (Russell 2021).

2. The collaborative development process of *Parlour Sounds*

> . . . It was a woman vacuuming,[4] a housewife maybe, or maybe not even a housewife,[5] and just stuck, just so stuck. I think we all know that feeling. And then finding a couple of things that kind of sound of what she feels like inside. She finds a way to open her mouth even if it's just for a couple of moments. At the end, she's back to dusting and her mouth is closed again.[6] It ends at this kind of suspension. I guess tomorrow, she wakes up and she vacuums again. There is no emancipation. You just see that repeated as a loop. In some ways, it's honest, you know? For a short while, there are sparks of sound and noise. Maybe that's the thing, pitches are the thing that feel like they're never ending, but the bits that there are noise, those are the bits that are freeing . . .
>
> —Peyee Chen (2020), soprano and collaborator in *Parlour Sounds*

Parlour Sounds was commissioned by Sound and Music, a national organisation for new music in the United Kingdom, as part of their Embedded composer-in-residence scheme. The ambitious, collaborative methodology of this multi-part intermedia project was in some measure influenced by the context and circumstances of Alessandrini's residency, which included institutional partners based in three different countries: in addition to the London-based Sound and Music, Red Note Ensemble in Scotland and the Conservatoire National Supérieur de Musique et de Danse de Paris (CNSMDP) were part of the collaboration, with production support from the Edinburgh International Science Festival, Sound Scotland, and theatre professionals engaged for the project. Alessandrini was in residency with Red Note Ensemble over the course of more than one year, from late 2015 until the premiere and reprise in spring 2017, including "shadowing" some of the ensemble's activities during that period—ranging from meetings to educational workshops to concerts—in addition to collaboratively planning the production of *Parlour Sounds*. This unusual situation allowed Alessandrini to shape not only the multimedia work itself but also the conditions in which it was created and developed, while gaining an understanding of the workings of the ensemble and getting to know its members *in situ*. Sound and Music engaged stage director Cathie Boyd to come on board as a project consultant, in addition to a stage manager engaged by Red Note Ensemble, Valentino Fabbreschi.

---

4 See MF14.2.

5 In conversations between Alessandrini and Chen about the character, they decided to leave the identity of the woman ambiguous in relation to the home space she is cleaning: the question whether she is performing these tasks in her own home, or whether she is performing paid labour in someone else's home, is left unanswered. Chen's costume—consisting of plain clothing, comfortable shoes, gloves, and a household apron—was chosen to leave open this ambiguity. This practical costume also allowed Chen to comfortably perform her dramatic tasks.

6 That is, humming—also called *bocca chiusa*—vocal techniques are employed at the end of the piece, and are subsumed within the instrumental textures. See MF14.1.

While the original commission was for members of Red Note Ensemble and soprano Peyee Chen, a partnership with the CNSMDP[7] permitted students from its professional diploma programme[8] to participate in the project, contributing to the collaborative, exploratory, and experimental nature of the project. The resulting composite ensemble consisted of ten musicians, with five each from Red Note and the CNSMDP programme respectively, in addition to Peyee Chen and the conductor, Simon Proust. With a duration of approximately forty minutes, *Parlour Sounds* comprised the first part of a diptych for this instrumentation, with a second dramatic work planned for 2022–23 to close the cycle.[9] The first performances of *Parlour Sounds* in 2017 were bookended by two compositions composed for the occasion by students from the CNSMDP, mentored and aided by Alessandrini in the rehearsal and development process. The call for student participation invited composers—ranging from undergraduate to doctoral students—to engage with two key themes of the project, which will be elaborated upon in the next section: (1) employing creative means to explore technological paradigms and their applications; and (2) integrating homemade and/or household objects or appliances into a technological apparatus by transgressively transforming their usual function.[10]

The *Parlour Sounds* project was realised in the context of an attempt to create a non-hierarchical structure in which roles, responsibilities, and creative agency were distributed and fluid, rather than delimited and fixed. One of the most important aspects of this collaborative methodology was skill sharing, particularly in the application of technology. Performer agency was dependent not only upon the interaction design employed in the project—including the design of instruments and interfaces—but also on each performer's process of technological engagement over the course of the project, as well as upon the contributions of performers to the interaction design process.

This collaborative process was informed by Alessandrini's previous experience of interface/instrument and interaction design for *Mondgewächse* (2014), an inclusive multimedia performance commissioned and produced by ShareMusic & Performing Arts. The circumstances of this evening-length performance were somewhat similar to those of *Parlour Sounds*, in that it was also the fruit of a year-long residency and involved the combined effort of two ensembles composed of five musicians each, with varying degrees of experience: in this case, musicians from the established contemporary music ensemble Gageego! joined forces with the newly-formed In:fluence Ensemble, whose

---

7   With funding from Diaphonique, a non-profit organisation funding projects in contemporary music involving cooperation between France and the UK.

8   Diplôme National Supérieur Professionnel de Musicien (DNSPM) and Diplôme d'Artiste Interprète (DAI), 3e cycle supérieur.

9   The performers and institutional and funding structure are not the same for this second staged work.

10 The call for projects distributed to students of the CNSMDP included the following text provided by Alessandrini: "Les projets pourraient adopter une forme de technologie comme métaphore compositionnelle, ou bien intégrer la technologie dans les dispositifs mêmes de la pièce, en utilisant des appareils insolites et artisanaux, détournant des objets de la technologie quotidienne, etc." (The projects could adopt a form of technology as a compositional metaphor, or integrate technology into the means of the piece itself, through the use of unusual or handmade devices, by repurposing technological objects of everyday life, etc.)

members were drawn from participants of ShareMusic workshops and previous large-scale projects. In this ambitious and many-faceted project, combining the music and interface/instrument design of Alessandrini with the interactive video of audiovisual artist Freida Abtan, "the collaborative development process was a necessary step to offer real agency to performers whose inclusivity needs vary significantly" (Alessandrini and Abtan 2020, 2).

3. THE HOME AS A SITE OF WORK, CREATIVITY, AND TECHNOLOGICAL TESTING GROUND

> For there is no other aesthetic problem than that
> of the insertion of art into everyday life.
>
> —Gilles Deleuze, *Difference and Repetition* (1994, 293)

The dramatic content of *Parlour Sounds* speaks to the question of technological paradigms and their social and institutional contexts. A review of the premiere from the Scottish *Herald* newspaper provides a succinct summary: it "tells the tale of a 1960s housewife who explores and creates sound by utilising her standard, everyday surroundings" (Heggie 2017). The work derives its title from the sitting-room setting, in which the protagonist of the monodrama—portrayed by soprano Peyee Chen—explores various ways of making sound by interacting with the technology that she finds at home, including kitchen devices, housekeeping aids, and other household gadgets, which have been transformed into musical interfaces/instruments through circuit-bending and physical computing techniques. The performance consists of a series of "vignettes" and ensemble movements, which flow from one to another. Chen performs housekeeping tasks in the vignettes, which then give rise to musical works in the ensemble movements, as if these ensemble pieces were the fruit of her imagination, prompted by her everyday actions of home labour.

Figure 14.1a–b.

Figure 14.1a–b. The sitting-room setting of *Parlour Sounds*, Edinburgh International Science Festival.

The household environment has multiple functions in relation to cyber-feminist perspectives on technological paradigms and the collaborative, non-hierarchical structure ambitioned by this project. First and foremost, the work is a feminist commentary on access to artistic creation. This primary theme was recognised by the *Herald* review, which identified the creative aspirations of the protagonist within the confines of her commonplace home environment: "While much of the piece is entertaining and fun (a hoover playing a 'moothie'[11] for instance), overall the work is deeply profound. The claustrophobia and sense of unharnessed potential energy is rife, leading the audience to question Chen's character, and her need to create art from the mundane" (Heggie 2017).

While there is a specifically feminist aspect to this claim on the space of the home as a site of creation—one that is specific to the domain of music technology, as we will see shortly—its narrative themes are also a part of the larger, feminist-informed critical collaborative methodology, which favours an inclusive process over a rigidly-structured artistic production in which creators and consumers are cast in fixed roles. To continue the epigraph of this section:

> The more our daily life appears standardised, stereotyped and subject to an accelerated reproduction of objects of consumption, the more art must be injected into it in order to extract from it that little difference which plays simultaneously between other levels of repetition, and even in order to make the two extremes resonate—namely, the habitual series of consumption and the instinctual series of destruction and death. (Deleuze 1994, 293)[12]

The home is as well a site of economic activity, though not necessarily recognised and redistributed as such. The identity of women's unpaid labour at home has long been discussed in the context of Marxism (Federici 1975),

---

11 *Hoover* is a British English term for a vacuum cleaner, while *moothie* is a specifically Scottish word for a harmonica. The reviewer (Heggie 2017) is referring to a vacuum cleaner that has been electronically modified through real-time processing of electromagnetic signals, which does indeed fortuitously encounter a harmonica in the opening vignette of *Parlour Sounds*. See MF14.2.

12 The complete passage: "Perhaps the highest object of art is to bring into play simultaneously all these repetitions, with their differences in kind and rhythm, their respective displacements and disguises, their divergences and decentrings; to embed them in one another and to envelop one or the other in illusions the 'effect' of which varies in each case. Art does not imitate, above all because it repeats; it repeats all the repetitions, by virtue of an internal power (an imitation is a copy, but art is simulation, it reverses copies into simulacra). Even the most mechanical, the most banal, the most habitual and the most stereotyped repetition finds a place in works of art, it is always displaced in relation to other repetitions, and it is subject to the condition that a difference may be extracted from it for these other repetitions. For there is no other aesthetic problem than that of the insertion of art into everyday life. The more our daily life appears standardised, stereotyped and subject to an accelerated reproduction of objects of consumption, the more art must be injected into it in order to extract from it that little difference which plays simultaneously between other levels of repetition, and even in order to make the two extremes resonate—namely, the habitual series of consumption and the instinctual series of destruction and death. Art thereby connects the tableau of cruelty with that of stupidity, and discovers underneath consumption a schizophrenic clattering of the jaws, and underneath the most ignoble destructions of war, still more processes of consumption. It aesthetically reproduces the illusions and mystifications which make up the real essence of this civilisation, in order that Difference may at last be expressed with a force of anger which is itself repetitive and capable of introducing the strangest selection, even if this is only a contraction here and there—in other words, a freedom for the end of a world. Each art has its interrelated techniques or repetitions, the critical and revolutionary power of which may attain the highest degree and lead us from the sad repetitions of habit to the profound repetitions of memory, and then to the ultimate repetitions of death in which our freedom is played out" (Deleuze 1994, 293).

in terms of separating the family and home from the labour market (Cooper 2017). While the identity of the protagonist vis-à-vis the domestic space she is working in remains ambiguous,[13] such that she could be in either her own home or that of her employer, there is a degree of dissatisfaction expressed in the portrayal of the household tasks that lends them a negative valence; whether the protagonist's resentment is due to the conditions of her employment or the inherently exploitative nature of a system where housework wages are not paid or expected, nor equally shared between partners, is left open to the spectator. The sound-making potential of the housekeeping appliances becomes both an outlet for the protagonist's frustration and at times, a source of playful and joyful exploration. Siloed from capital, this art-making is less commodified and seemingly boundless in the home setting of *Parlour Sounds*. Domestic items that are such potent signifiers of women's subjugation are now avant-garde instruments. While the intricacies of economic and sexual politics extend beyond the home and its objects, historical female creators in music technology who sought creative freedom have at times found productive refuge in their homes as an alternative to institutional studios, and women working in technology have used the transformation of household objects into electronic interfaces/instruments in order to engage with issues around the valorisation of women's labour. We will look at examples of both these phenomena, and how they play out in *Parlour Sounds*, in sections 4 and 5.

Thus, in addition to the larger significance of situating the creative act in the home space, the *mise en scène* of making art in a commonplace home environment in *Parlour Sounds* overtly makes reference to its specifically feminist project. By focusing on household appliances that constitute technological developments predominantly designed for and marketed to women, *Parlour Sounds* engages with a uniquely female perspective on technology. Its setting in 1960s Britain was chosen as a time and place in which technological innovations for home use—ranging from household appliances to high-fidelity ("hi-fi") sound equipment—were often targeted towards a female audience, even if traditional sources such as journals and magazines constructed a "serious, powerful, masculine home listener" (Perchard 2017, 373). As Wajcman writes,

> Capital's interest cannot be supposed always to coincide with that of men as a sex. As we have seen, some technologies are designed for use by women in order to break the craft control of men. Thus gender divisions are commonly exploited in the power struggles between capital and labour. In this way, the social relations that shape technology include those of gender as well as class. (Wajcman 1991, 52)

Indeed, the post-war culture of consumerism and women's increasing work in the home—cleaning, cooking, decorating, maintaining—slowly changed the very niche, male hobbyist narrative for hi-fi audio to an aspirational middle-class product like washing machines and vacuum cleaners. Advertisements

---

13   See footnote 5.

for hi-fi audio machines featured women or legs of women, and the products themselves started incorporating more plastic which had a modern and warm connotation, as well as emphasising "touch" in its design to appeal to the "sensitive" woman (Perchard 2017, 384, 387). As a result of the female-inflected marketing of hi-fi music appliances to UK households, women, music, and technology are inextricably linked in the home environment portrayed in *Parlour Sounds*;[14] this context sets the stage for the protagonist, and is referenced by one of the interfaces, in which a vintage radio houses a microprocessor and speakers transmitting electronic sound (see figure 14.2, and video documentation at https://patriciaalessandrini.com/ParlourSounds).[15]

Figure 14.2a–c.

---

14 According to Perchard (2017) the woman listeners in the home of this period would have been lost to history if not for the inclusion of alternative primary sources such as journals in research on this subject to supplement the more readily available male-biased hi-fi audio journals. This is another instance where habitual methodologies may hide and reinforce biases.
15 The electronics pictured are a BeagleBone Black computer board with a Bela Cape for audio capacity, using Pure Data for the sound design. This interface was designed by Patricia Alessandrini and Jack Armitage in the Augmented Instrument Lab of Queen Mary University, London.

Figure 14.2a–c. Repurposed vintage radio interface.

4. The home as an alternative studio space

> if you had heard her
> chanting as she ironed
> you would understand form and line
> and discipline and order and
> america.

—Lucille Clifton, "study the masters" from *Blessing the Boats* (2000, 25)

Making household objects into musical instruments both subverts the objects from their usual functions and expands the boundaries of what may constitute a musical interface/instrument. By drawing on a gestural language derived from household labour in the performance on specially designed interface/ instruments, the design of these interfaces/instruments valorises labour traditionally associated with women. As Wajcman writes,

> Certain kinds of work experience, in particular men's, is recognized as "technical" and legitimated as expertise. Women's knowledge and skills have been traditionally undervalued. Contesting this involves re-examining the accepted definitions of expertise and challenging the sexual division of labour which sustains them. Technical competence is certainly not the only source of male power, but it is an important one, especially in relation to women. (Wajcman 1991, 165)[16]

Instrument and interface builders have engaged with women's undervalued labour—in particular, domestic labour—by taking inspiration from house-keeping devices that are intersectionally charged with the association of this labour. In Jocelyn Ho and Margaret Schedel's *Women's Labor* project, domestic tools are "imparted with newly foregrounded materiality—that is, sonic, sentient materiality" (Ho, Schedel, and Blessing 2020, 501) by repurposing them as musical instruments. Beginning with the Embedded Iron, a sensor-filled 3D-printed vintage iron that pairs with a wooden ironing board with built-in speakers, and continuing with the Umbrella Rotary Dryer and the embroidery hoop, the intention is to "bring the material objects of women's often unpaid, unrecognized domestic chores into an active ontological correspondence with participants both as users/performers and as audience" (ibid. 2020, 503). With workshops, commissioned compositions from female-identifying composers, public performances, and installations, the audience in each situation is encouraged to reflect upon the social/feminist history of tools in the context of both feminist theory of domestic labour and feminism in music technology. In their publications on the *Women's Labor* project, Ho, Schedel, and their

---

16　Wajcman (1991, 25) also writes: "It is impossible to divorce the gender relations which are expressed in, and shape technologies from, the wider social structures that create and maintain them. In developing a theory of the gendered character of technology, we are inevitably in danger of either adopting an essentialist position that sees technology as inherently patriarchal, or losing sight of the structure of gender relations through an overemphasis on the historical variability of the categories of 'women' and 'technology.'"

collaborator Matthew Blessing cite other examples of engagement with domestic spaces and objects in electronic music and intermedial art, such as *Fashionably Late for the Relationship* by R. Luke DuBois and Lián Amaris Sifuentes, in which a bedroom suite is staged in Union Square, New York, in order to use technology to "play . . . with conceptions of time, femininity, and intimacy" (Robertson 2007) and Nicolee Kuester's *Conversation Piece No. 1*, in which the act of hair combing is augmented by Mari Kimura's MUGIC sensor (cited in Schedel, Ho, and Blessing 2020, 501n30).[17]

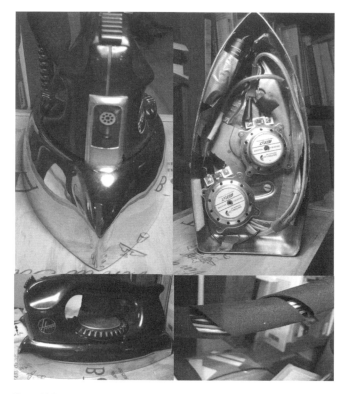

Figure 14.3.

In addition to the vintage radio interface and modified vacuum cleaner discussed in the previous sections (3 and 2, respectively), *Parlour Sounds* employs a vintage iron with embedded electronics.[18] Similar to the vintage radio, the iron interface contains embedded sensors and speakers, which in this case are transducers that cause the metal body of the iron to resonate, as well as any resonant body it comes into contact with, such as an ironing board.[19] The iron itself was also equipped with position sensors, and a microphone was placed in

17 On the MUGIC sensor, see https://mugicmotion.com/.
18 As for the vintage radio, the vintage iron was designed and constructed in the augmented instrument lab by Patricia Alessandrini and Jack Armitage, using a BeagleBone Black board with a Bela Cape, running Pure Data. (See footnote 15 above.) See MF14.3.
19 A metal ironing board was used for this purpose, with relatively thin fabrics to optimise the contact between the iron and the board.

Figure 14.3. Several views of the vintage iron interface.

the steam hole (see figure 14.3). The processor and amplifier for the transducers were placed outside the iron, rather than in its interior as for the vintage radio. As irons from the 1960s were often equipped with cloth-bound electrical cords, the wires leading to and from the processor and amplifier were bound together using a striped pattern imitating those vintage cords (see figure 14.3, and video documentation at https://patriciaalessandrini.com/ParlourSounds).

The commonality of the iron in these two projects—*Women's Labor* and *Parlour Sounds*—provides an opportunity for a comparison in implementation and conceptualisation of the interfaces in relation to the physical and cultural affordances of the household objects. In *Parlour Sounds*, the iron-interface is designed to have the same feel and approximate weight as the vintage iron it is built from, and to use the gestures of ironing in performance with it. Although the mechanics of the original iron have been removed, the solid handle and hollowed-out metallic body of the iron maintain a certain heft, while the microphone, sensors, and transducers mounted in it further contribute to its weight. Its sound-making is dependent upon the act of ironing: through the sensor data, it is programmed to be silent when in the vertical resting position, and to receive vocal (or other) sonic input from the microphone situated near the top, and then to play sound when in the horizontal ironing position, tuned to the pitch material detected by the microphone while in the upright position. By manipulating the iron as one would when ironing, the performer is able to change the sound in two ways: movements picked up by the sensor modify the timbre of the sound synthesis, and manipulating the iron vis-à-vis the ironing surface permits physical filtering of the sound from the transducers.[20] Conversely, the iron of *Women's Labor* is designed to be light and easy to manipulate freely, to allow the performer to use both the gestures of ironing or other gestures.[21] The authors of *Women's Labor* emphasise the lightness of the design and its relationship to expressivity, as they describe taking measurements "from an antique iron that was too heavy to manipulate expressively" (Schedel, Ho, and Blessing 2019, 378).

These contrasting examples illustrate the multiplicity of possible meanings called up by the musical employment of a household object in a feminist context. In *Parlour Sounds*, the iron-interface is entirely performed upon using gestures derived from female-associated labour, to directly valorise that labour: that is, the more accustomed a performer is with the act of ironing, the more at ease they will be in performing with the iron-interface, as they will already have learned its gestural language and have a feel for the weight of the iron in their hand. In *Women's Labor*, the iron-interface is freed from its weight and functional gestures, opening it up to new gestural possibilities. Each performer in their manner posits a reaction to the weight and function of the iron, either by emphasising it or subversively eschewing it. Each engages differently with the

---

20 See MF14.3.

21 While the authors of *Women's Labor* focus on ironing gestures in the publications cited here (Schedel, Ho, and Blessing 2019, 2020), discussion of the project by Jocelyn Ho and Margaret Schedel in a panel at Stanford University with Pamela Z on 19 March 2021 revealed that the gestural possibilities of the iron-interface are not limited to ironing (Z, Ho, Schedel, and members of the fff ensemble 2021).

symbolic representation of ironing as a housekeeping act women perform for others: in *Parlour Sounds*, Peyee Chen irons a large dress shirt—presumably not her own[22]—while in *Women's Labor*, different patterns and textures of ironed fabric initialise the sonic palette.

In considering women's labour and its valorisation in these two projects, it is important to take into account not only what methodologies are involved in the design of the interfaces, but what labour may be involved in the making of their component parts, and the social, political, and ecological impacts of these production processes. There are, in a sense, four forms of labour present in these iron-interfaces: (1) the female-associated labour referenced by their form, and manifested in performance; (2) the labour of musicians learning to use the interface and performing with it; (3) the labour of designing and producing them; and (4) the labour involved in the production of their constituent parts. The sonic cyberfeminist project by its nature requires attention to issues of equity and inclusion in all four stages, including the potential exploitation of workers in the fourth category, whose oppression is often both racialised and gendered (Tamirisa 2021). While this fourth category of labour is not made explicit onstage in these works, a consideration of it is built into the design process, which minimises dependence upon the labour of mass production, and favours low-cost elemental production over high-end prefabricated technology.

The divergent design methods employed in the two iron-interfaces—one repurposing the body of a vintage iron, one recreating the shape of an iron by 3D printing it—exemplify two transgressive methodologies that stand in contrast to the common employment of costly commercial audio equipment and computers in music technology: up-cycling and DIY. These approaches allowed the designers to circumvent the purchase of manufactured parts in building the body of their respective iron-interfaces, and to limit commercial purchases to the greatest degree possible to smaller electronic components. While 3D printing may present its own problems in terms of access, cost, and sustainability of materials, it has undoubtedly revolutionised DIY design for artists and makers, and holds the potential to circumvent capitalist modes of commercial production and delivery. Up-cycling is not only environmentally sustainable, but offers a rebuke to the profit-driven culture of planned obsolescence and the market-driven quest for innovation in interface design and music technology as a whole (Hayes and Marquez-Borbon 2020).[23]

The process of up-cycling in relation to planned obsolescence and technological opacity was raised in the presentation of the *Parlour Sounds* project at the Sonic Cyberfeminisms conference hosted by the University of Lincoln in

---

22 Once again, the relationship of Peyee Chen's character to the home environment she is performing housekeeping labour in remains ambiguous, in terms of whether she is performing housework for her own family in her own home or for an employer (see footnote 5 and discussion in section 3).

23 Lauren Hayes and Adnan Marquez-Borbon write that "the market demands of the neoliberal university . . . have underpinned academia's drive for innovation" in the design of New Interfaces for Musical Expression (NIMEs) (2020, 428). They go on to say that "While the new and novel 'N' of NIME—supported by the prevalence of demos—could be thought of as aligning with their logic of 'innovation'—often assumed to be tied to the agendas of funding bodies and governmental agencies, where research is guided and driven specifically by economic demands—there may be cases where this produces both inventive as well as anti-inventive outcomes" (Hayes and Marquez-Borbon 2020, 431).

2017,[24] in which Alessandrini described how her research on the design of irons quickly led her to the conclusion that recent models did not lend themselves as easily to the separation—or repair—of individual components as earlier models. In addition to the practical problem posed by modern models, the ethical preference was to upscale a non-functional, second-hand vintage object rather than taking apart a functional, mass-produced model in order to repurpose it, as the latter approach would in a sense "undo" the labour producing the original iron. In a subsequent conference presentation by Alessandrini on design methodologies, the relationship between the transgressive form of the interface or other artefact, on the one hand, and the equitable consideration of all actors in the process of making and performing with it, on the other, was further elaborated: "An artefact can only be as transgressive as the process producing it. . . . It is only through radical identification with all actors in the process of production that true transgression in design is achieved" (Alessandrini 2018). Walter Benjamin's concept of *aura* (Benjamin 1968) was applied here to a repurposed object and its history, how it came into the hands of the designer, and from whom. The process of radical identification consisted in part of considering each component's trajectory and therefore, for instance, executing *Parlour Sounds*' interface design and other design projects without recourse to Amazon's delivery service to buy parts, because of its exploitative labour conditions (Alessandrini 2018; Klippenstein 2021).

Even more than in its physical computing interface design, the area in which the principles of DIY, up-cycling, and low-level production are most present in *Parlour Sounds* is in its use of circuit bending to create entirely analogue electronic instruments from electronic components and repurposed appliances or objects. As we will see in the next section, this technique plays a key role in its cyberfeminist conceptualisation of an "outside-the-studio"—or perhaps even, "post-studio"—approach to sound art and creative music technology.

5. The home as an alternative studio space

While the home can be charged as a confined space of household labour for women, it has paradoxically served as a site of freedom and exploration in electronic music in its function as an alternative workspace to male-dominated institutional studios. There are parallel histories to the institutional developments of electronic music, with key developments, inventions, and artistic contributions—spanning both analogue and digital forms—made by figures such as Carla Scaletti, Wendy Carlos, and Éliane Radigue outside institutional electronic music studios, in their own personal studios, often in home environments (Heying 2018–19). Another parallel line is traced by "handmade" (Collins 2020)—in a sense, "homemade"—electronic instruments created through the DIY techniques commonly referred to as circuit-bending, a practice particularly suited to home environments as it does not require standard computers or studio equipment (Ghazala 2004).

---

24   See https://soniccyberfeminisms.wordpress.com/.

Although an artist may choose to work outside institutional studios for a multitude of reasons—to avoid the constraints of institutional methodologies or aesthetics, or simply because the work does not require conventional studio equipment—forms of bias, exclusion, and/or the social dynamics of the studio environment are often at play. Today, enrolment for music technology degrees in the United Kingdom remains primarily white and male (Born and Devine 2015). While women's inclusion in science, technology, engineering, and mathematics (STEM) have seen some advancements in recent years, music technology remains predominantly male (Mathew, Grossman, and Andreopoulou 2016; Female Pressure 2020). The absence of women from the musical canon, masculine vocabularies in musical discourse, and the gendered character of instruments all factor into the "musicalised male hegemony" (Born and Devine 2015, 151).

In 2017, Alessandrini served on a team of convenors—led by long-time activist and scholar Liz Dobson, one of the founding directors of the Yorkshire Sound Women Network (YSWN)[25]—of the Activating Inclusive Sound Spaces conference (see AISS 2017), which identified a need to "activate safer spaces" for music production institutionally, and called for the recognition of sound artists working outside institutional spaces such as electronic music studios due to the socio-political conditions of those spaces and other circumstances:

> A significant amount of data (on festivals, labels and clubs, union membership, academic conference attendance, and course application) concretely demonstrates that our music and sound industries are predominantly male and ethnically homogeneous (white). Research has shown how assumptions are made about who is associated with digital music and sound production practices, raising fundamental questions about how our environments and communities influence and shape them and our industries. . . . In particular we need to amplify the voices of people creating and producing independently without institutional support, to understand their perspectives and their views about how circumstance shapes practice. (AISS 2017)

In Madison Heying's extensive research on Carla Scaletti, the Kyma system she co-created, and the Kyma user community (Heying 2019), she describes the factors that led Scaletti to develop Kyma outside the historical Experimental Music Studios (EMS) of the Music Department at the University of Illinois Urbana-Champaign—where she was studying composition at the time—and to eventually start her own company.[26] Heying cites Schedel's historical research on electronic music studios, which highlights the "'operational characteristics'" of professional studios that had their "own signature sound which came not only from the equipment itself," but from social pressures that "'exert a considerable influence on the range and type of compositional operations which may be satisfactorily executed'" (Schedel 2007, 26, interpolating a quotation from Manning 2004, 152, as quoted by Heying 2019, 26). Scaletti found that "to do the things I really wanted to do in computer music, I was going to have to

---

25 See https://yorkshiresoundwomen.com/about/.
26 The Symbolic Sound Corporation, co-founded with her partner, Kyma co-creator Kurt Hebel.

learn to make the tools myself" (Scaletti 2015, 14, as quoted in Heying 2019, 32). Kyma was thus created out of personal aesthetics and technological goals, in order for Scaletti to work outside existing frameworks of pitch and linear time in electronic music, the predominant paradigms of the EMS.

Originally designed for Scaletti's own compositional projects, multiplicity and flexibility of function were reflected in Kyma's design: "With Kyma, users had the utility of a music studio, coupled with developments in personal computers and communication technology, which enabled them to establish personal music production studios, often in their own home" (Heying 2019, 162). Heying goes on to quote Schedel once again, on the advantages of a home studio: "primarily, it liberates the composer, promoting flexibility and freedom of self-expression" (Schedel 2007, 32, as quoted in Heying 2019, 162–63). In her broader research on women and studio dynamics, Heying applies Nirmal Puwar's concept of *space invaders* (2004) to the misogyny and alienation experienced by Daphne Oram, Wendy Carlos, and Tara Rodgers—in addition to Scaletti—that spurred them to abandon academic and commercial institutions to pursue "aesthetic, technical, and social freedom" in their self-built home studios (Heying 2019, 216).

6. Composing electronics collaboratively outside the studio environment

> Ever seen anyone make sounds with an egg slicer?
>
> —Publicity text for the avant-premiere performance
> of *Parlour Sounds* at the Barn, Banchory (Barn 2017)[27]

The "outside the studio" paradigm is not only referenced by the setting and content of *Parlour Sounds*—in which the protagonist experiments with sound in a home environment—but also applied in its collaborative creative methodology in several respects. The two interfaces discussed above—the vintage radio and iron—can be deployed anywhere through the use of their onboard speakers and integrated microprocessor. The same is true for the purely analogue electronic instruments employed in *Parlour Sounds*, which were created through circuit-bending techniques by Alessandrini and noise artist and instrument-maker Ewa Justka. In relation to the previous section on the interface/instrument design, the analogue instruments were even more elemental in their design from basic components, and were all created either in collective workshops or collaboratively in the apartments of Alessandrini and Justka. Performance or improvisation on these analogue instruments was also created through a collaborative compositional process, in which the performers themselves played a key creative role.

---

27 Publicity furnished by the Barn and the Curious series of Sound Scotland, who were the co-producers of the avant-première and hosted the workshop period discussed in this section.

Because the analogue electronic instruments were designed to be open-ended and multiplicitous in their applications, with several options for touch and/or sonic input built into each, performance on them was largely left open to the performers' own creation and improvisation through an educative work-shopping process that took place over the course of Alessandrini's Sound and Music residency. As a first step, Peyee Chen came to London to attend a circuit-bending workshop by Nicolas Collins organised by Alessandrini.[28] As a result, Chen was able not only to better understand the principles of circuit-bending design and brush up on instrument-making skills such as soldering, but also to make her own instrument, which she was able to practise with prior to the first workshops and rehearsals. In the meantime, the student performers from the CNSMDP were invited to one of the four Sound Kitchen sessions at the Gaîté lyrique during Alessandrini's residency there with the Ensemble Intercontemporain, where they were able to observe a circuit-bending workshop by Alessandrini and a performance by the workshop participants, as well as compositions by Alessandrini featuring live electronics.[29]

During a subsequent workshopping residency of the *Parlour Sounds* project at the Barn in Banchory, the students of the CNSMDP participated in a workshopping session featuring a variety of analogue electronic instruments, and were able to experiment with them while learning more about them. Through repeated workshopping and rehearsing with the instruments over the course of the Banchory residency, an improvisatory prelude was composed, in which each student participant had their role and took cues from one another and Chen, who performed at the same time with her modified vacuum cleaner.[30] This led to a noise-heavy prelude scene full of wild energy and spontaneity, yet with enough consistency to be reliably repeated over the course of multiple performances. The Banchory residency also allowed Chen and Alessandrini to further collaborate on dramatic interludes featuring the analogue instruments, including one in which Chen's writing—using the conductivity of a graphite pencil—becomes part of the circuit.[31]

Each step in the process of building, trying out and repairing or altering the analogue electronic instruments, and composing for them—all of which Chen actively played a role in—was thus performed entirely outside the studio, with much of it taking place on the set of the production. To close the loop of the collaborative circuit, so to speak, the audience members were invited onstage at the end of the performance to try out the instruments and ask questions about them; this was very much in keeping with the pedagogical mission of the host of the premiere, the Edinburgh International Science Festival. While the interfaces played a crucial expressive role in Chen's performance, as they were designed for specific gestures and musical situations related to the domestic labour she portrayed on the stage, the analogue electronic instruments proved

---

28 In January 2017 at Goldsmiths College, where Alessandrini was teaching at the time, see https://www.gold.ac.uk/calendar/?id=10447.

29 See https://patriciaalessandrini.com/blogs/notes/posts/sound-kitchen-ii-avec-les-solistes-de-l-ensemble-intercontemporain-a-la-gaite-lyrique for the full programme.

30 See footnote 11 for a description of the modified vacuum cleaner and MF14.2.

31 See Barn (2017), the documentation at https://patriciaalessandrini.com/ParlourSounds, and MF14.1.

to be especially popular during the audience demos, as their large variety of sounds and modes of sound-making lent themselves to the curious audience members' experimentations.

This multifaceted outside-the-studio process shows that the distributive and inclusive nature of the cyberfeminist project is situated not only in the non-hierarchical connectedness of actors in the process—composers, performers, designers, and so on—but also across categories of composition, improvisation, and performance, as well as interface, instrument, and environment. This interconnectedness is described by Simon Waters in his writing on interactive music:

> I follow Impett[32] . . . in understanding music as a complex dynamical system, whether one is talking about its organisation as acoustic fact, or about its consolidation in culture as a (social) practice embodying behaviours, beliefs and actions. And here I'm concerned to apply this model for understanding complex interactions to the distinctions between the terms: *performer*, *instrument*, and *environment*. The terms reify the corporeality (bodilyness) of the first, the goal-orientedness of the second, the otherness of the third. What is *lost* in this set of distinctions? (Waters 2007, 2)

7. FUTURE CYBERFEMINIST PERSPECTIVES FOR MUSIC TECHNOLOGY

> Sonic cyberfeminisms is something that is done and practised, as well as something that is thought about and reflected on.
>
> —Annie Goh and Marie Thompson, "Sonic Cyberfeminisms: Introduction" (Goh and Thompson 2021b, 9)[33]

In both its content and methodology, *Parlour Sounds* applies distributed, cyberfeminist principles to propose an alternative to dominant paradigms of electronic music, thereby proposing a theoretical framework in which roles and distinctions between composition, design, improvisation, and performance are blurred. In particular, its inclusive collaborative methodology offers a counterpoint to traditional notions in the male-dominated field of electronic music of solitary studio composition by a single author, as skill-sharing and workshop-

---

32 In the epigraph of the article, Waters (2007, 1) quotes Impett (2001, 108): "Music is understood as a dynamical complex of interacting situated embodied behaviours. These behaviours may be physical or virtual, composed or emergent, or of a time scale such that they figure as constraints or constructs. All interact in the same space by a process of mutual modelling, redescription, and emergent restructuring."

33 The full passage reads, "Thus, we aim to make clear our understanding of cyberfeminism as a feminist practice of steering: in this case, highlighting the complex imbrication of gender, sound and technology that both endures and transforms, whilst attending to but also moving beyond questions of representation and inclusion. We do so at a time when the gendered makeup of different audio technocultures is subject to increasing scrutiny. Including contributions from activists, artists and composers alongside scholars is intended to highlight the limitations of academic knowledge production to which many of us in the academy are bound, and all too often unable to acknowledge subservience to. Sonic cyberfeminisms is something that is done and practised, as well as something that is thought about and reflected on."

ping grant performers agency to creatively shape their interpretative roles. In order for the theoretical framework proposed here to be effective in future practical applications beyond *Parlour Sounds*, however, it needs to be reactive to the changing situation in music technology: perhaps most significantly, developments in machine learning (ML) and artificial intelligence (AI) are posing new problems of ethics, power-relations, access, and exclusion. These issues are in part addressed in Alessandrini's project dating from 2019, *Ada's Song*, a homage to Ada Lovelace in which AI processes are applied both in the compositional process and in performance, in the piloting of an instrumental robotics system called the Piano Machine.[34] Two complementary notions are at the forefront of this work: Ada Lovelace's insistence on human responsibility and agency in her theorisation of AI, and keeping "humans in the loop" (Wang 2019) in AI-assisted composition and performance, including the control of automata/robotics.

The framework proposed by the *Parlour Sounds* project, in which the relationship between the cyberfeminist principles reflected in the content and its application in a distributive process are key, may potentially be beneficially applied to some of the ethical problems raised by AI. *Parlour Sounds'* application of principles to process can be related directly to calls for greater transparency, inclusion, and ethical responsibility in design for AI: at each level of the process, the designer must be responsible for *how* design is done, that this *how* is intricately related to the *why* of the design, and will determine how value systems may subsequently be coded into AI (Meierling 2021). The skill-sharing and educative methods of *Parlour Sounds* are also relevant here: workshops for inclusion in electronic music and other creative domains have spanned both analogue and digital technologies, and some have focused specifically on coding, including ML and AI.[35]

There are other renewed challenges posed by AI that call for further reflection upon and adaptation of the theory and practices outlined in this chapter. Just as access to professional studio equipment and mainframes of early computing was often only available to those affiliated with the institutions that housed them, and thus presented problems of bias, exclusion, and a lack of diversity among its users, the data and computing power used in complex ML and AI processes is similarly restricted to resource-rich companies and universities, thereby presenting similar problems in regard to inclusion. Thus, the practical need for institutional access, which had been lessened by the increased access to personal computers and free software from the 1980s on, is once again heightened by the computing needs for complex ML and AI

---

34 The Piano Machine was first designed and produced by Alessandrini in collaboration with Konstantin Leonenko in 2017. It uses physical computing techniques to mechanically excite the individual strings of the piano. See https://patriciaalessandrini.com/pianomachine for more information and documentation.

35 For example the Code Liberation Foundation, as well as workshops and developments by Rebecca Fiebrink and other researchers in ML and AI (Gillies et al. 2016; Parke-Wolfe, Scurto, and Fiebrink 2019). Other examples of organisations working across digital and analogue technology (in a primarily Anglophone context) include SoundGirls, TECHNE, TITWRENCH, Women's Audio Mission, Women in Sound Women on Sound (WISWOS), Women Produce Music, and the aforementioned YSWN (Thompson 2018).

processes. This new frontier for access and inclusion in music technology requires an increased prioritisation of strategies to fundamentally change the institutional dynamics of the field of electronic music. As this access is in essence virtual rather than physical, the distributive "out-of-the-studio" methodology proposed by *Parlour Sounds* and the cyberfeminist principles it is based upon may be particularly relevant in addressing these issues.

The success of the cyberfeminist project relies on its geographical inclusion and intersectionality, which requires both structural change in the field and creative distributed strategies for broad demographic and geographical reach (Tamirisa 2021). As this chapter is being completed approximately one year into the global Covid-19 pandemic, it is more apparent than ever that networked strategies for education, skill-sharing, workshopping, and performance will play a key role in future music technology. As for virtual computing, these techniques have their own unique technical requirements—in particular, broadband access—which once again pose challenges to inclusivity, and often require community infrastructure and/or institutional support.[36]

While most of the discussion in this chapter has focussed on *Parlour Sounds'* collaborative methodologies and its situation of design and experimentation outside traditional studio spaces, it is vitally important to note the institutional context in which it was made, and the need to not only create alternative spaces but also have an impact on the social dynamics, priorities, and structures of music technology and associated fields. *Parlour Sounds* benefited from the open-ended and supportive embedded structure provided by Sound and Music, which has invested resources in recent years to improve access to developmental opportunities and establish best practices for their programmes.[37] However, in the absence of a generalised acceptance and enactment of best practices and shared goals for inclusion by all the institutional and individual partners, *Parlour Sounds* was nonetheless subject to hindrances caused by ambient gender bias in the male-dominated fields of electronic and contemporary music.

One of the female-identifying performers commented on the gendered dynamics encountered in the mounting of the production: "I think if Patricia were a dude, they wouldn't have reacted in the same way, even if she spoke and asked for things in the same way, and that was surprising and kind of not okay" (Zhu 2020). Another example was the lack of female-identifying, non-binary, or gender-queer candidates for the open call for scores from composers of the CNSMDP, which some of its faculty lamented as due to systemic problems of gender bias in the area of composition, conducting, and *écriture musicale* at that

---

36 While there are freeware options for videoconferencing, as well as for low-latency, uncompressed audio through the use of free and open-source software such as Jacktrip (from the Center for Computer Research in Music and Acoustics—CCRMA), these tools require a minimum of internet access, speed, and reliability to be used effectively in pedagogical and/or performance situations.

37 See for instance Sound and Music's Fair Access Principles: https://soundandmusic.org/our-impact/fair-access-principles/.

institution,[38] in addition to the general lack of non-male representation in European contemporary music institutions (Fure 2016).

Thus, a key takeaway of this project is that articulating goals for access, inclusion, and equity is not sufficient; best practice guidelines need to be clearly explicit and intentionally opted-into by all partners in order to create the safer, more inclusive spaces ambitioned by initiatives such as AISS and projects such as Sonic Cyberfeminisms;[39] this process will be all the more important given the complex ethical and technical challenges posed by virtual computing and networked performance. Inclusive practices cannot merely sit alongside exclusive ones, and thus need to actively contribute to the remediation of institutional bias and discrimination. It is our hope that the cyberfeminist-informed collaborative methodology critically outlined and analysed here may contribute to these efforts, while exemplifying some of the creative and technological contributions to music technology this methodology affords. The collaborative methodology of *Parlour Sounds* and its design principles can serve as a basis for efforts towards diversity, inclusion, and equity that is not simply surface-level, but proposes an alternative structure for performance practices. Drawing upon experience from this production, the importance of social engagement with inclusion and ability can serve as a means towards creating a methodology more generally applicable in collaborative projects relating to music technology.

REFERENCES

Alessandrini, Patricia. 2018. "Repurposing, Transgression and Aura: Material, Means and Methods in Design." Conference presentation Manifestival 2018: Symposium for Artful Design, Stanford, CA, November 2018.

Alessandrini, Patricia, and Freida Abtan. 2020. "*Mondgewächse*: a Collaborative Methodology for Inclusive Audiovisual Mappings in Instrument Design." Short paper and demo presentation, International Conference on New Interfaces for Musical Expression, Birmingham.

Allen, Amy. 2016. "Feminist Perspectives on Power." In *Stanford Encyclopedia of Philosophy*, Fall 2016 ed., edited by Edward N. Zalta. Accessed 24 April 2021. https:// plato.stanford.edu/entries/feminist-power/.

Barn, the. 2017. "Curious: Parlour Sounds. Patricia Alessandrini and Red Note Ensemble." Facebook, 31 January 2017. Accessed 26 April 2021. https://www.facebook.com/watch/?v=10158305658610529.

Benjamin, Walter. 1968. "The Work of Art in the Age of Mechanical Reproduction." In *Illuminations: Essays and Reflections*, edited by Hannah Arendt, translated by Harry Zohn, 219–53. New York: Harcourt Brace Jovanovich. Essay first published 1936 as "L'œuvre d'art à l'époque de sa reproduction mécanisée" (*Zeitschrift für Sozialforschung* 5 [1]: 40–68).

---

38 According to correspondence between Alessandrini and the CNSMDP administration, there was only one female-identifying composition student who would have been eligible to participate in the project. Among factors that may have affected recruitment and admissions were the controversial statements made by the CNSMDP director at that time. See for instance Le Monde and Agence France-Presse (2013).

39 Mandatory policy opt-ins are already in practice by a number of organisations running workshops, hackathons, and so on. See for instance, the 2020 Hacksmiths Code of Conduct, https://github.com/hacksmiths/code-of-conduct.

Born, Georgina, and Kyle Devine. 2015. "Music Technology, Gender, and Class: Digitization, Educational and Social Change in Britain." *Twentieth-Century Music* 12 (2): 135–72.

Butler, Judith. 1990. *Gender Trouble: Feminism and the Subversion of Identity*. New York: Routledge.

Chen, Peyee. 2020. Interview by Julie Zhu, Zoom, 20 November 2020.

Clifton, Lucille. 2000. "study the masters." In *Blessing the Boats: New and Selected Poems 1988–2000*, 25. Rochester, NY: BOA Editions.

Collins, Nicolas. 2020. *Handmade Electronic Music: The Art of Hardware Hacking*. 3rd ed. Abingdon, UK: Routledge.

Cooper, Melinda. 2017. *Family Values: Between Neoliberalism and the New Social Conservatism*. New York: Zone Books.

Deleuze, Gilles. 1968. *Différence et Répétition*. Paris: Presses universitaires de France. Translated by Paul Patton as Deleuze 1994.

———. 1994. *Difference and Repetition*. Translated by Paul Patton. New York: Columbia University Press. First published as Deleuze 1968.

Federici, Silvia. 1975. *Wages against Housework*. Bristol, UK: Falling Wall Press.

Female Pressure. 2020. "FACTS Survey 2020." 4th edition, of the FACTS Survey. Accessed 26 April 2021. https://femalepressure.files.wordpress.com/2020/03/facts2020survey-by_femalepressure.pdf.

Fure, Ashley. 2016. "GRID: Gender Research in Darmstadt: A 2016 HISTORAGE Project Funded by the Goethe Institute." GRID: Feminist Activism during Darmstädter Ferienkurse 2016. Accessed 6 May 2020. https://griddarmstadt.files.wordpress.com/2016/08/grid_gender_research_in_darmstadt.pdf.

Ghazala, Qubais Reed. 2004. "The Folk Music of Chance Electronics: Circuit-Bending the Modern Coconut." In "Composers inside Electronics: Music after David Tudor," special issue, *Leonardo Music Journal* 14: 96–104.

Gillies, Marco, Rebecca Fiebrink, Atau Tanaka, Jérémie Garcia, Frédéric Bevilacqua, Alexis Heloir, Fabrizio Nunnari, et al. 2016. "Human-Centered Machine Learning." In *CHI EA '16: Proceedings of the 2016 CHI Conference Extended Abstracts on Human Factors in Computing Systems*, 3558–65. https://doi.org/10.1145/2851581.2856492.

Goh, Annie, and Marie Thompson, eds. 2021a. "Sonic Cyberfeminisms," special issue, *Feminist Review* 127 (1).

———. 2021b. "Sonic Cyberfeminisms: Introduction." In Goh and Thompson 2021a, 1–12.

Haraway, Donna J. (1985) 1991. "A Cyborg Manifesto: Science, Technology, and Socialist-Feminism in the Late Twentieth Century." In *Simians, Cyborgs, and Women: The Reinvention of Nature*, 149–82. New York: Routledge. Chapter first published 1985 as "Manifesto for Cyborgs: Science, Technology, and Socialist Feminism in the 1980s" (*Socialist Review* 80: 65–108).

Hayes, Lauren, and Adnan Marquez-Borbon. 2020. "Nuanced and Interrelated Mediations and Exigencies (NIME): Addressing the Prevailing Political and Epistemological Crises." In *NIME'20: Proceedings of the International Conference on New Interfaces for Musical Expression*, 428–33. Accessed 26 April 2021. https://nime.org/proceedings/2020/nime2020_paper83.pdf.

Heggie, Miranda. 2017. "Music Review: Red Note Ensemble, Summerhall, Edinburgh." *Herald* (Scotland), 14 April 2017. Accessed 25 April 2021. https://www.heraldscotland.com/life_style/arts_ents/15225854.music-review-red-note-ensemble-summerhall-edinburgh/.

Heying, Madison. 2018–19. "A Room of One's Own: The Independent Studios of Women Making Electronic and Computer Music." Paper presented at Stanford University Music Department, 25 February 2019, and at the annual meeting of the American Musicological Society, San Antonio, TX, 1–3 November 2018.

———. 2019. "A Complex and Interactive Network: Carla Scaletti, the Kyma System, and the Kyma User Community." PhD thesis, University of California, Santa Cruz.

Ho, Jocelyn, Margaret Schedel, and Matthew Blessing. 2020. "Revaluing Women's Labor through Material Engagement with Musical Instruments Built from Domestic Tools." In *Why Sentience? 26th International*

Symposium on Electronic Arts, ISEA2020: Proceedings, 501–4. Accessed 6 May 2021. https://isea2020.isea-international.org/PROCEEDING_041120_LR.pdf.

Impett, Jonathan. 2001. "Interaction, Simulation, and Invention: A Model for Interactive Music." In *Artificial Life Models for Music Applications*, edited by Eleonora Bilotta, Eduardo Reck Miranda, Peitro Pantano, and Peter M. Todd, 108–19. Consenza, Italy: Editoriale Bios.

Klippenstein, Ken. 2021. "Documents Show Amazon Is Aware Drivers Pee in Bottles and Even Defecate En route, Despite Company Denial." *Intercept*, 25 March 2021. Accessed 26 April 2021. https://theintercept.com/2021/03/25/amazon-drivers-pee-bottles-union/.

Le Monde and Agence France-Presse (AFP). 2013. "Femme et chef d'orchestre? Le compositeur Bruno Mantovani n'y croit pas." *Le Monde*, 10 October 2013. Accessed 27 April 2021. https://www.lemonde.fr/societe/article/2013/10/10/femme-et-chef-d-orchestre-le-compositeur-bruno-mantovani-n-y-croit-pas_3493601_3224.html.

Manning, Peter. 2004. *Electronic and Computer Music*. Rev. and expanded ed. New York: Oxford University Press.

Mathew, Marlene, Jennifer Grossman, and Areti Andreopoulou. 2016. "Women in Audio: Contributions and Challenges in Music Technology and Production." In *Proceedings of the 141st Convention of the Audio Engineering Society (AES)*, paper 9673.

Meierling, Chris. 2021. Design Research Spot Lecture, Designing Machine Learning, Stanford University course taught by Michelle Carney and Emily Callaghan, 3 February 2021.

Old Boys Network. 1997. "100 Anti-Theses of Cyberfeminism." Presented at First Cyberfeminist International, Hybrid Workspace, conference, Documenta X, Kassel, September 1997.

O'Neil, Cathy. 2016. *Weapons of Math Destruction: How Big Data Increases Inequality and Threatens Democracy*. New York: Broadway Books.

Parke-Wolfe, Samuel Thompson, Hugo Scurto, and Rebecca Fiebrink. 2019. "Sound Control: Supporting Custom Musical Interface Design for Children with Disabilities." In *NIME'19: Proceedings of the International Conference on New Interfaces for Musical Expression*, 192–97. https://doi.org/10.5281/zenodo.3672920.

Perchard, Tom. 2017. "Technology, Listening and Historical Method: Placing Audio in the Post-War British Home." *Journal of the Royal Musical Association* 142 (2): 367–99.

Puwar, Nirmal. 2004. *Space Invaders: Race, Gender and Bodies Out of Place*. Oxford: Berg.

Reiche, Claudia, and Verena Kuni, eds. 2004. *Cyberfeminism: Next Protocols*. New York: Autonomedia.

Robertson, Campbell. 2007. "She's Got a Date and Only 72 Hours to Prepare." *New York Times*, 9 July 2007. Accessed 26 April 2020. https://www.nytimes.com/2007/07/09/arts/09slow.html.

Russell, Legacy. 2021. "Ain't I a Womxn? What Glitch Feminism Can Teach Us Now." *Hyperallergic*, 27 January 2021. Accessed 27 April 2021. https://hyperallergic.com/616359/aint-i-a-womxn-what-glitch-feminism-can-teach-us-now/.

Scaletti, Carla. 2015. "Looking Back, Looking Forward: A Keynote Address for the 2015 International Computer Music Conference." *Computer Music Journal* 40 (1): 10–24.

Schedel, Margaret. 2007. "Electronic Music and the Studio." In *The Cambridge Companion to Electronic Music*, edited by Nick Collins and Julio d'Escriván, 24–37. Cambridge: Cambridge University Press.

Schedel, Margaret, Jocelyn Ho, and Matthew Blessing. 2019. "Women's Labor: Creating NIMEs from Domestic Tools." *NIME'19: Proceedings of the International Conference on New Interfaces for Musical Expression*, 377–80. https://doi.org/10.5281/zenodo.3672729.

Tamirisa, Asha. 2021. "Sonic Activism in the Integrated Circuit." *Feminist Review* 127 (1): 13–19.

Thompson, Marie. 2018. "Sonic (Cyber) Feminisms: Questions, Strategies and Contestations." Keynote presentation given at the Mutek Festival, Montreal, 21 August 2018.

Wajcman, Judy. 1991. *Feminism Confronts Technology*. Cambridge: Polity Press.

Wang, Ge. 2019. "Humans in the Loop: The Design of Interactive AI Systems." Stanford University Human-Centred

Artificial Intelligence (HAI), 20 October 2019. Accessed 27 April 2021. https://hai.stanford.edu/news/humans-loop-design-interactive-ai-systems.

Waters, Simon. 2007. "Performance Ecosystems: Ecological Approaches to Musical Interaction." EMS: Electroacoustic Music Studies Network—De Montfort/Leicester. Accessed 26 April 2021. http://ems-network.org/IMG/pdf_WatersEMS07.pdf.

Z, Pamela, Jocelyn Ho, Margaret Schedel, and members of the fff ensemble. 2021.

"Panel | Pamela Z, Margaret Schedel, Jocelyn Ho, fff ensemble." Moderated by Patricia Alessandrini and Julie Zhu. Center for Computer Research in Music and Acoustics—CCRMA, Stanford, 19 March 2021. Vimeo video, 1:27:58, uploaded by "CCRMA," 19 March 2021. Accessed 26 April 2021. https://vimeo.com/510395686.

Zhu, Julie. 2021. Interview with participant(s) of *Parlour Sounds*, Zoom, 20 November 2020.

Changing the Vocabulary of Creative Research

The Role of Networks, Risk, and Accountability in Transcending Technical Rationality

Ambrose Field

University of York, UK

PROLOGUE

This chapter seeks to question the ontology and underpinning discourse of "composition as research," proposing that for too long the artistic community has accepted without modification an uneasy mapping of questions and frameworks from the sciences onto the processes, contexts, and situations of artistic creativity. However, this is not a straightforward claim for inapplicability, rather a call to action to address the contemporary demands of an interdisciplinary research landscape where complexity, context, risk, and emergence play a significant part in research that exceeds the boundaries of that which can be described by technical systems alone.

The chapter notes that artistic creation is articulated through culture by a complex and networked service-dominant logic, rather than a linear supply chain of artistic "goods" from creator to perceiver. In doing so, it suggests that the arts function as a complex system and that traditional research models for creative practice—often themselves based on linear relationships between research process and research outputs—have consequently become crystallised around nineteenth-century values of artefact production and singular points of knowledge ownership.

A starting point to disrupt these links is offered through a modification of the vocabulary of how creative research is framed in scholarly practice. The straightforward idea of the *creative question* is introduced to supplement the classical notion of the *research question*, so that a dependence on the act of translation between textual and non-textual domains in encapsulating enquiry in creative research can be reassessed. Risk, within this untranslated remit, changes behaviour from a force to be mitigated to an agent for enabling emergence and exploration. Broader, interdisciplinary research domains today encompass an experimental system far wider than that which can be described by technical rationality alone. To this end, *artistic accountability* is proposed as a challenge to *procedural justification* in the academic presentation of musical composition research, with a view to enabling contextual discourse that is outward looking and connective by default.

INTRODUCTION

This chapter highlights ways in which the discourse of creative practice research can flourish within the more generalised context of institutional higher education. It is not designed as additional fuel for the fire of "composition as research" debates, previously extensively discussed by other authors (particular themes relevant to this work are documented in Harrison [2013]; Croft [2015]; Reeves [2016]; Armstrong [2020]). This chapter poses some alternative points of view designed to help resituate creative practice research within the academic landscape of the twenty-first century.

Theoretical and applied research have traditionally inhabited different institutional contexts and academic discourses, but increasingly today these domains are not artificially separated where it is not relevant to do so (for example, in AI, safety critical research, complex systems). Schön ([1983] 2016, 24) noted that theoretical research could be thought of as the object of "scholarship" and applied research, in general terms as something that happens with regard to industry or practice-based professions. He comments that applied research was often an activity undertaken by different people to those who concern themselves with theoretical problems. However, value judgements drawn from distinctions between practice, theory, role-descriptions, and workflow have leaked into music academia over time without reference to the interconnectedness musical creativity has across the domains that constitute it: for example, musicology could be thought of as a scholarly *performance* of musical ideas, the formation of computer code as a *creative* action, and performance as an *articulation* of culture. In the past, distinctions between pure and applied research were most visible in the sciences. This separation has been decreasing in higher education due to an increase in challenge-based research and the prevalence of funding streams aligned to problems of global significance. Despite this convergence it is likely that academia will retain "pure" maths and "applied" engineering: a robust knowledge of the disciplinary is important in its own right and informs interdisciplinary developments. Similarly, it will remain important for performers to study performance technique to an advanced level in order to articulate artistic ideas. However, it is the awareness of an external context beyond discipline boundaries that can help complete the *experimental system* (see below) and form a springboard for interdisciplinary connections.

In music, an unfortunate and unnecessarily reductive segregation of the discipline by workflow (composers compose, performers perform) has been legitimised by past practice—in particular, through the nineteenth-century European conservatoire pedagogy of "reverence for the composer" (for a full discussion, see Rubinoff [2017, 477]) and the establishment of musicology in some university departments as an activity that was to be applied retroactively to performance or composition and not in combination with them (see Rink [2003, 304]; Cook [2013] also highlights a contemporary understanding where musicology is informed by performance and vice versa). The lived reality of creativity today is for many artists not a separation between the applied and the theoretical, or the practical and the technical, it is more a complex, layered, and interdependent integration of these domains. This is strongly evidenced in the work of Assis (2014, 21) in discussion of *assemblages* as a tool for understanding the interconnected nature of research in creative practice. To avoid artificial separations between workflow, roles, and people and what they might or might not be expected to accomplish, it is necessary to move beyond the constraints of thinking of music research as a *supply chain* of "outputs" and "products." Notions of distributed creativity, when brought together with aspects of contemporary economic theory can provide useful perspectives in this regard as "value" today is rarely located in things or products alone.

Creativity acting through networks

Distributed creativity (Clarke and Doffman 2017) situates composition as an activity that is not solely undertaken by isolated individuals and instead foregrounds a networked relationship between the nodes within it and the surrounding context. While distributed creativity and actor–network (Latour 1996) theory describe inter-relationships between nodes and contexts, composition possesses unique capabilities in being able to generate artefacts at particular points within a network and at *the same time* generate new knowledge that informs how the links within the network might themselves be assembled and reassembled. For example, a musical performance may change the way those who listen to it understand a particular space or occasion: meanwhile such situations may or may not have been part of a particular purposefully designed network of distributed creative practice. However, these dynamic changes to the network are important in determining the human impact of the performance. A more flexible theory is perhaps required to account for this shifting set of connections between objects and contexts to link together the *relationships* that articulate and generate *human value* (as opposed to "economic value"). If it is possible to define these relationships, then articulating diversity (of all forms—human and artistic) within creative musical research becomes correspondingly more achievable.

Lusch and Vargo ([2006] 2014) have tackled this problem in contemporary economics and marketing theory, proposing that a shift has occurred between goods-based logics and service-based logics (SD logic). Goods-based logic involved "value" being created from the development and supply of finished products to market: in musical terms almost exactly corresponding to a nineteenth-century model of music production where composers made a work, performers performed it, and the audience listened without substantive influence over the nature of what they were consuming. Goods-based logic helped gatekeepers (traditionally publishers, venue managers, radio stations, and now media platforms and content aggregation systems) preserve boundaries between the job descriptions of performer, composer, and audience. Service-dominant logic replaces goods-based logic where products were shipped along a linear trajectory from designer to end user, were unchangeable, and were not sculpted in any way as an interactive part of that relationship. SD logic challenges the view that value exists in the goods alone. Much has changed within music over the last century: we understand creativity to be not solely located within a particular artefact but to be part of a much wider cultural process that encompasses the creation, reception, and cultural situation of music. It is also worth noting that the workflow segregation of nineteenth century goods-based logic is mostly visible in Western classical music and not in culture where stronger integration between creative practice, performance, audience, and society has already dissolved those boundaries or does not recognise them from the outset.

Due to the adoption of service-dominant logic within the marketing toolkit of contemporary music publishing and consumption, the commercial value in establishing *networks* of creators and consumers is clear. The platform—either online or physical, serves as the aggregation and distribution agent, with a gatekeeping functionality that defines brand and the distinctiveness of the platform (see Brousseau and Penard 2007, 101). However, this process is one of selection and it is beneficial for the platform itself to maintain a workflow segregation between artwork producer and consumer. Although value in the wider creative economy is driven through the SD logic of networking—in particular via relationship marketing aided by social network systems, doing so via closed commercial platforms in music still sustains a goods-based logic in the application of corresponding creative practices where it has been repurposed as a tool to aid new types of gatekeeping by platform service providers. Given that these practices exist within the economics of contemporary artistic consumption, it is therefore not surprising that in institutional research infrastructure, and in the education of creative practitioners, a goods-based view of "outputs" and measurable "product" still exists (see Piccini 2002), even though creative practice itself operates highly effectively through truly networked relationships to deliver *human value*. When embedded within a relational system, goods logic serves to enshrine views of creative knowledge as being capable of encapsulation in an "output," rather than in the relationships it has created, or expressed through technical rationality to the exclusion of how it has changed the context and relationships that surround it. Meanwhile, service-dominant logic situates all participants and their connections *within* the bounds of a broader system, moving the focus away from product as an isolated entity towards a situation where community and the network shapes the operant resources contained within *the whole system*. This system is the *experimental system of creative practice* (see below).

Is composition then a service? Perhaps not in the sense of it being subservient to other domains—it is, however, a body of human knowledge that can change in response to the environment in which it is placed. Composition, as an activity, can very much be concerned with the extension and evolution of relationships rather than the generation of goods—objects that are solely explainable in terms of the processes that made them. Nonetheless, forms of interdisciplinary creativity flourish through networked SD logic where ensembles of all kinds generate their own material using curiosity-driven exploration via a blend of composition and performance, or within a wide spectrum of community music practices, or through the "live art" of performance-based or technology enabled installation. In short, designing music with SD logic in mind enables stronger links to be made with the cultures and communities in which it is situated. It would therefore be of benefit to widen institutional design, pedagogy, and funding discourse to take into account networked practices and community and cultural relationships where creativity is not segregated between roles that carry goods-based logic identifiers, such as "composer," "performer," and "audience."

EXPERIMENTAL SYSTEM

To characterise scientific research as a sequence of tests and experiments of a reductive kind would be just as inappropriate as it is to claim that all parts of a compositional process are the sole product of "inspiration" (rather than planning, technique, craft, hard work, or happy accidents, all of which can coexist under the broader heading of "creativity"). However, institutionalised instrumental indicators of research success may challenge the idea that research rigour can interact with creativity: instead, I will argue that "rigour" in the true sense of the word is essential to creativity and forms the backbone of *artistic accountability* (see below). It operates in a multi-dimensional way binding the strands of creative enquiry together, rather than being perceived through a measurable quantum of objective truth within a linear research methodology. Rigour forms both part of the act of creativity and reflection-in-action on creativity in a way that makes it difficult to separate the two: it brings together Dewey's concepts ([1934] 1958, 46) of *doing* and *undergoing*. However, research rigour in creative practice may not necessarily be found in post-hoc justification a priori, as this type of rigour is not a specific linear sequence of events and observations that become visible and apparent if "good process" is followed. It is more difficult to pinpoint *research rigour* in complex systems where outputs do not match inputs, where the development of knowledge may occur in nonlinear ways. That does not automatically mean the latter process is *not rigorous*: a heightened sense of research rigour is required to keep the multiple strands, contexts, and overlapping threads of enquiry aligned. Such a multidimensional sense of research rigour is captured in late twentieth-century views of scientific research processes. In environmental biology, Hans-Jörg Rheinberger has proposed the idea of the *experimental system*, enabling the widening of the importance of context within experimental research (as documented by Assis 2014,

48). Experiments conducted as reductive entities, Rheinberger argues, risk not interacting with information generated by the real world in which tests and experiments are conducted. The technical rationality of reductive methods is called into question as the only source of truth about research: while it may establish facts, these often need to be evaluated in wider frames of enquiry than those encapsulated by reductive processes alone. And so it is with musical composition. The experimental system of musical composition depends on contextual and cultural interactions, on human relationships *and* on creative processes. How these are aligned can either be a significant part of the compositional process (especially when considering whether a service-based logic for creativity is applicable) or inconsequential (for example, music created entirely in the abstract, if that were possible). Rheinberger (2015, 172) argues that it is the relationship between ideas within the experimental system and those outside it that creates knowledge. Composers are free to configure the component parts of their experimental systems as discrete units, or to create a highly networked and dependent set of interactions. Furthermore, some properties of the networks described within the experimental system of creativity can only be found through *emergence* (see Goldstein 2013, 81–83). Emergence can be thought of as the act of making visible the latent properties of a system through exploration and discovery. As such, emergence as an idea is closely allied to creativity.

Research gaps, risk, and creativity

The identification of "research gaps" forms a fundamental part of research methodology in science disciplines and also serves to strengthen technical rational arguments traditionally constructed to establish the *validity* of research. Without the identification of research gaps, multiple different versions of similar ideas would proliferate, work would be duplicated, and the process of "advancing knowledge" would ultimately break down. Finding a research gap lies at the heart of positivist methodologies to pinpoint an *original contribution*. Research gaps can be typically found by scanning literature horizons and developing contextual awareness, as well as through other methods (see Bryman 2012, 50–75). In doing so, they also create the rationale to clear a discursive space in preparation for *adding new knowledge*. While such methods can apply to creative research, or research about creativity, it does not follow though that they will be called upon in the same ways within musical composition. Composers, for instance, may wish to be fully contextually aware of previous music with similar characteristics in style, performance practice, genre, or cultural situation. However, they might also wish to challenge existing constructional methods, or use established theory as a tool to circumvent the normal through articulating a new artistic vision. It is therefore unlikely that any single piece of a creative output will fill a *creative gap*: therefore, any idea of creative output itself being able to address specific *research gaps* might be problematic as there is no singular generalised, peer-reviewed solution from which a future body of work can "progress."

Research methodology is most often communicated about through the written word: an act that would involve translation for creative practices, making a surrogate expression of research that is one step removed from the research processes being undertaken.[1] Meanwhile, it is important to note that the actual practice of research in many disciplines is non-linguistic in nature, and that it may also be accountable for by technical rationality. Yet in creative practice, a reliance on technical process as the *most visible* driver for research methodology needs to be questioned, in that there is no individual *methodology* that can by default legitimate an original contribution. In the arts, it is possible for the duplication of workflow and process to lead to different and unexpected results, due to the ability of artistic practice to occupy a rhizomatic relationship within a broader, contextually situated, experimental system. If replication of workflow—even in a few instances—can lead to originality, then the notion of identifying a research gap in creative practice as a proxy for originality needs to be supplemented with additional contextualising information. The idea of *artistic accountability* presented below is introduced to address this.

TECHNICAL SYSTEMS AND TECHNICAL PRACTICES

In previous work (Field 2021), I have described the relationship between *technical systems* and Rheinberger's concept of *experimental system*. In summary, technical systems are a subset of an experimental system, yet they lack visibility of the complete context that surrounds them within an experimental system. From the point of view of compositional discourse, technical systems could describe methods of harmony for example, or a particular electronic music sound process, but expecting a documentation of this to encapsulate the entire *creative envelope* (see below for further discussion) in such a way that it forms the totality of the perceived experience may not be possible.[2]

While understanding technical systems is a necessary part of many creative processes, isolating technical practices and then using them as a proxy for artistic experience can be problematic particularly if they become elevated to a status where they are charged with representing creativity itself. Beale, Schofield, and Austin (2018) show that even where technical systems have a close relationship with artefacts, it is not possible to fully account for *experience*. In an archaeological study of computer mice from the 1980s, despite knowing the design and the use cases (a high level of knowledge about the artefact from the outset), it was not possible to interpolate significant information with regard to how people themselves would have felt using them or for individual preferences in doing so. As a result, the technical descriptions of an artefact cannot themselves form a complete contextualised evidence base about that artefact—shown here within even the most generic and globally familiar of

---

1 This is not an argument against communicating about creativity through written expression, which is valuable in and of itself.
2 While acknowledging that it is perfectly possible for a single process to be responsible for the entire creative envelope of a musical work, even in this case the technical rationality of a procedural description will still not fully translate into what the music actually sounds like.

objects. On this basis, technical practice alone can only be one of the available tools in imagining the past or understanding music from across the globe: how culture and context can be creatively integrated with technical practice is paramount in providing a functional experimental system within which constraints and opportunities can be explored. With this in mind, it is valuable for music education to engage in *historically and culturally informed creativity* alongside performance approaches.

ADJUSTING THE VOCABULARY FOR CREATIVE RESEARCH

This chapter proposes that the traditional vocabulary of research needs to be supplemented, rather than replaced or adjusted, to bring the workflow, outcomes, and contexts of creative practice research into sharper perspective, starting with the basic foundations of research process—the research question. In research that exists outside the field of creative practice, the process of discovery is guided by the *research question* and generating a significantly robust set of research questions forms an integral starting point. The research question defines how ideas are to be defined, shaped, and executed. Notably, research questions themselves can be delivered through investigative practice and do not necessarily need to be always "answered" in the form of experimental proof—this is only one type of response to a research question. There already is tremendous latitude within the remit of the "research question" to accommodate many types of research in practice. However, a number of underlying assumptions prevent this discourse from mapping entirely successfully onto creative practice. These are that:

- the research question itself is expressed through the use of text/language (rather than through sound, visual, or other sensory processes);
- the final response to the research question is normally captured through text/language;[3]
- it should be held as a constant yardstick against which "progress" can be measured.

It is notable that these characteristics can be mutable in reality to varying extents depending on the project concerned, but that they are also ones by which traditional assumptions of scholarship, such as those embedded in nineteenth-century views of scientific method (see Bauer 1992) are based. Assis (2018, 97) provides a helpful point of departure in this respect, identifying that creative practice research—across a variety of different domains and media—can be thought of as *assemblages* (drawing on Deleuze) of layered systems, rather than singular, linear trajectories of discovery. The critical processes used to evaluate and discuss research should surely match the nature of work being created: yet this discussion can often instead match normative templates drawing on technical practices and existing methods by way of legitimation. However, just as with the archaeology of the computer mice mentioned above, only the creative work itself can fully communicate the layered, dynamic, and

---

3 In applied research, the extent to which this is the case may vary.

complex connections between art and context (socio, cultural, geographical, situational) regardless of how precisely technical attributes have been documented. In this respect, there is a gap between how *artistic* reception practices and *research* reception practices in creative work operate as systems.

Nattiez (1990, 18) comments that communications science has developed significantly since Roman Jakobson's model of linear information transmission from sender to receiver. Contrast this with how institutionalised research itself as a system works today: instrumentalised measurement is built on the foundation of linear relationships between "research question" and the production of "outcome." Extending this analogy, in musical communication and reception, Nattiez suggests that receivers have as much relevance to the *message* as creators through the idea of *esthesis*: likewise, in systems of research, is the path really a straight transmission from question to outcome, and can the *esthesis of research* (the outcome) influence the *poeisis* (the research question)? Therefore, a type of research question is required where outcome is permitted to be legitimate even in cases where it does not align at all with the creative starting points, yet still describes a purposeful track of critical enquiry and creative curiosity.

In contemporary research methodology, the complexity of experimental systems means that research questions can be mutable, that answers may not always occur in the domain of the question (and indeed, may occur in tangential domains or in cross-disciplinary contexts) and that experimental settings depend on context for their evaluation. Yet, in some institutional contexts such as research assessment exercises or faculty assessments, it still seems that the values from pre-twenty-first-century scholarship are today applied to creative practice research. This is increasingly problematic as science and the arts and humanities do not need to be thought of as polar opposites despite the continued governmental simplification of convenience in determining national funding priorities. Creative practice is, in a way, the ultimate complex, context-dependent system. By necessity, outcomes need to or exist within their contextual surroundings and the poeitic starting points and challenges of research may, depending on the nature of the project, have the opportunity to lead to creatively valid but ultimately unrelated end points. The working practices required to investigate the "questions" may change as an understanding of the creative issues they represent also evolves.

To this end, the reductive idea of a research question needs to be supplemented to accommodate the non-linear and complex nature of creative enquiry, not because it is deficient for its intended function. A research question, in a traditional sense, acts as a marker in a linear system of knowledge transmission.

THE CREATIVE QUESTION

I am hesitant to add the word *question* in expressing the idea of *creative questions*. However, I am not referring to question in the sense that question needs a corresponding *answer*, instead, this concerns an enquiry-based process that a particular idea, challenge, or stimulus involves. In a research context, this system importantly is more than considering a stimulus as a starting point. Creative issues can be precisely specified through their own unique expression in relevant media. Without translation into language, non-linguistic creativity can itself pose complex issues as the focus of enquiries that are challenging, thought-provoking, or indeed, questioning. The *process of focused creative enquiry* stemming from a creative question may be a differentiator between creative research and creativity in a more general sense. A creative question in this respect can serve to encompass those non-linguistic, non-textual questions: for music, these questions can be posed by sound itself. I am defining *creative question* as a type of research question specifically intended as a pragmatic research tool for use within creative practice. Creative questions should ideally have a status equal to research questions and this is necessary to help avoid reducing the scope of artistic discourse to areas that can only be substantiated through technical rationality.

At the root of a creative question is a challenge or exploratory proposition exposed by the artistic material or the artistic practice itself. It may also require cross-domain or interdisciplinary knowledge to formulate; yet importantly, there is no need to *translate* this challenge or material into other forms of discourse for it to function as a creative question and subsequently enable research processes. Should it be necessary to express a creative question in linguistic form, this of course may be possible and desirable for communicating about research, although as with any translation, information losses may occur.

A creative question could include:

- artistic materials that hold the potential for *future development*;
- "what-if" questions posed through combinations of materials, contexts, and cultures that are examined through practice.

The purpose of creative questions is to *enable* enquiry by means of an investigative working practice. In such a workflow, art meets craft and technique joins forces with context to provide the tools necessary for discovery-based, creative enquiry. Style becomes not a constraint or limitation, but a vehicle for investigation of new possibilities. According to the Frascati research manual (OECD 2015), research must confront the researcher with surprising and novel propositions: creative questions provide a framework for the exploration of those propositions as a way to *probe the unknown* rather than to validate the known. Lastly, creative questions function as tools to investigate emergent behaviour: focusing enquiry to provoke new and unexpected behaviours of materials, allowing the evaluation and identification of the properties of emergent structures. What appears as a continuum between an unexpected outcome and an expected outcome in the linguistic representation of creative questions may not be relevant or may not even connect to the space of available musical responses.

Perhaps creative questions can have answers, but not in the sense of literal answers. Creative answers are more than an initial response or reaction: they are carefully planned and executed items of knowledge in their own right brought about through research. Although expressed through media other than text, creative questions can be far from generic: by keeping their integrity in sound, visual, or symbolic forms of artistic expression,[4] we should expect that what constitutes answers can also occupy the same artistic domain.

In summary, creative questions:

- · embody a sense of exploration and critical enquiry;
- · investigate artistic issues directly in the relevant medium, rather than in translation;
- · can be answered, but not necessarily in the literal meaning of reply or simplistic free-form response. Creative answers are the effects of *informed* artistic exploration. They address the issues posed by the original ideas and can also result in the creation of additional creative questions;
- · allow for the idea of emergence to influence research enquiry;
- · should be held open to challenge and new directions of exploration or even their own redefinition as work progresses.

ARTISTIC ACCOUNTABILITY

In order for creative questions to have similar properties to research questions as resources that are called upon to shape enquiry, it is necessary to form a bond between them and the ways in which they are represented in discourse. The concept of artistic accountability is proposed to help unite the *creative envelope* (below) with creative questions in a way that does not require post-hoc theorising to discover. Artistic accountability is the glue that binds research, practice, and experience together. This can take the form of a linguistic expression of knowledge that might not be possible to hear in the music, rather than a description (translation) of musical features and constructions that are already available within the music through listening to it. Artistic accountability is not justification: justification concerns the legitimation of ideas, whereas accountability concerns the authentic generation of ideas within a defined artistic vision.

Having a consistent artistic vision doesn't necessarily mean sticking to one type of material or a single set of realisation processes, nor is it a call for the rejection of technical rationality where it becomes necessary in accounting for that vision—instead, to enable artistic accountability, technical rationality should be aligned, and not post-theorised, to the art being created. For example, composition can retain a consistency of artistic vision even when materials used to express the design ideas change during development. Artistic accountability is ultimately straightforward: the documentation and discourse of creative work should, in an honest, thorough, and accountable sense itself *believe in all aspects* of that work. Accountability is not a tool to graft external legitimacy onto creative work.

---

4 Such as poetry, for example.

ARTISTIC ACCOUNTABILITY AND RISK

Creating artistic accountability demands a reappraisal of the qualities of risk, acknowledging that risk is not a factor to be mitigated but instead, an integral and enabling part of creative processes. Artistic risk is not economic risk or bureaucratic risk. Yet, in institutional research discourse, is unnecessary complexity generated through aligning the notion of risk in creative practice to such meanings? Commonly, risk is thought of as a negative quantity, which needs normalisation or mitigation through actions. Risk is there to be *minimised*. In creativity, the situation is different: risk becomes a positive force, creating opportunity where none previously existed. *Artistic risk* can be safely *maximised* if required (yet, sometimes the bureaucracy of style and genre are introduced to regulate it). Consequently, reducing exposure to artistic risk also constrains the scope of experimental practice in creative research.

Risk can result in outcomes that are not always possible to pre-think or pre-calculate, and this element forms part of the workflow of creative investigation. Although unmanaged risks are built in to manageable structures in order to explore, refine, and create, this process *is not* mitigation. In business, mitigation is mostly about control (even where risk-taking itself is deliberately part of a planned sequence of actions), course-correcting a variance from the expected, managing back towards the known direction of strategy. It should be noted that in musical composition this process *also* happens: composers may predefine a structure and generate materials specifically to fit. However, risks are not mitigated in an economic sense: creative material that does not fit the underlying strategy will itself need modification, exploration, or curation, and sometimes it is necessary to change the overall plan itself and abandon the strategy by which the risks are themselves addressed. Ultimately, most creative risks can carry an element of individual choice and these acts of evaluative self-determination can lead to a working research practice that is individual, yet is also informed, pragmatic, and flexible. Such behaviour does not emerge from following a risk register and inhabits the wider context of the experimental system of creativity. Artistic accountability therefore helps connect the domain of risk to the creative vision of the artist or community.

THE CREATIVE ENVELOPE

Research processes often require a higher-level formalisation to encapsulate the initial proposition within a wrapper of both specific methodology and subject-domain expectations for processes and outcomes. In social science, the synthesis of process and method can be encapsulated within normative forms of *research design*. The research design is not usually expected to change dramatically or itself evolve along tangential avenues as work progresses. However, such formalisations are frequently used in evaluative processes where the success of research is also related back to the core proposition. Finding a form to encapsulate the space of possibilities in which creativity can take place can be problematic when it comes to the interaction of creative practice with institutional research reporting. Ideally, creativity would exist within a space that is flexible, yet bounded by artistic goals that themselves may be mutable, revisited, or change over time. Creative practice is effectively a form of *dynamic* research design. In order to help address the gap between artistic process and research accountability, the notion of a *creative envelope* is proposed here as a way of expressing the research design for a creative project in an accountable, yet sufficiently flexible manner.

The *creative envelope* is drawn from a synthesis of the idea of an "envelope" as a high-level expression of the limits of available possibilities for creative development and the idea of an envelope being a boundary between an object and the broader surrounding environment, as it is in the architectural concept of a *building envelope* (see Kumar and Raheja 2016). These two ideas combine to define the space of available creative options, and how those options in practice become demarcated with respect to others. Having a creative envelope avoids the need for imposing a single pre-designed methodology of investigation where it is not relevant to the artistic objectives under development; meanwhile, it acknowledges that design and process will relate both to the materials being worked upon and to their reception in practice. In architecture, the boundary between the contents of the envelope and the outside environment is an entity charged with being more than the facade of a building: it is an expression of culture, human values, and design considerations. The building envelope concerns how people connect to materials and as a consequence, how the reception and experience of design can map onto the parameters of creation. In music, materials and contexts have their own affordances that determine the nature of the creative envelope in their artistic realisation. Without thinking of a creative envelope as *both* a boundary and a flexible container, the "knowledge" of creativity risks being framed instead by technical rationality alone. Technical rationality is a quantity that can be traded, creates a goods-logic of knowledge supply, and obscures the networks of complex interaction that might underpin an artistic creation. Building design offers another useful parallel: a *tight building envelope* may concern internal structures that are relatively impermeable and inaccessible to the surrounding environment, and a loose building envelope may offer the opportunity for greater interface between the building and situation. A creative envelope then is not simply an expression of the boundaries of artistic possibility: it is formed from a combination of starting intentions, design constraints, creative enquiry processes, emergent properties, evaluative thinking, and dynamic processes (such as chance, change, and other forms of complex interaction) all mixed together in a non-linear way. The idea of the creative envelope is proposed as a tool to help flatten this multidimensional space, creating a zone for creative enquiry that is flexible, yet entirely definable when it is aligned to *artistic accountability*.

CONCLUSION

The ideas presented above are personal views and will not be fully generalisable for all forms of creative endeavour. They are intended to be helpful in rethinking the presentation of creative research within existing research frameworks, arguing for new and subject-appropriate ways of framing creative research. However, due to the nature of creativity where subverting the normal, or commenting on, extending, and reframing ideas comes with a flexibility to be as process driven or as inspirational as required, exceptions to ontologies will always emerge and are to be expected. To this end, creating a bridge between different modes of research across disciplines, accounting for practices where research unites enquiry with creativity, is a necessary developmental step in today's increasingly interdisciplinary research culture. *Artistic accountability*, the *creative envelope*, and the idea of the *creative question* are proposed as ways in which the institutional research discourse around creative practice can be opened up with integrity to the work involved and people who make it.

REFERENCES

Armstrong, Thomas. 2020. "Picking Up the Pieces: An Autoethnographic Journey into Artistic Research." Paper presented at the virtual conference The Autoethnography of Composition and the Composition of Autoethnography, Glasgow, 17–18 June 2020. Accessed 27 April 2021. https://openresearch.surrey.ac.uk/esploro/outputs/conferencePaper/Picking-Up-the-pieces-An-Autoethnographic-Journey-into-Artistic-Research/99527423602346.

Assis, Paulo de. 2014. "Epistemic Complexity and Experimental Systems in Music Performance." In *Artistic Experimentation in Music: An Anthology*, edited by Darla Crispin and Bob Gilmore, 41–54. Orpheus Institute Series. Leuven: Leuven University Press.

———. 2018. *Logic of Experimentation: Rethinking Music Performance through Artistic Research*. Orpheus Institute Series. Leuven: Leuven University Press.

Bauer, Henry H. 1992. *Scientific Literacy and the Myth of the Scientific Method*. Urbana: University of Illinois Press.

Beale, Gareth, John Schofield, and Jim Austin. 2018. "The Archaeology of the Digital Periphery: Computer Mice and the Archaeology of the Early Digital Era." *Journal of Contemporary Archaeology* 5 (2): 154–73.

Brousseau, Eric, and Thierry Pénard. 2007. "The Economics of Digital Business Models: A Framework for Analyzing the Economics of Platforms." *Review of Network Economics* 6 (2): 81–114.

Bryman, Alan. 2012. *Social Research Methods*. 4th ed. Oxford: Oxford University Press.

Clarke, Eric F., and Mark Doffman. 2017. *Distributed Creativity: Collaboration and Improvisation in Contemporary Music*. New York: Oxford University Press.

Cook, Nicholas. 2013. *Beyond the Score: Music as Performance*. New York: Oxford University Press.

Croft, John. 2015. "Composition Is Not Research." *Tempo* 69 (272): 6–11.

Dewey, John. (1934) 1958. *Art as Experience*. New York: Capricorn Books. First published 1934 (New York: Minton, Balch & Co.).

Field, Ambrose. 2021. "Redefining Progress at the Intersection of AI and Artistic Research." In *Experience Music Experiment: Pragmatism and Artistic Research*, edited by William Brooks, 249–62. Orpheus Institute Series. Leuven: Leuven University Press.

Goldstein, Jeffrey. 2013. "Complexity and Philosophy: Re-imagining Emergence; Part 1." *Emergence: Complexity and Organization* 15 (2): 77–103.

Harrison, Scott D., ed. 2013. *Research and Research Education in Music Performance and Pedagogy*. Dordrecht: Springer Netherlands.

Kumar, Gireendra, and Gaurav Raheja. 2016. "Design Determinants of Building Envelope for Sustainable Built Environment: A Review." *International Journal of Built Environment and Sustainability* 3 (2): 111–18. https://doi.org/10.11113/ijbes.v3.n2.127.

Latour, Bruno. 1996. "On Actor-Network Theory: A Few Clarifications." *Soziale Welt* 47 (4): 369–81.

Lusch, Robert F., and Stephen L. Vargo, eds. (2006) 2014. "Service-Dominant Logic: What It Is, What It Is Not, What It Might Be." In *The Service-Dominant Logic of Marketing: Dialog, Debate, and Directions*, 43–56. New York: Routledge. First published 2006 (Armonk, NY: M. E. Sharpe).

Nattiez, Jean-Jacques. 1990. *Music and Discourse: Toward a Semiology of Music*. Translated by Carolyn Abbate. Princeton, NJ: Princeton University Press. First published 1987 as *Musicologie générale et sémiologie* (Paris: Christian Bourgois).

OECD. 2015. *Frascati Manual 2015: Guidelines for Collecting and Reporting Data on Research and Experimental Development*. OECD. Accessed 29 April 2021. https://www.oecd-ilibrary.org/science-and-technology/frascati-manual-2015_9789264239012-en.

Piccini, Angela. 2002. "An Historiographic Perspective on Practice as Research." PARIP (Practice as Research in Performance: 2001–2006), University of Bristol. Accessed 27 April 2021. http://www.bris.ac.uk/parip/t_ap.htm.

Reeves, Camden. 2016. "Composition, Research and Pseudo-Science: A Response to John Croft." *Tempo* 70 (275): 50–59.

Rheinberger, Hans-Jörg. 2015. "Difference Machines: Time in Experimental Systems." *Configurations* 23 (2): 165–76.

Rink, John. 2003. "In Respect of Performance: The View from Musicology." *Psychology of Music* 31 (3): 303–23.

Rubinoff, Kailan R. 2017. "Toward a Revolutionary Model of Music Pedagogy: The Paris Conservatoire, Hugot and Wunderlich's *Méthode de flûte*, and the Disciplining of the Musician." *Journal of Musicology* 34 (4): 473–514.

Schön, Donald A. (1983) 2016. *The Reflective Practitioner: How Professionals Think in Action*. Abingdon, UK: Routledge. First published 1983 (New York: Basic Books).

Designing Audience–Work Relationships

Marko Ciciliani

University of Music and Performing Arts Graz, Austria

INTRODUCTION

In this chapter, I investigate the relationship between audience members and the presentation of an audiovisual work, as well as the extent to which this relationship can be designed as an aesthetic experience by applying particular set-ups and possibilities for interaction.[1] My focus will lie on works that combine aspects typical of concert situations and of installations, works that create a particular situation through which audience members encounter the work. In order to differentiate between various set-ups, as a point of orientation I first establish a short catalogue of attributes that typically distinguish concert situations from installations—specifically, such installations that aesthetically include the space in which they are presented. Although this catalogue is based on simplifications—as I show below, there are many examples, even historical ones, where concert works are imbued with characteristics of installations and vice versa—its purpose is to provide a set of criteria that will help differentiate the qualities of individual arrangements. In this context, the chapter's focus will lie on works using a set-up that can be seen as a hybrid between the concert and the installation categories, creating a particular situation through which audience members encounter the work in question. Furthermore, the role of audience participation will be investigated in these contexts, specifically through possibilities for interacting with elements of the presented works. Complementary to the set-up, interaction is considered another means of shaping and designing the audience–work relationship.

After providing a historical perspective on hybrid works and my personal motivation for exploring such settings, the aspects I will discuss in this chapter refer to durations and temporal delimitations, contractions and expansions of attention, considerations of proxemics and social aspects within artworks, audience participation, and the role of narrativity and memory. In order to directly compare different solutions using hybrids in between concert and installation settings and different audience–work relationships, I will discuss three audiovisual projects that I created in the recent past: *Anna & Marie* (2018–19), *Rave Séance* (2020), and *Why Frets?* (2020, in progress).

---

1   This article has been written as part of the research project GAPPP, funded by the Austrian Science Fund FWF as AR 364-G24.

Modes of perception induced by concert settings and installations

Many works in the field of installation art[2] place importance on the aspect of space. Even when sound is not emitted through spatially distributed sound sources, the relationship of sound and a particular acoustic situation often gains particular relevance. When the space becomes part of the work, the boundaries between what lies inside and what lies outside the work often become blurred. This applies both to the work's temporal organisation—when no clear beginnings or endings can be identified—and to its audiovisual material. Concert situations usually provide clear demarcations as to what belongs to the presented artwork. In the temporal dimension, this is designated by well-defined beginnings and endings of pieces, while in terms of material, the performers' musical intentions usually declare what lies inside and outside the presented work—for example, the coughing of an audience member or a musician's loud page turn are not considered part of the work.[3] In an installation situation, the boundaries of time and material can be less distinct, however. Many installation works do not have clear beginnings and endings, and the surrounding space often becomes a buffer zone that only gradually transitions between the work of art and the outside world. As a result, sounds that originate not in the set-up of the installation but in the neighbouring environment also are often perceived as part of the overall situation belonging to the work: unlike the cough of an audience member during a concert, accidental sounds are more likely to be integrated into the experience of an installation. In an installation, all present elements thus establish relationships of varying qualities and hierarchies. What takes place in between them creates what Gernot Böhme describes as atmospheres, which "are always spatial, 'borderless, poured out, at the same time placeless, i.e. not localizable,'[4] they are poignant and powerful emotions, spatial carriers of moods" (2013, 29, my translation). Böhme emphasises that atmospheres have an ephemeral quality but nonetheless form a substantial part of an aesthetic experience. While atmospheres always influence modes of perception—in concerts just as much as in installations—in the latter they tend to be perceived as part of the work, or at least as part of the experience that is facilitated by the work, while in the former they are usually considered to be more circumstantial and therefore not part of the work proper.

When Anne Ring Petersen compares photography with installations, she states: "Where photography selects one single perspective for its viewer, installation art opens up for many perspectives and leaves it up to the viewer to choose" (Petersen 2015, 14). I propose that this applies in much the same way to concert situations and installations if visitors are allowed to move freely in the space: the ability to choose their location in relation to the work gives audience members a form of agency that they do not have in a traditional concert situation.

---

2 I also include all kinds of sound installations in the term *installation*.
3 Although the latter is also the result of the performer's intention, it is motivated not by musical considerations but by practical necessities in the performance.
4 Here, Böhme is quoting Hermann Schmitz.

However, in installations changes of perspective do not take place only by physically taking various positions in the space, but also by successively directing the focus of attention to a variety of phenomena. Such meandering shifts of attention are facilitated if the situation offers a certain degree of redundancy, meaning that the visitor can move their attention away from a particular phenomenon and direct it elsewhere without being concerned that they might miss a unique event. This is yet another aspect where concert works often differ: these works tend to be characterised by more concentrated organisations of material and far fewer redundancies; moments of distraction can thus give the audience member the impression that they have missed something. In installations, the spatial flexibility and continuous accessibility usually also accentuate a social quality in the experience. The possibility of "meandering attention" also allows for encounters with other visitors. This is less likely in concerts because of the gravity of attention that pulls towards the performance area, which throws the audience members back on themselves, turning the listening experience to a solitary one (Schröder 2014, 29).

Before the term *installation art* became common, such arrangements in space were referred to as *environments* or *environmental art*. The term *environment* seems more suitable than the later *installation* for describing the quality of the encounter between audience members and the work of art. An environment encompasses the individual and accordingly suggests the adoption of a "wide-angle" perspective in order to comprehend it. Nikos Papastergiadis and Amelia Barikin refer to this mode of perception as the "ambient perspective," which they describe as a response to a "contemporary condition": "Attention is now dispersed. It is not concentrated towards a singular point in the horizon" (Papastergiadis and Barikin 2015, 81). Such a "singular point" would be more similar to a concert work, which demands full focal attention.

Finally, installations that are spatially spread out introduce an additional layer or temporality that is established by the audience member's movement while exploring the space. Concert works create their own structured temporal organisation, which is affected only by the audience member's state of concentration. The sonic layers of installation works are usually also arranged and structured in time; however, an additional temporal layer results from the exploration of the space, an exploration that is necessary in order to experience the work more comprehensively. This temporality "is not a mechanical chain of extraction and construction, but an iterative process of selecting and interlacing" (Papastergiadis and Barikin 2015, 83), and this is precisely what Michael Fried criticised as art's "theatricality" in his seminal article "Art and Objecthood" (Fried [1967] 1995). Fried attacks "literalist art," by which he refers to practices of minimalist sculptures that were not meant to be self-contained but also included the environment as part of an expanded situation. Exploring such an expanded artwork requires time and movement, which Fried designates as theatre: "theatre and theatricality are at war today, not simply with modernist painting (or modernist painting and sculpture), but with art as such" (ibid., 139). Fried's fierce criticism is interesting because it shows the radicality of the departure from modernist paradigms ("focal attention" on a work) introduced by those works that expand beyond their objecthood into the atmospheric and ambient realm ("meandering attention").

Table 16.1 provides a summary of the aforementioned differences between concert works and installation works.

Attributes of concert works	Attributes of installation works
Temporally delimited	Temporally open
Single layer of temporality	Double layer of temporality
Concentrated material	Redundant material
Close focus of attention	Wide-angle attention (ambient perspective)
Atmosphere is circumstantial	Atmosphere is part of the work
Solitary situation	Social situation

Table 16.1.

While these attributes are simplifications, they nevertheless designate pronounced tendencies in the two areas. The following sections will explore these tendencies and discuss hybrid forms applied in particular works.

Hybrids in historical perspective

Various aspects that are quite typical of installations have already entered into many concert works, sometimes even long before the existence of installation art as an artistic practice. This can be observed, for example, in the application of timescales that exceed what is usually considered practical in concert pieces. In the Romantic period, operas and symphonic works already took on epic lengths—Anton Bruckner's Eighth and Ninth symphonies are close to ninety minutes in duration, Gustav Mahler's Third around one hundred minutes, and some of Richard Wagner's operas last more than five hours. While these lengthy pieces are very dense in their musical material, structure, and variety, the experience of duration took on a fundamentally different character when combined with scarce or redundant forms of material. A well-known first example of such a work is *Vexations* by Erik Satie, composed in 1893. Consisting of only eighteen notes, it requires 840 repetitions that add up to a duration of around eighteen hours (Prendergast 2003, 7). The first reported complete performance, however, did not take place until 1963 in New York, a time and place where minimalist concert pieces with extreme durations were being explored by various composers, for example by La Monte Young in his *Compositions 1960* or in pieces like *The Second Dream of the High Tension Line Stepdown Transformer* of 1962.[5]

---

5   In the domain of film, long durations with minimal material were explored at the same time in New York, too, including by Andy Warhol in his films *Sleep* (1963), which shows his partner John Giorno sleeping for the duration of five hours and twenty minutes, and *Empire* (1964), showing a static shot of the illuminated Empire State Building in New York with a running time of approximately eight hours.

338

Table 16.1. Typical attributes of concert and installation works.

Besides minimalist reductions of material, it is also noteworthy that the displaying of processes became the focus of some artists' interest. Compositions like *Pendulum Music* by Steve Reich (1968) or *I Am Sitting in a Room* by Alvin Lucier (1970) set a process in motion that no longer is actively influenced following its initiation. The piece ends when the process comes to a halt, or—in the case of the latter work—when "it reaches the point of diminishing returns" (Lucier [1980] 1995, 86). This approach differs quite fundamentally from more traditional compositional approaches in which the composer is in control of all sonic details from beginning to end. In process-oriented works, attention focuses upon a process that then takes its course. Once the process becomes clear to the audience, it also allows for predictability and thus produces a redundancy that provides space for meandering attention.

Starting in the 1950s, many works in the context of happenings or Fluxus allowed the audience to move around freely during performances, which facilitated an "ambient perspective" when encountering works that were often multilayered. The relationship between the audience and the presentation thus became an aspect of the artistic design (Kirby 1965, 25). In the field of music, similar explorations of new modes of presentation took place, for example at the renowned Philips Pavilion at the World's Fair in Brussels in 1958, where the compositions *Concret PH* by Iannis Xenakis and *Poème électronique* by Edgard Varèse were presented in a multi-speaker setting to a non-seated audience. The former piece was played while the audience was entering the space. During the presentation of the latter work, a double projection of a film of static, mainly black-and-white photographs was displayed that had been arranged by Le Corbusier. Additional projections of images were shown during the presentation along with a light design of changing coloured light patterns. The visual artistic concept also extended to the design of the entire building, for which both Xenakis and Corbusier were responsible (Nanz 2006, 20–24).

More recently, it is not uncommon for composers to experiment with combinations of attributes typical of installations and attributes that are characteristic of concert pieces. Furthermore, curators of festivals often place performances in contexts for which the works were originally not intended, which sometimes entails a fundamentally different experience. In 2016, for example, several string quartets by Dmitri Shostakovich were performed simultaneously at the Wien Modern festival in Vienna. During this event, the audience was also allowed to move between the string quartets, which were spatially distributed in the concert hall (Weidringer 2016).

Personal motivations

In my own work, I had felt the need to find alternatives to the proscenium-type[6] concert format for some time. Since most of my projects are concert works that also contain visual elements (mostly video, light, or laser projections), it feels plausible to arrange the performance space in a way that resonates with the work's artistic content or focus. In a previous publication, I drew a comparison between the presentation of an audiovisual work and an act of enunciation, in the sense that an audience is addressed in a particular way (Ciciliani 2017). In this earlier paper, I distinguished between the enunciated, that is, the work proper, and the act of enunciation, that is, all the circumstances that are part of its presentation, which includes not only the act of performance but also other circumstances, such as the architectural design, its demographic function, light conditions, and so on. With this comparison, I aimed to raise awareness of the many aspects that lie both within and outside the work that affect the experience of a performance. Such a "widened lens" or ambient perspective is "a way of addressing both the feedback between the producer and the receiver of aesthetic meaning, and the wider social context in which media operate to generate new dynamics in the cohesion and dispersion of focus and attention" (Papastergiadis and Barikin 2015, 86). While the ambient perspective that installations evoke has a strong appeal to me as an aesthetic experience, at the same time I also feel drawn to the focal attention that performances evoke. As a result of this, in the recent past I explored hybrid formats that combine attributes of both concert works and installations, searching for particular modes of communication, and in consequence designing specific encounters between audience members and the work in question that are suitable for the given project.

Durations and temporal delimitations (*Rave Séance* and *Why Frets?*)

In my project *Rave Séance* I created an installation-like set-up with a circular arrangement of five tables. Four of these tables provide space for up to twelve audience members to sit down on pillows. Other audience members can move freely in the space around those tables. A time-variant light design accentuates the circular shape of the arrangement with five long bar lamps that are also arranged circularly around the tables, and five spotlights that are positioned under the tables, pointing inwards towards the centre of the arrangement.

---

6 The term *proscenium* designates the arc or frame that encloses the performance area. The term *proscenium-style* is a more generalised form, designating any performance where the stage area is the focus of attention. I prefer to use the term *proscenium-style* instead of *stage-based*, for example, because the former refers to the framing of the action onstage, which thus describes what lies inside and outside the work. This also extends to a clear division between performance area and audience. I therefore extend the meaning of the proscenium to a stage of attention during the presentation of a work.

In this central area, laser projections are displayed at various points in the piece (plate 16.1).[7]

At the fifth table, I am seated in my role as performer. While the audience tables are equipped with large buttons that are illuminated at various points and allow for interaction, my table holds a touch-sensitive controller and a modular synthesiser. I am present as a performer for the entire time this work is presented, operating the electronics and at certain points also using my voice, which is heavily processed.

I refer to *Rave Séance* as a performative installation. It does not have a specific start and end and the audience can enter and leave as they please. The audio-visual material never repeats in identical ways, but it is organised in so-called cycles that are structured similarly, each of them lasting between twelve to twenty minutes. At the premiere of this work at the A Dela? festival at Ljudmila, a venue in Ljubljana, Slovenia, on 27 August 2020, I performed for three hours, starting at eight p.m. and finishing at eleven p.m. A second shorter perform-ance took place on 15 September 2020 at the Audio Mostly Conference at the IEM in Graz, Austria. To avoid marking a "beginning" of the performance, in both cases I started with no audience in the space, so the work was already underway when the first audience members entered.

As the performance element is very present in this project, clear temporal demarcations would have given it the character of a concert piece. As I envis-aged an event that is stretched out over a longer period, I composed a circular form that repeats seamlessly in non-identical ways. In this way, I created redun-dancy on the level of the material. The cycles were composed in such a way that there were extended periods of time when my role as performer was quite passive. However, when I used my voice, light fixtures that were pointed at me were turned on, which created a strong point of emphasis, placing myself as performer at the centre of attention. Other points of emphasis were marked by the turning on of the laser or by moments when audience members were able to interact with the performance by pressing the buttons on the tables. The possibility of interaction was indicated by turning on the lights in the buttons (plate 16.2a–b).

Overall, my impression was that this project successfully combined aspects that are typical of a concert piece with aspects that are associated with installa-tion works. The extended duration, combined with the alternatives offered to the audience of standing, sitting, or moving around, introduced a fluidity that usually is not found in concert works. At the same time, the cyclical form con-tained dramatic moments when attention was drawn towards particular events, such as the vocal section, the laser designs, or the modes of interaction. With regard to the steering of attention, I would say that these were moments of contraction, or moments when attention converged to a point, while alterna-tively there were also moments that encouraged a more ambient perspective and a meandering of attention. In summary, I would say that this combina-

---

7   A detailed description of the work, along with a video trailer, can be found at http://www.ciciliani.com/rave-sceance.html.

tion of an installation-like set-up and a performance created dynamic shifts of attention—contracting and expanding—depending on whether attention was attracted to certain events or let loose by exposing it to textures involving greater redundancies.

With regard to temporal organisation, I found myself in a very different situation when working on a net-art website, which forms part of my project *Why Frets?* (started in 2020 and still in progress). This project as a whole comprises a series of websites as forms of audiovisual net-art, an audiovisual installation, a performance lecture for PowerPoint and electric guitar, and a composition for three electric guitars. While working on this net-art website, I created a virtual 3D space in which the user can navigate and interact with various objects that are present in the virtual space (plate 16.3). The movement and the interactions all entail dynamic changes in the sound layers that accompany the experience.[8]

Initially, I approached this project as an interactive sound installation in virtual space with a fixed number of elements distributed in the environment that were related to sonic events exhibiting different qualities and behaviours. My original idea was that I wanted to give the user a sense of liveness when interacting with the project, and convey the impression that she or he is acting as a performer in the virtual scenario. While working on this project, I increasingly felt dissatisfied with the arrangement of a virtual installation as it did not incite the engagement I was looking for, and I was lacking a sense of direction and development. As I wondered how I could enforce the impression of a performance, I decided to go the opposite way to *Rave Séance*: instead of extending duration in order to avoid the impression of a concert work, here I decided to introduce a clear beginning and end in order to support the impression of a performance. Both projects provided almost contrary points of departure. While in *Rave Séance* it was the performance that formed the main focus and that I felt the need to counterbalance, in the net-art project I found myself with a static situation that was devoid of any directionality. I introduced this directionality by designing a dramaturgy of events, where certain user behaviours unlocked new possibilities. Instead of only introducing new events, other objects that offered interactions disappeared after a certain number of events had been triggered. Furthermore, I added texts that appeared in reaction to events just triggered, which inserted aspects of a story. I address the aspect of narrativity in greater detail in the section "Asynchronous presence in *Why Frets?*" below.

Contractions and expansions of attention (Anna & Marie)

In my introduction to *Rave Séance* in the preceding section, I described moments of contraction and expansion of attention that took place during the performance. In this section I present the set-up of *Anna & Marie* and observe how similar changes of attention occurred as in *Rave Séance*, while the set-up and the mode of presentation in both works differed strongly.

---

8 The website can be found at https://whyfrets.iem.sh.

In 2019 my project *Anna & Marie* was presented over a period of three days at the Donaueschinger Musiktage in Germany. *Anna & Marie* is a concert piece for two violinists—one playing electric violin and the other Baroque violin—and generative electronics performed in the environment of an installation. The entire set-up encompasses two navigable 3D environments that are projected onto two large screens, nine illuminated panels, light design, torsos of dolls, and wireless earpieces that are scattered across the floor. Large beanbags were distributed in the space, which allowed the audience to sit comfortably and change orientation as they pleased. Over the course of the three days of the festival, a total of eight individual performances were presented that all differed from each other in both musical and visual terms. In between the performances, the environment was available as an installation. Every performance ended with a unique audiovisual state that led seamlessly into the installation mode: sound textures of different characters and qualities, light designs with different sets of colours, and a story that could be followed on the scattered earpieces in the form of a recorded dialogue. The narrative was different after each performance.

During the installation phase, the audience had the possibility of interacting with the environment in various ways: tablets were distributed throughout the space that could be picked up and pointed at the nine panels, leading to the generation of an augmented reality with additional visual phenomena and sounds (plate 16.4). Furthermore, the audience was able to move through the 3D spaces presented on the main projection screens using game controllers. During the performances, the violinists navigated these 3D spaces by playing their instruments.[9] In the following, I will focus on how the overall situation and mode of perception changed between the different states of this work—that is, whether a performance was taking place, or whether the space was being presented to the audience as an audiovisual installation.

During the concerts, the violinists stood in two positions in the space about ten metres apart from each other and facing in different directions (plate 16.5). Both stood next to one of the screens with the 3D environments that related to their actions. From most positions in the space it was not possible for the audience to see both violinists and their screens at the same time, hence the audience members usually focused on one of the two players in turn. During the performances, audience members could use the earpieces that were randomly scattered throughout the space to follow the storyline that was being generated in real time by the playing of the musicians. The number of available earpieces was deliberately lower than the number of audience members, which led some of the visitors to share a single earpiece, while others passed theirs on to other people during the performance. On a subtle level, this introduced social exchange—facilitated by the informal seating on the large cushions—which is rather uncommon for conventional concert formats. Otherwise, the audience behaved in a similar way to classical concerts in the sense that they avoided

---

9   For a detailed description of the project, please refer to Ciciliani and Lüneburg (2021); additional information and detailed video documentations can be found at http://www.ciciliani.com/anna--marie.html.

unnecessary physical movement and remained quiet. Due to the set-up in the space and the scarcity of earpieces, the experience of the performance was necessarily fragmented, as it was impossible to follow both violinists' actions throughout, and it was unlikely that anybody would follow the complete story-line on an earpiece. The playing of the violinists along with their navigation in the 3D environments that they controlled formed the centre of attention. While the other elements of the set-up such as the nine illuminated panels, the light design, and the dolls, receded into the background of the experience, the violinists not only strongly contributed to the general atmosphere but also unobtrusively offered points of distraction that allowed for meandering attention.

As mentioned above, the audiovisual setting of the installation emerged directly from the preceding performance. In this situation there were no predominant centres of attention. Now, however, the possibilities for interaction were larger for the audience members. While it was not forbidden for the audience to move around in the space during the concerts, the overall situation discouraged it as this would have blocked other audience members' lines of sight and would have created noise, which could have been felt to disturb others. During the installation phase, however, it felt more appropriate to move around than to sit in one place. Forms of interaction available to the audience included the aforementioned use of tablets for the generation of augmented reality, the use of game controllers to move through the 3D environments, and the use of the earpieces to listen to the version of the story that had been generated during the most recent performance (plate 16.6). Altogether, in my impression, the overall situation was quite typical for an installation, in the sense that there were manifold different phenomena that could be addressed in turn, and which established relationships of different qualities with one another. The overall material had a redundant quality that facilitated meandering attention and did not impose the feeling that one needed to be quiet to avoid disturbing other visitors.

The sonic part of the installation consisted of a sound layer that was distributed throughout the space. While this sound layer constantly changed, its general character nevertheless remained the same. The interactions of the audience with the augmented reality and the 3D environment also produced additional sources of sound that complemented the autonomously playing sound layer. Depending on the number of visitors and their activities, the overall sonic situation was sometimes denser than at other times. This entailed a different social situation than during the performance. While in the latter, there was potentially a more direct sort of exchange between audience members due to the sharing of the earpieces, during the installation parts the audience actively contributed to the overall sonic state, which affected not only their personal experience but also the experience of everybody else present in the space.

To summarise, *Anna & Marie* combines an installation and performances in turn in the same space. The performances are embedded in the environment of the installation, while the sound material and narrative of the installation depends on the preceding performance. In contrast to a piece such as *Rave Séance*, where the performance lasts for the entire duration of the presentation, in *Anna & Marie* there were distinct performances at set times, and phases in between during which the installation could be experienced. To what extent did modes of perception change between the performance and the installation? While during the performances, the overall set-up already led to a somewhat fragmented experience, there nevertheless were strong foci of attention and the overall character of a more conventional concert situation, which led to corresponding behaviour on the part of the audience. The installation, however, encouraged meandering attention to a much greater extent than the concert performances. The shift from concert to installation and vice versa can be described as a contraction and widening of a "lens" of attention. The experience of the installation in my perception clearly asked for an ambient perspective, whereas the concert was characterised by focal points of attention.

The social and proxemics (*Anna & Marie*, *Rave Séance*)

In this section I would like to reflect on how the set-up of a space, the positioning of the elements of a work in relation to the audience, and olfactory design affect social aspects and sensations of intimacy. As points of orientation, I apply several criteria that Edward T. Hall described in his investigations regarding proxemics (1966), which he defines as "the term I have coined for the interrelated observations and theories of man's use of space as a specialized elaboration of culture" (ibid., 1).

Hall differentiates four categories of distance that elicit distinct social behaviours and ways of perceiving other people: intimate, personal, social, and public space. Each of the categories is characterised by different modes of perceiving another person. For example, when we are very near to another person (intimate space), we can often smell them, but due to our close proximity, we have to move our eyes actively in order to visually capture their entire face. From a distance out of arm's reach, we can keep our eyes steady and see the person's entire face, but the distance is usually too great for olfactory perception. Moreover, when in "intimate space," conversations can take place by whispering or talking very softly, while larger distances require louder speech. In the following, I will apply proxemic considerations not only to the relationship between audience members and performers in a hybrid situation, but also to the relationship between the artwork and audience members. Although an encounter with another person is very different from being exposed to an artwork, I contend that the distance at which we encounter individual elements of the latter nevertheless entails different qualities in the aesthetic experience. In this case, too, Hall's differentiated observations are helpful for understanding these qualitative differences. Figure 16.1 shows a summary of Hall's classifications and the characteristics of each category.

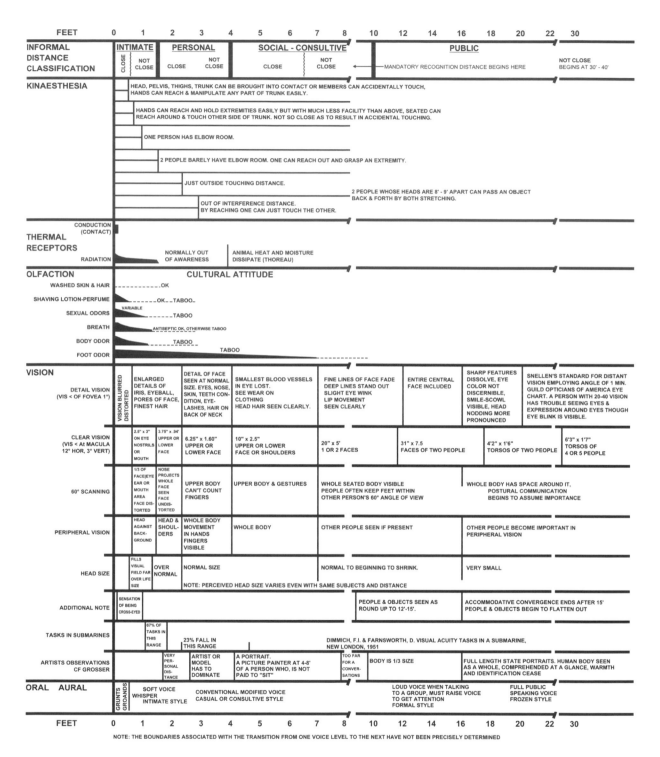

Figure 16.1.

Figure 16.1. Table of proxemic perception according to Edward T. Hall (1966, 126–27).

In *Anna & Marie* and in *Rave Séance* I came up with specific set-ups and arrangements to design the space in order to generate different qualities of intimacy. While in *Anna & Marie*, I intended to create a general atmosphere of intimacy between audience members and the various phenomena in the space, in *Rave Séance* I additionally aimed to create intimacy within a smaller group of audience members and the performer. The main subject of *Anna & Marie* is the lives of two female anatomists and wax-model artists who lived in the eighteenth century. The video projections and the panels that were distributed throughout the space all showed images that related to their works. The size of the space at the premiere was seven by twenty metres. At a height of three meters, the ceiling was relatively low when seen in proportion to the surface, which gave it the character of a domestic room rather than a public concert hall. During the concerts the room was rather densely populated, which meant that audience members were sitting within what Hall calls "personal space" (that is, within arm's reach), which is not an unusual arrangement for concert situations. While the focus of attention gravitates towards particular phenomena in the space—during the concerts, these were the performances of the two violinists—I would argue that the feeling of physical closeness to another person is not felt as strongly as in direct interpersonal encounters. Since the violinists' performance area was neither elevated nor otherwise demarcated (apart from the presence of a music stand), audience members and the performers were closer to each other than in standard concert situations, however. The distance between the violinists and the closest audience members was less than one and a half metres, which, according to Hall, falls into the close end of "social space." Since in *Anna & Marie* the violinists were standing while the audience was seated on cushions on the floor, there was an additional vertical distance, which, in social as well as in typical concert situations, designates relationships of dominance and subordination. Another small detail worth mentioning is the earpieces that audience members used to follow the narrative. By holding a piece of equipment against their ear, they brought it into their closest intimate space, which also involved the sense of touch. The sense of intimacy was intensified as the narrative was told as a dialogue between the two protagonists. In my impression, listening to this personal conversation with an earpiece evoked a feeling of eavesdropping, as if one were intruding into someone else's intimate sphere.

During the installation phases of *Anna & Marie* the performers were absent, but proxemics could be observed between the individual components of the artwork and audience members. The earpieces were available to the audience in the same way as during the concert. In addition, when audience members used the tablets to generate augmented reality, they had to come relatively close to the panels—about one to two metres—which, according to Hall, is between the far end of "personal space" and the close end of "social space." Due to the design of the augmented reality, audience members also had to physically move around the panel with the tablet—merely standing still would not have enabled them to access all the information displayed. In sum, the proximity and physical engagement when using the augmented reality created

347

a contact between the audience member, the tablet, and the panel that was more involved and personal than if the audience member had encountered the panel as a painting in a gallery. The same can be said about the navigation in the 3D space that was offered to the audience, which also demanded their active participation. A last aspect that played a subtle but noteworthy role is olfaction. Since the protagonists of the story were wax artists, I set up two hidden pots filled with beeswax on hot plates, so the entire space was filled with its odour (plate 16.7). As mentioned at the beginning of this section, in social situations the perception of smell only occurs in intimate proximity. The goal of the olfactory design was to involve yet another sense in a way that relates to the subject of the work, and thereby to also enhance a feeling of intimacy with the presented lives of the protagonists.

In *Rave Séance*, the set-up was confined to a much smaller spatial area than in *Anna & Marie*. Its circular arrangement of five small tables had a diameter of about five metres. Although audience members could also move outside this circular arrangement, I focus my discussion on those who sat at the tables. As mentioned before, four of the five tables were available for the audience, while the fifth table was reserved for me as the performer. Up to three people could sit on cushions at each table, which means that the distance between them was within the close end of "personal space." The distances between the tables were also relatively close, so even audience members sitting at adjacent tables were still within the far end of "personal space." The hierarchical difference between performer and audience members was minimised in this set-up and the intention was to create a sense of togetherness between the audience members sitting at the tables and myself as performer. Nevertheless, I should mention that hierarchy was still maintained as I used an entire table for myself, while up to three audience members had to share a single table. Also, unlike the audience members who were sitting on small cushions on the floor, I was sitting on a low chair, which created a small but noteworthy difference in vertical distance, which also suggested a hierarchy. The choice of a chair for myself was not part of the original plan but turned out to be a practical necessity, since otherwise I would not have been able to operate the equipment positioned on the table. The circular set-up of the tables meant that the audience were looking at other audience members who were sitting on the opposite side of the arrangement. The purpose of the circular arrangement was literally to also create an "inner circle" that included the performer, but excluded the audience members standing at the periphery who had not found a place at the tables. The "privileged" role of the audience at the tables is underlined by the possibility of interaction offered to them by means of the large buttons positioned in front of them on the small tables. Laser projections—occurring at certain points during the performance—are projected on the floor in the middle of the circular arrangement. For the audience members at the tables, the projection is thus very close (partly within arm's reach). They also look down on the projection, which in my understanding underlined the impression that the projection was in their personal space, rather than a detached phenomenon they beheld from a distance.

In summary, while the set-up of *Anna & Marie* mainly aimed at creating intimacy between audience members and the different elements in the space that related to the subject of the work, in *Rave Séance* the goal was to create a particular intimacy between audience members and the performer. The set-up of the space in both cases determined a social situation in the sense that relationships among audience members and between audience members and performer(s) were consciously designed. The differentiations of the qualities of proxemics help us understand how these social relationships were constructed in greater detail. I also consider these qualities meaningful when applied not only to interpersonal relations but also to the relationship between audience members and the inanimate components belonging to the work. For clarity, I offer a reduced and simplified version of Hall's table in figures 16.2 and 16.3. Here, I graphically display the discussed aspects of proxemics as they were applied in these two projects, which allows for direct comparison. The tables show at a glance that in *Rave Séance* the spatial arrangement was more compact than in *Anna & Marie* and that in the former many phenomena occurred within the ranges of "intimate" and "personal space."

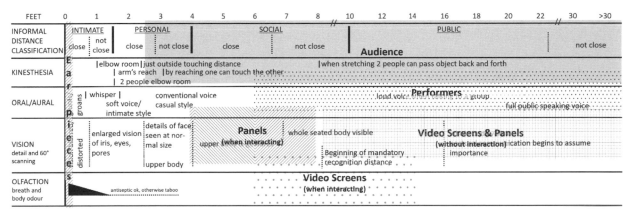

Figure 16.2.

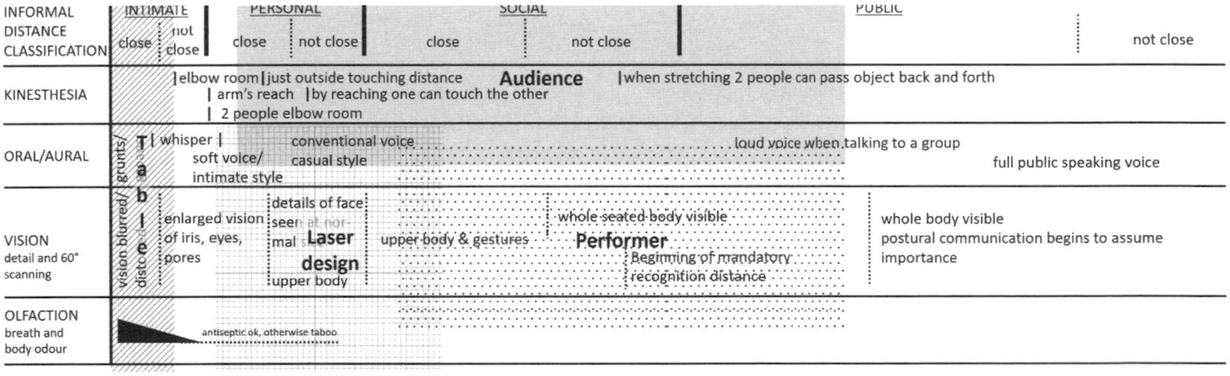

Figure 16.3.

Figure 16.2. Proxemics in *Anna & Marie*, superimposed onto Edward T. Hall's simplified chart of proxemic perception.

Figure 16.3. Proxemics in *Rave Séance*, superimposed onto Edward T. Hall's simplified chart of proxemic perception.

An additional aspect that has an impact on the relationship between audience members and the presented work is whether audience members can actively interact with the components, which will be discussed further in the following section.

AUDIENCE PARTICIPATION (*ANNA & MARIE*, *WHY FRETS?*, *RAVE SÉANCE*)

In all three projects presented in this chapter, I offer the audience active participation to different degrees. In *Anna & Marie*, as described above, this participation takes place via the augmented reality features and the navigation in the 3D environments. In both cases, the audience forms their own personal experience with a particular medium, while at the same time they also generate sound that is perceived by all other audience members in the space, and thus adds a shared experience. In the net-art example of *Why Frets?*, due to its virtual web-based nature, the encounter with the work is solitary. As mentioned above, here my goal was to give the user the impression of being the performer. In *Rave Séance*, finally, all interactions take place by pressing a large button when its built-in lamp is lit. Depending on the section of the work, pressing the button either causes harmonic changes in a synthesised texture or activates solenoids and shaker motors that are attached to the tables, which provides the audience members at the tables with an—often unexpected!—haptic experience.

Although the influence I provide audience members with is certainly noticable, it is always kept within rather constrained boundaries when seen in relation to the overall work. The audience's behaviour can definitely influence the character of a performance, as is the case when I compare the two performances of *Rave Séance* in the summer of 2020 that took place first in Ljubljana and a few weeks later in Graz. In Ljubljana, some audience members were waiting eagerly for the next moment the buttons in front of them lit up, indicating that an event could take place. Once the buttons did light up, some audience members would hit them with forceful, large gestures that often were louder than the effect actually triggered. Perhaps they recognised that when the button was triggered, the lights would also turn off on all other twelve buttons, meaning that everybody would have to wait until the lights came on again in order to create the next trigger. Unexpectedly for me, a playful competitive situation evolved within a group of audience members where each person tried to be the first to react when the lights went back on, while they seemed rather oblivious to the actual effect of the interaction. Contrary to this, the audience members in Graz only triggered the buttons occasionally and much more discreetly and quietly. But even with a "hyperactive" audience such as the one in Ljubljana, their interactions cannot influence the progress of the work and its formal outline. The effect of the interactions remained confined to the moment when they occur, with no long-term consequences.

My main motivation to include audience participation is not so much an interest in letting the audience co-create or co-perform the piece. Rather, I see it as a way to design the relationship between the work and audience members.

I want to give them the possibility of becoming part of the performance event, even if the influence they have is strongly contained. I often find composing for and designing audience participation challenging. First of all, the interaction has to be perceived as meaningful by the audience members, which means that the effects have to be well integrated into the work as a whole. If the impact on the work is overly superficial, it will likely be perceived as too banal and uninteresting. Conversely, too strong an impact might destroy the identity and integrity of the performance, which might be perceived as arbitrary and unsatisfactory for the audience. A good balance therefore needs to be struck between these two extremes. Another challenge is how to communicate to the audience that they can make use of interactive functionalities. Verbal instructions often feel inappropriate and not aesthetically fitting in a particular context, so other means often have to be found (in *Rave Séance*, for example, I indicated the interaction by providing the buttons that light up when they are "active"). Beyond that, audience members often behave differently to my original expectations and not always to my liking. In Ljubljana, for example, I was on the one hand very pleased that the audience members reacted so enthusiastically to the given possibilities of interaction. On the other hand, I was less content when the act of interaction dominated what was actually happening artistically during the performance. At times I was even worried that they would destroy the tables, which had been specially built for this project. For me, every performance is a learning experience that afterwards often led me to adjust the details of the algorithmic implementation of the interactions—in other words, adjusting the leeway that I permit the audience.

Incorporating the possibility of interaction for audience members means relinquishing part of the control, which—admittedly—I usually try to keep restricted within clear boundaries. However, at the same time I do consider it an exciting aspect to work with, and an important means of designing the relationship between the audience and the presented work.

ASYNCHRONOUS PRESENCE (*WHY FRETS?*)

The ambient perspective, or the concept of atmosphere, is based on the co-presence of a multitude of phenomena in time and space that form a network of relationships. However, as mentioned above, the project *Why Frets?* consists of a series of events and works that are not experienced simultaneously: a sequence of websites that I consider a form of audiovisual net-art, an audiovisual installation, a performance lecture for PowerPoint and electric guitar, and a composition for three electric guitars. Most of these works cannot be experienced simultaneously. Nevertheless, I conceived them as phenomena that relate to one another in ways similar to the various elements of an installation: a network of relationships that gives rise to a particular atmosphere and a particular aesthetic state. A shared space and time provides the basis for the co-presence of phenomena within installations; so where does this happen in *Why Frets?* if there is no shared space? The realm where these disparate elements of the work come together is the memory of the audience member: after successively experiencing the different components of the work, it is only there that the relationships between the individual entities can evolve.

The question arises of the extent to which the interrelationships between the various elements of this work differ from more traditional collections of works that are conceived as a series, for instance, Maximilian Marcoll's *Amproprifikationen* (2016–), or transmedia works with various entities such as Ryoji Ikeda's *micro / macro* (2015). Although each entity of *Why Frets?* can be experienced as self-contained, the larger concept of the overall work can only be grasped when several, if not all, of its components have been experienced. In this sense, a balance between autonomy and interdependency is at play between the individual elements: they are complete and at the same time incomplete when seen in isolation. In order to intensify the unfolding of relationships between the different elements, I made use of a narrative that extends across the different parts of the project, akin to transmedia storytelling. Stories can create emotional bonds between the audience and the aesthetic experience, and they can provide memorable anchor points that are easier to recall and therefore also facilitate the establishment of connections between story fragments. In this particular case, the story that is told is a fictitious history of the electric guitar. The story elements of the overarching narrative underpin all the different parts of *Why Frets?*, although while the story is told more explicitly in the performance lecture and the net-art sections, it is more concealed in the installation and the concert piece. Moreover, in the net-art sections and the audiovisual installation, interactive elements allow audience members to take on a more active role in the experience of the artwork. Audience participation is thus another aspect that is applied in order to enhance the memorability and the connectedness between the different elements.

In summary, in *Why Frets?* I aim at evoking in audience members what Papastergiadis and Barikin described as the ambient perspective. However, here the ambient perspective takes place differently. It is not a dispersion of attention across various phenomena that are co-present in time and place. Furthermore, since every element is encountered individually, there is nothing that could lead to what I described above as meandering attention. Instead, the ambient perspective is maintained in that the individual parts of the work extend beyond themselves. Although each one of them is to a certain extent self-contained, the connecting element of storytelling suggests a continuation that is only fulfilled when the experience of the various parts is combined. This also connects the different parts as an aesthetic experience that forms across different media. In other words, the storytelling acts as a glue that fuses aesthetic experiences of different qualities that are brought together only in the audience member's memory but could otherwise not converge to form a unified experience.

CONCLUSION

In this chapter, I presented three recent projects of mine as examples of works that combine characteristics of performances and installations, while affordances for interaction are offered for audience members. My intention was to show on the basis of these case studies that the selection of a particular set-up combined with audience participation forms, shapes, and designs the relationship between audience members and the work they encounter.

As early as 1965, Michael Kirby wrote in reference to happenings that they attempt to "alter the audience-performance relationship . . . and to use this relationship artistically" (1965, 25). More than fifty years later, the designing of audience–work relationships has been widely explored across many disciplines. However, only rarely have the implications of set-ups and interactions been analysed carefully and from the inside perspective of artistic practice, as is characteristic of artistic research. This chapter represents an attempt to better understand how audience–work relationships can be designed as an artistic and aesthetic means of expression.

REFERENCES

Böhme, Gernot. 2013. *Atmosphäre: Essays zur neuen Ästhetik*. Rev. ed. Frankfurt am Main: Suhrkamp.

Ciciliani, Marko. 2017. "Token of Enunciation in Multimedia Performance." In *Proceedings of ICMC/EMC International Computer Music Conference 2017*, 127–34. Shanghai: ICMA.

Ciciliani, Marko, and Barbara Lüneburg. 2021. "Anna & Marie, a Performative Installation Built on Ergodic." In *Ludified: Artistic Research in Audiovisual Composition, Performance and Perception; Game Elements in Marko Ciciliani's Audiovisual Works*, edited by Marko Ciciliani, Barbara Lüneburg, and Andreas Pirchner, 89–125. Berlin: Green Box.

Fried, Michael. (1967) 1995. "Art and Objecthood." In *Minimal Art: A Critical Anthology*, edited by Gregory Battcock, 116–47. Berkeley: University of California Press. Essay first published 1967 (*Artforum* 5 [June]: 12–23). Book first published 1968 (New York: Dutton).

Hall, Edward T. 1966. *The Hidden Dimension*. Garden City, NY: Doubleday.

Kirby, Michael. 1965. *Happenings: An Illustrated Anthology*. New York: E. P. Dutton.

Lucier, Alvin. (1980) 1995. "'Every Room Has Its Own Melody': 'I Am Sitting in a Room' (1970)," interview with Douglas Simon. In *Reflections: Interviews, Scores, Writings, 1965–1994*, edited by Gisela Gronemeyer and Reinhard Oehlschlägel, 86–95. Cologne: MusikTexte. Interview first published 1980 in *Chambers*, by Alvin Lucier and Douglas Simon (Middletown, CT: Wesleyan University Press), 33–39.

Nanz, Dieter A. 2006. "Neue Klänge, Varèse und das Poème Électronique." In *Edgar Varèse und das Poème électronique: Eine Dokumentation*, edited by Dieter A. Nanz, 20–24. Basel: Paul Sacher Stiftung.

Papastergiadis, Nikos, and Amelia Barikin. 2015. "Ambient Perspective and Endless Art." *Discipline*, no. 4, 80–91.

Petersen, Anne Ring. 2015. *Installation Art: Between Image and Stage*. Copenhagen: Museum Tusculanum Press.

Prendergast, Mark. 2003. *The Ambient Century: From Mahler to Moby—The Evolution of Sound in the Electronic Age*. New ed. London: Bloomsbury.

Schröder, Julia H. 2014. *Zur Position der Musikhörenden: Konzeptionen ästhetischer Erfahrung im Konzert*. Hofheim: Wolke Verlag.

Weidringer, Walter. 2016. "Viel mehr als Chaos: Schostakowitsch total." *Die Presse*, 13 November 2016. Accessed 2 January 2021. https://www.diepresse.com/5117463/viel-mehr-als-chaos-schostakowitsch-total.

Appendix

Online Materials

As further reference to chapters 2 (Rosenboom), 4 (Warde), 5 (Brown), 9 (Romero), 11 (Fantechi), and 14 (Alessandrini and Zhu) in this book, an online repository of multimedia files was created to enhance the reading of the relevant chapters. The material is hosted on the website of the Orpheus Institute, Ghent. These examples, which should be viewed in connection with a reading of the relevant articles, may all be accessed under the URL: https://orpheusinstituut.be/en/sound-work-media-repository.

Patricia Alessandrini is a composer/sound artist creating compositions, installations, and performance situations that are frequently interactive and theatrical. Through these intermedial formats, she actively engages with the concert music repertoire, and issues of representation, interpretation, perception, and memory. Her works are often collaborative, and engage with social and political issues. She researches embodied interaction and immersive audiovisual experience, including instrument design for inclusive performance. Her works have been presented in the Americas, Asia, Australia, and over fifteen European countries. She is also a performer and improviser of live electronics. She was composer-in-residence at the 2010 soundSCAPE festival, and featured in ICELab with the International Contemporary Ensemble in 2012. In 2015–16 she was featured as a composer, curator, and educator in four concert and outreach events by the Ensemble InterContemporain, as part of the Sound Kitchen series at the Gaîté lyrique.

She studied composition and electronics at the Conservatorio G. B. Martini di Bologna, Conservatoire National de Strasbourg, and IRCAM, and holds two PhDs, from Princeton University and the Sonic Arts Research Centre (SARC), Queen's University Belfast, respectively. She has taught computer-assisted composition at the Accademia Musicale Pescarese, composition with technology at Bangor University, and as a lecturer in sonic arts at Goldsmiths College, and is currently an assistant professor of composition at Stanford University, where she performs research at the Center for Computer Research in Music and Acoustics (CCRMA). Her works are published by Babelscores, and may be consulted at patriciaalessandrini.com.

Alan F. Blackwell is Professor of Interdisciplinary Design at the University of Cambridge Department of Computer Science and Technology. During his early career as an industrial automation engineer in his native New Zealand, he pursued hobbies in philosophy, comparative religion, and orchestral music. Those broader interests led eventually to an extended master's by research in artificial intelligence, investigating topics of commonsense planning in the physical world, which were not too distant from those being explored by Philip Agre at the same time. Like Agre, Blackwell's subsequent interests both started from and challenge narrow interpretations of AI, resulting in a critical technical practice that habitually crosses disciplinary boundaries. He has convened and supported a variety of distinctive research communities, including those for the interdisciplinary study of diagrams, the psychology of programming, and live coding as a critically informed performance practice. His current post as Director of Cambridge Global Challenges allows him to shape research that advances sustainable development goals drawing on a wide range of academic disciplines, while offering opportunities for more specialist enquiry, such as questioning the role of AI in relation to low-income populations and indigenous knowledge systems.

Nicholas Brown is a composer, performer, and writer. His musical works have been widely presented at international festivals and venues such as Huddersfield Contemporary Music Festival, the BBC Promenade Concerts, Three Choirs Festival (UK), Sonorities (Belfast), Science Gallery Dublin, Scenkonstmuseet (Stockholm), Concertgebouw Brugge, and Turner Contemporary (Margate). He has also composed two scores for silent films, which have been released by the British Film Institute. As a writer and researcher, he has published journal articles and book chapters on issues in contemporary musical practice, especially the use of digital technologies in computer-assisted composition. He holds the post of Ussher Assistant Professor in Sonic Arts at Trinity College Dublin and is an associate researcher at the Orpheus Institute, Ghent. For more information, see www.nicholasbrown.co.uk.

Marko Ciciliani is a composer, audiovisual artist, performer, and researcher based in Austria. The focus of his work lies in the composition of performative electronic music, mostly in audiovisual contexts. Interactive video, light design, and laser graphics often play an integral part in his compositions. Ciciliani's works have been performed in more than forty-five countries across Eurasia, Oceania, and the Americas. They have been released on five full-length CDs and three multimedia books. In addition, his music can be found on more than a dozen compilation CDs.

Ciciliani is Professor for Computer Music Composition and Sound Design at the Institute for Electronic Music and Acoustics (IEM) of the University of Music and Performing Arts Graz. Since 2013 he has regularly been invited as a coach to the multidisciplinary course LAbO in Antwerp, for which he served as Artistic Director in 2020 and 2021. In 2014, 2016, and 2018 he was a tutor at the Summer Courses for Contemporary Music Darmstadt. Ciciliani was granted funding for the artistic research project GAPPP—Gamified Audiovisual Performance and Performance Practice, which was funded as part of the PEEK program of the Austrian Science Fund and ran from 2016 to 2021. The results of this research, which examined the artistic potential of elements from computer games in the context of audiovisual composition and performance, was published as the monograph *LUDIFIED* (Berlin: TheGreenBox). http://www.ciciliani.com and http://gappp.net.

New York born and raised, **Nicolas Collins** spent most of the 1990s in Europe, where he was Artistic Director of STEIM (Amsterdam), and a DAAD composer-in-residence in Berlin. He is a professor in the Department of Sound at the School of the Art Institute of Chicago and a research fellow at the Orpheus Institute, Ghent. From 1997 to 2017 he was Editor-in-Chief of the *Leonardo Music Journal*. An early adopter of microcomputers for live performance, Collins also makes use of homemade electronic circuitry and conventional acoustic instruments. His book, *Handmade Electronic Music: The Art of Hardware Hacking* (Routledge), now in its third edition, has influenced emerging electronic music worldwide. www.nicolascollins.com.

Notes on Contributors

Agostino Di Scipio is a composer, sound artist, and scholar. He graduated in composition and electronic music from the Conservatory of L'Aquila and was later appointed a doctor of research at University Paris 8. His work with live electronics and sound installations include unusual approaches to sound generation and transmission, creating "man-machine-environment" networks of sounding interactions. He has been an artist-in-residence at several institutions worldwide. His music is available on various labels (including RZ Edition, Neos Records, Chrysopeé Electronique, Wergo, Neuma, Stradivarius, Die Schachtel). With pianist Ciro Longobardi, Di Scipio published a large-scale realisation of John Cage's *Electronic Music for Piano* (Venice Biennale 2012, available on Stradivarius). With saxophonist and political agitator Mario Gabola he established the Upset duo, exploring recycled analogue circuitry. With Dario Sanfilippo, he established the Machine Milieu project, exploring chaotic dynamics and autonomic behaviour in multiagent systems. His output also includes two chamber music theatre works, with poetry reading and electroacoustics: *Tiresia* (with poet Giuliano Mesa) and *Sound & Fury: A Theatre of Sounds, Noises and Sometimes Voices* (based on excerpts from Shakespeare's *The Tempest*).

Di Scipio has extensively researched and lectured on the history and politics of sound and music technologies, and published papers, essays, and monographs on related matters. He was Professor in Electroacoustic Composition at the Conservatory of Naples (2001–13) and today holds the same position in his hometown, L'Aquila; he has also been a guest professor at numerous educational institutions. https://agostinodiscipio.xoom.it/adiscipi/index.html.

Daniela Fantechi is an Italian composer and researcher. She studied composition at the Conservatory of Florence and at Kunstuniversität, Graz, with Beat Furrer, Clemens Gadenstätter, and Georg Friedrich Haas, and received a master of musicology degree from the University of Florence. In 2016 she participated in Kultur Kontakt's artist-in-residence programe in Vienna, and in 2017 Steiermark's St.A.I.R artist-in-residence programme in Graz. In 2011 she joined the ensemble Blutwurst (www.blutwurst.it), whose research is devoted to the acoustic exploration of sustained tones and slowly transformed pattern of sounds. Since 2017 she has also been a member of Azione_Improvvisa, an ensemble focused on the exploration of new sound identities in the field of contemporary music (www.azioneimprovvisa.com). Her work focuses on the exploration of the sonic possibilities of acoustic instruments, combining aspects of traditional composition and extensive research on sound, through its modes of production. Her current research project concerns the composition of instrumental music implemented with a specific use of piezoelectric microphones. Fantechi is currently a doctoral researcher at the Orpheus Institute, Ghent, within the research cluster Music, Thought and Technology (orpheusinstituut.be/en/projects/music-thought-and-technology). Her compositions have been performed in Italy, Austria, Spain, Portugal, France, England, Switzerland, Belgium, and Germany.

Ambrose Field is a composer whose work has been performed on three continents. His album *Being Dufay* (ECM Records 2071) toured to thirteen nations as a live performance. His vocal piece *Pod Twoj□ obron□*, for the Polish National Chamber Choir, was specifically commissioned to honour the eightieth birthday of H. M. Górecki. For his work with technology, he is a three-time recipient of the honorary award at the Prix Ars Electronica. Interdisciplinary creative questions underpin his output. Field's series of architecturally informed compositions *Architexture* make use of specific acoustics of a site to inform how a score is crafted. His cycle of pieces for solo flute, *Quantaform Series*, which rethinks the relationship between performer and environment, is the subject of a film made with the support of the Arts Council UK and National Lottery Heritage Fund (2019). Field is Dean of Arts and Humanities at the University of York, UK, where he was previously Head of Department of Music from 2013. Field was appointed to Honorary Professorships at the Beijing Institute for Advanced Innovation, and at the China National School of Music, China Conservatory, in 2018.

Karim Haddad was born in Beirut, Lebanon. He was a student at the National Conservatory of Beirut and studied philosophy and Anglo-Saxon literature at the American University of Beirut. After a degree in musicology at Paris IV Sorbonne, he entered the CNSMD, Paris, at which he obtained six prizes (harmony, counterpoint, fugue, orchestration, analysis, and composition) as well as the Diplôme Supérieur de Composition with distinction. He worked notably with Alain Bancquart, Paul Mefano, Brian Ferneyhough, Klaus Huber, Karlheinz Stockhausen, and Emmanuel Nunes. In 2020, he obtained the degree of Doctor of the Sorbonne University in "Music, Research in Composition." He currently works as a researcher and development officer at IRCAM within the Musical Representations team. His works have been performed by soloists of the Itinéraire, Contrechamps, and 2e2m ensembles, the Diotima Quartet, the Radio-France Philharmonic Orchestra, the Berlin Staatsoper, the SIC ensemble, and the instrumental ensemble Futurs-Musiques, at various festivals such as the Festival Présence de Radio-France, the Agora Ircam Festival, the Lucero Festival, and the Gulbenkian Foundation's Rencontres Musicales.

Composer, trumpet-player, and writer **Jonathan Impett** is Director of Research at the Orpheus Institute, Ghent, and Associate Professor at Middlesex University, London. At Orpheus he leads the research group Music, Thought and Technology, investigating the implications of technological concepts for all aspects of music creation, practice, and understanding. His music explores new modes of construction and representation, combining score, electronics, AI, installation, and improvisation. A recent series, "presence and resonance," builds new musical constructs from historical sources using wave models as an appropriate way of manipulating time-based phenomena. The electroacoustic improvisation project Three States of Wax sets out from Michel Serres's notion of material as a nexus of information, transformed in every interrogation. His monograph *Luigi Nono and Musical Thought* was published in 2019, the first comprehensive study of the composer's work. He is also a member of the Orchestra of the Eighteenth Century and the Amsterdam Baroque Orchestra.

Thor Magnusson is Professor in Future Music at the University of Sussex and a research professor at the Iceland University of the Arts. His work focuses on the impact digital technologies have on musical creativity and practice, explored through software development, composition, and performance. He is the co-founder of ixi audio (www.ixi-audio.net), and has developed audio software and systems of generative music composition, written computer music tutorials, and created two musical live coding environments. He has taught workshops in creative music coding and sound installations, and given presentations, performances, and visiting lectures at diverse art institutions, conservatories, and universities internationally. Magnusson is currently the Edgard Varèse Guest Professor at Berlin's Technische Universität. Magnusson's monograph *Sonic Writing: The Technologies of Material, Symbolic and Signal Inscriptions* (Bloomsbury Academic, 2019) explores how contemporary music technologies trace their ancestry to previous forms of instruments and media, including symbolic musical notation. The book underpins the current research of the MIMIC project (www.mimicproject.com), where Magnusson has worked on a system that enables users to design their own live coding languages for machine learning (www.sema.codes). Magnusson is currently running an ERC Consolidator project, Intelligent Instruments, researching human perception of intelligent musical instruments, embedded with machine learning and other AI (see http://sonicwriting.org/blog/intent). For further information see http://thormagnusson.github.io.

Scott McLaughlin is an Irish composer and improviser based in Huddersfield, UK. He started out as a shoegaze/experimental-rock guitarist before studying music in his twenties at the University of Ulster, after which he undertook an MA/PhD at the University of Huddersfield. Currently, Scott lectures in composition and music technology at the University of Leeds, and co-directs CePRA (Centre for Practice Research in the Arts). His research focuses on contingency and indeterminacy in the physical materiality of sound, exploring material agency and recursive feedback systems in constraint-based open-form composition. Currently, Scott is an AHRC Leadership Fellow on the Garden of Forking Paths project exploring composing for contingency in clarinets (forkingpaths.leeds.ac.uk).

Lula Romero is a composer of electroacoustic and acoustic music and a doctoral candidate at the University of Music and Performing Arts, Graz, Austria. She holds degrees in composition, piano, and art history. In her compositional work she explores the phenomenon of space in music with regard to structure and material and its relation to theories and practices of feminism and questions of social equality. Romero has been awarded the GIGA-HERTZ

Production prize 2014 by the ZKM | SWR Experimentalstudio Freiburg, the Kompositionsstipendium 2015 and 2012 and the Berlin–Rheinsberger Kompositionspreis 2011, among others, and the Residence at the Deutsches Studienzentrum Venedig (Venice) 2017 by the German Government. In 2019 her CD *Ins Offene* was released by Wergo in the Edition Zeitgenössische Musik series produced by the Deutscher Musikrat. Her works have been performed by the SWR Symphony Orchestra, KNM Berlin, Vertixe Sonora Ensemble, Duo Hellqvist/Amaral, Nieuw Ensemble, Kairos Quartet, and Zafraan Ensemble, among others, while her music has been commissioned by festivals such as Donaueschinger Musiktage, MATA (New York), SPOR (Aarhus), Mixtur (Barcelona), and the Sonification Festival (Berlin). She lives and works in Berlin. For more information, see www.lularomero.com.

David Rosenboom is a multifaceted composer-performer, interdisciplinary artist, author, and educator known as a pioneer in American experimental music. His multi-disciplinary, post-genre composition and performance has traversed ideas about spontaneously evolving musical forms, languages for improvisation, new techniques in scoring, cross-cultural and large-form collaborations, performance art and literature, interactive multi-media and new instrument technologies, generative algorithmic systems, art-science research and philosophy, and extended musical interface with the human nervous system. A feature article in *The Wire* magazine about his life and work begins, "Biofeedback, intelligence swarms, solar vibrations and generative opera are among the utopian possibilities proposed by US composer David Rosenboom during 50 years of navigating new frontiers of music and technology" (J. Cowley, September 2014).

Rosenboom was Dean of the Herb Alpert School of Music at California Institute of the Arts from 1990 to 2020, where he now holds the Roy E. Disney Family Chair in Musical Composition. Earlier position highlights include: Richard Seaver Distinguished Chair in Music, CalArts; Darius Milhaud Professor of Music, Mills College; founding music and interdisciplinary professor, York University (Toronto); Artistic Coordinator, Electric Circus (New York); and Creative Associate, Center for Creative and Performing Arts, State University of New York (Buffalo). He regularly performs and speaks in international venues, and his work is widely recorded and published. During his fifty-year retrospective at the Whitney Museum of American Art, the *New York Times* referred to him as an "avatar of experimental music" (A. Tommasini, 24 May 2015). https://davidrosenboom.com.

Ann Warde is an experimental composer, sound installation artist, and independent scholar, and a recent NYSCA/NYFA Artist Fellow in Music/Sound from the New York Foundation for the Arts. Her music has recently been presented during residencies at the Virginia Center for the Creative Arts, the Tone Deaf Festival at Queen's University, Canada, and the European University Cyprus Interfaces Project. Her study of composition and ethnomusicology led to a Mellon Postdoctoral Fellowship in music at Cornell

University, after which her work with sound shifted, focusing for the next decade on applications of audio technology to the analysis of whale sounds at Cornell's Lab of Ornithology. Subsequently, as a US-UK Fulbright Researcher at the University of York, and alongside investigations of spatial audio techniques in music composition and bioacoustics, she developed interests in American philosophy. Recent and forthcoming publications include chapters in *Sound Art and Music: Philosophy, Composition, Performance*; *Experience Music Experiment: Pragmatism and Artistic Research*; *Women in Pragmatism: Past and Future*; and *Sounds, Ecologies, Musics*; and the articles "Hidden Encounters: Seeking Unpredictable Yet Responsive Interactivity" (in *The Global Composition 2018 Proceedings*) and "Points of View: Doubtful Sound" (in the online journal *Echo*).

Laura Zattra holds PhDs from the Sorbonne University and Trento University. She is a research associate in the Analysis of Musical Practices Research Group, IRCAM (Paris), and IreMus (Sorbonne University). She teaches History of Electroacoustic Music and History of Sound Design in Cinema on bachelor and master's programmes, and was an invited lecturer on the Master of Arts Sound Studies and Sonic Arts programme at the Universität der Künste in Berlin (2018) and the Estonian Academy of Music in Tallin (2021). She is co-editor-in-chief of *Musica/Tecnologia* (Firenze University Press), founder of www.teresarampazzi.it, and a member of the editorial board of *Projet Analyses* (Ircam, Paris). Her research has been funded by grants from the French CNRS, the French Labex CAP (Sorbonne Paris 1), the University of Padova (2006–12), IRCAM-CNRS, Paris, the University of Calgary (SSHRC grant, collaborator), and DeMonfort University, UK. She has published over eighty articles, book chapters, and conference papers. Her books include *La notazione della musica elettroacustica: Scrutare il passato per contemplare il futuro* (with S. Alessandretti, 2019), *Live-Electronic Music: Composition, Performance and Study* (Routledge, with F. Sallis, V. Bertolani, and I. Burle, 2018); *Studiare la Computer Music: Definizioni, analisi, fonti* (2011); *Presenza storica di Luigi Nono / Historical Presence of Luigi Nono* (with A. I. De Benedictis, 2011); *Musica e famiglia: L'avventura artistica di Renata Zatti* (2010); and *Vent'anni di musica elettronica all'università di Padova: Il Centro di sonologia computazionale* (with S. Durante, 2002).

Julie Zhu is a composer, artist, and carillonneur. Her work is visual and aural, operating on an expansive definition of score, striving for expressive algorithm. She entangles various media, from mural painting and sculpture to performance and video, and collaborates with artists from different fields to create experimental chamber experiences. Her scores range from hair cast in clear resin to temporary tattoos to traditional orchestration, and have been performed by the JACK quartet, Quasar, Line Upon Line, Marco Fusi, Longleash, PROMPTUS, and TAK ensemble, among others. As a professional carillonneur, Zhu has presented concerts and lectures throughout Europe and North America. She was appointed carillonneur at

Saint Thomas Fifth Avenue in New York City in 2015. Zhu studied at Yale University (BA mathematics, BA art), the Royal Carillon School (Diploma carillon performance), Hunter College (MFA art), and at present, Stanford University (DMA composition).

Index

A

Aaron, Sam, 20, 31, 32
    See also Collins, Nicolas, and Sam Aaron, works by
Aaronson, Scott, 48, 75
Abtan, Freida, 299, 314
Activating Inclusive Sound Spaces (AISS), 308, 314
Adam, Alison, 16, 32
Adams, Rachel, 16, 32
Adams, Tony E., 127, 133, 135
Adler, Guido, 278n2
Adorno, Theodor W., 235, 245
Afroz, Sadia, 24, 32
Afshordi, Niayesh, 59, 75
Agamben, Giorgio, 120, 121, 133–34, 188
Agon, Carlos, 260n7, 266, 275, 276
Agre, Philip, 8–10, 13, 15, 17–19, 21, 22, 29–31, 32, 45, 46, 49–50, 74, 75, 89–95, 99, 101, 102, 119, 123–24, 127, 130–33, 134, 154, 156, 159, 168, 169, 172, 173, 188, 197, 231, 244–45
    Computation and Human Experience, 17, 92, 231
    Pengi, 18
    "Toward a Critical Technical Practice," 89–90, 93–94
Akrich, Madeleine, 220, 228
Alessandrini, Patricia, 12, 295–317
    Ada's Song, 312
    Mondgewächse, 298
    Parlour Sounds, 12, 295–302, 304–7, 309–14
Allen, Amy, 296, 314
Amacher, Maryanne, 41
Amaris Sifuentes, Lián, 304
    See also DuBois, R. Luke, and Lián Amaris Sifuentes, works by
Amazon Mechanical Turk, 23
Amcoustics, 207n10
    Amray, 202n9
    Amroc, 207n10
Amoore, Louise, 21, 32
André, Mark, 214n12
    …auf III…, 214n12
Andreopoulou, Areti, 308, 316
Antunes, Luís, 48, 75
Apple, 16, 79n1
Appleton, Jon, 175, 188
Arieff, Allison, 86, 87
Aristotle, 38
Armitage, Jack, 302n15, 304n18
Armstrong, Thomas, 320, 332
Arnellos, Argyris, 180, 189
Ashley, Robert, 81, 165
    Music with Roots in the Aether, 81
Assayag, Gérard, 266, 276
Assis, Paulo de, 175, 176, 189, 321, 323, 326, 332
Augmented Instrument Lab, Queen Mary University, 302n15
Auslander, Philip, 171, 173, 189
Austin, Jim, 325, 332
Auyang, Sunny Y., 40, 75

B

Bach, Carl Philipp Emanuel, 108–10
    Abschied von meinem Silbermannischen Claviere in einem Rondo, 108–10

Bach, Johann Sebastian, 20, 82, 119, 226
    Inventions, 226
    Musical Offering, 119
Badiou, Alain, 118, 134
Baird, Davis, 219, 228
Banzi, Massimo, 86
Barad, Karen, 158n4, 169, 197, 217
    Meeting the Universe Halfway, 197
Barandiaran, Xabier, 181, 189
Baranski, Sandrine, 175, 189
Baratin, Marc, 38, 75
Barbaras, Renaud, 180, 189
Bardzell, Jeffrey, 30, 32
Bardzell, Jeffrey, Shaowen Bardzell, and Mark Blythe, works by
    Critical Theory and Interaction Design, 30
Bardzell, Shaowen, 30, 32
    See also Bardzell, Jeffrey, Shaowen Bardzell, and Mark Blythe, works by
Barikin, Amelia, 337, 340, 352, 353
Barkati, Karen, 177n11, 189
Barrett, Margaret S., 287, 291, 293
Barrett, Steven F., 112, 115
Barthélémy, Jean-Hughes, 187, 189
Barthet, Mathieu, 174n6, 193
Bartolani, Valentina, 174, 193
Bateson, Gregory, 36, 75
Battier, Marc, 175, 189, 193
Battistelli, Giorgio, 283
Bauer, Henry H., 326, 332
Bayle, Laurent, 291
BeagleBone Black, 302n15, 304n18
Beale, Gareth, 325, 332
Beatles, the, 87
Beckett, Samuel, 118
Beethoven, Ludwig van, 120
Behrman, David, 79, 85n11, 174nn
    Cello with Melody-Driven Electronics, 85n11
Bekker, Paul, 278n3
Bela Cape, 302n15, 304n18
Bellemare, Marc G., 18, 33
Belton, Olivia, 16, 32
Bender, Emily M., 22, 32
Benjamin, Walter, 177, 307, 314
Béranger, Sébastien, 177n11, 189
Berger, John, 118, 134
Berio, Luciano, 279–83, 287, 290
    Thema (Omaggio a Joyce), 282
Bernardini, Nicola, 171, 175, 189
Berry, David M., 126, 134
Bertolani, Valentina, 171, 189
Bertoncini, Mario, 174n3
Bevilacqua, Frédéric, 312n35, 315
Bich, Leonardo, 180, 189
Birbaumer, N., 48, 75
Birtwistle, Harrison, 285
Biset, Sébastien, 184, 189
Blackwell, Alan F., 9, 15–33
Blanton, Jimmy, 29
Blessing, Matthew, 303, 305, 315, 316
Blythe, Mark, 30, 32
    See also Bardzell, Jeffrey, Shaowen Bardzell, and Mark Blythe, works by

Bochner, Arthur P., 127, 134
Boden, Margaret A., 220, 228
Boehner, Kirsten, 110, 112, 115
Boethius, 132
Bogue, Ronald, 187, 189
Bohm, David, 56, 75
Böhme, Gernot, 336, 353
Bonardi, Alain, 177n11, 189
Bonnet, François, 57, 75
Borgdorff, Henk, 215, 217
Borgo, David, 185, 189
Born, Georgina, 110n7, 114, 115, 132–33, 134, 308, 315
Boulez, Pierre, 121–22, 128, 134, 168n14, 169, 174n4, 252n3, 257–60, 262n8, 265, 275
    Penser la musique aujourd'hui, 259, 262n8
    Third Piano Sonata, 259n5, 260
Boutard, Guillaume, 278, 293
Bovermann, Till, 31, 32
Bowers, John, 82n4, 83, 174n6
Bown, Oliver, 182n19, 185, 189–90
Boyd, Cathie, 297
Brahms, Johannes, 278n3
Braidotti, Rosi, 212, 217
    Nomadic Subjects, 212
Brauchli, Bernard, 108, 115
Braun, C., 48, 75
Braxton, Anthony, 44, 77
Brennan, Michael, 24, 32
Bresson, Jean, 266, 276
Britten, Benjamin, 278n3
Brousseau, Eric, 322, 332
Brown, Nicholas G., 10, 105–16
    As I Have Now Memoyre, 114n12
    Undulatory Theory of Light, The, 105, 112, 113–15
    Vanishing Points, 105, 108–10
Brown, Tanya M., 48, 75
Bruckner, Anton, 338
    Symphony No. 8, 338
    Symphony No. 9, 338
Brün, Herbert, 95–97, 99, 102
Brün, Michael, 95n2
Bryman, Alan, 324, 332
Buchla, Donald, 52
Burle, Jan, 174, 193
Butler, Judith, 296, 315

C
Cade, David E., 100, 102
Cage, John, 11, 40–41, 75, 87, 100, 115, 118, 128, 153, 158, 174, 175n9, 195, 196, 235, 245, 279, 280, 282
    Cartridge Music, 174
    Fontana Mix, 282
    Imaginary Landscape No. 1, 175n9
    Lecture on the Weather, 40–41
Calambokidis, John, 100, 102
California E.A.R. Unit, 59
    apek, Karel, 23
Cardew, Cornelius, 168
Carlos, Wendy, 307, 309
Carpentier, Sarah M., 48, 75
Carter, Elliott, 121
Cassidy, Aaron, 199
Cassin, Barbara, 38, 75

Center for Computer Research in Music and Acoustics (CCRMA), 313n36
Centore, Leandro, 174, 190
Centro di Sonologia Computazionale (CSC), 280, 283–84, 290
Ceriani, Miguel, 174n6, 193
Chadabe, Joel, 174, 190
Charles, Ray, 67
    Message from the People, A, 67
Chemero, Andy, 119, 134
Chen, Peyee, 297–300, 306, 310, 315
Cheshire, Tom, 21, 32
Chitman, Karl, 32
Choi, Insook, 51, 75
Chowning, John, 279n4
Chuck, 84
Ciciliani, Marko, 12, 13, 149–52, 335–53
    Anna & Marie, 151–52, 335, 342–45, 347–49
    Rave Séance, 149–50, 335, 340–42, 345, 347–51
    Why Frets?, 150, 335, 340, 342, 350–52
Centre International de Recherche Musicale (CIRM), Nice, 285
Clark, Andy, 119, 134, 188n22, 190
Clark, T. J., 118, 134
Clarke, Bruce, 172, 180, 187, 190
Clarke, Eric F., 123, 134, 321, 332
Clementi, Aldo, 283
Clifton, Lucille, 303, 315
Code Liberation Foundation, 312n35
Collins, Nick, 19–20, 32, 84, 106, 115, 190
    Baroqtronica: The Art of Machine Listening, 19–20
    Ornamaton, 19–20
Collins, Nicolas, 9, 10, 79–87, 174, 307, 310, 315
Collins, Nicolas, and Sam Aaron, works by
    Titan, 20–21
Composers Inside Electronics, 174n2
Conservatoire National Supérieur de Musique et de Danse de Paris (CNSMDP), 297–98, 310, 313, 314n38
Cont, Arshia, 177n11, 190
Conway, John Horton, 156
    Game of Life, 156
Cook, Nicholas, 321, 332
Coons, Edgar E., 56, 75
Cooper, Melinda, 301, 315
Copernicus, Nicolaus, 50
Costa, Madalena, 48, 75
Cottrell, William, 48, 75
Cox, Geoff, 125, 134
Cozman, Fabio G., 22, 33
Craft, Robert, 278n3
Craig-Martin, Michael, 126, 134
Crick, Francis, 219
Croft, John, 119, 134, 186, 190, 320, 332
Cross, Ian, 24, 26, 33
Cross, Nigel, 279, 288, 292
Cuartielles, David, 86
Cunningham, Merce, 84

D
Dack, John, 293
Dahlstedt, Palle, 185, 190
David, Shay, 110, 112, 115
Davies, David, 111, 113n9, 116

Davies, Hugh, 174n3, 175, 190
Davies, Sarah Rachel, 7, 13
Davis, Miles, 87
De Benedictis, Angela, 281, 282, 289, 290, 291, 292, 294
DeLanda, Manuel, 121, 134
Deleuze, Gilles, 168, 169, 299, 300, 315, 326
de Libera, Alain, 38, 75
Demers, Joanna, 235–36, 245
    Listening through the Noise, 235
De Poli, Giovanni, 281n7, 292
Derrida, Jacques, 215
Descartes, René, 74, 122, 131
d'Escrivan, Julio, 19
Devine, Kyle, 308, 315
Devlin, Kate, 16, 32
Dewey, John, 105n2, 323, 332
Dharmawan, Dwiki, 72
d'Heudieres, Louis, 164–65, 169
Diaphonique, 298n7
Dieter, Michael, 89–90, 93, 95, 102, 112, 116
    "Virtues of Critical Technical Practice, The," 89
Dillon, James, 285
Di Scipio, Agostino, 10, 171–94
Döbereiner, Luc, 200n4
Dobson, Liz, 308
Dodge, Martin, 8, 13
Doffman, Mark, 123, 134, 321, 332
Dompier, Steve, 79n1
Donatoni, Franco, 283
Donaueschinger Musiktage, 202, 211n11, 343
Donin, Nicolas, 278, 290, 291, 292, 293
Dourish, Paul, 19, 30, 32 33
    Where the Action Is, 30
Dreyfus, Laurence, 226, 228
DuBois, R. Luke, 304
DuBois, R. Luke, and Lián Amaris Sifuentes, works by
    Fashionably Late for the Relationship, 304

E
Eco, Umberto, 213, 217, 280, 292
Ede, Jim, 20
Edinburgh International Science Festival, 297, 299, 310
Einstein, Albert, 219, 228
Eldridge, Alice, 185, 189
Ellis, Carolyn S., 127, 133, 134, 135
Emmerson, Simon, 171, 176, 177, 178, 191, 277n1, 292
Ensemble Intercontemporain, 310
Erickson, Kristin, 52, 75
Etxeberria, Arantza, 181, 191
Evangelisti, Franco, 174n3
Experimental Music Studios (EMS), University of
    Illinois Urbana-Champaign, 308, 309
Experimentalstudio des SWR, Freiburg, 174n5

F
Fabbreschi, Valentino, 297
Fabbriciani, Roberto, 282n9
Faber, Sarah E. M., 48, 75
Fahlbusch, James A., 100, 102
Faia, Carl, 277, 279–80, 285–92
    "Collaborative Computer Music Composition and
    the Emergence of the Computer Music Designer,"
    285–86, 290

Fantechi, Daniela, 11, 231–45
    Hidden Traces, 233–34, 238, 243
    PianoMusicBox_1, 233–34, 238, 243
    Residual, 233–35, 238, 243
Faraday, Michael, 113, 116
Federici, Silvia, 301, 315
Feenberg, Andrew, 173, 175, 187, 191
Feld, Stephen, 132
Female Pressure, 308, 315
Ferneyhough, Brian, 7, 13, 120, 128, 134
fff ensemble, 305n21, 317
Fiebrink, Rebecca, 312n35, 315, 316
Field, Ambrose, 12, 319–33
Finlay, Janet, 30, 33
Fluxus, 278n2, 339
Forsythe, Diana E., 18, 33
Fortnow, Lance, 48, 75
Foucault, Michel, 41, 75, 112, 116, 296
4i system, 284
Francesconi, Luca, 285
Frangella, Luis, 41
Franken, Daan, 181, 193
Franssen, Maarten, 106, 116
Frascati Manual, 328
Fried, Michael, 337, 353
    "Art and Objecthood," 337
Friedan, Betty, 16
Friedlaender, Ari S., 100, 102
Friedman, Batya, 107, 116
Fritz, Claudia, 24, 26, 33
Froese, Tom, 172, 180, 191
Fuller, Buckminster, 41
Fure, Ashley, 199, 314, 315
Furrer, Beat, 214n12
    FAMA, 214n12

G
Gaburo, Kenneth, 35–36, 52, 75
Gaburo, Virginia, 49, 75
Gageego!, 298
Galileo Galilei, 50, 75
Garcia, Jérémie, 312n35, 315
Garland, Alex, 16
    Ex Machina, 16
Gebru, Timnit, 22, 32
Gemeinboeck, Petra, 182n19, 185, 190
Gentle Fire, 174n3
Ghazala, Qubais Reed, 307, 315
Gibson, James J., 183, 191, 236, 245
Gillies, Marco, 312n35, 315
Giorno, John, 338n5
Glass, Philip, 87, 278n3
Glover, Richard, 123, 135
Gödel, Kurt, 38
Godlovitch, Stan, 111, 116
Goehr, Lydia, 216, 217, 226, 228, 278n2, 292
Goh, Annie, 296, 311, 315
Goldberger, Ary L., 48, 75
Goldstein, Jeffrey, 324, 332
Goldstein, Rebecca, 38, 76
Google, 18
    DeepMind, 18
GPT-3, 22, 23
Grainger, Percy, 175n8
    Free Music 1, 175n8

Graves, Alex, 18, 33
Green, Owen, 174n6, 179, 191
Greenstadt, Rachel, 24, 32
Griffiths, Dave, 31, 32
Grisey, Gérard, 128, 132
Gritten, Anthony, 118, 134
Gross, Matthias, 121, 134
Grossman, Jennifer, 308, 316
Grotthuss, Dietrich Ewald von, 108
Groupe de Recherches Musicales (GRM), Paris, 281n8
Guarnieri, Adriano, 283
Guattari, Félix, 168, 169, 187, 191

H
Habbestad, Bjørnar, 236, 245
Haddad, Karim, 11, 247–76
    Etüde No. 6 ". . . où ton âme en le somme gît
    cachée, . . . ," 267, 274
Hacksmiths Code of Conduct, 314n39
Hall, Edward T., 345–47, 349, 353
Hallowell, Ronan, 172, 191
Halpern, Megan, 7, 13
Hamman, Michael, 175, 185, 191
Hannay, Alastair, 187, 191
Hansen, Mark B. N., 172, 180, 184, 187, 190, 191
Haraway, Donna, 12, 154, 156, 163, 169, 197, 212, 217,
    296, 315
    "Cyborg Manifesto, A," 296
Harman, Graham, 114, 116
    Art and Objects, 114
Harrison, Scott D., 320, 333
Harvey, Jonathan, 279, 285, 287, 290
Haydn, Joseph, 120
Hayes, Lauren, 306, 315
Hebel, Kurt, 308n26
Heggie, Miranda, 299, 300, 315
Heidegger, Martin, 114n15, 275, 276
Helms, Johanna Evelyn, 280n5, 292
Heloir, Alexis, 312n35, 315
Hennion, Antoine, 175, 191
Hermano, Mara L., 8, 14
Hermes Ensemble, 233–34
Hertz, Garnet, 115, 116
Heying, Madison, 307, 308–9, 315
Hildebrand, John A., 100, 102
Hindemith, Paul, 175n8, 291
    7 Triostücke, 175n8
Hinton, Milt, 29
Ho, Jocelyn, 303, 305, 315, 316, 317
Ho, Jocelyn, and Margaret Schedel, works by,
    Women's Labour, 303, 305–6
Hoffmann, E. T. A., 23
Hogan, Ed, 15, 33
Hölderlin, Friedrich, 11, 248, 276
Holert, Tom, 215, 217
Holland, Simon, 226, 228
Holst, Imogen, 278n3
Hörl, Erich, 172–73, 187, 191
Horst, Maja, 7, 13
Hui, Yuk, 125, 134, 155, 169
Huron, David, 119, 134
Husserl, Edmund, 30
Hutchins, Edwin, 119, 123, 135
    Cognition in the Wild, 123

I
I Ching, 41, 153
Ihde, Don, 105n2, 116
Ikeda, Ryoji, 352
    micro / macro, 352
Impett, Jonathan, 7–14, 102, 117–35, 173, 175n7, 191,
    228, 242–43, 245, 311, 316
Industry, The, 68
In:fluence Ensemble, 298
Ingold, Tim, 157, 169
Inoue, Satoko, 72
IRCAM, 109n6, 174n5, 177n11, 280, 285–86, 287, 291
Iverson, Jennifer, 278, 292
Ives, Charles, 87

J
Jacktrip, 313n36
Jakobson, Roman, 327
Jaynes, Julian, 68, 76
Jeremijenko, Natalie, 115, 116
Joachim, Joseph, 278n3
Jobs, Steve, 79n1
Johnson, Janice, 15, 29
John-Steiner, Vera, 286, 291, 292
Jonas, Hans, 181, 192
Jones, Stacy Holman, 127, 133, 135
Jørgensen, Sven E., 184, 192
Josel, Seth, 233, 234, 243
Joseph, John, 100, 102
Justka, Ewa, 309

K
Kahn, Douglas, 279n4, 293
Kaiser, Jeff, 185, 189
Karplus, Kevin, 82, 87
Kauffman, Stuart A., 39, 64, 76
Kavukcuoglu, Koray, 18, 33
Kaye, Joseph "Jofish," 110, 112, 115
Keijzer, Fred, 181, 193
Keil, Charles, 185n20, 192
Kelly, Caleb, 111, 116
    Gallery Sound, 111
Kermick, Jüri, 225
Kerner, Hannah, 101, 102
    "Too Many AI Researchers Think Real-World
    Problems Are Not Relevant," 101
Kettle's Yard, 20
Kimura, Mari, 304
    MUGIC, 304
King, Elaine, 118, 134
Kirby, David, 7, 13
Kirby, Michael, 339, 353
Kitchen, Rob, 8, 13
Kittler, Friedrich, 125–26, 135
    "There Is No Software," 125
Klaucke, Inga Maria, 19
Klauer, Giorgio, 175n7
Klippenstein, Ken, 307, 316
Komito, David Ross, 43, 76
Krakauer, David C., 45n7, 76
Krenek, Ernst, 278n3
Kuester, Nicolee, 304
    Conversation Piece No. 1, 304
Kuhn, Thomas, 131
Kuivila, Ron, 79, 80, 85, 174n6

Index

Kumar, Gireendra, 331, 33
Kuni, Verena, 296, 316
Kunz, Werner, 19, 33
Kusumo, Sardono W., 72
Kyma, 308–9

L

Lachenmann, Helmut, 128
Landy, Leigh, 277n1, 293
   "But Is It (Also) Music?," 277n1
Lang, Fritz, 16
   Metropolis, 16
Latour, Bruno, 128–29, 135, 172, 175, 180, 183, 191, 192, 321, 333
Laugier, Sandra, 38, 75
Laville, Frédéric, 172, 184, 192
Le Corbusier, 339
Lenat, Douglas B., 18, 33
Leonenko, Konstantin, 312n34
Leroi-Gourhan, André, 188n21, 192
Leroux, Philippe, 279, 285–86, 287, 289
   M, 285, 289
Lewenstein, Bruce, 7, 13
Lietti, Alfredo, 280, 281, 293
Ligeti, György, 119
Lim, Liza, 199
Liszt, Franz, 278n3
Lokhorst, Gert-Jan, 106, 116
Lorenz, Martin, 200n4
Losano, Mario, 182n18, 192
Loud Objects, 84
Love, Karlin, 287, 291, 293
Lovelace, Countess of (Augusta Ada King), 312
Löw, Martina, 214, 217
Lucier, Alvin, 79, 81, 100, 155, 174, 198–99, 216, 339, 353
   Bird and Person Dyning, 198–99, 216
   I Am Sitting in a Room, 339
Lüneburg, Barbara, 343n9, 353
Lupone, Michelangelo, 175n7
Lusch, Robert F., 321, 333
Lutzenberger, W., 48, 75

M

Maar, Dora, 118–19
MacLean, Alex, 125, 134
Maderna, Bruno, 280–83, 290
   Notturno, 282
Magnusson, Thor, 11, 175, 176, 185, 192, 219–29
   ixi lang, 223
   Sonic Writing, 226
   Threnoscope, 11, 220–28
Māhina-Tuai, Kolokesa Uafā, 32
Mahler, Gustav, 338
   Symphony No. 3, 338
Mainzer, Klaus, 48, 76
Maldacena, Juan, 60, 76
Mancilla, Roberto Gustavo, 180, 192
Mann, Robert B., 59, 75
Manning, Erin, 166, 167, 169
Manning, Peter, 175, 192, 308, 316
Manoury, Philippe, 177n11, 192
Marcoll, Maximilian, 352
   Amproprifikationen, 352
Margolina, Tetyana, 100, 102

Marquez-Borbon, Adnan, 306, 315
Martin, Aengus, 185, 190
Martirano, Salvatore, 46
Marx, Karl, 301
Massumi, Brian, 125, 135, 166, 167, 168, 169
Mathew, Marlene, 308, 316
Maturana, Humberto, 172, 181, 192
Max/MSP, 287, 290
Mayer-Kress, G., 48, 75
McBurney, Peter, 185, 190
McCormack, Jon, 185, 189
McCormick, Lisa, 171, 192
McCulloch, Andrea R., 48, 75
McDonald, Mark A., 100, 102
McGregor, Wayne, 20
McIntosh, Anthony R., 48, 75
McLaughlin, Scott, 10, 153–69
   Endless Mobility of Listening, The, 161
   whole is encountered by going further into the parts, The, 162
McLean, Alex, 223, 229
McMillan-Major, Angelina, 22, 32
Meierling, Chris, 312, 316
Melton, William, 278n2, 293
Menke, Christoph, 211, 216, 217
Merelo, Juan Juliano, 181
Mesnick, Sarah L., 100, 102
Messiaen, Olivier, 58, 121, 175n8
   Fêtes des belles eaux, 175n8
   Quartet for the End of Time, 58
Milhaud, Darius, 175n8
   Suite for ondes Martenot and piano, 175n8
Miller, Cassandra, 164, 165, 169
Mnih, Volodymyr, 18, 33
Montero, Miguel, 48, 75
Monteverdi, Claudio, 87
Moore, Brian C. J., 24, 26, 33
Moore, F. Richard, 106–7, 116
Moreno, Alvaro, 181, 189
Moreschi, Bruno, 22, 33
Morin, Edgar, 176, 184, 187, 192
Mozart, Wolfgang Amadeus, 108
Muhly, Nico, 128, 135
Mulholland, Paul, 226, 228
Mullen, Tim, 48, 69, 77
Müller, Felix, 184, 192
Mumma, Gordon, 85n11, 174n2, 175, 192
Mundry, Isabel, 214n12
   Penelopes Atem, 214n12
Murail, Tristan, 177n11, 192
Musica Elettronica Viva (MEV), 174n3

N

Nāgārjuna, 43
Nanz, Dieter A., 339, 353
Nattiez, Jean-Jacques, 327, 333
Network Music Festival, 20
Neuhaus, Max, 174
New Grove Dictionary of Music and Musicians, The, 277n1
Niblock, Phil, 224
Nijholt, Anton, 37, 76
Nöe, Alva, 119, 135
NoMus, 280, 283, 290
Nono, Luigi, 120, 128, 174n5, 278n2, 279–85, 289, 293
   Das Atmende Klarsein, 282

Intolleranza 1960, 282n9
    La fabbrica illuminata, 283n11
    Prometeo, 284–85
Novati, Maria Maddalena, 280, 290, 293
Nunnari, Fabrizio, 312n35, 315
Nü Soundworks, 109
Nyström, Erik, 201n6, 217

O
Obama, Barack, 23
O'Callaghan, Casey, 115n16, 116
Odum, Eugene P., 173n1, 192
Oestreich, William K., 100, 102
O'Hagan, Peter, 259n5, 276
Old Boys Network, 296, 316
Oliveros, Pauline, 87
Ollivier, Harold, 42, 76
O'Neil, Cathy, 295, 316
OpenMusic, 260n7, 266, 267, 272, 273
Oram, Daphne, 309
Orpheus Institute, 227
Owens, Jessie Ann, 124, 135

P
Panaccio-Letendre, Charlotte, 176, 192
Papastergiadis, Nikos, 337, 340, 352, 353
Papert, Seymour, 225, 229
Parisi, Luciana, 8, 13
Parke-Wolfe, Samuel Thompson, 312n35, 316
Pask, Gordon, 182n19
    Colloquy of Mobiles, A, 182n19
Pasquier, Philippe, 185, 193
Pénard, Thierry, 322, 332
Peirce, Charles Sanders, 37, 51, 76, 91, 102
    Illustrations of the Logic of Science, 51
Penderecki, Krzysztof, 283
Peng, C.-K., 48, 75
Penrose, Roger, 60n13, 76
Perchard, Tom, 301, 302, 316
Pereira, Gabriel, 22, 33
Perkis, Tim, 80n2
    Mouseguitar, 80n2
Petersen, Anne Ring, 336, 353
Phelan, Peggy, 171, 192
Philips Pavilion (World's Fair, Brussels), 339
Picasso, Pablo, 118
    Guernica, 118
Piccini, Angela, 322, 333
Pickering, Andrew, 30, 33, 161n11, 168, 169
Piekut, Benjamin, 129, 135, 168, 169
Pinch, Trevor, 278n2, 293
Plessas, Peter, 278, 293
Plot, Martín, 67, 76
Pollini, Maurizio, 283
Poulin, David, 42, 76
Pound, Ezra, 268, 276
    Antheil, 268
Pourhasan, Razieh, 59, 75
Pousseur, Henri, 174, 192, 280
Prendergast, Mark, 338, 353
Prominski, Martin, 173n1, 184, 192
Pronestì, Laura, 280, 293
Proust, Joëlle, 56, 76
Proust, Simon, 298
Pure Data, 302n15, 304n18
Puwar, Nirmal, 309, 316
Pythagoras, 132

Q
Quéré, Louis, 172, 184, 192

R
Radigue, Éliane, 307
Raff, Joseph Joachim, 278n3
Raheja, Gaurav, 331, 333
Rameau, Jean-Philippe, 132
Rammert, Werner, 172, 176, 184, 192
Rancière, Jacques, 89, 102, 216, 217
    Dissensus, 89n1
    Politics of Aesthetics, The, 89n1
Random Dance, 20
Rau, H., 48, 75
Rebelo, Pedro, 174n6
Rebughini, Paola, 181n16, 192
Redhead, Lauren, 123, 135
Red Note Ensemble, 297–98
Reeves, Camden, 320, 333
Reich, Steve, 87, 339
    Pendulum Music, 339
Reicha, Anton, 122
Reiche, Claudia, 296, 316
Reid, Sarah Belle, 65
Rembrandt, 23
Rheinberger, Hans-Jörg, 323–25, 333
Riley, Terry, 85n11, 87, 223
Rink, John, 321, 333
Risset, Jean-Claude, 279n4
Rittel, Horst W. J., 19, 33
Ritter, Petra, 48, 75
Roads, Curtis, 235, 240, 244, 245
    Microsounds, 240
Robaszkiewicz, Sébastien, 109n6, 116
Roberts, Sara, 38n1
Robertson, Campbell, 304, 316
Roche, Heather, 165n12
Rodà, Antonio, 281, 293
Rodgers, Tara, 309
Romero, Lula, 10, 11, 195–217
    displaced, 211n11
    MTRAK (מטרקא), 197, 200–201, 211, 214–16
    Parallax, 197, 202–11, 213–16
Romitelli, Fausto, 285
Rosch, Eleanor, 180, 193
Rosenboom, David, 9, 13, 35–78, 137–48
    Battle Hymn of Insurgent Arts, 66–67
    Champ Vital (Life Field), 59
    Choose Your Universe, 65–66, 140
    Earth Encomium, 64–65, 138–39
    Experiment, The (scene from *Hopscotch*), 68–71, 142
    In the Beginning—, 59
    Natural Scores, 65–66, 140
    Nothingness Is Unstable, 64–65, 138–39
    On Being Invisible, 51, 69
    On Being Invisible II, 69
    Portable Gold and Philosophers' Stones, 69
    Predictions, Confirmations and Disconfirmations, 46
    Quartet for the Beginning of a Time, 58–63
    Ringing Minds, 69
    Summary History of Humans in the World, A, 40
    Swarming Intelligence Carnival, 72–73, 143–48
    Two Lines, 44
    Unverifiable Intuitions, 71–72
    Zones of Influence, 59

Rosier-Catach, Irène, 38, 75
Rubinoff, Kailan R., 321, 333
Russell, Legacy, 296, 316
Rusu, Andrei A., 18, 33
Rutz, Hanns Holger, 185, 192

S

Saccone, Chiara, 233, 234
Saladin, Mathieu, 174, 193
Salimpoor, Valorie, 48, 75
Sallis, Friedmann, 171, 174, 189, 193
Salter, Chris, 171, 193
Sanden, Paul, 171, 173, 176, 177, 193
Sanfilippo, Dario, 185, 190, 193
Satie, Erik, 338
    Vexations, 338
Saunders, Rob, 182n19, 185, 189
Sawyer, Keith, 289, 293
Scaletti, Carla, 307, 308–9, 316
Schaeffer, Pierre, 55, 77, 236, 240, 245
Schauffler, Robert Haven, 120, 135
Schechner, Richard, 171, 193
Schedel, Margaret, 303, 305, 308, 309, 315, 316, 317
    See also Ho, Jocelyn, and Margaret Schedel, works
    by,
Schmitz, Hermann, 336n4
Schnell, Norbert, 109n6, 116, 175, 193
Schoenberg, Arnold, 122, 127, 131, 135, 247, 276
Schofield, John, 325, 332
Schön, Donald A., 320, 333
Schröder, Julia H., 337, 353
Schumacher, Patrik, 122, 135
Sciarrino, Salvatore, 279, 283, 285, 290
    Perseo e Andromeda, 290
Scurto, Hugo, 312n35, 316
Seago, Allan, 226, 228
Searle, John, 17
SEGMOD, 200, 211
Sengers, Phoebe, 30, 33, 110, 112, 115, 116
Sennett, Richard, 130, 135
Serres, Michel, 131–32, 135
Sève, Bernard, 278n2, 293
Sève, Lucien, 176, 193
Shapin, Steven, 278, 293
SharcMusic, 299
Sharon, Yuval, 68, 78
    Hopscotch, 68
Shen, Kelly, 48, 75
Shmitchell, Shmargaret, 22, 32
Shostakovich, Dmitri, 339
Sidharta, Otto, 72
Silver, David, 18, 33
Simondon, Gilbert, 129, 135, 181n16, 187, 188, 193
Skinner, Damian, 32
Small, Christopher, 98, 102, 176, 193
Smalley, Denis, 241, 245, 277n1, 292
Smith, George, 36, 78
Smith, Wadada Leo, 44, 78
Smith-Brindle, Reginald, 120, 135
Snyder, Bob, 239, 245
    Music and Memory, 239
Somerson, Rosanne, 8, 14
Sonic Arts Union, 87, 174n2
Sonic Cyberfeminisms, 314
Sound and Music, 297, 310, 313
Sound Girls, 312n35
Sound Scotland, 297, 309n27

Spatz, Ben, 158n7, 169
Spencer-Brown, G., 42, 78
    Laws of Form, 42
Spinoza, Baruch de, 126
Stapleton, Paul, 185, 193
Steen-Andersen, Simon, 199
Stewart, John, 181, 193
Stiegler, Bernard, 188n21, 193
Stjernfelt, Frederik, 37, 51n8, 78
Stockhausen, Karlheinz, 127, 174n3
    Mikrophonie I, 174n3
Stolfi, Ariane de Souza, 174n6, 193
Stravinsky, Igor, 278n3
Strong, Alex, 82, 87
Studio di Fonologia della RAI (SfM), Milan,
    280–83, 287
    Archivio dello Studio di Fonologia, Associazione
    NoMus, 280, 283
Studio für elektronische Musik, WDR, Cologne, 278,
    281n8
Suchman, Lucy, 19, 33
Sun Tzu, 65, 78
    Art of War, The, 65
SuperCollider, 84, 106n3, 214, 223, 224, 225
Symbolic Sound Corporation, 308n26
Szlavnics, Chiyoko, 199

T

Tamirisa, Asha, 306, 313, 316
Tanaka, Atau, 48, 78, 312n35, 315
Tarkovsky, Andrei, 248, 276
    Sculpting in Time, 248
Taste of Honey, A, 15, 17
    "Boogie Oogie Oogie," 15, 17, 26, 28, 29
Tatar, Kıvanç, 185, 193
TECHNE, 312n35
Tenney, James, 279n4
Thom, René, 44, 49, 78
Thompson, Evan, 180, 181, 193
Thompson, Marie, 296, 311, 312n35, 315, 316
Thoreau, Henry David, 41
Tidhar, Dan, 19
TITWRENCH, 312n35
Trocco, Frank, 278n2, 293
Tudor, David, 79, 80, 84, 87, 174
Turchet, Luca, 174n6, 193
Turkle, Shelly, 225, 229
Twain, Mark, 67, 78
    Battle Hymn of the Republic (Bought Down to
    Date), 67

V

Vaccarini, Marina, 280, 293
Vaggione, Horacio, 111, 116
Valle, Andrea, 174n6, 240, 245
van de Poel, Ibo, 106, 116
van Duijn, Marc, 181, 193
Varela, Francisco J., 172, 180, 181, 192, 193
Varèse, Edgard, 235, 245, 339
    Poème électronique, 339
Vargo, Stephen L., 321, 333
Vear, Craig, 226, 229
Velvet Underground, the, 223
Veness, Joel, 18, 33
Verrando, Giovanni, 175n7
Vesely, Dalibor, 122, 135
Vidolin, Alvise, 279–85, 286, 289–90, 292, 293

Index

Viñao, Alejandro, 285
Virtual Violins project, 24–26, 28
von Bertalanffy, Ludwig, 179n14, 194
von Foerster, Heinz, 35, 36, 54, 55n11, 68, 75, 176, 180, 194

W

Wagner, Richard, 338
Wagstaff, Kiri, 101, 102
    "Machine Learning That Matters," 101
Wajcman, Judy, 295–96, 303, 316
    Feminism Confronts Technology, 296
Walshe, Jennifer, 164
    THIS IS WHY PEOPLE O.D. ON PILLS, 164
Wang, Ge, 312, 316
Wang, Zheng, 48, 75
Warde, Ann, 9, 89–103
Warhol, Andy, 338n5
    Empire, 338n5
    Sleep, 338n5
Waters, Simon, 172, 175n7, 179, 185, 194, 237, 245, 311, 317
Watson, James, 219
Webber, Melvin M., 19, 33
Webern, Anton, 247
Weidringer, Walter, 339, 353
Weiss, Gerhard, 182, 194
Weisstein, Eric W., 159, 169
Weizenbaum, Joseph, 16
Welby, Victoria, 91–92, 102
    What Is Meaning?, 91, 92
Weston, Alex, 278n3
Wien Modern, 339
Wikipedia, 23

Wilkie, Katie, 226, 228
Williams, Christopher, 162, 169
Wimsatt, W. C., 43, 78
Wishart, Trevor, 108n5, 111, 116, 241, 245
    On Sonic Art, 108n5
Wolff, Christian, 85n11, 96
Wolpe, Stefan, 175n9
Women in Sound Women on Sound (WISWOS), 312n35
Women Produce Music, 312n35
Women's Audio Mission, 312n35
Woodhouse, Jim, 24, 33, 26
Wright, Peter, 30, 33

X

Xenakis, Iannis, 107, 116, 132, 339
    Concret PH, 339

Y

Yorkshire Sound Women Network (YSWN), 308, 312n35
Young, Erin, 68
Young, La Monte, 87, 223–24, 338
    Compositions 1960, 338
    Second Dream of the High Tension Line Stepdown Transformer, The, 338

Z

Z, Pamela, 305n21, 317
Zattra, Laura, 11, 12, 174, 193, 277–94
Zhu, Julie, 12, 295–317
Zuboff, Shoshana, 22, 33
Zuccheri, Marino, 279–83, 286–87, 289–92, 294
Zurek, Wojciech H., 42, 76

Editor
Jonathan Impett

Authors
Patricia Alessandrini
Alan F. Blackwell
Nicholas Brown
Marko Ciciliani
Nicolas Collins
Agostino Di Scipio
Daniela Fantechi
Ambrose Field
Karim Haddad
Jonathan Impett
Thor Magnusson
Scott McLaughlin
Lula Romero
David Rosenboom
Ann Warde
Laura Zattra
Julie Zhu

Production manager
Heike Vermeire

Managing editor
Edward Crooks

Series editor
William Brooks

Lay-out
Studio Luc Derycke

Cover design
Lucia D'Errico

Cover image
© Speculum humanae salvationis,
GKS 80 folio, the Royal Danish
Library, 47 verso.

Typesetting
Friedemann BV

Printing
Wilco, Amersfoort
(The Netherlands)

© 2021 by Leuven University Press /
Universitaire Pers Leuven /
Presses Universitaires de Louvain.
Minderbroedersstraat 4
B-3000 Leuven (Belgium)

ISBN 978 94 6270 258 5
eISBN 978 94 6166 366 5
https://doi.org/10.11116/9789461663665

D/2021/1869/38
NUR: 664

*This book is published in the Orpheus Institute
Series.*

The Orpheus Institute Series encompasses monographs by fellows and associates of the Orpheus Institute, compilations of lectures and texts from seminars and study days, and edited volumes on topics arising from work at the institute. Research can be presented in digital media as well as printed texts. As a whole, the series is meant to enhance and advance discourse in the field of artistic research in music and to generate future work in this emerging and vital area of study.

RECENT TITLES IN THIS SERIES:

– *Experience Music Experiment: Pragmatism and Artistic Research*
  William Brooks (ed.)
  2021, ISBN 978 94 6270 279 0

– *Machinic Assemblages of Desire: Deleuze and Artistic Research 3*
  Paulo de Assis and Paolo Giudici (eds.)
  2021, ISBN 978 94 6270 254 7

– *Performance, Subjectivity, and Experimentation*
  Catherine Laws (ed.)
  2020, ISBN 978 94 6270 231 8

– *Listening to the Other*
  Stefan Östersjö
  2020, ISBN 978 94 6270 229 5

– *Aberrant Nuptials: Deleuze and Artistic Research 2*
  Paulo de Assis and Paolo Giudici (eds.)
  2019, ISBN 978 94 6270 202 8

– *Voices, Bodies, Practices: Performing Musical Subjectivities*
  Catherine Laws, William Brooks, David Gorton, Nguyễn Thanh Thủy,
  Stefan Östersjö, and Jeremy J. Wells
  2019, ISBN 978 94 6270 205 9

– *Futures of the Contemporary: Contemporaneity, Untimeliness, and Artistic Research*
  Paulo de Assis and Michael Schwab (eds.)
  2019, ISBN 978 94 6270 183 0

ORPHEUS
———
INSTITUUT

Orpheus Institute
Korte Meer 12
B – 9000 Ghent
Belgium
+32 (0)9 330 40 81
www.orpheusinstituut.be

The Orpheus Institute has been providing postgraduate education for musicians since 1996 and introduced the first doctoral programme for music practitioners in Flanders (2004). Acting as an umbrella institution for Flanders, it is co-governed by the music and dramatic arts departments of all four Flemish colleges, which are strongly involved in its operation.

Throughout the Institute's various activities (seminars, conferences, workshops, and associated events) there is a clear focus on the development of a new research discipline in the arts, one that addresses questions and topics that are at the heart of musical practice, building on the unique expertise and perspectives of musicians and maintaining a constant dialogue with more established research disciplines.

Within this context, the Orpheus Institute launched an international Research Centre in 2007 that acts as a stable constituent within an ever-growing field of inquiry. The Orpheus Research Centre is a place where musical artists can fruitfully conduct individual and collaborative research on issues that are of concern to all involved in artistic practice. Its core mission is the development of a discipline-specific discourse in the field of artistic research in music.